FLYING THE OREGON TRAIL

FLYING THE OREGON TRAIL

BY

MAURICE BRETT

CIRRUS ASSOCIATES

PUBLISHED BY:
Cirrus Associates (S.W.),
Kington Magna,
Gillingham,
Dorset,
SP8 5EW UK.

ISBN 1 902807 05 7

PRINTED IN ENGLAND BY:
Hillman Printers (Frome) Ltd,
Handlemaker Road,
Marston Trading Estate,
Frome,
Somerset,
BA11 4RW.

PHOTO SCANNING BY:
Castle Graphics Ltd,
Nunney,
Nr. Frome,
Somerset,
BA11 4LW.

DISTRIBUTORS:
Vine House Distribution Ltd,
Waldenbury,
North Common,
Chailey,
East Sussex,
BN8 4DR.

COVER: Chimney Rock, Nebraska. Photo: the author.

ALSO BY THE SAME AUTHOR: *"A Sunday Flyer,"* published 2000.

DEDICATION

Although he is not around now to see this book in its final printed form, I would like to dedicate this to the memory of my old friend, the late Bill Kee, of Twin Falls, Idaho, without whom the germ of the idea behind the flight would never have originated. It was he who, having shown me local sites, excited my interest further with the gift of a copy of "The Oregon Trail Revisited," Gregory Franzwa's book about where and how to view traces of the Trail.

Also to Gregory Franzwa for his enthusiasm in the formative days, to Barbara Magerl of OCTA (Oregon–California Trails Association) who did so much to assist in every way, and to Gerry Schwam, an American fellow member of the DH Moth Club who saw to the nuts and bolts in the flying department.

CONTENTS

FOREWORD

by

BARBARA MAGERL

As new Vice President of the Oregon-California Trails Association (OCTA), it was exciting to hear about an Englishman at the national convention in Scotts Bluff, Nebraska in 1985. Especially exciting because I was also Public Relations Chairman and the gentleman was going to fly the trail the next year – a great story with lots of advance time. We met briefly at Ft. Laramie at convention's end. So briefly I wasn't sure why someone from the other side of the 'pond' was interested in an historic US trail when too few Americans appreciated this thrilling epic in our history.

Maurice Brett's description of his research and tedious transferring to roller maps impressed me deeply. The thought of someone flying in an unfamiliar country, seeking traces of trails more than 150 years old, while worrying about roller maps, altitude, updrafts, fuel, storms, etc. awed me! "What a dedicated man he is," I thought. "Or maybe a crackpot." But once he mentioned Jimmy Stewart and invoked the name Narcissa Whitman, I was solidly in his corner!

Having a corporate sponsor to cover expenses made it a dream come true. However, as the dream became a nightmare, I was personally saddened. With great admiration I read communiqués as he steadfastly pasted together the pieces of the dream and enlisted two chums and three spouses. Spunky people all, I decided.

For moral support I contacted a London correspondent and his article appeared in our local "KANSAS CITY STAR" newspaper. That led another Kansas City journalist to write an item on Brett's flight which appeared in the brand-new "SMITHSONIAN AIR & SPACE MAGAZINE."

On a scorching hot day in 1986, a jubilant handful of OCTA members, City of Independence, Missouri representatives, and some media turned out to welcome the Brits. I'll never forget one young reporter inspecting the wing and remarking, "It's made of fabric!" Ah! to be so young. After an evening of English wit, in true trail tradition reluctant OCTA members had to bid the pioneers goodbye. With the same sense of excitement as earlier travellers, they 'went West.'

In 1988 my husband and I hosted the Bretts when they returned for an OCTA convention in St Joseph, Missouri, and showed them some local trail in a leisurely fashion. In 1993 Maurice advised us that he would be going to Oregon, for a flying adventure. Reunion denied, I decided, but Fate is curious. In Baker City, Oregon for the OCTA convention, my husband and I were driving on our own to the Whitman Mission.

Realizing the unusual amount of small plane traffic in an underpopulated area, I followed a hunch. Result: a reunion with Maurice – at a small airfield, of course.

With all its suspense and challenges, and humor, this story unfolds the excitement of a man and his friends fulfilling a dream: in essence, the same story played out by the thousands of Americans who 'went West' in the 1800s. Perhaps this book will inspire others – whether puddle-jumpers or land huggers – to follow the Oregon Trail, or their own personal dream.

A personal note: as I understand it, Maurice's journey was partly inspired by a Jimmy Stewart film, *"At the Bend of the River."* It was filmed in 1951 mostly in Oregon when I was visiting my oldest brother there. One day he had an emergency call from the film company saying they urgently needed a generator up on Mount Hood. My kind brother allowed this film fanatic to tag along on the delivery. What a thrill – and what preparation for a role I would play much, much later.

Barbara Magerl
Past-VP OCTA, Founder–Trails Head Chapter OCTA

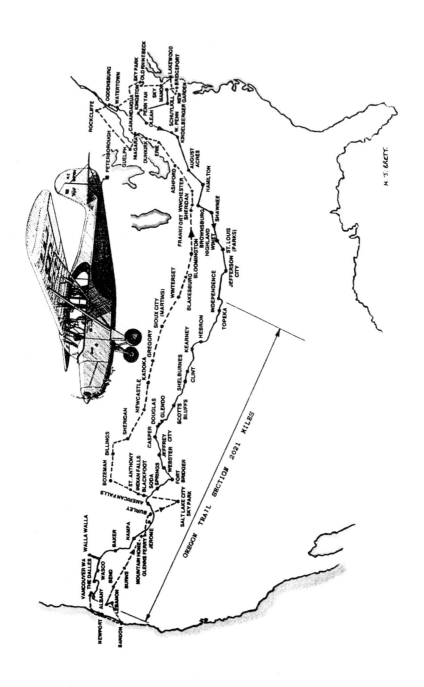

OREGON TRAIL SECTION 2021 MILES

N. J. BRETT.

INTRODUCTION

This book is about a real-life adventure in the '80s (the 1980s) – an out-of-reach dream come true for three ordinary English couples, whose families had departed the nest leaving them free to indulge in a literal flight of fancy. For the author, then 60 years old, it was in fact fulfilment of two such daydreams. One was to follow the whole route of the Oregon Trail in the only way possible in these days. The other was to experience just a little whiff of the old barnstorming days of flying under the wide blue skies of North America whilst making a double coast-to-coast crossing. At the same time, the opportunity was taken to indulge in a kind of pilgrimage, to join in with the sesquicentennial celebrations of the first crossing of the continent by a party of men and women.

In recent history the United States of America has tended to be seen in the role of leader and provider of goods and advanced technology to, with few exceptions, the rest of the world, which makes it all the more difficult to realise that less than 170 years ago it was thought impossible to drive wagons across the North American continent, or for women and children to make the overland journey.

In 1836, a small party of missionaries set out from the State of New York, led by Dr Marcus Whitman, to establish a Presbyterian Mission in Oregon. Two wives accompanied the missionaries, and thus were the first white women to make the journey. Having proved it possible both for women and wagons to make the overland crossing, they were succeeded by increasing numbers of settlers following their tracks over the Oregon Trail.

Perhaps the majority of the settlers were farmers from the old West, such as the States of Illinois, Missouri, Indiana and so on, suffering from the effects of the Depression of 1837 and years of hot dry weather which parched the land. Others were immigrants from every part of Europe and Scandinavia, attracted by the lure of free land and a new start in life. The settlers' numbers were swollen in 1849 by the influx of the 'Forty-Niners,' heading for the gold fields of California in the great Gold Rush.

Between the years of 1841 and the turn of the century, 300-400,000 people made the hazardous journey over the Trails, with around 100,000 wagons. Amazingly, some of the tracks made by these wagons can still be seen today, in places so clearly that they can be followed as easily as any modern road, in others only visible in conditions when the crops or the lighting circumstances are just right. Of the 2,021 miles of the Oregon Trail from Independence, Missouri to Oregon City, Oregon, some 300 miles of ruts remain to be seen.

Peak years were during the 1850s and 1860s, 52,000 taking to the Trail in 1852, the highest number in any year; the last great year was 1869, when the inter-continental railroad was finally completed. In 1856, the wagon trains were augmented by the Mormon Handcart Companies, made up of teams of five people pulling trek carts each carrying 500 lb. Whether pulling carts or accompanying ox-, mule- or horse-drawn wagons, most walked for the whole of the way, averaging around 15 miles per day. They started west when the grass was six inches high, to ensure feed for the animals, and hoped to reach their destination four to five months later, before the snows appeared on the Blue Mountains.

Not all of those that set out reached their goal. It is estimated that 30-45,000 died along the way, mostly from diseases such as cholera, accidents involving guns, axes, falling under wagon wheels etc., or from bad weather conditions. Despite the popular impression to the contrary, just a few died from skirmishes with Indians, mostly in the period of 1863-64. Whatever their ultimate fate, they had taken part in perhaps the greatest known emigration in the history of mankind, more people over a greater distance than any that had gone before – and they had done so entirely of their own volition.

Starting in Independence, Missouri, the early pioneers traversed the rolling prairies for 300 miles to the Platte River. They followed that river as it meandered across the Plains for another 400 miles, then crossed a sage desert to the Sweetwater River, covering another 150 miles to the Rockies. Three hundred miles of sage desert and mountains took them to Fort Hall on the Snake River. They crossed more sage desert, at times high above the Snake, running 500 feet down in its deep gorge, to Fort Boise. The Trail then wound up through the Blue Mountains, to the mighty Columbia. From the Dalles, the wagons were either floated down the hazardous waters of the Columbia to the Willamette valley, or hauled across the fearsome Cascade Mountains over the Barlow Road to Trail's End at Oregon City.

Because the Trail route lies in areas where access is difficult or impossible, e.g. through major highway intersections, cultivated farm land, Indian Reservation lands, or reservoirs, it is now not possible to drive, walk or ride over much of the Trail. The only way to follow the whole route now is to fly over it, and until very recently surprisingly few people have attempted that. In fact, the author believes that this flight could have been the first in which a crew set out to fly the whole length, with sufficient information in the way of special charts to ensure a reasonable chance of keeping exactly to the defined Trail route.

That the flight took place at all was due to the help given by many people and organizations, both in the UK and the USA: to mention just a few, the members of the Stevenage Flying Club, Gerry Schwam, an American member of the DH Moth Club, OCTA (the Oregon–California Trails Association) and two of its members in particular, Gregory Franzwa and Barbara Magerl, Hiram Walker (UK) Ltd (Canadian Club), none of whom I can ever thank enough. And, of course, the unflinching and untiring support of the other members of our team. At least, they now share that rare sense of achieving the seemingly impossible that must be akin, however minusculely, to what those who made the original journey felt when they rolled into Oregon City.

Part 1 of this book tells of how the project came about: the search for sponsorship to make it possible; the winning of an international Club Challenge Competition which was to fund the transporting of two old biplanes and eight participants across the Atlantic in order to make the flight over the Oregon Trail; the logistics behind what became a quite complex operation; its cancellation at the last possible moment; and the determination to keep it alive which resulted in a reduced party of three pilots and their wives setting off for the States.

Part 2 covers the acquisition of a little 40-years-old, 65 hp monoplane with which to make the flight: the subsequent journey, on a day-by-day basis, by two pilots in the aircraft and the third pilot and three wives in a large station wagon, from east to west covering the whole length of the Oregon Trail.

Finally, Part 3 describes the flight back: the return to Salt Lake City from where the ground party flew back home after 4 weeks and 6,000 miles on the road; across the Rockies to New Jersey via the Little Big Horn, Mount Rushmore, the Badlands, an Antique Fly-In, various aviation museums in Dayton, Ottawa and Old Rhinebeck, Niagara Falls and the forests of Ontario, the flight being completed in the wake of Hurricane Charlie. Before returning the aircraft to its previous owners it had flown 128 hours, covered 7,500 miles, landed at 80 airfields and crossed both Pacific and Atlantic coasts.

One last thought: the project came about to satisfy a desire to travel the whole length of the Trail route, to understand the nature of the country over which it lies and to gain an impression of what the pioneers faced. What emerged was a demonstration of how impossible it is, for people of our time, to even begin to appreciate what it must have been like for those who set out, all those years ago, on one of mankind's greatest adventures.

PROLOGUE

"Switches off?" Brian's query echoed round the grey stillness.

I checked that the ignition switch was 'Off' before answering: "Switches off."

Brian placed both hands on the propeller blade and nudged it against engine compression: "Fuel on?"

It was and I replied: "Fuel on."

And so on, through the brief start-up sequence, shorter than usual because this engine required neither priming nor sucking-in.

"Brakes on?"

"Brakes on."

"Throttle set?

"Throttle set."

"Contact?"

Clicking the switch on through two positions, pressing harder on the brakes and pulling the stick back with my right hand, I called: "Contact."

Brian swung the propeller blade smartly down, the engine coughed once, and then again, before settling into an even tickover. There was the same old thrill as the machine awoke: a tremor of life surging through all points of contact – stick, seat, brake pedals, floor boards and throttle lever.

The oil pressure gauge needle flicked round to a steady 30 and I eased the throttle forward a fraction until the rev counter settled at 1,000 rpm. But it would be four minutes before the oil temperature gauge registered above its low mark of 100 deg F. Then we could carry out a full-power run-up and check the drop in revs as each magneto was switched off and on in turn, followed by a test for carburettor icing and, finally, be on our way.

There was nothing else that had not already been checked. Maps to hand, harness tight, watch set to stopwatch mode and zeroed, fuel contents indicator dancing on the 'Full' mark. Outside, there was no sign of life on the field; with such a low overcast, hilltops fuzzy in the mist, a hint of drizzle in the air and the warning of thunderstorms, only "mad dogs and Englishmen" were out in the midday murk!

At this time we should have been 250 miles away. Now, all we could do was to go up and have a look at conditions from the air, in the hope that the gradual improvement was not all imaginary and would be sufficient to let us keep going far enough to escape this confounded clag.

Four minutes seem much longer when you are waiting impatiently for them to pass, and I found myself thinking back over the events that had finally led us here to Sky Manor, New Jersey – still scarcely able to believe that at last all the man-made obstacles were overcome ...

PART 1: PRELUDE

CHAPTER 1
IN THE BEGINNING

Until my wife Irene and I, back in 1950, saw the film "Where the River Bends," which was set in Oregon in the beautiful country around the Columbia river and told of a group of pioneers trying to reach Oregon City, we had really not known anything of Oregon. Then it became for us as for so many before, a sort of Eldorado, a place that one day we would just have to see for ourselves. At the time, it seemed beyond the bounds of possibility, but the desire to do so never quite went away.

What enhanced the desire was my correspondence with a couple of like-minded aviation enthusiasts in California and Oregon (Bill Kee and George Mazon), which continued until their deaths in 1993 and 1998 respectively. We did eventually get to visit them both, in 1979, Bill by that time having retired and moved back to his home town, Twin Falls in Idaho.

Meanwhile, I had learned to fly, and founded the Stevenage Flying Club in order to operate a 4-seat biplane (a Thruxton Jackaroo *[Fig. 1]*, converted from a DH.82A Tiger Moth) at the lowest possible cost. This we flew around England, Scotland and Wales and, having no radio or other navigation aids, learned how not to get lost and how to avoid the worst of the unpredictable weather this tight little island could throw at us.

In a way, our flying was somewhat akin to the early barnstorming days, operating mostly from small grass fields and farm strips, taking up any who would fly with us, asking only that they replace the fuel we used in doing so. We quickly learned to carry out our own maintenance and overhauls under the watchful eyes of friendly engineers who had the necessary licences to keep the authorities happy. Where our activities differed greatly from the real barnstormers in the States was that here we were limited in the distances that could be flown; in one day's flying we could run out of land to fly over, no matter which direction we took, and some of us yearned to fly in the wide open spaces that existed across 'The Pond.'

Our first Jackaroo (G-APAL) was written off in 1968 after an argument with some power lines (with no damage to the occupants), the Club replacing it with another of the same type (G-AOIR). In the process of rebuilding it, 'PAL was eventually converted back into a Tiger Moth *[Fig. 2]*, my eldest son Alan (by now a suitably licensed engineer) and I completing the work in 1984. Neither of us intended to keep the Tiger Moth for more than perhaps a year in view of the high upkeep costs, but that one year raised the possibility of doing something about satisfying that great urge to fly across the States.

There was now another reason for flying in the USA. When in 1979, and again in 1981, my wife and I had toured around the Western States, we had come across marked stretches of the Oregon Trail. What had started then as idle curiosity had by now grown into a desire to traverse the entire length of the Oregon Trail, to see first hand the sort of country the pioneers had travelled, so impressed had we become with the story of this vast westward migration. There was now only one way in which to follow exactly the course of the Trail and that was by air. It was also the only way in which I could do it in a single visit within the confines of a holiday from work (four weeks maximum).

There was of course just one big, seemingly insurmountable, problem – that was the cost. A few years earlier, when the Tiger Moth looked to be nearer completion than it actually was, another old colleague, George Cull, had mentioned that he knew of empty containers being shipped to or from the USA and these were big enough to accommodate several small aircraft. When I had suggested we might ship the Club Jackaroo and the Tiger in such a container, George looked further into it and sadly came back with a negative answer: what was more, the cost of hiring and shipping a container was around £3,000 each way. That ought to have been the end of it, but the dream kept resurfacing.

What we needed was the sort of financial backing that was being handed out to all sorts of eye-catching projects, by companies desperate for media cover to promote their name and product. Alas, I could see little media attention being forthcoming for the sort of flying we were contemplating, which we thought would be a pretty ordinary, everyday activity for our opposite numbers in the States.

However, the difficulty we had encountered in obtaining any information about the Oregon Trail suggested that there might be scope for an educational approach – perhaps a TV documentary or coverage for such as the National Geographic Society. The trigger came with the realisation that video cameras were now small and light enough to carry on aircraft such as the Tiger Moth, and with the new-found capability of running tapes for three hours it would be possible to mount the camera externally and let it run for the whole of the maximum flight time of a Tiger. The resulting tapes could be edited to provide a commercially viewable tape – or so it seemed at the time. Had I been even a little more knowledgeable about the subject, the idea would have died there and then, so it only goes to prove the worth of the saying: "Where ignorance is bliss 'tis folly to be wise."

It was enough to set the wheels in motion. The Club members liked the idea of shipping the two aircraft off to the States with an itinerary which would allow all the pilots to share the flying, providing we could obtain financial backing to cover at least the cost of shipping the aircraft out and back. George offered to produce copies of a report to be sent to possible sponsors if I would write it, and this was done over the Whitsun holiday in 1984, aiming at summer 1985 for the flight. Copies of the report were sent to some 25 prominent companies over a 12-month period.

Cost estimates amounted to just over £12,000, covering aircraft shipping; hire of a small truck to take spares, fuel, luggage, camping gear and supplies; cost of fuel and oil for the aircraft and truck; air fares for six pilots; and insurance cover. Individuals would cover their own daily expenses and the costs of any family they wished to take with them. We anticipated that considerable assistance would be forthcoming with fuel and air fares and possibly even shipping and hire car costs from suppliers in return for publicity. The flight was thought to be newsworthy simply because as far as we could ascertain no one had flown over the Trail from beginning to end, certainly not in two old biplanes shipped over from England and flown by British crews.

Meanwhile, there was much work to do. The Tiger Moth first flew in June 1984 and it took several months to shake out all the bugs, with a persistent rigging problem that didn't want to go away. High on the agenda were: the need to establish the operating parameters for flying the Trail, such as height and speed; the ease of following a largely invisible route; a means of mounting and operating video and still cameras etc.

First attempts at flying over a nearby section of occasionally visible Roman road were most discouraging. The big problem was in handling any sort of map of a scale large enough for identifying individual buildings and picking out tracks. A small hand-made section of map covering about five miles at a scale of ½ inch to the mile was drawn and oriented so that we would fly up it (it is not easy to identify ground features and read place names when flying say southwest using a north-orientated map – if turned so that features on the left of the route on the map match those that appear to the left on the ground etc., the wording is upside down).

Relating the map to the ground was easy enough if held at eye level, and we soon determined that the ideal height and speed to fly at were 500 ft and 60-70 mph. At this height we could usefully identify features up to around three miles away. What proved impossible was the timely location on the map of the next feature to look for – by the time I had found it, we had flown past it. Attempts to hold the position on the map with a finger showed the need for an extra hand – one to hold the control column, one to hold the map and one to fix the position on the map, ignoring the need to have a controlling hand on the throttle. At 500 ft the Tiger could not be left to its own devices whilst the pilot was scanning the map; an increase in noise indicated it was rapidly returning to earth and a reduction meant we were about to stall!

Fig. 1. Thruxton Jackaroo G-AOIR, one of the two aircraft originally intended to be used for the Oregon Trail Flight. A four-seat cabin conversion of a Tiger Moth, powered by the same 130 hp Gipsy Major engine, this belonged to the Stevenage Flying Club. *(Photo: G.A. Cull)*

Fig. 2. 1939 de Havilland Tiger Moth G-APAL, here shown in prewar RAF markings carrying its RAF serial no. N6847. This aircraft was rebuilt by the author and others after flying into power lines in 1968, and was to have been flown by the author as the 'camera ship' and 'lead aircraft.' *(Photo: Mike Vaisey)*

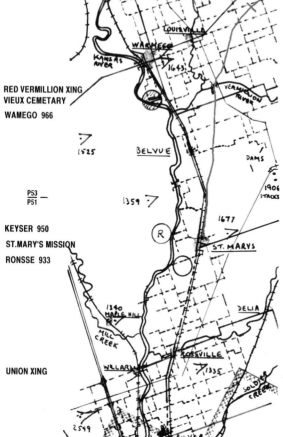

RED VERMILLION XING
VIEUX CEMETARY
WAMEGO 966

P53/P51

KEYSER 950
ST.MARY'S MISSION
RONSSE 933

UNION XING

Fig. 3 (above). The roller map case mounted on the upper left side longeron of a Tiger Moth and protruding into the slipstream. The two knobs at the side are for positioning the map under the fixed cursor line.

Fig. 4. A section of the map roll at St. Marys, west of Topeka KS. The roll is 5.4 in. wide, the map width of 3.5 in. (=14 miles) starting 1.2 in. from the left edge. The Trail route (original in green) follows the railroad past St. Marys, then WNW to the Red Vermillion Crossing and on to the northwest. Red triangular symbols (obstructions with heights above ground) point north. Brown circles are small airfields (name and height in margin). P51/P53 refers to pages in Franzwa's book *"Maps of the Oregon Trail."*

The answer was to make a continuous roll strip map, passing under a cursor which would fix our last known position – one hand to roll on the map to the next feature and one hand to fly the aircraft *[Fig. 3]*. What was not so simple was how to do it. The six 52 in x 41 in US Sectional Aeronautical charts we used as a basis were drawn to a scale of 1:500,000 (roughly 1/8 in to a mile). The 133 charts we had showing the Oregon Trail route in detail were at ½ inch to a mile. By reducing the Trail charts photographically to ¼ inch to a mile and projecting the Sectionals onto them at the same scale it was possible to draw up a new strip map combining the required features of both at an acceptable scale *[Fig. 4]*. The strip was 3½ in wide, giving a 14 mile-wide swathe – when the Trail route wandered too close to the edge of the strip, that section was ended and a new one started at an appropriate angle to the previous one, and so on. Even so, it required a roll 42 feet long to cover the 2,021 miles of the Trail, hand-drawn in seven colours, a feat that occupied some 200 hours of painstaking effort.

The other factor that gave much food for thought was the determination of the flight schedule. Neither aircraft was equipped with wheel brakes, depending instead on a tail-skid for slowing and limited steering, which meant that landing on out-of-wind concrete runways was not practical as the skid provided no control on hard surfaces. This constrained us to finding airfields with grass or dirt runways, at just the right distance apart to allow for a reasonable daily schedule. We restricted ourselves to early-morning flying both to avoid hot and high take-off problems (wings provide less lift when the temperature is high and the airfield is on high ground, due to lowered air density under these conditions) and to avoid filming into the sun.

With a flight duration of 2½ hours (after allowing a 30-minute safety margin) we could reckon on a maximum stage length of roughly 150 miles assuming a 15 mph head wind. It would not be practical to plan for more than two stages a day as we wished to finish flying before midday to avoid the highest temperatures and turbulence. Also, every stop consumed at least an hour by the time we had refuelled etc. Other factors such as the location of suitable airfields would drop this to around 250 miles a day, which would be quite enough for the ground crews to aim at.

Thus we should reckon on nine days flying over the Trail, plus a full contingency day to cover the possibility of bad weather or maintenance problems with the aircraft. We settled on ten days plus four days to get from our East Coast base to Independence Missouri. It was of course important to arrive at a schedule we were confident of adhering to in order to allow the sponsor's publicity people to plan maximum coverage.

The return flight would be a different kettle of fish. With no media attention to worry about we looked forward to a real barnstorm on the way back, the only scheduled item being that of the transport back to

England. The winds would be behind us, and with no camera work to worry about we could fly as long as conditions and our own endurance would allow.

During the following winter I made contact with Gregory Franzwa, author of a number of books on the Oregon Trail, including the maps I used as a basis for my strip-map. I pestered him with a wide range of questions, in answering some of which he referred me to books about the Whitmans, who established a Mission at Walla Walla. These revealed yet another fascinating adventure and an important date – they had travelled over the Trail in 1836 and the missionaries' wives were the first white women to travel overland to Oregon. 1986 would see the 150th anniversary of their epic trek and there would be bound to be celebrations somewhere along the route that we could join in with, hopefully with advantage to us all.

So far we had only negative responses from the recipients of our Report, and the time came when we decided to postpone the flight to 1986, now enhanced by being a special anniversary year. By mid-1985 we had no further progress to cheer us, but I decided that I would have to go ahead with plans to visit the States to clear up more questions. I had by now joined OCTA (the Oregon–California Trails Association) and decided to attend their Convention at Scottsbluff, Nebraska. This would give me a chance to try out my map in the air at the invitation of Ritch Rundstrom at Kearney. A Pan Am pilot, he owned a Piper Cub which would be ideal for the job, and having heard of our planned flight had written to me offering to help in any way he could.

That trip cleared up a number of points: the map worked fine; I discovered what to look for in the way of trail ruts; I met a fine bunch of people who convinced me we were doing the right thing with our planned flight; and the weather gave me a fright, with winds of 60 mph the night I arrived in Denver, and hailstorms that blocked roads with three feet of ice. At least the latter convinced me of the need to find hangar accommodation overnight for our fabric-covered aircraft!

Before departing for the States I had one last-minute job to do. It seemed that Canadian Club (the whisky distillers) were running a "Club Challenge" competition. Any challenging activity a Club would like to undertake, but were unable to carry out on the grounds of excessive cost or inexperience, could be entered for the competition; a small number of winners (chosen for their media appeal) would be funded by Canadian Club to carry out their activity with maximum publicity. It was obviously set up with us in mind! The only snag was that we did not hear about it until several weeks after the closing date for entries, but I entered anyway, sending them a copy of our standard Report.

CHAPTER 2
THE CHALLENGE

On my return from the States in late August 1985, I had expected to find either a rejection of our entry in the Canadian Club Challenge competition due to late entry, or an acknowledgement of receipt. There was neither and as the weeks sped past I assumed that it had sunk like a stone, especially as the winners were to be announced early in October.

All the more surprising then to receive a phone call on October 1st from the PR agency handling the competition. A very young-sounding Gary informed me that we were virtually certain to be one of the winners and it was just a matter of the judges checking our *bona fides* and validity of our figures. Announcement of the winners was now to be delayed to mid-November but he would contact me again within a week. Funding would cover all the costs incurred including members' daily expenses; they would like to visit us and see the aircraft, but in the meantime could we update the report with any changes following my visit to the States and could they have it within 48 hours? That of course gave little time for a proper review of the figures and all I could say was that the timing of the flight should be in June/July rather than August, but that I would send them a fully updated report in about a week's time.

The new figures took into account the desire to follow the Whitmans' route from Canandaigua in New York State (which increased the mileage and number of members taking part) and to join in with the sesquicentennial celebrations to be held there and in Walla Walla (which would increase the publicity value); also the extra costs of including members' daily expenses and the sinking value of the pound against the dollar (which that winter fell almost to parity).

The week passed and no call came from Gary, and it was to be five weeks before we heard from him again to fix a meeting on November 8th. The press announcement was now deferred until the end of November and we were asked if we could transport the Tiger Moth to London and erect it in the basement ballroom of the Royal Lancaster Hotel, where the reception was to be held. He obviously had no idea of the work involved in dismantling, preparing for transport and re-erecting the Tiger Moth, and then repeating it all over again and getting it back to flying condition. But we did it, and were proud to see how well it looked, glittering under the ballroom lights.

Meanwhile, we had much other work to do, including renewing the Certificate of Airworthiness for the Jackaroo. A formidable list of tasks was drawn up and split fairly evenly on a voluntary basis between the members. We arranged to meet regularly to review progress on completing the tasks which were: identification and provision of the spares we would need; installing and testing radio, intercom and emergency locater transmitters for both aircraft, and radio for the ground crew; provision of video and still cameras, films and tapes, and mounting them on the aircraft; arranging transport for people, and packing and shipping for the aircraft and spares, and provision of the support vehicle; providing camping equipment and survival gear in case crews were to force-land in the more remote areas; rostering the ground and air crews (surprisingly difficult and tedious with continually changing require-ments); and arranging flight schedules and routeing, airfield clearance, maps and charts and briefing notes for the crews and publicity people.

Unfortunately, the delays and poor communication we had faced from the outset persisted right through our dealings with the agency people. When they wished to contact us they did so, usually requesting some action within 48 hours; when we wanted to contact them they were never in the office and requests for them to call us back or respond to letters were ignored. This made it very difficult to determine what progress they were making with tasks they had undertaken themselves, such as booking air passages, shipping for the aircraft, hire of cars, provision of video equipment etc, all of which they were hoping to obtain free or at reduced cost in return for media exposure. In the end we arranged all except the videos ourselves, which proved very fortunate as it turned out.

Pressure to get everything completed never eased off right up to the time we left for the States, and a full-dress rehearsal planned for around Easter was for various reasons not carried out until the Spring Bank Holiday, only a week and half before the planned shipping date. The rehearsal was intended to prove aircraft operating procedures (speeds, heights and spacing), use of the roller map and supporting charts in the Tiger Moth, intercom, air-to-air communication, video and still cameras photography, fuel consumptions and even crew endurance (some had never flown six hours in one day). Timing was important as we needed all the equipment to be available and still leave time to correct any shortcomings. As it happened we had not obtained a video camera, but were using both a remote-controlled fixed Leica (R4 with a 60 mm f2.8 Macro-Elmarit lens) and a hand-held M6 with a 90 mm f2.8 Tele-Elmarit lens.

The planned flight was to be south-westerly over the route of the pre-historic Icknield Way from near our base at Gransden, then over the equally ancient but more visible Ridgeway, westwards through the Thames Valley, and along the post-Roman Wansdyke, a system of defensive earthworks leading towards Bristol, landing at Badminton to complete the first leg. From there we would turn northward over the River Severn to pick up Offa's Dyke, a great defensive ditch which marked the old border between England and Wales. After landing near the northern end, we would head back south-east to home, following disused railways. In order to prove the use of the roller map, I drew the route on a strip map similar to the one prepared for the Oregon trail.

This would give us practice in following now-invisible routes, footpaths, earthworks and ploughed railways, as well as some rugged hill country in the Black Mountains. In all, a distance of nearly 500 miles, involving three landings and about eight hours flying. That should prove something, one way or another.

Delays in completing the tasks plus poor weather took us right up to the Bank Holiday Monday, with only one further weekend available after that if we failed to make it. The weather forecast for the Monday was not good, but it was flyable with an estimated wind strength of 17 mph and a possibility of rain or fog in the south-west. We were due to meet at Gransden at 08.00 and when I arrived the wind was rattling the corrugated iron hangar doors and straining the windsock nearly horizontal. Broken cloud layers promised almost anything but visibility was not too bad.

By the time we were airborne, our schedule had quietly slipped an hour, a not unusual occurrence. We ran into trouble straight away as John, my crew member, could not hear me though I could read him quite well over the intercom. By trial and error I established that I had to deepen my voice and turn my head when speaking so that the slipstream pressed the throat mike against my throat instead of away from it! Similarly we could not establish communication with the Jackaroo and never did throughout the flight. By the time we had sorted out the intercom we had strayed way off the route and only by using knowledge of the local terrain did I regain it. That would be something to watch out for over the Trail, where my local knowledge was non-existent!

The next thing we learned was that it was essential for me to have a copy of the air chart to hand. At one point in trying to follow a circular path round an air traffic zone I was blown off course and off the strip map, and then had difficulty in identifying our position, John by this time having also lost his place on his chart. Fortunately we had no further problems in that respect but those two occurrences were sufficient to show the error of our ways – when flying over the Trail we always had a copy of the Sectional for each crew member!

Of the Icknield Way we saw no sign, but the Ridgeway, with its chalky tracks and paths, was easy to identify, as were the steep embankments of the Wansdyke. Offa's Dyke was patchy, at times there being no evidence of it whatsoever, at others just a well-worn footpath, but over long stretches there were deep furrows that pointed the way, much as I imagined we would see over the Oregon Trail.

In climbing up over the Black Mountains we got caught at low altitude on the lee side of a steep ridge. Buffeted by the downdraughts curling over the rim, the Tiger proved incapable of climbing clear of them, able to do no more than match the steep slope of the ridge as we rode up to the top of the hill. I could have turned away and circled clear of the turbulence (an option not always available where there is a succession of ridges), but I was interested to see how well the Tiger could cope. The Jackaroo following behind and some 500 ft higher had no such difficulty. That experience made me resolve not to get caught again in such circumstances – next time there may not be an easy way out!

On the first leg we shot a full roll of film on the fixed camera to check if we now had the remote control bugs sorted out. We had, but now another problem presented itself. We had encountered pretty damp conditions early on, with drizzle and mist, but were not prepared for the effect this had on the camera lens. It looked to be completely opaque, as if it had been struck by a stone and had splintered; on closer examination it turned out to be internal condensation with no way of removing it. All we could do was to turn the aircraft so that the camera faced into the sun and hope that it would dry out. It never did fully, but sufficiently so to warrant shooting another roll on the way back.

Our second leg ended at a small airfield on top of the hills outside Welshpool, some two-thirds of the way along the Dyke. What with our late start and an extra hour on the ground at Badminton, plus a pleasant rest at Welshpool we deemed it sufficient to fly straight back from there. We had proved most of what we had set out to do and learnt quite a lot, and it would still be a six-hour flight by the time we landed at Gransden. The flight home following the disused railways was a doddle in comparison with the concentration required on the outward legs, but it was encouraging to know that we could follow the roller map as well as we had in the later stages.

When we flew the aircraft into the British Aerospace airfield at Hatfield on the evening before we were due to dismantle them for shipping, relations between ourselves and the agency had become even more strained. A crunch point had been reached when it became obvious that Gary had not done any of the things he had insisted on taking on, and was unlikely to complete them by the scheduled time. He was going to hand us a cheque for everything but the shipping, which of course was the biggest item of expenditure and which he was still hoping to obtain free of charge. The amount now being talked about was well short of what was needed, and we observed that it would not cover the insurance premium. I don't think they had stopped to consider indemnity cover until then, their attitude being that it was up to us as to whether we took out insurance.

We had been negotiating for $1M (million) indemnity, and had found it very difficult to get any insurer to quote a figure; when they did the cost was roughly twice what we had been led to expect, and this had to be passed back to Canadian Club for approval. The outcome was a request by their lawyers to increase it to $5M. When we obtained a quote for that amount and passed it on, the cover required was raised to $15M. Eventually we were able to give a quote for the new figure, when it was upped yet again to $25M, and we were still trying to obtain that when the shipping date was reached. When we refused to dismantle the aircraft without a written assurance that the shipping costs would be paid we were told that the whole thing was off and in its place were offered a weekend trip to Vancouver to visit the '86 Expo! The next day the local papers and radio were stating that the flight was off because the US aviation authorities would not allow it!

This of course was unacceptable to the team members after the immense amount of work that had been put in, not to mention the out-of-pocket expenses incurred. We had lived, eaten, slept, and breathed this project too long to be put off like that. The upshot of it all was that three of us, Brian Hargrave, George Cull and myself, together with our wives Sonia, Jean and Irene respectively, decided to go ahead, with or without the help of Canadian Club, and show that the reasons given for it being cancelled were patently without foundation.

It had been a condition of the competition that winners were not to approach the Canadian Club management for any reason at all, but now we had nothing to lose by doing so. Faced with our version of the story, and a new proposal to hire American aircraft with a reduced team (there now being insufficient time to ship out our own aircraft) the UK Manager could not have been more helpful. It was finally agreed that providing we could obtain the necessary indemnity cover they would agree to pay the costs of a team of three and the use of a single aircraft and hire car (the original costs were seemingly to be shared by both US and UK branches, the former now apparently having pulled out). Surprisingly, we were asked to make no mention of Canadian Club's involvement – no logos, no stickers, no publicity.

Despite the manager's instructions to the agency that we were to be paid immediately, the cliff-hanging continued until the last moment, the cheque finally coming to hand less than 48 hours before we left for the States, and not without continual chasing.

By the time we had shared the payment amongst the team members who were not going the amount we received per head was way down on what was required, but it was still well worthwhile, and at least gave some recompense to those unfortunate enough not to go. All this should be a warning to winners of competitions to read the small print, keep a very close eye on the ball until it is safely in the net, and to take nothing for granted!

Regarding the hire of an aircraft of similar performance (so that we would not need to change the schedules), the nearest we could get at such short notice was a 1946 65 hp Aeronca Champion ("Champ"), though even this had to be on a 'buy and resale' basis, the resale figure being reduced by the equivalent hire charge – seemingly the owner had little faith in our returning the aircraft safely. By selling my share of the Tiger Moth (which I had always planned to do after our return) I was able to raise the purchase price of the Champ. We were most fortunate in that Gerry Schwam, a fellow DH Moth Club member in Philadelphia, who was to have been involved in setting up base camp for assembling and re-crating the two biplanes, was on hand to negotiate use of the Champ, so that when we arrived in the States all we had to do was hand over the money! Gerry, like Ritch Rundstrom, had written to us on hearing about our original plans, offering to help.

We had been unable to clinch any deals on video equipment and my resources were stretched enough to not wish to purchase the equipment. Besides, a BBC TV producer had told me that we should use Super 8 mm ciné film in preference to domestic standard video if we wished to do anything with it. I knew nothing about cine-filming, but a friend of mine lent me a camera, unfortunately too late to have time to carry out any trials. It was even at too short notice to be able to buy reels of film locally, and there was no time to travel down to London to get any or to send away for it. We took the camera with us and fortunately obtained some film in the States with the help of our OCTA friends. But we were literally shooting blind, with no chance of feedback as to whether the results would be any good.

All too suddenly, it was the day before our leaving date. That day rushed by in a frenzy of last-minute activity to the point where it seemed impossible that there would be time to get everything completed. Even on the morning of departure there were little jobs still to be done and I nearly missed the flight trying to make a last-minute call to my bank.

In the airport lounge, I checked for the 'n'th time over all the details. Suddenly, I realised that I had forgotten the name of the American bank at which we were to collect our Banker's Order for payment for the aircraft we were buying. All I could recall was that it was "The First ...... Bank" in Philadelphia. Unbelievably, it was not written on the paperwork from my own bank, and in desperation, I searched for a telephone. All to no avail, as the only one I could find in the departure lounge would respond only to a Telecom credit card, which I did not possess!

I was still searching for a coin-box phone, when my now-frantic wife found me and screeched a warning that if we didn't run we would miss the plane. They had already announced "last calls" for boarders!

But we made it, and still hardly able to believe that it was all now actually happening, we sat back in relief as our aircraft took off for Philadelphia. What we had left undone would have to stay undone unless it could be dealt with over there.

'Now' was a little oasis of relaxation – who knew, or at that moment cared, what problems tomorrow would bring?

PART 2: EAST-WEST

CHAPTER 3
CLEARING THE DECKS

It was cloudy when we left Heathrow and cloudy when we arrived at Philadelphia, but that was about all that the weather had in common at the two places. The east side of the States was suffering one of its usual high-summer bouts of sweltering humidity, with a high hazy overcast and distant, towering banks of cumulo-nimbus thunderheads, threatening something highly unwelcome. The sun filtered through so that emerging from the aircraft was a little like entering a greenhouse, the air heavy, humid and hot.

Gerry Schwam was waiting to meet us when we arrived and helped us to collect our hire car. We had originally enquired about a large estate wagon so that we could seat six and take all our luggage in comfort. But the quote had been so high that we settled on a saloon (in local parlance, sedan), thinking our requirements for six seats would be very limited. Imagine our surprise then to be confronted with the largest estate car we had ever seen *[Fig. 5]*. It seems they had taken our enquiry as an order and once started it had not been stoppable – no matter, they still charged us only for the saloon.

The size of the thing had all the wives twittering about whether they could cope with it but, by the time we handed it in at Salt Lake City, they had become quite accustomed to it. As it happened it was just as well we had it – by the time it had swallowed up all our gear and the six of us there was little room to spare – and we did need it as a six-seater quite extensively in the first few days before setting out for the West!

Of course, in the States, everyone is able to cope with such large monsters from birth, so that when you hire one, nobody expects to tell you how to drive it. But Brian, who was doing the initial spell of driving, wanted, not unreasonably, to know what all the knobs and buttons and controls were and what they did. That took a little while and a lot of explaining before an 'expert' was produced. Even so, most of the minor controls were the subject of much experimentation from then on. Brian's initial driving lesson was round the collection car park, to the consternation of the security men at the exit. They seemed convinced that there was something sinister about this large white estate that kept rushing up to the exit and then turning back in.

I don't think we ever did sort out quite how to cope with the tailgate. This seemingly could only be opened or locked shut with the electrically-operated window wound down. Certainly the crew found out the hard way that all was not what it seemed when, on accelerating from some traffic lights, the gate swung open and distributed most of the load over the roadway. That provided no small degree of interest and amusement for the local population.

Brian enjoyed the low-speed acceleration and braking more than the rest of the crew! They soon found that any loosely-stowed cases would slide to the back when he took off, and rush forward to thump into the back of the seats when he braked. The rear-seat passengers quickly became quite adept at anticipating when he was going to brake hard, and then turning round and catching the bigger cases before they struck!

Gerry gave us a conducted tour round part of the city en route to the motel he had booked for us that night, the most memorable part of the drive being through the beautiful Fairmount Park along the east bank of the Schuylkill River. This gave us a totally different view of the city than the more depressing one, along Broad Street, that we encountered on every subsequent journey to and from our motel at Willow Grove on the northern outskirts.

We arranged to go out to Sky Manor airport, in New Jersey, the next day (Saturday) to see the Aeronca Champion [Fig. 6] that Gerry had located for us and, if we felt that it was suitable, to finalise the deal. What I had overlooked was that the banks were closed that day and we would not be able to arrange payment until Monday. To complicate the situation, the weather was marginal for flying, with heavy thunderstorms building up, and thick mist and low cloud forecast until Monday.

We went out and had a look at the aeroplane but could not fly it due to the bad weather. Gerry introduced us to Bill Smela who, with his wife Maryjo, operated SkyArts, which seemed to cover every conceivable activity associated with light aircraft and gliders. They owned the Aeronca, which they used to convert nosewheel-trained pilots to fly what are universally now referred to as "taildraggers." Bill looked a typical cigar-chewing, fast-talking car salesman, and it was not until later that we learned how false this impression was.

As for the Champion, what we saw was not exactly inspiring; in our ignorance of the Aeronca wing structure and method of mounting the ailerons, it seemed as if the brackets supporting the latter were loose. It looked to lean slightly to one side and have a degree more dihedral on one wing than the other. At first, it proved totally impossible to get the engine cowling fasteners to engage and I had visions of the cowling coming adrift in flight. The spartan interior and paucity of instrument-ation was no bother – it had all the essential instruments we needed. It even had an oil temperature gauge, which we didn't have in the Tiger, admittedly in much cooler conditions. There was no radio but we did not use one at home so that was no problem either.

When we climbed in we found the door would not latch shut and had to be secured by a home-made iron catch. The sliding windows fitted on the left side of the cabin demanded patience to move without jamming. There was no mixture control fitted, although one would be necessary at the altitudes at which we would be flying over the mountains.

28

In the door pocket was a broken piece of weathered and time-worn wood, like a short stick. Something about it stopped me from throwing it away, it having a small vee cut in one edge which looked to have some purpose in being there. Suddenly I twigged that it was probably a dipstick, the coarse calibration of the rotating ball fuel gauge presumably not being sufficiently reliable when the fuel tank was nearly empty! Sure enough, on inserting it through the filler there was just enough of the broken end left to be able to touch bottom without letting go! There was to come a time when I would be grateful for that little broken stick!

With its stubby, deep fuselage and ridiculously short undercarriage legs, so that it looked to be suffering from 'duck's disease' (its bottom too near the ground), aesthetic appeal was sadly lacking. But, although the paintwork was peeling in one or two places, the little aeroplane had a friendly and reassuring look about it. Like our familiar and well-tried Jackaroo at home, it was clearly accustomed to working hard for its living.

Bill convinced us that the loose aileron brackets were OK and that they were designed to enable the ailerons to float to the correct position when raised or lowered; later, when we had a chance to look at the manual, we found this was so. Its large side windows would enable us easily to photograph the ground using a hand-held camera in the back. The substantial wing-struts would serve to mount the fixed, remote-control camera. There were tubular struts inside the cabin on which to mount my roller map case, and still have a good view of the ground.

The Champ had two other prime factors going for it: one was an engine with only 600-odd hours from new; the other was that I had just enough money to buy it and no more. With the latter point in mind we all agreed, with varying degrees of enthusiasm, that the Champion should do what we wanted if its performance measured up to Bill's claims.

Actually, Bill seemed to be having second thoughts, when he realised that we really did intend to fly it across the Rockies to the Pacific coast and back. This trip was calling a lot of bluffs, including mine! Driven into a corner and pressed for an answer as to whether he thought the Champ could do what we wanted, he agreed, almost reluctantly, that it could.

Even so, he took me to look at a more powerful and later version and extolled its undoubted advantages over the Champ – greater speed, higher ceiling, longer range, heavier load capability, fitted radio, blind flying panel, more comfortable seats, you name it etc. It really was more suitable but so was a helicopter and I couldn't afford one of those either!

He observed that if we encountered really bad weather the Champ could not run away fast enough. It had insufficient endurance to dodge aside and wait for bad weather to pass. If we tangled with downdraughts over the mountains it could not climb fast enough to get out, etc. I could only give him my stock answer: "If it gets that bad we won't fly." Pity, it would have been safer to have had that other machine, but it was the Champ or nothing and the latter made it more of a challenge anyway!

We agreed to come back the next day if the weather was OK for flying; I was anxious to make the altitude check flight and thus know that we would go ahead with the Champ. Meanwhile, on the way back to Gerry's place for an evening meal, we did a spot of sightseeing and tourist shopping round the old Colonial town of New Hope, on the Delaware River, where we were introduced to bagels ("Sixty years old already and never eaten a bagel? Man, you haven't lived!").

So passed Saturday without any flying, and Sunday likewise for the same reasons. Sunday morning was our first experiment with the Weather Information Service. Standing under the dripping awning outside the motel, we used a call-box phone to dial the toll-free Flight Service Station (FSS) to obtain the local forecast, on the face of things easy enough to do. Pilots all over the USA have been accustomed to doing this since before they learned to walk. Problem was we had already had several unsuccessful brushes with the telephones, which didn't help, but now we ran into another snag.

One needed to be familiar with the local geography to know which of the confusing array of area names to call for the airfield conditions required. Brian, who was the most familiar of the three of us with the new-fangled art of radio-telephony, was appointed the task of talking to the weather man. When he did eventually locate the correct FSS for the area he failed to make much sense of the jargon which was hurled at him at break-neck speed in full-blown, nasal American. But we got the general gist that it was pretty horrible flying weather, too bad even for ducks, and was likely to stay that way for the rest of the day! We retired hurt.

At least it gave us a chance to visit Washington DC. This enabled the guys to satisfy a long-held ambition to look over the Smithsonian National Air and Space Museum, and for the gals to see the Capitol and the White House. That weekend also served to introduce us to the severity of American thunderstorms. The torrential downpour we encountered in Washington as we took our leave was so bad that, in company with every other driver, we had to pull into the side of the road and stop. The wipers simply could not cope with the amount of water hurled at the windscreen – we literally could not see where we were going even at a walking pace! When we returned to our motel there was a Niagara Falls off the roof outside our room where the gutters and drains were totally inadequate to carry the volume of water.

The ladies also took the opportunity, throughout the weekend, of learning how to handle the car in preparation for the coming long drive. Round and round and round the motel driveways and car park they went, the monstrous size of the car gradually shrinking as they became accustomed to it. Some of the motel overnighters thought this was a new form of entertainment laid on by the management, and came out to cheer them on! But it was a while before the girls felt reasonably happy about driving it in traffic, Sonia being the first and bravest in driving most of the way to Washington.

Our plan for Monday was for me to phone Leitz in New York in order to make arrangements about collecting the cameras they were to loan us: for me to call at the bank to pick up the banker's order for the cash for the aircraft; for us then to call on Gerry to pick up the Narco transceivers that were to be loaned to us; and for us then to drive out to Sky Manor to do some flying, the weather now having relented a little. We confidently anticipated being able to clear all the jobs by midmorning and have lunch at Sky Manor. We still had not learned how long the simplest tasks take.

Suffice it to say we were still trying to find our way to Gerry's office by midday, the roads, last seen at night, looking entirely different in daylight. When we got there Gerry had not received the radios and promised to try and get them to us as soon as they arrived.

Neither had things happened as anticipated with the cameras, and they would not be ready to collect until Tuesday at the earliest. This was a major setback as we could not make the brackets for mounting them on the aircraft until we had them. As with the ciné camera, there would be no opportunity to check them out in the air, process the film and view the results. My worst fears were now materialising – we could have the fixed camera aiming at the wrong point and not know it. Similarly the exposures could be incorrectly adjusted for the conditions. And of course, the remote control for the fixed camera, with which initially we had so many problems in the UK, could do the same again and us be not aware of it.

To crown it all, there was still confusion over the name of the bank, there being two banks in the city with the word 'First' in the title. Naturally, we picked the wrong one initially. The one we wanted had no local branches in our vicinity and we had to drive a considerable distance for a branch that would handle the transaction. Not an entirely auspicious start! Somehow, we got everything sorted out and made it to Sky Manor by mid-afternoon.

Bill Smela was a difficult individual to find and pin down. If not piloting the big Cessna Bird Dog used for glider-tugging, he was probably buried in a fuselage, somewhere in the hangar, with a blow-torch in his hand. When we finally tracked him down he mentioned that over the weekend he had fitted an altitude mixture control and showed us a small knob on the instrument panel.

At last I was able to climb aboard the Champ with Bill and take the first check-ride with him. It turned out to be far worse to handle on the ground than in the air. Initially, it took much concentration to be able to steer the wayward thing where you, and not it, wanted to go (it obviously preferred to proceed tail-first). It was necessary to anticipate which way it would swing next and apply corrective rudder before the swing developed, the rudder having a delayed action effect. The art lay in not having to keep jabbing the brakes to bring it back from where it should not have been.

Despite a very noticeable, protesting squeak from the rudder pedals when they were pressed either way, Bill was able to taxy the Champ without any noticeable noise from them. But my progression down the taxyway, to the end of the runway, was accompanied by their running commentary on how badly I was anticipating which way and how far the wretched thing was going to swing next. It was amazing how quiet they became within a few days!

In the air, the short, fat little fuselage also dictated constant attention to the ball and turn indicator. This showed how well you were keeping the aircraft's controls co-ordinated – too much rudder for the degree of aileron applied meant the ball skidded off to the opposite side. With time, keeping the ball central would, like the taxying, become second nature.

But in the meantime, Bill Smela, sitting good-humouredly in the back, patiently growled his stock quotation for this situation: "Kick the ball" (i.e. kick the rudder bar on the side to which the ball swung). This he had apparently had dinned into him when taught to fly by a grizzled old Service instructor. It seemed that, although the Champ was a fairly docile little machine most of the time, it could bite the unwary by spinning off a badly co-ordinated turn at low speed. "Kick the ball" – I heard that repeated over my shoulder all the way across the States and back, whenever the wretched thing moved off centre.

A whole hour of 'circuits and bumps' sped past, with me making several quite inexcusably bad touchdowns when I landed from Tiger Moth height (a foot or so higher than that of the Aeronca). They were not exactly helped by a 10 mph crosswind, though we could reckon on having to cope with much higher crosswinds than that.

Something else that had to become second nature was the correct use of the carburettor heat control to prevent carburettor icing. This manual control, vital to the safe operation of the Continental engine in the Champ, was not needed on the Gipsy Major engines fitted in our own aircraft. After forgetting to use it several times on the approach to land, I eventually got used to it and Bill pronounced himself satisfied that I was safe to let out on my own.

There followed a few solo circuits, then at last we could carry out that altitude check! Brian, being the heavier of the other two, came up with me, together with what we hoped was a representative load. It was about 7.15 in the evening by the time we took off, and the Champ was noticeably slower in the climb than when only Bill had been aboard with me. It was a beautiful, sunny, hazy evening when we took off. Up till then, I had only flown round the circuit at low altitude, and other than taking grim note of the string of pylons marching across the line of the runway, had not really paid much attention to the surrounding scene.

Now, as we climbed higher, we could see a very large river a few miles to the west, the Delaware, gleaming dully through the evening haze. As we circled, we started to pick out several adjacent airfields and a few prominent features which ensured that we were always able to spot our own base. A rough check on our rate of climb over the first few thousand feet indicated it to be around 300 feet per minute – nothing earth-shattering but we were not going in for altitude records!

Brian, sitting in the back, had a Sectional map and was checking the ground features as we climbed. Suddenly he asked: "Have you been watching the compass lately?"

I had to confess I had only vaguely been doing so, idly watching to see north come up on each circle we made.

"Well, I have been for the last couple of circuits and have not yet seen south appear!", said Brian. "You watch it, and see what I mean."

Sure enough, once past north, the compass card slowed as it went through east and then stopped at about 120 degrees, though the aircraft was still turning! I watched pop-eyed as, after a few seconds, it swung smartly back through north to settle on about 240 degrees, before recommencing its leisurely anti-clockwise rotation to match our slow rate of turn! Once again, as it reached 120 degrees it repeated the process.

Well, there had to be a south in there somewhere; no compass I had ever heard of disliked south so much as to omit it altogether. So I tried creeping up on it from the opposite direction, circling now anti-clockwise. But the compass would have none of it. Either it was ashamed to admit that it had no south reading or it simply did not like south! We would have to see Bill about that one when we got down.

After about an hour of steady climbing we decided that the Champ's climb rate had dropped almost to zero. I still had full control so we had not reached the ceiling, but the stalling speed seemed very close to our cruise speed. The altimeter showed 11,000 ft, which was all that we were asking of the Champ. We had tried the operation of the new mixture control, kidding ourselves that it really did have an effect, but not entirely convinced!

With the shades of night beginning to draw in below we decided to call it a day. It may not be appreciated by everyone that at dusk, an aircraft at 11,000 ft may be flying in bright evening sunlight, though at ground level the sun has long since slipped below the horizon. By the time we had rejoined the circuit, lights could be seen here and there although there was still ample light to see to fly.

We tackled Bill about the compass and were surprised at his reaction – he seemed to think we could manage without one, suggesting if he could not correct ours we could perhaps fit a car compass on the windscreen! He was pulling our leg of course, and he fitted another the next day. The only problem was that he repositioned it from the instrument panel to a new mounting on the wing cabane struts, way above the pilot's eye level. This because he thought the mixture control he had fitted on the panel, adjacent to the compass, had adversely affected it.

That night we all settled into a local motel, though the proprietor would not have been flattered by the ladies' remarks about the general state of things. We had little choice at that time but we only stayed there the one night. At least the sight of myriads of fireflies dancing in the grounds provided a new topic of conversation!

Next morning was a truly summery day, with clear blue sky and zephyr breeze – had the weather now changed our way? I had to drive over to New York to pick up the cameras from Leitz and the wives joined me to see a little more of the scenery. It was late afternoon by the time we got back to Sky Manor and I expected to find that George and Brian had done their check-rides with Bill. This unfortunately was not so, as Bill had not been available all day. He fitted them in that evening and then started in on making up a mounting for the camera.

George had used his time in applying some lettering on the side of the fuselage below the cabin window, outlining who we were and what we were doing. Brian had been checking out the radios, Gerry having flown in with them that afternoon. That was his last visit and I missed the chance of a final chat with him before we left for the great unknown. Not only that, but I also missed a flying visit by the unique Pitcairn Autogyro – the only prewar autogyro flying anywhere in the world!

That evening, Maryjo and I sorted out all the paperwork and I emerged the proud, if temporary, owner of a 1946 Aeronca 7AC Champion, registration NC2979E, with strict instructions to bring it back in one piece. It had been in the family for too many years for it to be otherwise!

Brian and I decided to spend the night on the floor of the little Clubhouse in our sleeping bags, so that we could make an early start if the weather was good. George and the harem drove off to find a motel a little closer to Canandaigua, to give themselves a better chance of arriving there before 1.00 pm next day. To our eyes, the sky that night looked just right for good weather the next morning, but Bill cast an experienced eye at it and cheerfully forecast fog and low cloud, which would not shift before midday, if then! He perhaps was cheerful because it would give him time to finish off in the morning the camera mount he had been making for us. He was that confident about it that he made no attempt to finish the mount that night.

Sure enough, at crack of dawn when we woke and looked out, thick mist filled the valleys. The crests of the hills stood out sharp and clear against a narrow reddish streak of sky beneath a solid blanket of cloud. We thought that presaged another fine day, once the sun burnt it off: unfortunately it never got a chance to. The cloud cover thickened to fill the gap above the hills. We could do nothing but watch miserably as, within an hour, the hilltops disappeared. When we phoned the FSS for a weather report, it sounded as if we would not be moving at all that day, with a forecast of continuing fog and thunderstorms. The outlook was just as bleak for the next few days as well!

We used the time to good effect, Brian taking the opportunity to check-swing the compass, i.e. compare the compass reading at eight or more points with a calibration compass. The effect was startling. Sure enough, the compass did read at all points, south dutifully coming up in the correct sequence. But the check swing also revealed that, even with full compensation adjustment, there were residual errors of between +40 and -37 degrees (known as compass deviation).

This meant that every time we took a reading we had to add or subtract the error in order to get a true value, e.g. to indicate that the aircraft was heading North (360 deg) the required compass reading was 325 deg, and for East (90 deg), 130 deg [Appendix 3]. While virtually all aircraft magnetic compasses have deviation errors, it is rarely more than 5 degrees, which means that the reading is usually somewhere near the required figure. Such a large error also meant that the rotating card was either too sluggish or far too sensitive at different points of the compass. The slightest turn of the aircraft while on a southerly heading sent it swinging wildly while it tried to fit in all those extra degrees before reaching east or west.

There was no time to do anything about it – we would have to learn to live with it! Brian later made up a large deviation card to mount over the hole left in the instrument panel when the compass was moved up to the cabane struts. At least we now knew what we were up against and so could make allowance for it; I shudder to think of how we would have managed without that knowledge on the few occasions when we were forced to fly a compass heading.

The other thing we did was to test-mount the camera as soon as Bill had finished. It was not aligned vertically or horizontally as well as I would have liked, but at least it had a substantial platform mounted on a rigid, well-braced strut [Fig. 7]. We ran the remote control cable down the strut and up through the cabin window, leaving the push-button controller dangling from the cabane strut convenient to my left hand.

Meanwhile, during the morning, the phone lines between Sky Manor and Canandaigua grew pretty warm as both ends tried to establish what the situation was. Sadly I had to inform my good friend Dr Marvin Rapp, who was organising the local Whitman sesquicentennial celebrations, that we would not be able to get to the lunchtime reception he had arranged for us. Not just a lunch, but the local TV and Press would be expecting us, and I feared that it would not look good for Marvin if no one from our party was present.

To make it worse, at Canandaigua the sun was blazing down from a clear blue sky and he, and no doubt others, found it difficult to understand that conditions at Sky Manor could be so bad as to prevent our leaving. The thought that we were letting everyone down, including ourselves, did not help, but the fact remained that with so many unknowns and firsts it would have been foolish to jeopardise the whole expedition on the first day.

Flying a strange aircraft, with a compass we had not yet learned to trust, using unfamiliar maps over unfamiliar terrain, was not a good base from which to tackle marginal weather conditions, whose sudden ferocity we had witnessed in awe from the ground only days before. I miserably surveyed our chances of getting out sometime that day and came to a conclusion that if we did not, we could be stuck there for days or even weeks from what the locals were saying! Later, we became sufficiently used to all these then unknowns that we flew under conditions almost as bad; if only our visit to Canandaigua could have been on even the second day out!

CHAPTER 4

SESQUICENTENNIAL AT CANANDAIGUA

Around midday I could stand it no longer. We had been up since 5.30 and all we had seen for our pains was one aircraft movement the whole morning. That was a Tri-Pacer which had flown out on instruments under a lowering sky at around 10.00, almost immediately disappearing into cloud. He had full radio-navigation and blind-flying equipment and an instrument rating which allowed him to fly under IFR (Instrument Flight Rules), none of which we had. But by 12.00 there was a visible lifting of the cloudbase and we could just distinguish the tops of the nearby hills from the underside of the clouds. True, there was still the odd low rumble of thunder, and we had seen occasional flashes from within the clouds off to the southeast, but we were going northwest! And up that way, if we could break through, were clear blue skies!

Brian and I discussed the prospects with Bill Smela, and though he did not give it his blessing he raised no real objection. He suggested it would be better to skirt well south of Allentown, making our turning point the airfield at Quakertown. That way we had plenty of easily recognisable features, could land at the airfield there if conditions were too bad, and would be well clear of the control zones. If we could get over the 1600 feet high foothills of the Appalachian Mountains we would be able to assess whether we could make it to Schuylkill County airport, near Pottsville, for our first away landing and refuelling stop.

I decided we would load up as if we were on our way and take off for a circuit of the airfield. If the clouds would let us up to 1000ft above the airfield, and visibility was such that we could see where we were going, it was worth having a try at it – we could always come back!

Remembering the trouble with lens condensation on our dummy run, in somewhat similar conditions back home, we decided not to fit the camera on Bill's newly finished mounting. With all our gear shoehorned into the cabin, Brian was quite a snug fit in the back without too much room to move his feet around, and it took him a little while to sort out where to put his essential navigating gear and the Narco. If ever we were going to need the latter it would be over these first few legs in the murk!

We said our farewells to our new-found friends and wandered out onto the wet, deserted airfield. The gloomy scene overhead, with its mottled blanket of light and dark grey clouds, and the unrelenting mists over the valleys, looked only marginally improved, and I had a grim feeling we could well be back within a few minutes. The Champ started easily enough, Brian climbed into the rear and eventually pronounced himself settled, and suddenly, there were no more reasons for not getting on with it! Maryjo waved to us from the club house as we taxied out.

A well-behaved wind of about 10 knots blew straight down runway 24 and at 12.20 EST (Eastern Summer Time) we were airborne. At least, by taking off from the end adjacent to the parking area, I had been saved the embarrassing nagging from the rudder pedals, which had accompanied my earlier waltzing down the half-mile of taxyway to the far end! Although now somewhat more loaded than on my previous flights, the Champ lifted easily into the damp and heavy atmosphere. We soon found ourselves dodging thin wisps and tendrils under a scattering of rain and storm clouds, whose bases were generally about 1000 ft above the higher ground.

There was a thick, continuous blanket above these lower clouds, too high to be of any concern to us except for the gloom it settled over all below it. Now we could see that in the direction we were travelling we had misty visibility of about three miles in between the showers, and took heart from the fact that we would be able to dodge the latter and still maintain roughly the required heading.

Even the compass acted as a compass should on this first leg. Although there was a deviation factor of −15 deg to take into account, this was largely offset by the large (to our eyes) local magnetic variation of 12 deg W, with virtually no offset necessary to counter wind drift. Consequently, for our track of 248 deg we needed to steer 246 deg, comfortingly close, though with compass graduations spaced at 5 deg we were not going to fly that accurately!

Within a few minutes of taking off and setting course our first major landmark drifted past under our nose, the Delaware River with the busy, small community of Frenchtown on our left. There was no time to gaze at that, other than to recognise the bridge we had motored over several times. Bright blue streaks of lightning, a mile or so ahead and to our right, flashed briefly from a small black cloud and disappeared into a misty valley, the accompanying thunder roll easily audible above the muffled roar of the engine.

We swung clear of that cloud and several more in the area that sporadically spat their flashes at the ground. Strangely, although this was the closest that I had flown to an active thunder storm, there was no sense of danger, more of intense interest to see such a firework display from the air rather than, as usual, from the ground. Perhaps this was because the storm clouds were quite small and isolated and it was easy to keep clear of them.

Brian sat in the back with his ear glued to the Narco, seemingly oblivious to all that was going on around him, while he twiddled the knobs and squirmed this way and that in an effort to improve reception. Because we had not had the requisite 16 hours in which to charge the batteries, the volume had to be turned up past the point at which distortion made the weak signal unreadable. At least for a while he satisfied himself that with more power we should obtain usable VOR transmissions. As I had heard from Schuylkill, in answer to the questionnaire I sent out from the UK, that they were looking forward to our visit and were not bothered about us calling them on the radio, we had no problems in that direction.

At first, we were in and out of light rain, and the shining road surfaces below confirmed that it was pretty wet down there too. But as we progressed westward, the rain eased off almost completely, though the mist and scattered storm clouds persisted. We soon found ourselves at home with the maps, the main differences being the colouring and the fact that the charts did not show the woods, of which there was a sprinkling below. Despite our twisting and turning to dodge the blacker clouds, Quakertown soon appeared as expected, with the broad stripes of the Pennsylvania Turnpike crossing a few miles beyond. Here we changed to a more northerly course and our compass error increased at the new heading, so that instead of steering 285 deg we needed 256 deg. At least it was breaking us in gently!

Ahead we had another major highway to watch for as a check that we were on track, expecting to cross highway Interstate 78 (I-78) obliquely at Lenhartsville. Now we were crossing shallow ridges and misty wooded valleys and the low height at which we were forced to fly restricted our view of what lay in the next valley. Identifying our track was by best-guess compass course and rapid recognition of major features, so it was not surprising that by the time we came upon I-78 we were 3 miles off course. We crossed by the town of Hamburg, identified by State Highway 61 crossing I-78 and by the twin railways and river which would conveniently lead us straight to Pottsville. Here also we crossed the Appalachian Trail, running from Maine almost down to Atlanta in Georgia, though we were too busy looking elsewhere to notice it!

Pottsville proved to be a busy-looking, semi-industrial town, still quite small but larger than any we had seen to date. Now we were running into thicker and gloomier cloud cover, with a particularly nasty looking storm upwind of us. We were tempted to drop into the small private airfield of Chim, just outside Pottsville, rather than our destination field. The latter lay on top of a 1700 foot high plateau, 700 ft higher than Chim, and much closer to that storm cloud! But as is often the way, matters got no worse and we climbed up over the higher ground, still clear of the storm.

Circling warily round the airfield, conscious of the now very close thunderstorm, we looked in vain for a windsock. Brian was having no luck with his attempts to contact the tower on the radio, so we needed sight of the windsock to decide which runway to land on. Before I found the 'sock, I realised that a Cherokee that I had spotted taxying out was now lined up at the end of runway 29 and, as I watched, started his take-off run.

Now, although it is not unknown for pilots to unwittingly land downwind for some reason or other, I have never known one to take-off downwind if there is any sort of breeze blowing. Consequently we gave up our fruitless search for the windsock and lined up to land in the direction in which the Cherokee had just taken off. The end of the runway was close to the rim of a steep-sided valley, crossing which, we ran into quite turbulent air swirling up over the edge.

The runway threshold was coming up faster than expected and the Champ did not want to sit down in the gusty conditions. With the engine throttled right back we still seemed to be going too fast and then suddenly, I had to hold off to prevent the Champ touching down – something was wrong, it had not handled at all like this at Sky Manor! At the last moment, I caught sight of a windsock out of the corner of my eye. It was a dirty khaki affair that looked no more than six feet above the long, brown hay grass between the runway and the taxyway and it was pointing *the wrong way*. So that was it – I was committing the cardinal sin of landing downwind!

At this point the Champ, tail-down and power off for a three-pointer, still a foot or so in the air and with a groundspeed some twenty miles an hour faster than normal for landing, decided it had had enough. It banged itself very noisily onto the runway, scrunching me down in my seat. From the noise and the jarring shock, it sounded and felt as if the undercarriage must have folded up or the fuselage structure had broken and bent!

Not content with that, the maniacal machine now darted uncontrollably to the right, heading in a tightening curve for the rough ground beyond the runway. Despite my left foot pushing both rudder and brake pedals to the floor it continued its headlong swerve, with the left wheel locked, the tyre screeching in protest, now making straight for a blue runway light mounted on a short stake. Whether we hit the light or not we shall never know but at least the rough ground slowed us, and the brake started to pull the aircraft straight, just preventing a damaging groundloop. After an eternity, our mad bumping, bouncing and clattering through the knee-high grass was halted. We just sat there for a moment or two, recovering our breath and letting the adrenaline settle, wondering miserably how much damage we had sustained.

Miraculously, the engine was still ticking over quite unconcernedly and there there was none of the roughness one would expect if the propeller had been damaged. The aircraft sat markedly left wing low and there seemed no doubt that at very least, an undercarriage leg was bent, but I feared that it would prove much worse. What a way to arrive at our first away landing! Was this to be as far as we would get? What an ignominious end to the great adventure.

Looking out to both sides, a cursory examination showed nothing obviously broken, but it was clear that we would not be able to tell until the machine was on clear ground. Gingerly, I opened the throttle, needing full revs to get the aircraft to move at all. It lurched forward, heaving itself up out of a dip and waddled uncertainly across the rough, the handling feeling all wrong. Yet, once onto the Tarmac taxyway, things seemed pretty normal, with the Champ as usual wanting to wander whichever way took its fancy.

We slunk up to the refuelling bay, hoping not too many people had witnessed our 'arrival'. Switching off, we miserably climbed out, both of us expecting to see some evidence of catastrophic damage. But there was none. The propeller was unmarked, there were no tell-tale wrinkles in the fabric, the aircraft still sat slightly one wing low as usual and, unbelievably, close examination revealed no sign of damage anywhere! They surely built them tough in those days!

Far from there being anybody watching, the vast expanse of concrete in front of the hangars was deserted, the only sign of life being a distant tractor approaching at great speed from the far end of the hangars. It was driven by an amiable fellow whose scruffy overalls showed that he was the guy that did all the work to keep the place going. Ted turned out to be extremely friendly and very interested in what we were doing. He knew all about our coming from the correspondence we had had, and was desperately anxious to contact a reporter from the local newspaper, who had also been expecting us but had now given up waiting. We had a coffee while we waited, and tried once more to make some sense of the weather forecasts. They only confirmed what we already knew – it was fine where we were going and bad where we were!

Meanwhile, the Cherokee had returned and it seemed that the pilot had taken off downwind deliberately in order to avoid the thunderstorm we had seen sitting off the end of the runway. He volunteered the information that there were still thunderstorms north of us, but that if we could clear the next range of hills we should be in the clear, with only low ground beyond that. We were now of course very late, and offering our apologies for not waiting any longer (Ted had been unable to contact his reporter), we took our leave.

Regrettably, we had no time to take more than a perfunctory look at the thriving new museum that was being created there – out on the line were a Dakota, Mitchell, PV-2 Neptune, Harvard, Valiant and Cornell, all looking immaculate.

The earlier, unusual handling of the Champ was explained when we turned to taxy across the wind, the gusts swinging the tail and rocking the wings. We had a long squeaky progression down to the far end of the

4600ft long runway – none of this macho downwind take-off nonsense for me. We had all we needed of downwind handling effects impressed on us when we landed!

We took off into a wind that was stronger and more turbulent than when we had landed but the overcast and light drizzle were no worse. Now the compass error was more noticeable – to fly almost due north the required reading was 323 deg! Our track led us at right angles across successive long, high ridges, well-wooded, each with roads, railways and rivers in the extensively populated valleys in between. Now it was difficult to be sure we were on track, with only an occasional confirmation that we were on course.

At least we had no need to avoid troublesome thunderstorms on this leg. We even had time to reflect on the fact that only 200 years before, this had been Frontier country, when the woods below could have been harbouring hostile Indians and grizzly bears!

Gradually the weather started to improve, with a lifting cloudbase and even occasional breaks in the solid cover. At the highest point on our track, 2,585 ft near North Mountain, the cloudbase was at least another 1,000 ft above the thickly wooded top. By halfway we were flying over undulating parkland, in warm sunshine under scattered cumulus, though the wind was quite variable, requiring constant changes in compass heading. With the sun came increased visibility, which became almost unlimited under clear blue skies by the time we approached our destination airfield. This was Penn Yan, easily identified by its location at the northern end of Keuka Lake. We could have been in another world from that we had left at midday!

On the final run-in to Penn Yan we had to dog-leg round the Control Zone at Elmira, passing midway between there and Ithaca. These were names I had come across when reading about the Whitmans' journey of 150 years earlier. Now I was seeing the country for the first time and adding a little flesh to the bones of the images I had formed. Marcus Whitman had taken his newly-wed bride Narcissa from her home town of Amity (now Belmont), setting out in thick snow the day after their marriage, almost due east for Ithaca. There they collected two Nez Perce Indian boys who were to accompany them to Oregon, first calling at Rushville to visit Marcus' mother before embarking on their epic journey.

It was difficult to visualise how the attractive parkland landscape unfolding below would have appeared 150 years ago. Only a mere 40 years or so after the western frontier of the newly independent United States had been pushed farther west, it would probably have still been extensively forested, the majority of the farms and small communities now to be seen still waiting to be hacked out of the woods. Almost certainly, the beautiful and natural Finger Lakes would have been little changed, and with the primitive roads then in existence, would no doubt have formed a time-consuming barrier to anyone journeying between Ithaca and Rushville.

Circling Penn Yan we were struck by its deserted air. Not a soul in sight, neither could we see a windsock, despite careful searching. Fortunately there was drifting smoke from a nearby bonfire and I made no mistake about landing into wind; even so it was an untidy arrival and I was glad no one was watching. Thinking about it later I realised we were a lot heavier at the back than when doing my check-out with Bill Smela, and that would probably account for the Champ's anxiety to proceed tail-first at the slightest relaxation of attention, once the tail was down. We taxied near to the pumps and switched off, at which point we spotted the windsock! It was on a short mast mounted on top of the hangar, and was of a type that was new to us, but which rapidly became familiar. Instead of the usual all fabric sock which would hang limply against the pole when there was no wind, this differed in being drawn over a light frame for the first third of its length, so that there was always part of it horizontal, with the outer two-thirds free to hang limply from the end of the frame or stream out in the wind.

My first thought now was to phone someone at Canandaigua to let them know we had arrived. The aircraft that were to escort us into Canandaigua had evidently given us up for lost and the problem now was to know which of several airfields in the area we were expected at. The flight office was also deserted but at least it had a toilet, a drinks machine and a telephone, which we made use of in that order!

At least we would have made use of the phone if only we could have found a number to ring. I had no reply from Marvin's number and then we were stuck for whom to ring next. Fortunately at that point a new entrant appeared on the scene and we had found someone who could escort us in to Canandaigua. He also produced our first reporter, who was quite unlike the image created by Hollywood and TV – he was actually very polite and quite knowledgeable about what we were doing. Full marks!

Our escort was to be a magnificent Boeing Stearman PT-17, in vintage yellow Air Force trainer colours. What a picture it made, against a background of the beautiful Finger Lakes in the now bright evening sun. Our destination turned out to be a fine little grass airstrip on the outskirts of town – the Champ obviously appreciated landing on the lush green, making up for all her earlier misdemeanours with the lightest and smoothest of touchdowns to date!

By the time we had the Champ tied down for the night and had collected all our assortment of rubbish from inside, our transport had arrived and we were soon on our way to a reunion with our ground party. It seemed they had done us proud, George, guessing that we would be held up by the weather, driving furiously to arrive on time for the reception and standing in for us in grand style. At least Marvin Rapp had some of the party to put in front of the TV cameras and talk to the reporters, and make a speech at the reception lunch he had laid on. There had understandably been great confusion as to when we would actually arrive or even if we would arrive at all, and several local pilots had been standing by most of the afternoon, making occasional sorties in the direction of Penn Yan to see if we had reached there.

There passed a most pleasant evening, during which we met, over a leisurely and vociferous dinner, many local people involved with the Whitman Celebrations. There were more speeches from both sides of the Atlantic and by the time we broke up many who had never met in the morning were acting as if they had known each other all their lives! Afterwards, Marvin showed me round some of the places we should have visited in the afternoon had we been on time and, something I considered a great honour, took me to meet Robert Moody, the Town Historian, an octogenarian and an authority on the Whitmans who, despite the late hour and his advancing years, had waited up especially. We were all well looked after by local people that night, who took us into their homes and showed us real American hospitality, and arranged transport to get us back to the airfield in the morning. The real tragedy had been our inability to get to Canandaigua on time and I still feel a sense of guilt at having let them down after so much thought and planning had gone into making us welcome.

CHAPTER 5

GOING WEST

Having split up for the night, each couple staying with a different host, we planned to meet up at the airfield in the morning, as early as seemed prudent in the light of our activities of the night before. Brian and I aimed to get away long before 08.00 if possible. Due to one of those silly little misunderstandings which are prone to arise in circumstances such as these, each of us had one set of air charts and thought that the other set, which we needed with us, was in the car with George and Jean. We were ready to go long before they appeared, so it really hurt when we found we had both sets of maps all the time!

Meanwhile, I busied myself with mounting the fixed camera, whilst Brian worked out the compass headings to fly. We had agreed to leave the compass deviation table with him. When there were such unbelievable errors involved, I had no desire to wrestle with the mental arithmetic required to sort out what numbers to hold on the compass. We could not afford the time to get lost through my adding when I should have been subtracting, or through not believing the results of the calculations. Track, 229 deg: wind 10 mph from 250 deg, giving course 232 deg: add local magnetic variation, 10 deg west, 242 deg: deduct 15 deg compass error deviation (at 240 deg), steer 227 deg. Today the numbers on all four legs would look reasonably believable!

On arrival at the airfield, around 06.45, it had been a beautiful, calm, sunny morning with not a cloud in the sky, quite unlike the forecast fog and low cloud. But, as time rolled on, a few small puffy cumulus clouds drifted across; more ominously, a low haze on the southern horizon began to sprout bulging cumulus tops. By 08.35, when we finally took off, it was into a stiffening breeze and there was a little more cloud than blue sky with the sun beginning to yawn in anticipation of a complete rest later on!

Sure enough, as we proceeded southwest towards Olean, after a minor detour over the town of Canandaigua, the clouds became more heavily swollen, settled lower in the sky, and took on an altogether more greyly threatening look. In fact, it was not so much that the clouds were lower but that the ground was coming up to meet them. At Canandaigua, the airfield height was 800 ft above sea level, but Olean was 2,135 ft up in the Allegheny Mountains, higher than any airfield that either of us had used.

Only too well aware of the rising ground ahead, we were becoming a little apprehensive about the narrowing gap between cloud base and hilltop. Fortunately, despite the now gradually thickening haze, we had no difficulty in picking out Olean's single Tarmac runway, overlooking a steep-sided valley.

In order to save time at Canandaigua, we had forsaken breakfast for an early arrival at the airfield, intending to eat at the first airport which sported a restaurant. But at Olean we looked in vain for food and had to be satisfied with their fine coffee. Here we tried to get an update on the weather, but suffered the same fate as on previous occasions – we were unable to translate the gibberish that snapped out of the phone at us! At least we understood that it sounded anything but good for small VFR (Visual Flight Rules) aircraft! There was an intriguing instrument in the flight office which purported to show the wind speed and direction; unfortunately neither we nor any of the locals could relate what it showed to what could be seen outside!

What with refuelling, seeking food and weather information, and the usual long taxy from and to the runway, just over an hour had elapsed by the time we were airborne again. Now, what few breaks in the cloud were remaining when we landed had long since closed up and the haze had thickened to mist. The first part of our route took us across a 2,400 ft-high range within ten minutes of takeoff. We decided that, if we could stay clear of clouds as we crossed the highest point, it should be safe to continue – if not, we would turn back to Olean.

Cloud base proved to be around 3,000 ft and, beyond the ridge, looked to remain at the same height, so we cautiously pressed on. There was a feeling of having passed a point of no return – ahead was a half hour of flying before the plateau dropped below 2,000 ft. If the cloud base lowered to join up with the mist we would be looking for somewhere to land in a hurry!

Fortunately, we did not realise that for the same distance ahead there lay a wall-to-wall, solid carpet of trees (like nothing either of us had ever encountered before), part of the Allegheny National Forest. Had we done so, we would probably still have been at Olean a week later! There were just a few swathes cut through the unending trees but these would have been of no use to us in an emergency; some unthinking persons had filled them with power lines and pylons. So for an ageless 30 minutes we apprehensively watched the gradually darkening, unbroken layer of cloud ahead, the ever-thickening mist, our Mickey Mouse compass, and the dense cover of trees very close below.

The gap between treetops and cloud base remained little more than 600 ft for much of the time. In such conditions one listens very attentively to the hopefully regular beat of the motor, and hears all sorts of alarming noises which were not noticeable before! Initially we were helped by the VOR signals picked up by our little transceiver. But that soon used up the power in the still not fully-charged batteries, happily not before we had established the required compass heading on which to fly.

The mist quickly thickened to reduce visibility to some 2 or 3 miles which did nothing to help! New York State gave way to Pennsylvania without revealing the fact to our eager eyes. An early landmark, the small town of Bradford, which should have been visible just two miles southeast of our track, slid past unobserved. We knew it was out there somewhere as, early on, we crossed a road leading to it. After that, apart from the power line breaks, there were barely any tracks through the trees, and no clearings, roads or habitation that were in our range of vision.

There was time to conjecture that many of these trees would have been here when the young American Republic was pushing its Frontier westward. Some, even earlier, when the British and French Colonials were contending the area. And some when the only intruders were Indian hunters of the local Wenro tribes, before the coming of the white man!

Good things are not the only ones to come to an end and, after what seemed an eternity, the trees relented and yielded up a deep valley, with a long narrow stretch of water – the Allegheny Reservoir. At the same time, there was a distinct brightening of a narrow sector of the clouds ahead. According to our charts, the land should drop more rapidly beyond the low ridge on the far side of the valley. At last we were able to fix our position and could hardly believe that we were no more than a mile off track. It was not only the sky that was lighter!

Now there was another airfield, Scandia, to run to if conditions worsened – we reckoned we could find it readily enough, just four miles west of the reservoir, if we had to turn back. We even discussed whether to divert to Scandia there and then in the hope that things might improve later, but decided to keep going while we could. Things were more likely to worsen and it was essential to break out of this eastern belt of high humidity if we possibly could. 'Pressonitis' is the term commonly and disparagingly applied at home to this line of thinking, but I have a more sympathetic understanding now of how pilots get themselves into the situations to which it is applied!

Sure enough, past the ridge the land almost imperceptibly started to drop, noticeable more by the increasing gap between cloud base and ground than anything else. Even more significant was the continuing improvement in the light, which indicated that the cloud cover was thinner and thus gave hope that the sun would eventually break through. It was also good to see increasingly larger clearings in the trees, with occasional roads and small hamlets. It is always a comforting feeling, when flying a small aircraft, to see open spaces large enough to land safely in if necessary.

It seemed a good idea on this and later stages to practise using the fixed wing camera. We were satisfied that the camera was correctly aligned with the aircraft centre-line, fore and aft, so that as long as I flew towards an object, it should lie within the lens' field of view. But it was angled a little too steeply downwards and tilted some 10 degrees horizontally. We also needed to check what happened to the film advance drive when the remote control button was pressed!

The procedure then, was first to point the aircraft at the target and add a little power. Left hand off the throttle to pick up the remote controller, find the button and check the exposure counter number. Look out at the camera and pull the stick back until the camera seemed angled up sufficiently. Then ease the stick over to the left to tilt the aircraft about ten degrees to bring the camera level, with a little top rudder to hold it all together. Press the button and check that the number clicked up by one. This all had to be done rapidly because of the transient nature of all the elements. At least there was plenty of opportunity to practise on the way to Independence, though there would probably be no opportunity to have the film processed in order to assess the results.

What really concerned us most about the camera was the degree of vibration it was subject to. The wing strut had looked substantial and vibration-free, with a small jury strut to dampen out vibrations at mid-span. But with the heavy camera mounted on it, the wind pressure and springy nature of the mounting set up an oscillatory motion which had the camera nodding visibly and very rapidly.

There was not a lot I could do to counteract that. We set the camera shutter controls for speed priority, and hoped that the sun would shine sufficiently brightly to enable the camera to operate at 1,000th-second speed, despite our slow speed, 100 DIN film. That just might be sufficient to cancel out the effect of the vibration!

Of equal concern was the fact that the whole wing vibrated noticeably in sympathy with the camera! The effect on handling and performance was negligible, but for some reason I kept thinking of James Stewart's Mr Honey, in the film of Nevil Shute's story *"No Highway,"* and his theories about metal fatigue!

Operating the cameras from the back seat was no easier. The window glazing was not clear enough to shoot through, so we opened the rear sliding panel on the left side (which had a bad habit of jamming at crucial moments). To point the camera through the opening, the rear seat occupant had to lean well forward, anything left on his lap sliding immediately into the hidden depths. If I sideslipped, even gently, to give a better angle for the camera, a roaring draught blasted through the open window and swirled any loose papers round the cabin, as well as raising the noise to a level which precluded conversation.

Later on, when George was filming, he found that the only way he could aim properly (being a little shorter than Brian) was to undo his lap strap and crouch forward, our heads now in close proximity. He had to take care not to receive a blow in some vital part from the rear stick, which could be waggling around violently as I attempted to hold a line in sometimes turbulent conditions.

We flew for a further hour and a half, more or less on the same course, initially with very few opportunities to confirm our position. Below, the forest had given way to pleasant, rolling parkland, but still with very few identifiable towns or villages. The roads on our charts were so few and far between that when we did come across their counterparts below, we could not be certain whether they were those, or others too minor to be shown. There always seemed to be more than we expected! The same applied to small rivers and streams. The only thing we were certain of was that the wind was now quite variable, calling for constant changes of heading for correction. For instance, when we crossed our first major highway, I-80, near Clarion, we were ten miles east of track!

Eventually, the inevitable happened, and we came across a pattern of features that defied matching with anything on the map. There was a railway, a small town, some main roads, a small airfield with a single N-S runway, and what appeared to be float planes on an adjacent river. I circled while we decided, by process of elimination, that Zelienople had more matching and fewer mismatching features than any other airfield in the vicinity. We were not at all convinced that this was correct but were not sure to what extent one should expect such features to match.

If our identification was correct, we were four miles north-west of track and our destination airfield was just eight miles due south. There was a long pause, while Brian did some complex sums before announcing that, to fly south, I needed to steer 205 deg. After eight minutes, if we were right, this heading should take us over Kindelberger. It would also lead us to Greater Pittsburgh International Airport, twelve miles further on, so we could not take any chances.

When Kindelberger failed to appear at the appointed time and, equally worrying, nothing else seemed to match our map, we turned 90 degrees left to start a circular search. The mist was thickening and dirtier, which suggested we were close to a large industrial area as expected, and there were now more supporting signs of this beneath us.

Almost immediately, we spotted a small, single-runway airfield nestling in a N-S valley, with a railway, roads and industrial buildings nearby. This field had nothing in common with Kindelberger! Neither did it share the endearing habit, of many other US airfields, of having its name painted on the runway. What was more, we could find no matching airfield in the expected area on the chart.

We were temporarily unsure of our position ('lost') and the fuel contents gauge showed that we really ought not to continue blundering around much longer, looking for something we could identify. More importantly, the presence of a major industrial city and its International

Airport, lurking somewhere in the surrounding murk, suggested we had better land and obtain a 'position fix,' and some fuel, without further ado!

As we joined the circuit (or 'pattern,' to use the vernacular), a tractor and gang-mower could be seen cutting the grass to one side of the runway, but no other sign of life. By the time we had landed, the tractor had disappeared, but now we saw a group of workmen who were busy renovating the airport buildings. Incredibly, they knew neither the name of the airfield nor the nearest town, having been brought there by truck in the morning and collected at night! Showing one of them the map produced a negative response – he could not read a map! Maybe they mistrusted this lost airman with a foreign-sounding accent! Faith in humanity was restored when we found someone filling a bucket at a nearby stand-pipe, who turned out to be a pilot washing his aircraft.

It appeared we had landed at West Penn, near Tarentum, about eight miles east of Pittsburgh and twenty miles east of Kindelberger. The airfield was not attended on weekdays and there was no fuel available. However, hearing that we were a little concerned about the amount we had left, and realising that we could easily get lost again in this murk, he kindly offered us some that he had drained from his tank. That was enough to restore confidence in our ability to reach our destination. Unable to pinpoint the airfield we had identified wrongly as Zelienople, we guessed that it was probably near Cooperstown, some nine miles south-east of track. We had persistently been blown south-east, which suggested that the wind had been a good deal stronger than forecast.

By the time we left, it was very warm. From take-off, rate of climb was noticeably down as we turned over a high, tree-clad ridge to the north of the airfield. Now that we knew where we were, life seemed much sweeter, with plenty of highways, railways and other features to identify from our map. The last major feature before Kindelberger, four miles east of the field, was a main highway (probably I-79). Sure enough, four minutes after crossing it, a tiny airstrip, recognisable in the mist only by having several aircraft parked on the grass, came into view about 400 yards to the right. Without the parked aircraft we would not have seen it, and indeed, nearly lost it in circling to land. So Lady Luck had not entirely deserted us – or had she?

We landed bumpily on its single, 1,500 ft-long, very rough dirt runway, located between rising ground on either side. A solitary petrol pump was adjacent to one end of the runway, with a hangar and lean-to outhouse tucked several hundred yards away down a slope. We taxied past a heavily oil-stained run-up area to the pump which, though old and dull was magically marked '80 octane,' switched off and climbed stiffly out into the very hazy but hot sunshine.

We were suddenly aware, as if intruding into a previous time, of the almost eerie stillness and quiet, with no sign of life, not even a bird. The only sound was the eternal chirruping of the cicadas. Three or four picketed aircraft looked as if they had taken root, and there was a desolate, long-deserted air about the place. Were we to be stuck here now for hours and hours while the day wasted away? This was one of the airfields I had written to for confirmation of fuel availability and had received a welcoming reply – we could certainly do with some of that welcome right now!

Thinking there might be people at the hangar, but doubtful as they almost certainly would have emerged at the sound of an aircraft landing, we wandered down the hill. The doors were open and inside, surprisingly for the size of the strip, was a DHC Beaver, obviously used for parachute jumping. A large sign showed that the Clubhouse belonged to the Beaver Valley parachuting club and with sinking hearts we realised that there would probably be nobody about for some time. At least there was a very welcome cold drinks dispensing machine, though of an antiquated type we had not encountered before. Feverishly searching our pockets we found sufficient quarters for two drinks, and learnt the hard way, at the expense of one lot of coins, how to exchange them for bottles.

Trudging back up to the aircraft, we wondered miserably what we should do next. Down the adjacent dirt road was a distant house, again with no sign of life, and up the hill to one side of the strip was another. I reasoned that anyone at the house by the strip must have heard the aircraft land and would come out to investigate. Brian decided to try it anyway and miraculously produced an elderly occupant, who turned out to be the owner of the airstrip and pilot of the Beaver. Seemingly, the Champ had made so little sound on my usual throttled-back approach that he had simply not heard us, though I would have thought we would have made enough noise in taxying back. Perhaps we sounded too much like a tractor?

Suddenly, all was light and life. Sure, he had received my letter and was glad to see us even if we had not brought our two old biplanes, though he would have liked very much to have seen them. But ". . . this is a nice little Airknocker (slang for Aeronca) – they've been very popular for many years." He had quite a few hours on Champs but had never considered taking one across the Rockies – ". . . say, that should be quite a trip!". We felt honoured indeed.

He soon had some life-giving, 80-octane Avgas gurgling into the tank, though the rate of revolutions of the hands on the delivery dial made it look as if we would be there for some time yet. I had estimated we would need at least seven gallons, possibly as many as ten, to fill up, so was most surprised to see the tank overflow with only four gallons on the clock. Although I knew it must have taken more than that he only wished to charge us what was indicated; we compromised at seven, everyone seemingly happy at that.

Questioned about the local weather conditions and the likelihood of further deterioration, our new-found friend told us what we wanted to hear. He confidently predicted that, although it might be a little thicker down by the river at nearby Rochester, this was otherwise as bad as we would get. We could expect it to improve steadily westwards once we left the low-lying Ohio River region.

With the old man's cheerful farewells and wishes for a safe flight ringing in our ears, we lined up for take-off. With a full tank and high temperatures, the rough strip suddenly looked very short, even though I knew that 1,500 feet really should have been ample. In line with the end of the strip was a group of small trees and we had little to spare as we flew over them. Making a wide circuit in an effort to gain height, I circled back low over the strip to give a farewell wave. Encouraged by the vigorous reply, we got down to the more serious business of establishing the required compass heading while we could still check our track.

Visibility was, if anything, worse and deteriorating rapidly as we approached the river, climbing as hard as the little Champ would go. We needed 1,500 ft clearance above the city, and there were numerous high obstructions in the area, including one shown as 950 ft above ground level. We were slightly north of track as we crossed a bend in the river, some four miles from the airfield. To our eyes, accustomed to viewing the Thames as a wide river, the Ohio looked more like a lake.

Visibility was now down to less than half a mile, with the north bank just discernible as we flew along the south bank. Ahead, the sun reflected dully off the water, showing us the course of the river, and soon, a bright, white, pinpoint of light flashed insistently through the fog, almost dead ahead and just below our level. At first, alarm bells rang in my mind – was this another aircraft, perhaps a helicopter? We soon saw the reason both for the light and the deterioration in visibility. Huge smoking stacks and steaming towers of a large industrial complex loomed up, to match the "high-intensity, light-lit, group obstruction" symbol on the map.

At least, in flying a straight course along the gently winding river for some 22 miles, we were able to obtain a first-class, reliable check on our compass reading. This would stand us in good stead for the rest of the two-hour leg. Our new course was pretty well dead into wind, which had dropped considerably, making navigating easier. As we flew along the last six miles of the southern bank of the Ohio river, before it swung 90 degrees south of our track, we had left Pennsylvania and briefly passed across the tip of that absurd, north-pointing, 60 miles-long finger of West Virginia, on our way into Ohio.

Although visibility gradually improved as we flew west, it never bettered about five miles down sun, or two miles into the sun. The latter's searing disc was now sliding almost imperceptibly down the windscreen, to where it made viewing the high-mounted compass an eye-straining chore. I saw little of the scenery, what with the goldfish bowl visibility and the need to concentrate on not letting the compass card wander too far off the correct heading. The impression gained was of an undulating parkland of open spaces and sparse woods, with the occasional line of tall trees, farm buildings or silos standing ghostly in the mist.

After nearly two increasingly soporific hours, we started looking for our destination airfield, August Acres, some four miles beyond Johnstown, Ohio. The sun, even brighter now, was glaring golden through the windscreen, and to read the compass I had to screw up my eyes and shield them from the glare with my left hand. Because of the mist, there was no horizon to aid accurate flying and little to steer a straight path by, so reading the compass was a tiring and constant necessity.

The airfield boasted a single 2,100 ft turf runway, so was not going to be too easy to spot among all the little oblong green or golden fields below us. This was not of any great concern, as a 7-miles-long, narrow reservoir lay squarely across our track, some 5 miles beyond the airfield. I planned to obtain an accurate position on the near shore, then turn and fly back towards the field with the sun behind us. It worked beautifully, the hangars and mown grass strip, completely invisible on the first pass, appearing almost dead on our nose, the sun lighting up the buildings, and the orange-yellow windsock standing out sharp and clear.

Suddenly, as if a weight had been lifted from my shoulders, I was wide awake, and even the sun's glare was no longer a problem as I settled into a high, power-off approach. A line of low-voltage power cables, marked by brightly-coloured balls, stretched across the runway threshold, but we dropped steeply over these to make a feather-light touchdown on the smooth, short turf.

This was just what an airfield should look like! A friendly welcome awaited us, the owner of the field, Paul August, coming out to meet us. His generous offer, to drive us down to the nearby Center Village Pizza Place to sample their speciality 'subs,' was accepted with alacrity.

As Brian observed somewhat pointedly, 6 o'clock in the evening was a little late to be taking breakfast! Here we discovered for the first time just what 'subs' were, having been mildly mystified on seeing them advertised way back in Philadelphia. Short for submarines, so-called for their foot-long, cigar-shaped bread rolls, subs came with a variety of salad fillings. We tried, with some satisfaction, the house speciality, which seemed to have an abundance of everything in it. Certainly, even Brian's insatiable appetite appeared to have been saturated on this occasion. Paul's son turned up before we finished to offer us a lift back to the airfield.

Before we left for our meal we had supervised refuelling and for the first time since leaving Sky Manor were able to purchase engine oil of the required grade. "You can always recognise it because it comes in a black container, and don't use any other unless you have to," Bill Smela had warned us. He had also advised that, because it was more expensive than most oils, not all FBOs (Fixed Base Operators) stocked it, so it would be as well to carry a spare with us. By now we had used the spare we had brought with us from Sky Manor and needed topping up with more. At least, we had by now established that the engine used about one pint in three hours flying, which rate it maintained throughout the whole flight.

We quickly got away on our return, at 7.15 pm, aware that we still had well over 100 miles to go and that it would be getting dark by about 9.00 pm. It was a beautiful evening when we left, still a little hazy with a cloudless sky and a burning golden sun, unfortunately still right behind the compass. This day I had understood for the first time why American pilots appeared to be inseparable from their long-peaked, baseball-style caps and would gladly have worn one to lessen the sun's glare.

What with the bright sun and the once more increasing haze, I soon abandoned our featureless course once clear of the sprawl of Columbus. Diverting slightly south to London (!) enabled us to follow a friendly railway that brought us back on track some 30 miles further on at Xenia. At last I really could relax, forget that wretched compass, and watch the world go by!

As we neared Hamilton-Fairfield, where we were to stay overnight, the sun finally sank below the haze. The last eight miles were over entirely featureless ground and we started to look for the airport flashing beacon to guide us in. We both spotted a flashing amber light at the same time, and decided from its direction that it had to be the airport. Laying aside our maps we headed straight for it only to discover that we were homing in on a minor road accident, attended by a highway patrol car and fire engine, both flashing their amber lights!

Very interesting, nobody seemed to have been hurt, but now where was our airfield? In the gloom and mist, we could be within 2 miles of it and not see it! At which point Brian spotted another, more slowly-flashing light way off to our right and I turned disbelievingly towards it. Sure enough, it marked a great expanse of concrete and a runway. After a tight circuit over the terminal buildings, to look for wind direction and to let them know we were about, the while anxiously scanning for other aircraft, we landed and taxied thankfully up to the fuel pumps.

Climbing wearily out after Brian had untangled from the para-phernalia around the rear seat, we were met by a couple of youngsters who came to refuel us. They were brothers, very keen on flying and most interested in what we were up to. They proved most helpful and, unasked, made space in their own hangar for the Champ overnight (charging only tie-down rates), the first time the old plane had enjoyed such luxury for countless years. We were shown round their workshops which contained a Waco biplane in course of reconstruction and an old

Model A Ford car in beautiful condition, after which they drove us down to the Holiday Inn Motel. "No charge – glad to be of help." Such is typical American hospitality!

There followed a grand reunion in the foyer. To our great surprise, our ground crew had also just arrived. They were attempting to unravel the confusion resulting from our booking rooms from the airport and their attempt to do the same at reception. They had apparently phoned the airport on arrival in Hamilton and had been told we were on our way. What better could we ask? Only that we could have found a restaurant nearby, still open at the time we were ready to eat, after booking in and cleaning up! We were just too late to catch the local one and had to drive around town to find one still serving – mind you, it was around 10.30 in the evening so we had no grounds to complain!

Over a typical large meal we excitedly exchanged the day's experiences, the ground crew having had a hectic time to cover the mileage and stay on the right roads! They had decided to abandon a planned 25-mile diversion to Niagara Falls to save time, and had been disappointed in seeing nothing of the Lake Erie shore as they drove down I-90 to Cleveland. Encountering the same, or worse, foggy conditions as the air crew, they wondered how we had fared.

They too had found it very hot and sticky as the day wore on. From Cleveland, they had ridden the I-71 all the way down to the outskirts of Cincinnati, covering over 500 miles before finding our motel. They had tried several times, unsuccessfully, to phone intermediate airfields en route to find out how we were progressing, finally and thankfully getting through to Hamilton to establish that we had just landed. In retrospect, this was a great achievement and perhaps more than we should have called on them to do!

One last observation came from Brian before we turned in. Since leaving Sky Manor, we had flown more than 11 hours over areas densely packed with airfields. Yet in all that time we had not seen another aircraft in the sky, other than the Stearman that had flown with us into Canandaigua! What a change from conditions at home!

Mention of the hours we had flown reminded me of something else. We had travelled in one day the distance it had taken the newly-married Whitmans some two weeks to cover at the start of their epic journey from Rushville 150 years previously. They had journeyed first by horse-drawn sleigh through the deep snows of early March, finishing their journey to Pittsburgh by coach. From there, they travelled along the broad Ohio River by side-wheel paddle-steamer before taking a brief respite over a long weekend here at Cincinnati.

While travelling along the Ohio River, the Whitmans had encountered even more foggy conditions than we did, and with heavy rain as well. Then, steamboat traffic on the river had been heavy, but we had seen no activity on the water at all, a pattern repeated on every other major waterway we flew over. They could have had little idea what hardships awaited them – at least we knew roughly what lay before us.

Or did we?

CHAPTER 6

MEET ME IN ST. LOUIS

Once again we made an early start. Brian and I took the 'tank' (as the station wagon came to be known) into town at 06.00, joining a queue at the only restaurant due to open at that time, and sat and waited for it to do so. Our hopes for an early breakfast were dashed, as every one else in town had the same idea, and we might as well have had an extra hour in bed. As one of the locals said: "Food it might be, but fast it is not." We still had to return for Jean and Sonia, who were to accompany us to the airport in order to take the car back to the motel, and when they left us, time had trickled away to past eight o'clock.

There followed the now customary one-sided battle with the FSS weather forecast. Happily, Brian picked out sufficient to indicate that we could expect a slight improvement over the conditions of the previous day, which we now felt reasonably capable of coping with. What was far more disturbing was a frantic phone call from Gregory Franzwa just as we were leaving.

Greg had arranged, as far back as early June, that we were to land at a small airstrip in the grounds of Parks College, on the outskirts of East St. Louis. There was to be a reception committee, and Press and TV to meet us, providing we arrived early enough to make the early evening news broadcast (though Greg himself would have to be absent preparing for the OCTA Convention). So that was where our ground crew was due to meet us that evening.

I had tried to phone him the previous evening, with an update on our progress, with no more success than on several previous occasions. Failing that, I had called Barbara Magerl at Kansas City to ask her to try and contact him, with the news that we were on schedule.

Because Gregory had not heard from us after we left Sky Manor, all the arrangements had been cancelled, and the College airstrip we were due to land on had not been prepared (being still under bean crop). Instead, it was suggested we should land at the adjacent major airport, BiState Parks, and make our own arrangements from there.

It was not only unfortunate that we would now not have anyone to meet us and perhaps show us a little of St. Louis, it was darn near disastrous. Our ground crew would not know of the change in plans and there was no way we could contact them. Greg gave me a name and number to phone at Parks, so that we could leave a message for them if they arrived at the College and wondered why there was no one there to greet them. At least we would all be tired enough by the time we got to St. Louis to be relieved at not having to give any media interviews! I left the phone feeling rather like a small boy who had accidentally trodden on the toe of a favourite aunt.

We finally got away by 09.00, the weather quite warm with a hazy sun and mist limiting visibility to little more than a mile. The wind was light and initially southerly, so that we taxied nearly to the western end of the mile-long runway to take off, feeling almost lost by the time we reached an intersection that enabled us to exit onto it. Turning quickly onto course we got our first fix where we crossed the sluggish, brown, Big Miami River some three miles from the airport.

Now we were heading north-west to Brownsburg, a small field on the northern outskirts of Indianapolis. This was quite a northerly deviation from the shortest route to St. Louis, chosen only to satisfy the original request of the publicity people to visit as many large cities as possible on the way to Independence. The publicity requirement was long since dead, but having written to the airfield operators for clearance to use their field, I felt that we might as well leave the arrangement to stand. It would in any case be interesting to see the famous Speedway from the air.

Initially, we were able to establish our course from a railway running along on our right for some eight miles. The wind quickly swung round to the west, requiring a change of heading, but then settled down so that we were able to fly that heading all the way to our first turning point, north of Indianapolis. We were flying over farming land, with very few features to help positioning, but a large reservoir at about one third distance and another just 4 miles from our turning point gave us all we needed. Visibility gradually improved to between 5 and 10 miles but then dropped back to about 2 near the big city.

As we turned south-west towards Brownsburg, over the built-up areas to the north of the city, we needed help from the VOR, as we dare not stray too far south into the International Airport Control Zone. Brian was having problems as he could not relate the VOR readings to where we thought we were, but suddenly all was explained. A large white tower that came into view on our left was soon identified as the VOR radio beacon, and suddenly, as we circled the beacon, we sighted the grass runways and hangars of Brownsburg.

As half expected in view of the poor visibility, the airfield looked deserted, while a dilapidated row of single, lock-up hangars gave it a forlorn, run-down air. We taxied up to the pumps and switched off, being met by a nonchalant young man who quickly refuelled the Champ, but whose thoughts were on other things than us. We found much the same reaction in the flight office, which was a little surprising in view of the friendly letter received from the owner. However, we were grateful that they offered the use of the office telephone to try and get the FSS weather and an 'actual' (current weather situation at the destination) from Shawnee, our next airfield.

There was no change in the forecast, though it was thought by the locals that the mist would decrease as we went west. It was now very warm and humid and we were thankful for the usual can of something cold and fizzy before we left. A Piper Cub taxied out before us and we followed him down the field to the end of the runway, quite pleased to see another aircraft flying.

The flight down to Shawnee, some 65 miles to the south, was under much the same conditions as the previous leg, visibility at first actually worsening and the wind quite variable. As a result we saw no signs of the Speedway, though we should have been very close to it. After the first 7 or 8 miles we found that we were well east of track, so circled back over the I-40 to start again from a positive fix provided by a prominent aerial mast, our compass heading needing adjusting by ten degrees to compensate for a quite strong breeze which had sprung up from the west.

Over the last few miles, we had only to follow a major road and railway from Freedom, on the White River, past Worthington to just before Switz City to find the airfield (we thought!). It was still very misty, so that we did not spot the airfield where expected, less than a mile to our left. Brian, busy with his VOR readings, found that they did not match either. The result was that we circled in some confusion over a little huddle of buildings that we eventually decided had to be Switz City, and then backtracked along the road to a Y-junction in order to locate the airfield.

Sure enough, when we turned back down the right fork, the grass runway soon came into sight, with a huddle of hangars at the far end. We were surprised to find a small group of people seemingly waiting for us to arrive, including a local reporter. Although I had written to the Secretary, telling him that we would now be flying a Champ in place of our biplanes and would not need them to lay in any special supplies of 80-octane for us, the letter had not then arrived! Still, they did not allow that to detract from the warmth of their welcome or their interest in what we were doing. They delighted in showing us around the aircraft based there, which included a rare Luscombe Model T-7F, a frustrated WW2 military observation machine which did not make it as such.

We were driven to a local farm for supplies of Mogas, meeting there a local 'oldest inhabitant,' and invited to tuck in to some delicious, if sticky, spare ribs. Fortunately for our schedule, we gained an hour on the transition from Eastern time to Central time (CST), though when we got the weather forecast it looked as if we had boobed by staying so long. A cold front, preceded by severe thunderstorms, was forecast to move in from the west any time after 2.00 pm; local opinion was that it could be quite unpleasant if they materialised as forecast. On the basis of 'where ignorance is bliss' and our need to meet our ground crew in St. Louis that night, plus our admittedly limited experience to date in dodging the storms, we decided to give it a try. We could always turn back at the first sight of anything really nasty.

Once again, we had a good compass bearing check during the first nine miles, following a road and railway to Linton (where the magnetic variation switched from West to East), after which we headed out over open, featureless ground until we crossed the Wabash River (without spotting any cannonballs). Now in Illinois, the rest of the flight progressed without incident over the broad, flat farmlands and romantic sounding rivers – the Willow, Little Wabash, Kaskaskia and the Shoal to name just a few. Still misty, humid and very warm in the hazy sunshine, we had only occasional sightings of threatening thunderstorms, and none close enough to cause us any problems.

Now Brian managed to drop off to sleep in the noisy cabin. With his long legs folded up amongst the assorted paraphernalia we had spread all around him, scrunched up in that uncomfortable little rear seat, how I shall never know, but that he certainly did!

One comforting thought about the navigation on this leg was that our track was bounded to north and south by major highways converging on St. Louis, and even if we drifted off to either side we would see one or other of them. As the afternoon wore on, the problem of glare from the sun making compass reading difficult was solved by diverting north to the nearest of the highways, I-70, and following that down to the neat little grass airfield of Highland Winet. Though we kept a hopeful eye open for our ground crew on the I-70, we saw no sign of their big white station wagon.

We were met by the airport manager, Jim Luber, who had written specially to tell me he was now stocking 80-octane fuel. The grass on the runway was as smooth and green as he had said it would be – I was almost relieved that we would not be scoring it with the tailskids of our biplanes, though he was disappointed to find that we had come without them. It made no difference to the welcome we received, and when we said that we needed to ring Bistate Parks to get clearance to land non-radio, Jim arranged with another pilot, who was leaving for St. Louis in a Cessna 150 at about the same time as us, to fly with us and notify the tower we were coming in.

In fact, he did considerably more than that. After gaining permission for us to land our little taildragger into wind on the short cross runway, he landed in order to shepherd us in round the miles of taxyways and acres of concrete. When he saw we were safely parked, he gave us a cheery wave and went on his way. Brian was pleased to be able to use the radio to communicate with him once we had landed and the engine was throttled back to a tickover.

On the way in to Parks, with our Champ at maximum cruise power, the 150 was flying in a marked nose-up attitude, with flaps partly down, in order to keep down to our speed. We gathered that the Cessna pilot was highly delighted to have at last found something which was slower than his 150!

From a long way out, we could see the great Gateway (of the West) Arch in St. Louis, but in following our escort did not get close enough to it to make it worth photographing. In any case it was too dull for good pictures. We thought we would do better when we left the next day, in the light of the early morning sun. Although it was still fairly murky on the way into St. Louis, no sooner had we landed and switched off than the sun shone bright and clear. The high overcast that had shrouded it almost since we left Canandaigua was at last blown away, there now being a very strong wind blowing.

An airport official car drove out to meet us and show us where to tie down for the night, enquiring whether we needed fuel. Although we had only flown for 35 minutes from Highland, I always like to top up at every opportunity so said: "Yes please." Before we had finished our chores, an enormous, high-speed, high-capacity, commercial refuelling tanker drove out, dwarfing the Champ. No, they had no 80-octane, would 100LL do? It would, with which the operator, directed to the filler, gave an enquiring squeeze on the nozzle trigger and immediately flooded over the top with the shortest of bursts.

Puzzled, he asked where the wing-tank fillers were. When he recovered from the shock of there not being any, he looked at the gauges and said that they were registering such a small amount that he could not read them! We settled on 2¼ gallons and he went on his way, shaking his head in disbelief. He had probably used more fuel in starting up and driving over, running his pump motor and driving back, than he had put in our tank!

It was very, very hot, probably the hottest it had been, the searing heat from the sun being reflected back off the burning white concrete so that we were thankful to get into the cool of the airport air-conditioned lounge (where we subsequently sat and shivered!). More cans of cold drinks were consumed while we phoned Parks College to leave a message for our ground crew to meet us in the lounge. To our surprise and relief they turned up within half an hour of our phone call, though it turned out that, having found the bean field and the College, no message had been given to them and they simply assumed we had landed at Bistate Parks!

We set off to look for a motel, hopefully not too close to an airport. We crossed the mighty Mississippi, turned north to pass and gaze in awe at the equally impressive Gateway Arch, regretting that we were too late to be able to take the lift to the top, and sped on round the outskirts, keeping all eyes open for motels. When we found them, they were all congregated round Lambert International Airport, anxious not to miss the deplaning travellers. The latter were no doubt expected to be too tired to be kept awake by the constant stream of noisy jets, which was just what we did not want. Eventually, after an incredible amount of driving and having nearly completed a full circuit of the sprawling city, we finally found a comfortable and relatively quiet Knights Motel on the south-western outskirts.

Over a full and satisfying meal in the nearby restaurant we all caught up on each other's day's events. The ground crew had had another long, hot, hard drive, over relatively minor roads, in taking the shortest route from Cincinnati to St. Louis. Now they were looking for an alternative to starting out after we had left. We agreed to try a different approach in the morning, in which they would head west straight away, rather than backtrack east to the airport with us. Brian and I were to take a taxi to the airport, which was reckoned to be no more than perhaps five miles round the ring road. Tomorrow the journey to Independence would be a much shorter distance than any to date, so we all slept soundly that night, in anticipation of an early arrival next day at the start point of the Oregon Trail!

The Whitmans had arrived in St. Louis on March 29th, in the evening of a foggy, cold and damp day, 26 days after setting out from Rushville. If our journey was also foggy it had fortunately been anything but cold and damp! They at least stole a march on us by seeing round the city, even if they were not impressed with St. Louis, regarding it as old, neglected and dirty, especially the French quarter. Nor could we comment on their reaction to the old Roman Catholic cathedral, which is still standing today!

CHAPTER 7
INDEPENDENCE-BOUND

In accordance with the ground crew's new plan to take some of the hard work out of their driving, they dropped Brian and me, with our flight gear, at the restaurant adjacent to the motel at around 07.00 and started on their way, intending to stop for their first meal after an hour or so of driving.

The restaurant was already crowded and it took an hour to get through breakfast. Brian, fast becoming the most experienced in coping with the American telephone systems, undertook to order the taxi. He was away so long that I began to think he must have gone off to the cab company to do so! When he eventually came back 30 minutes later it was with a long tale of woe, though at least the taxi was on its way.

Brian had found two public phones, near the entrance, where a long queue had formed waiting for seats. After unsuccessfully trying to ring the cab company number, he got through to the operator who asked for his area code. That floored him as it was not shown in the booth and no one in the queue had any idea. Simple, he thought, ask at the cash desk. The girl there did not know either, so that Brian had to make a tour of the restaurant to find someone who did.

Back to the phone where the operator told him how many more coins to insert. He had just enough, but unfortunately, before he got them all in, the coin box became full and jammed, so that the phone went dead and he could not tell the operator! Neither could he get his coins back to try again! Just to make matters worse, someone was now using the other phone! When he eventually got on to the other phone, the new operator was very sympathetic, understood the situation and put him straight through to the cab company. But his troubles were still not over.

The receptionist wanted to know where we were to be picked up. "Denny's," said Brian, confidently.

"Which one?" said the girl.

"The one in St. Louis," from Brian.

"There are several Denny's in St. Louis, which one?" asked the girl.

No one in the by now somewhat amused queue could identify for Brian which Denny's we were in; they had simply turned off the highway when they saw the sign! At least this time the girl at the cash desk could give him the answer and an exasperated Brian finally beat a hasty retreat from the telephone.

From our seat, we had a commanding view of the approach road to the entrance and sat and waited for the cab to appear. And waited – and waited – and waited. We did not know how far the taxi had to come so were not sure how long was a reasonable time to allow. In the end, I made for the phone booth, armed with a fresh supply of coins, the local area code and the location of our restaurant, Brian having had more than his fill of telephones for the morning! The cab company could not at first understand why we needed to have been waiting for more than a few minutes, the girl eventually coming back to say that the driver had turned up at the restaurant, found no one waiting and returned empty! We just made it out to the entrance in time to see the second one appear!

Now we had another problem. The driver knew where the airport was, but to him there was only one – Lambert International. Just in time, we stopped him rushing off to the north of St. Louis but then found he had no idea where Parks was. Parks is in East St. Louis, and East St. Louis is not St.Louis – it is not even in the same State and he had rarely ventured across the river! After telling him that the previous evening we had crossed the river by the Gateway Arch, I began to get worried when, on the other side of the river, he turned north following the Chicago signs on the I-55. It seemed ages before we came to an intersection at which he could U-turn! We soon had the air charts out and were directing the driver by those, but airports are big places to drive round and even when we got there we must have tried every entrance before finding the right one!

Now some two hours late, we settled the overnight bill (no landing fee, no nonsensical charge for navigation facilities and only $4.00 for the overnight tie-down) and quickly cleared for take-off, despite a repetition of the morning murk of the previous three days. We put in a call to Jefferson City, our next stop, advising them of our ETA (Estimated Time of Arrival) as they had requested; their weather was fine and hazy, with thunderstorms forecast at about the time of our expected arrival.

Parks Air Traffic Control were very helpful when we phoned them from the reception desk. They understood our problems with the radio and cleared us to leave the ramp when we were ready. They gave us a green light signal for take-off on the nearest runway, even though this was not the one in use for the big jets. How different to the attitude of the Controllers on most self-important airports at home, who do their best to deter us from using them if we are non-radio!

Any ideas we had the previous evening about photographing the Gateway Arch in the morning sun had long since gone, the gloom being comparable to that we had encountered at Pittsburgh. I had intended to follow the Mississippi north from Parks, swinging round west where the Missouri flowed into it, but the mist was such that it seemed wiser to keep well clear of the control zones around Lambert and skirt south. So we crossed the wide, brown, sullen expanse of the Mississippi, heading out over the southern suburbs of St. Louis. I found it difficult to picture what the area must have been like when the Whitmans steamed up-river 150 years before – it may not even have followed the same course at that time. One thing was certain, the beautiful landscapes on the wooded shores referred to by Narcissa had long since gone, swallowed up by the ever-expanding scar of urban and industrial development.

We could see little more than a mile or so, our first sighting of the mighty Missouri being of a broad stretch of turgid brown water materialising out of the mist, looping lazily like an enormous snake. Fortunately, the further west we progressed, the sunnier and clearer it became. At Jefferson City, our first refuelling stop 110 miles to the west, visibility was probably around ten miles where clear of the dark, grey storm clouds now looming up. Brian was delighted to establish radio contact with the tower, sufficient for them to advise of the runway in use and to tell him what lousy reception they had of his transmissions!

There was a message waiting for us at Jefferson City to telephone Jim Morgan, a member of the Experimental Aircraft Association (EAA), who wished to fly out and escort us in. I quickly got through to him and gave him our intended route and height, it soon being obvious that we would meet up somewhere along the I-70. Jim warned us to look out for some violent storms that had passed over Independence, heading east, and to make sure that we went round them. He also advised me on the 'pattern' expected from visiting light-plane pilots on arrival at Independence, a low flypast along the runway being the done thing before landing. This is possibly related to the practice of making a low inspection run over unknown ground before making an emergency landing.

Several other pilots, members of the Missouri Pilot's Association (MoPA), had been waiting with him for some time to escort us in, but had now left as our lateness was attributed to the severe thunderstorms in the area. Wiser than us in the ways of such weather conditions, they prudently assumed we would not fly until later.

After taking off from Jefferson City, the midday heat made itself felt in the noticeably reduced rate of climb as we struggled to lift over a ridge to the north of the airport. We could see that there were some nasty little storms hanging over our intended north-westerly course, with lightning flashing over the town of Ashland. But there was a gap to the west. After some twelve miles we were able to swing back north and rejoin our route over Viertol Airport, near Boonville.

And not a moment too soon, as we met a bright red Citabria just west of Boonville, looking very smart in the bright sunlight, the storms suddenly all now behind us. We could not make ourselves understood to Jim on the radio, picking up little more than a stream of garbled croaks from him, even when flying alongside. However, we did get the message that he had George on board with him; at least the ground party had got there on time, once again beating us to it!

The terrain below was much as we had seen for the last two days, flat, open, farm and parkland, with the Missouri meandering along through the verdant fields. The broad, dual carriageway of the I-70 Interstate

Highway would lead us straight to Independence, which is virtually an eastern suburb of Kansas City. On the way we passed a most enormous scrapyard of light aircraft, with rows and rows of fuselages, and stack after stack of wings etc., covering many acres of ground. It reminded me vividly of the great scrapyards of military aircraft in Europe at the end of the war, particularly at Burtonwood Base Air Depot in Lancashire, where I was based briefly with the RAF.

As arranged, we formated loosely on Jim's Citabria until we could see the airfield. Then he peeled off and left me to make a low-speed pass above the runway, past several photographers at one side, before pulling up to make a normal circuit and landing. For once, we made a presentable arrival in front of an audience, one much bigger than expected, as we saw when waved in to where a small crowd was obviously waiting for us. As I switched off and opened the door, a round of applause greeted us, the first I have ever experienced on such an occasion!

When we climbed out, the heat hit us, and suddenly I realised how dry and parched I was. There was no opportunity to remedy this as we were swept off to where a smaller group stood in front of the rest. With relief I recognised Barbara Magerl, the OCTA Vice-President, who had done so much to help us with arrangements along the Trail. We were quickly introduced to Councilwoman Millie Nesbitt, representing the Mayor of Independence in the latter's unavoidable absence, and Bob Hawley, a City Councillor, together with Joe McMillan of the Missouri Pilots' Association (MoPA).

There followed speeches of welcome [Fig. 8], the presentation to me of a beautiful Key and the Freedom of the City of Independence, and a treasured Proclamation of Welcome bearing the Seal of the City, the 'Queen City of the Trails.' All our team were appointed honorary members of the MoPA and presented with their attractive red and white caps [Fig. 9].

Whilst still trying to recover from such a friendly, sincere and warm welcome, so totally unexpected, it was suddenly my turn, with TV cameras and microphone! What does one say in such circumstances, with expectant faces so obviously waiting for something they would like to hear? Never one for excelling at off-the-cuff speeches, whatever I said – and I cannot remember a word – seemed to keep everyone happy.

There followed more interviews and more introductions, meeting some very charming people. Parched and dry, I was very glad in the end to be offered a refreshing iced drink while arrangements were made to refuel and hangar the Champ, all 'on the house' by the airport owner, Mrs Vesta Ailshire, a charming lady of indeterminate years.

In finding space in the hangar, a resident Tri-Pacer was bundled outside by its owner, a silver-haired veteran who had that indefinable something which sets such pilots aside from the usual weekend flier. I felt most honoured and suitably humbled when, on further discussion in the cool of the airport office, it transpired that Ted was Edwin Schoch, an old barnstormer of the twenties who became a test pilot for McDonnell. He had done all the test flying of the unlikely-looking and correspondingly dangerous XF-85 Goblin, a parasite jet fighter designed to be carried internally by the Convair B-36 bomber. What a pity that time did not permit a longer acquaintance – I could cheerfully have gone on listening indefinitely to his tales of the old days!

Meanwhile, Jim Morgan, who turned out to be an easygoing, genial giant, more usually to be found in the captain's seat of a Boeing 747, had offered to fly me around to photograph Liberty Landing, which I knew we would have no chance of doing the next day. This I particularly wanted to view from the air, having been puzzled by several aspects when visiting it by car the previous year. In 1836, Liberty Landing was the farthest point west along the Missouri that the commercial steamboats served. It was here that on April 7th of that year, with the temperature 8 degrees below freezing at 9 o'clock in the morning, the Whitmans disembarked from the side-wheeler "Chariton" which had brought them from St. Louis. Independence Landing (also known as Wayne City Landing) had not at that time achieved the pre-eminence it did for a short period in later years.

As we flew over the river towards Liberty Landing, I watched with great excitement as a century-old ghost of the old man of the river emerged. Often over the past 18 months I had pored over old maps and charts of the area, trying to relate them to what I had seen at ground level and to Narcissa Whitman's diary entries. It was only after Richard Badders, a fellow OCTA member and an employee of the US Corps of Engineers, had sent me copies of 19th Century charts of the river, that they had started to come together.

From the air I was able to see why the Landing was now so far from the river and from the small community of Liberty. A new channel had been made years later, by US Army engineers, to cut off a great, three-miles-wide loop of the river. For the airborne, the original course still etched its distinctive trace though it was virtually invisible from the ground! And Liberty was on the nearest high ground above the earlier flood basin of the river. As on many occasions later, a brief sighting from the air explained all!

Jim offered to let me fly his Citabria, which I did after I had taken sufficient pictures. The Citabria is a beefed-up, higher-powered and more fully-equipped development of the Champion, and would have been an ideal mount for what we were doing. Time was too short to do all that I would have liked, knowing that the rest of the crew were sitting it out on the ground awaiting our return, and anyway I dared not get too attached to the Citabria!

All the subsequent arrangements had been looked after for us by Barbara, so we all went off to our motel, deciding that what we needed to do more than anything else was to put our feet up and relax for an hour or so, in preparation for the evening activities. It also gave me an opportunity to find out how the car crew had fared. They had benefited by the morning arrangements, arriving at Independence at about one o'clock, despite having been stopped for speeding. Fortunately the patrolman was very understanding and let George off with a kindly warning! They had met Barbara at the airfield and had time to book into the motel before we arrived. Even so, all agreed that we ought not to take any chance of a repeat of the aircrew's disastrous attempts that morning to get away on their own!

A dining hall had been reserved for our evening reception at a top restaurant, and there followed a long evening of excellent food, convivial companions and even more speeches; fortunately for us all, in the atmosphere that prevailed, almost anything anyone said was well received. That was just as well, as I believe most of the members of our party were feeling more than a little light-headed by the time the evening was out. Brian was feeling so tired, in fact, that he dozed off at the table!

Amongst the many kindly folks we met was Don Claybaugh, President of the Spearhead Chapter, Kansas Pilots Association, who was most insistent that when we landed for refuelling at Topeka, we should do so at Philip Billard Municipal Airport instead of, as planned, at Mesa Verde. As the latter had been chosen to suit our tailskid-equipped biplanes, and we were no longer restricted to turf runways, I could hardly refuse, especially when I learned that a reception had been planned for us there as well! What was more, he was planning to fly into Independence in the morning in order to escort us in his Cessna 150. When he heard that we planned to get away by 06.30 if at all possible, he just smiled and shook his head, suggesting that 10.00 would be a better time – it was just as well we did not lay a bet with him!

Our last act before bidding Barbara and her husband and other friends goodnight, was to be taken by them to see the old original log Court House. Finally, we were driven round the famous Independence Square, in an old tradition, so we were told, of "Winding the Clock," undertaken by emigrants the night before setting out West on the Oregon Trail! So ended another fantastic evening, not likely ever to be forgotten by any member of our team! Tomorrow we should all try to follow the emigrants' tracks.

Fig. 5. The big Ford station-wagon used by the ground crew to shadow the aircrew across the States and back to Salt Lake City. It easily swallowed all six of us, baggage for a month, and equipment for the flight.

Fig. 6. The 1946 65 hp Aeronca Champion NC2979E at Sky Manor on the morning of our departure for Canandaigua, waiting for the low cloud and mist to clear sufficiently to take our leave. A line of tall power pylons march unseen in the murk across the hills in the background. At least the delay gave us time to finish the camera mounting and swing the compass!

Fig. 7. Old NC2979E sitting in the evening sun at BiState Parks Airport, St. Louis. This shows the strut-mounted Leica and remote control cable to the cabin.

Fig. 8. The author and Brian Hargrave at Independence Memorial Airport, eyes now shaded by our Missouri Pilots Association caps (having just been made Honorary Members), about to receive the Key of the City of Independence from Councilwoman Millie Nesbitt, representing the Mayor, with City Councillor Bob Hawley. *(Photo: G.A. Cull)*

Fig. 9. 'Full house' at Independence Memorial Airport. L. to R. are Maurice and Irene Brett, Brian Hargrave, Jean and George Cull, and Sonia Hargrave. *(Photo: Bob Barrett)*

Fig. 10. Liberty Landing on the River Missouri, where the Whitmans disembarked in 1836, is marked by a cross. A great loop of the river (marked by a dotted line) was cut off when the Army Engineers changed the course of the river in 1896. This view from the air, looking NE, solved a puzzle for the author of how the Whitmans had seemingly landed so far from the river!

Fig. 11. Wayne City (or Independence) Landing, Independence. Wagons were hauled up the 200 ft high slope (centre) after disembarking. In the mid-19th century, the south bank of the river was closer to the foot of the slope.

Fig. 12. At last – the roll-map in use in the Champ. The universal mount is clamped to the strut at the left of the windscreen, while the camera remote control unit is positioned just below the map case. *(Photo: Brian Hargrave)*

Fig. 13. A small thunderstorm near Lawrence produced the only rain we met over the Trail. The Trail lies partly under the shining wet Highway 40, switch-backing the 'prairie' contours which the wagons would have gone round where possible.

Fig. 14. Don Claybaugh, our Kansas Pilots Association guide, circled to point out this field of 'crop-art' by Lawrence creator Stan Herd, representing the Kansas State Flower in Van Gogh's painting of a vase of sunflowers.

Fig. 15. The Union Ferry site on the Kaw (Kansas) River. The river is very wide here, and comparatively shallow (note the sandbanks).

Fig. 16. Red Vermillion Crossing and Vieux Cemetery (site on left). The earlier red girder bridge is now replaced by a modern concrete affair. The Trail crossing point is this side of the bridge.

Fig. 17. Scott Spring near Westmoreland KS, looking NW. The arrow points to an adjacent grave marker at the roadside. Here the author noted what looked like rut swales (marked on the photo by a white line) heading towards the Spring but not shown on the maps. These are not visible from the road.

Fig. 18. Another view of the ruts near Scott Spring, again marked by an adjacent white line on the photo. The location is to the east side of Highway 99, south of the rest area at Scott Spring.

Fig. 19. We looked in vain for some definite identifying features for the Black Vermillion Crossing, so cannot say for certain if this is it. If not, it must be typical of the sort of fording point used. Note the large tree in the river bed!

Fig. 20. The clump of trees marking the Alcove Spring site (upper arrow) and Independence Crossing (right arrow) of the Big Blue River, viewed looking south. Positive location of the trees hiding the Spring is the angled railroad level-crossing (lower left) near Schroyer and the pronounced kink in the road 600 yds down the hill.

Fig. 21. Having failed to locate the Hollenburg Ranch (due to a map error), finding the little concrete Tri-County Marker (near Lanham) provided a great boost to morale in the cockpit.

Fig. 22. Rock Creek State Park, showing the Trail swales curving round from the lower right corner, past the East Ranch Station and over the toll bridge (centre left). Scene of the infamous Wild Bill Hickok/McCanles gunfight in 1861. The Park Authorities run an ox-drawn wagon (seen just above centre) round the site.

Fig. 23. Flying across Elm Creek (nr. Hastings) looking for the marked ruts beyond the Stage Station site, we found not only those of the main Trail (above the upper white marker line) but another more prominent set running through a small pond to the north-east, in the same field (below lower marker line). This view is looking west-south-west.

Fig. 24. The ruts through the pond, looking straight down.

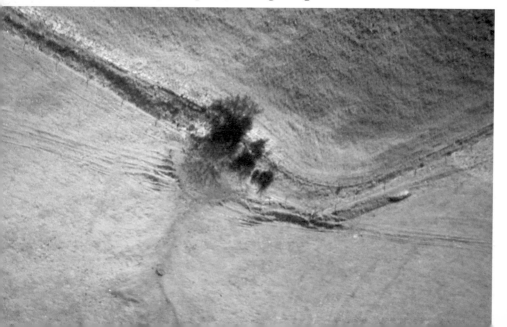

Fig. 25. Not strictly speaking an Oregon Trail feature, this picture of the bridge over the Big Sandy at Alexandria shows how well various markers stood out from the air. One of these is a Pony Express Centennial plaque.

Fig. 26. Skeins and channels of the Platte River near Lowell, Nebraska. Here a very high (1,163 ft) aerial mast stretches near-invisible supporting cables for hundreds of feet around.

Fig. 27. Fort Kearny looking NW along the sun-dappled Platte Valley. A reconstruction of the palisade built late in the life of the fort (never used in anger) can be seen to the left of site centre. The Trail (of which there is now no trace) passed along the north side. The later city of Kearney lies beyond the north bank of the Platte.

Fig. 28. Plum Creek Massacre Cemetery, looking south-west, is situated just off the dirt road south of Plum Creek and a mile and a half west of the massacre site.

CHAPTER 8
DAY 1:
ON THE OREGON TRAIL TO FORT KEARNY

Ever optimistic about timing, we all arranged to be up and about for an early breakfast. While the others made it by the appointed hour of six o'clock, Renie and I overslept and looked out bleary-eyed to see them lugging cases down to the car. Even though a little later than intended, we still had a problem in getting a meal at the required hour, so that it was gone eight o'clock before we arrived at the airfield. This taught us, in future, to religiously check the night before on the availability of breakfast when finalising the morning arrangements!

When we arrived it was to see that some kind person had moved the Champ out of the hangar and wheeled it down to the end of the flight line. This puzzled me considerably at the time as no one seemed to be aware of who had done it or when, and I privately felt this was taking hospitality a little too far – it was quite a long walk down to the end of the line!

Loading up with armfuls of assorted paraphernalia, Brian and I wandered along to where the Champ was parked, getting our feet soaking wet in the dew-heavy grass on the way. As we neared the Champ, I was beginning to feel that something about it was different. It looked the same as we had left it – and yet not! Closer still I realised I could not see the camera mount on the wing strut, and then that there was no sign of our Union Jacks or Oregon Trail wording on the side. A few more steps confirmed that this was not NC2979E but an identical aircraft, painted in the same authentic Aeronca colour scheme!

Cursing my own stupidity for the time wasted, and feeling very foolish to boot, I discovered eventually that it had been flown in after we had left the airfield. Of all the many Champions we came across, it was the only other one we saw in the original colour scheme, with exactly the same colour breaks and tones as ours.

Don Claybaugh was as good as his word and was waiting to greet us at the airfield. He was to escort us into the Philip Billard Municipal Airport at Topeka, and briefed us beforehand as to the joining procedure. Don was aware of the route we would be flying in following the Oregon Trail, and would keep well clear in the air. He also suggested that we look out for a local landmark near Lawrence, a field of 'crop-art' forming a mural of a vase of sunflowers (the State flower of Kansas), which he would circle to point out to us.

Brian was having problems in trying to stow all six feet of him and a multitude of items in the cabin, much of which had to be ready to hand. In addition to the sleeping bags, minimal overnight gear, spare quarts of

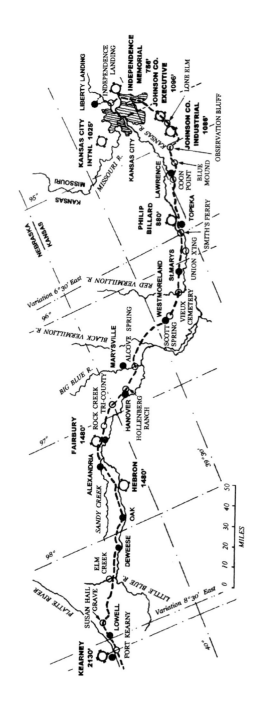

70

oil, three still cameras and boxes of film carried on the earlier stages, we now added the ciné camera and spools of film, two empty 3-gallon petrol containers, a half-gallon water container and paper cups, emergency rations, my roller map and and one or two vital tools. It was a very tight squeeze, especially now that the cameras and Trail maps were to be used in earnest.

But it was a special thrill to mount the roller map case on the cabin structure *[Fig. 12]*, knowing that at last it was there for the purpose for which so many hours work had been expended. If Aeronca's quoted 20 lb weight of disposable load looked a trifle minuscule in comparison with what we carried, we took comfort from the fact that we two English males weigh noticeably less than our American counterparts!

We got off at 09.30, only three hours later than intended! There were signs of thunderclouds to the north-west, as forecast, the sky was generally fairly overcast, with a light breeze, and it was pleasantly warm. Don thought that the forecast of thunder would keep some of the pilots away who might otherwise have come out to greet us at Topeka, many of them from quite a distance. We both agreed though that we should be able to dodge the storms or, at worst, land at some local airfield to let them pass.

Independence Memorial airfield is situated six miles to the south-east of the Trail Head at Independence Landing. That, and the need to climb to the legally required height of 1,500 ft at which to cross the city, gave Brian and I just a few brief minutes in the air to get ourselves settled in before our work started in earnest, but it was nothing like enough. When I turned over the site of the Landing, Brian was still trying to organise quick access to both the still cameras and the ciné-camera he was to use, as well as his radio and navigation equipment. The ciné-camera was now, for the first time, usable, as Barbara Magerl had obtained for us locally some 300 ft of film. Fortunately, I had taken all the stills I needed from the Citabria the day before, but it still left Brian needing two more hands when I suggested he shot off some ciné film of the Landing.

I was still fairly certain that the conditions under which the wing camera was operating would preclude it producing any usable pictures. As expected, it had not been possible to develop the first film we had shot, so there was no way of checking. Even so, I could not just abandon it without trying, especially as Brian had his hands so full. We quickly established another problem in using the hand-held cameras, which we never satisfactorily overcame, the full impact only becoming apparent when we developed our films back in the UK.

It was one thing for me to recognise the features to film, with the advantage of my special map and occasional prior knowledge. But it was quite another to convey their precise identification and location to the chap in the back, well enough for him to point the hand-held cameras at the right spot! Such features were often well spaced out. Giving as much warning as possible, I would circle slowly and throttle back to make myself better heard over the roar of the engine (if we were not too low), shouting above it and pointing to what I wanted photographed with the telephoto- or ciné- camera.

If I was lucky, he would not have been preoccupied with the radio: or trying to confirm position on his chart; or changing a film; or fishing around for some vital item (it was surprising what could lodge inaccessibly under the rear seat, mercifully well clear of any controls); or trying to prevent cramp in some nether part of his anatomy; or struggling not to catch up with the sleep he had lost the night before!

Don had soon caught up in his Cessna, and now sat discreetly slightly above and behind. After one or two checks to see how he was faring, and observing that he was invariably in more or less the same position, even after we circled several times, we were able forget him when concentration on other aspects dictated it. This was quite a relief, but at the same time it was good to know he was there and in radio communication with the outside world had we strayed into anyone else's zone or path.

Below, as we circled over the broad, brown Missouri, one's eyes were inevitably drawn to the smoking stacks of the white-powdered cement works, located on the south bank, just to the east of the Wayne City/-Independence Landing. Along the river bank, at the foot of the 300 ft-high, tree-covered cliff [Fig. 11], ran the rails of what has to be one of the most unlikely sounding and yet (thanks to Judy Garland) most well-known of railways – the Atchison, Topeka and Santa Fe RR!

The steep cliff road up which the wagoners had had to drive their reluctant charges looked innocuous enough from the air, a sound concrete surface now covering the slippery mud which once confronted the immigrants in the early spring. This was the start; from now on, we would be following every step of their way for the next 2,000 miles, measuring progress by the turning of the roller map which would be my guide and mentor.

Levelling off at 2,300 ft altitude, 1,500 ft above the city, I throttled back to our cruising revs of 2,100 to give an airspeed of around 75 mph. Brian glanced back at Don's Cessna and pointed out that he had 10 deg of flap down, as if to emphasise how slowly we were flying! The air was unexpectedly bumpy and I could not hold the machine level; perhaps it was just as well we had not got a video camera mounted on the wing as any viewers might have felt airsick watching the resulting tape!

Excitement was high as we headed south over River Road, which was thought to have taken the wagons to Independence Square, though there was nothing now to see to relate to the old Trail. The Trail turned to approach the easily identifiable Square from the west, and we circled to try and pick out from the surrounding trees the old log Court House, now moved one block south of the Square. From there we headed south, now following the old Santa Fe Trail, which was also used in the early years by those setting out for Oregon. It ran along Blue Ridge but at our height its gentle contours were meaningless.

I quickly lost count of intersecting roads, but two railways, which we had to cross obliquely, followed by a major highway, our old friend I-70, located our position. The Trail ran right through the middle of a major intersection, and I felt just a little satisfaction at being able for once to follow the Trail route more thoroughly than those on the ground!

Soon, we left Independence and passed onto Kansas City, Missouri (absolutely no connection and not to be confused with the outfit next door, Kansas City, Kansas!). There was nothing to indicate either transition, the urban sprawl continuing implacably across the invisible boundaries. The winding course of Blue Ridge Road (the old Santa Fe Trail), so remarkable for the fact that it was almost the only road that meandered amongst its grid-patterned neighbours, was easy to follow. It took us almost down to the next major highway, the US 71, the Trail route cutting straight through another even bigger and more complex intersection. Here, when travelling by car in the opposite direction the year before, I had failed miserably to locate the Blue Ridge Road, despite several circuits round the junction.

Satisfaction at the easier transition by air was short-lived. I wanted to photograph the site of the old Red Bridge over the Blue River, and try to pick out the first ruts that Franzwa had shown in his maps. Alas, from 1,500 ft over a disruptive pattern of trees and bushes, I could not pinpoint with any certainty even the bridge site, despite circling round and round trying to match ground and map. The location we photo-graphed turned out, on later examination of our slides, to be three-quarters of a mile south of the bridge.

By the time we left Kansas City we had survived the first and most hectic half-hour of flying over the route, had crossed the biggest urban complex that we would encounter anywhere along the Trail and had begun to get a feel for what was to follow. The fixed camera remote control appeared to be working, in that it was clicking over one number at a time. Brian was regaining his normal calm composure, though admittedly not yet happy about operating the ciné camera, air turbulence creating almost impossible conditions for filming. Ahead, the concrete jungle was giving way to open space and green fields. Perhaps, if I could remember to keep winding on my map roll, we might be able to follow its green line all the way, despite the fact that for most of the time there was nothing corresponding with it on the ground!

We had reduced the number of unknowns, and from now on the battle would be more with the elements than the technical aspects. Did the emigrants, I wonder, feel something of the same thing as they left the comparative safety of the United States, crossing the Western Frontier and heading out into the wilderness? If nothing else, emigrant diaries often noted a sense of loneliness at this juncture.

From now on, things became easier in that ground features were more widely spaced, giving us a little more time both to check what would be coming next and to look around us; also a mixed blessing, that of flying lower, our height from now on being around 500 ft above ground. From this height we could more readily recognise what lay below, but equally we could not see the distant pattern so well.

Turning west from the supposed Red Bridge site, we picked out the cemetery and drive-in theatre (since replaced by a very expensive shopping area) at New Santa Fe, and swung south-west across open fields for the first time. There was a little town of that name here, in the mid-nineteenth century, on the borders of Missouri and thus of the United States. And it was from here that the wagons rolled out across the unmarked Frontier, onto the wild open prairies and into Indian Territory. That cemetery and its name is all that is left now of the last town the immigrants saw until they reached Oregon City. Even the trees they left behind them here were reputed to be the last they would see, of any size and in any great numbers, until they reached the Boise River, within sight of the Blue Mountains in Oregon.

There was absolutely no sign of ruts over these long-cultivated areas and it was the wrong time of the year for tell-tale signs in the vegetation. At Stanley, the Trail cut close to a sports track and baseball field, and two miles further on, at our new low altitude, we had the first real opportunity of checking out the power lines shown in red on my map. Near Morse, we crossed a minor north-south highway, and sure enough, there were the cables, running alongside the road.

Here we had to give wide berth to an airfield, Johnson County Executive, all eyes peeled for any crossing air traffic. But the situation here was the same as at almost every airfield we had come across – other traffic was non-existent. I looked back up behind us, and sure enough, there was Don in his Cessna, seemingly unconcerned about our proximity to an active airfield. The old pioneers had one up on us at this point – they had trailed straight across the airfield!

Some five miles further on we came to the first notable feature on the Trail after Red Bridge, Lone Elm camp ground. Here, the emigrants spent their first night outside the United States, some 28 miles along their way from Independence, probably after two easy days travelling. Although the ¼-mile-square location was easy to establish, with the Lone Elm site amongst a clump of trees in the south-east corner, there was no evidence now of what may have been the greatest overnight concentrations of wagon trains along the Trail. Even at our low speed we had taken a little over half an hour to cover their two days of travel.

Unseen, a mile or two to our left, was a small private airstrip, with more to come. First was the large ex-Naval air station (Olathe), renamed Johnson County Industrial Airport when we passed it, but latterly the New Century AirCenter, the Trail crossing the boundaries of both airfields. Two miles beyond that was Gardner Municipal, for which the Trail showed a similar disregard! We were so busy keeping our eyes open for other aircraft (needless to say there were none), and counting off roads as we crossed them, that we had passed the junction of the Oregon and Santa Fe Trails before I realised it. There was probably nothing at all to see there, but it would have been nice to have noted such a historic spot in passing.

Now we turned due north for some six miles, the change in direction marking the first break point in my strip chart. As on our dummy run in the UK, this created no problems. The Trail ran along the edge of high ground above a small creek, nowadays largely hidden by trees. Suddenly, we were over the Sunflower Ordnance Works, whose barbed wire perimeter fence had stopped me from following the route in my car the previous year. From my loftier perch the reason for the high fence was obvious: rows and rows of the sort of little buildings one sees in ammunition dumps. I pretended not to notice, in the hopes that any quick-on-the-trigger, anti-aircraft missile operator would not really want to practise on us, taking comfort from the fact that it was not marked on the air charts as a Restricted Zone and was probably now disused! We later established that it was disused after the end of the war in Vietnam!

A mile and a half into the Ordnance Works, we swung through 90 deg to follow the Trail as it turned west, down a shallow escarpment from the highest point on the prairie for miles, named Observation Bluff by the emigrants. At the bottom, the Trail finally crossed the creek, whose very deep banks must have discouraged the wagoners from crossing higher up.

At this point, Don passed us and circled tightly just off to the north, as if to attract our attention to something below. A very minor diversion took us over a field with varied crops laid out to form a splendid representation of Van Gogh's painting of a vase of sunflowers (the State Flower of Kansas), which Don had mentioned earlier, the work of local 'crop-art' creator Stan Herd. Unfortunately, there were now no sunflowers in bloom but the shapes of the vase and flowers stood out clearly [Fig. 14] in what looked to be green plants, hay grass and bare earth. By now the early sunshine had given way to overcast, and suddenly the storms were on us again, creeping insidiously across our intended path from the south-west.

Some eight miles ahead was Blue Mound, a mile-long swelling on the surface of the flat plain, by the side of the Wakarusa River, where General Fremont on his early exploratory expeditions had camped. Anywhere else it would not be worth recording; but here it stood out for miles from the surrounding plain, treeless in emigrant days, to form an early, well-known landmark on the Oregon Trail. But not today! A thunderstorm was busily lancing blue lightning flashes in the direction of the town of Lawrence and had dropped a white veil over the Mound, blocking our way.

The only way to continue was to skirt north of Lawrence. There, easy-to-follow old faithful I-70 ran west, just north of the Trail, eventually continuing some five miles over the Trail itself. I-70 would, in fact, lead us almost straight to Philip Billard Municipal Airport at Topeka if the cloud continued to cloak our way west. Reluctantly we headed north-west, between Eudora and Lawrence, hoping to get past the latter before the cloud cut us off. We just made it, a brief shower pattering the windscreen as we crossed the wide Kansas River. Beyond Lawrence the way was clear. Now we could see the shining wet surface of Highway 40 as it switchbacked west *[Fig. 13]*. Here the route of the Trail alternated from one side to the other as the wagoners swung round the undulations which the modern road went over.

Meanwhile, we had a new hazard to watch for, with chimney stacks and aerial masts marked as high obstructions on my chart. At least these helped to fix our position! Soon, the Trail route and Highway 40 swung northwest to parallel I-70 near another old high-ground landmark, Coon Point, the two being coincident for most of the remaining 15 miles into Topeka. Though the plain was still relatively flat, the undulations, now like an ocean swell rather than hillocks, meant that here there was no way for the wagons to avoid a switchback route.

As we closed in to the airport, Don swung into the lead to position us in line with the runway in use and then turned off to one side. As at Independence, we made a low pass along the runway before landing – at last the Champ seemed to have got used to my ways and made no fuss about the latter! Flight time, two hours. Once again there was a small knot of people waiting to greet us, including the Airport Manager, City Admin. Officials, Officers of the KPA (Kansas Pilots Association) and Robert Richmond of the Kansas State Historical Society, with Press and local broadcasting photographers, video cameras and microphones. We met lots of friendly folk, shook many hands and exchanged speeches. The KPA presented us with their blue flight caps, a handsome wall plaque commemorating our flight, and made us Honorary Members.

Several other examples of the degree of hospitality which we were accorded stand out. While in the circuit, Brian had tried to talk to the tower and had made poor and intermittent contact. Hearing of this, a local organisation, Hetrick Aircraft, offered to look at our equipment to see if they could assist in any way. As a result, an external aerial was installed and the little Narco transceiver fitted up with a head-set and noise-cancelling microphone to try and reduce background noise, all without charge. If willingness alone could have solved our problems, there would have been none remaining – alas it seemed to confirm that all we needed was time to charge the batteries for the Narcos to live up to their reputation as the best!

Meanwhile, someone was busy filling our fuel and oil tanks with the correct grades and would take no payment for doing so. Perhaps most unexpected and therefore most impressive of all were the efforts of a delightful lady, Mrs Loueen Burrows from Hesston, a small town some 150 miles distant. She and her husband had driven all the way over that morning to bring a magnificent picnic lunch, for us and the welcoming party, entirely at her own expense; we sat at her table under her sunshade and enjoyed a welcome break and a feast to boot. It was now very hot and when we were getting ready to leave, she insisted on us taking an insulated container full of iced orange juice. The orange juice was soon consumed but the little red container served us all the rest of the way and is still with me today. It seemed that Loueen had enjoyed tremendously a visit to England, and this was her way of returning the friendliness she had found then!

How does one repay such warmth and good old Mid-Western hospitality? All we could do to reciprocate at that point was to wear with pride our blue KPA caps as we left. We were most grateful for these caps and between us we wore one of each of the KPA and MoPA caps from then on! We finally tore ourselves away just after one o'clock – now some 3¼ hours later than intended and at almost the peak heat of the day. There were still scattered thunderstorms about, but the forecast was that they would die out as we flew west. Now we were on our own, Don having carried out his self-imposed task of ensuring that we arrived safely at Topeka.

We took off to the north-west, crossing another railroad known to many in Britain only through the words of a song – the Rock Island Line (CRI&PR). The exact Trail route through downtown Topeka is seemingly not known with absolute certainty, so I felt quite justified in skirting the city to the north following Highway 24. This in any case coincided briefly with the Trail, west of the Kansas River crossing site. There, the river is impressively wide, and must have looked impossibly so to anyone standing on one bank, who had to swim their animals and float their wagons across to the other! The Kaw River, as it was often referred to in emigrant diaries, with a width of 600-700 ft, was the first big river crossing they had encountered though, later, others would dwarf it.

As yet, despite careful searching, we had seen no real evidence of the Trail, nor had we expected to this far east. But as we cut south-west from the small community of Menoken towards the Smith's Ferry site, following that green line that represented the Oregon Trail on my map, suddenly it had a counterpart on the ground. Crossing some indifferently cultivated fields, with bare or thin patches, a corresponding colour break showed up through the dark green crop ahead. A lighter-toned, poorly-growing swathe angled across the field towards the river, as far as a dirt road. The line was continued part way across the next field as a streak of bare earth.

I shouted excitedly to Brian to have a look, to get his opinion in case I was imagining it. We circled several times, but the line was only evident when we were flying along it, and then it pointed unerringly towards what I had identified as the site of Smith's Ferry. Location of the latter was pinpointed by an overhead power line running down to the river.

This was a great morale booster – so there *was* something to see after all, even when there was no indication of ruts on Greg's maps! Although we were to see nothing more for another half hour, it kept us on our toes from then on. We had no difficulty in following the route, now heading north of west from the ferry site, for much of the way under Highway 24, with the Union Pacific RR running alongside it. We diverted briefly to photograph the site of the old Union Ferry at Willard, where an older, alternate route from Topeka crossed the Kaw *[Fig. 15]*. The weather here was once more not conducive to good aerial photography, with occasional showers and a high overcast.

At St. Marys, we looked in vain for a sighting of the old Catholic Indian Mission, but could not recognise it! Four miles beyond the town, Highway 24 left the Trail route and from then on we were on our own as far as navigation was concerned – no more major highways to show us the way, until we reached our overnight destination, Kearney! It was back to counting off the miles and intersections and watching the rivers, railroads and power lines. When they deserted us, we would have to resort to the far less accurate process of following a compass course and noting elapsed times to calculate distance.

This way, we followed the Trail fairly accurately, locating the Red Vermillion River crossing, now spanned by a new concrete bridge instead of the expected iron girder bridge. This threw me at first, but there could be no real doubt about our location, with the old Vieux cemetery close by *[Fig. 16]*. Here was buried Louis Vieux, the old chief of the Pottawatomie Indians, who still have an Indian Reservation in the area.

It was difficult to imagine the scene at this idyllic spot when, in May 1849, a large wagon train encamped here and, in the course of a week, lost 40 or 50 of its members from cholera. Then, there were still enormous herds of buffalo roaming the plains, seeking and polluting the same water that the emigrants used for drinking and washing. Few were aware at that time of the necessity to purify the water by boiling, and the prevalent cholera epidemic needed little excuse to spread under such conditions. No doubt they would have needed all their strength to continue, the banks of the river being very steep and the current rapid.

The Trail coincided with gravel roads for much of the way to the Red Vermillion, but beyond that struck out across fields and open grassland to the small town of Westmoreland. Approaching the sites of Scott Spring (there are at least two) where Highway 99 nears Westmoreland, we saw our first ruts [Figs. 17 & 18].

They furrowed a short distance across a grassy field to the east of the road and deeply through rising ground. Once again, when in line with them they were very evident – viewed from the side they could have passed unnoticed. We circled several times, not because on this occasion there was any doubt about what we could see, but just to drink in the scene. Where Franzwa's Maps showed ruts to the west of the road we could find nothing. Our ruts pointed straight towards a rest area with a commemorative marker, but though we circled at very low level again and again over the adjacent site of the springs by the side of Rock Creek, we could see nothing that looked like a spring.

North of the town the route continued across country and we searched unsuccessfully for a marshal's grave marked on my map, circling several times and seeing nothing that we could positively identify. Neither could we see ruts marked over this stretch. Further on we had trouble in determining position with any degree of accuracy, the main problem being that roads and tracks could not always be matched with the map, either being present where there should have been none, or not turning up as expected.

We picked out the next river, the Black Vermillion, but could not pinpoint the Trail crossing [Fig. 19]. The river looped in an intricate fashion, far more so than the map showed, and despite flying up and down it for a short distance in each direction, the roads obstinately refused to match. What made it so frustrating was that we knew we were in the right area and must have flown back and forth across it!

Twelve even more featureless miles further on we started to look for the famous Alcove Spring. For long stretches there had been no fixes and I had to recourse to flying by that wretched compass for part of the way. The countryside had slowly changed from flat, along the Kansas River, to undulating plains with low hills and valleys. Cultivation was intermittent, with more grassland than wheat, but occasional silos dotted the scene. There were fewer trees now and the whole was beginning to look more like the prairies as I had imagined them to be.

There was a brief sign of life at some sort of sports gathering miles from anywhere, with dozens of cars glinting in the sun to our left, a small crowd and white banners. Now the sun was searing again through the upper windshield, the motor's even rhythm was boring through the background and I was beginning to be aware that we had been up a long time.

Suddenly, I was jerked into wakefulness by the realisation that there was a whole series of navigation features coming up. We had just crossed a long straight highway, US 77, and a mile or so ahead was a wide valley and a shining stretch of water. Hastily turning on my roller map, which I had neglected to do for some miles, we were obviously approaching the Big Blue River, and with any luck the famous Alcove Spring.

Slanting in from the left was a railway which, on our right, crossed a north-south gravel road at a very shallow angle. Incredibly, we were spot on track. Circling over the crossing we looked for some sign of the spring, a half-mile to the south. In the end I decided it had to be hidden among the small trees and bushes in the southern vee of the level-crossing. Later, in discussion with the ground party, who had successfully visited the site, we decided it was in the next clump of trees to the south [Fig. 20].

On again, over the Independence crossing of the Big Blue, and now once more there was the familiar pattern of the mile square grid of roads, which made trail tracking so easy. Or did it? Our next landmark was the Hollenburg Ranch, an old Pony Express Station, reputedly the only one to retain the original log buildings and setting. But here we found it impossible to pinpoint the ranch.

No matter how I tried, I could not match the pattern of roads and an adjacent railway line. In the end we found a ranch that almost matched, including having a couple of old log outhouses, and decided that would have to do until we knew better. Again, on our return, we found we had wrongly identified the building. This appeared to be due to the railway line having been re-routed at some time to run south of the ranch, into the adjacent town of Hanover, instead of, as Greg's map showed, to the north of both.

The error on the railway routing had thrown us almost a mile off track, and it took several more miles to get everything back in accord. That this was successful was shown by our seeing a little triangular concrete plinth appear under our nose, the Tri-County Trail marker, showing the transition from Kansas to Nebraska [Fig. 21]. When my map was right, we could pick out 3 ft-high markers – when it was wrong we could miss a ranch house! Given more time, we might have been able to carry out more successful sleuthing, but all we could do under the circumstances was to follow the map! Nor could we find the site of the next Pony Express Station, though this was hardly surprising, as nothing remained of that one.

For the next hundred miles or so, we would be following the Trail north-west along the wide, shallow valley of the Little Blue River, one-time Pawnee country and the scene of continual fighting between them and their traditional enemies, the Sioux. Over some stretches, the wagons had been forced to detour as much as three miles from the east bank to find suitable fording places over the many creeks running into the river; at others they ran close to the steep banks. Now a mixture of rolling pastoral parkland and cultivated fields, it made for a pleasant flight at our low level.

A few more minutes flying and we were circling over one of the more famous sites shared by the Oregon Trail, the old Stage Line and the Pony Express, namely Rock Creek Station, now a State Park [Fig. 22]. This is perhaps best known as the scene of the shoot-out between Wild Bill Hickok and the so-called McCanles Gang, though present-day understanding shows Hickok in a less favourable light than did the popular legend. Of more interest to us was the sight of the deep and wide swales (soil depressions, usually grassed-over, resulting from long periods of weathering of deep wheel ruts) of the Oregon Trail as they ascended the west bank of Rock Creek, the first that we had seen of those shown on the maps. It being Sunday, there were a few visitors walking the paths and we were rewarded by the sight of the Park's white-topped, ox-drawn wagon ambling round the site.

There was nothing more marked on my map until just beyond the town of Fairbury, where we looked for ruts and the well-known Winslow grave. Unfortunately for us, the Trail route here crossed another airfield. Again this called for a careful lookout for other aircraft (we saw none), and a detour to avoid the field. In mistakenly looking for a railed, rectangular plot we missed seeing the small obelisk marking the hilltop grave site. In fact we saw nothing identifiable of any of twenty or so sites shown on the map along this stretch, mostly those of now unmarked road ranches, stage and Pony Express stations or graves. Most of the former suffered burning, and their occupants violent death, at the hands of the Sioux and Cheyenne during the Indian wars of 1863-4.

That we were on track was confirmed by the number of Oregon Trail and Pony Express markers we came across, the route being very well marked in Nebraska [Fig. 25]. I had seen the circular Trail markers before, and it was easy at our low height to distinguish between the two types, the Pony Express markers being rectangular.

We were soon nearing our next stop, Hebron, scheduled stage length being 146 miles and 2 hrs 26 min elapsed time. The airfield was four miles south of the Trail and we had no difficulty in locating it. By now the sun was beating down from a nearly clear blue sky, the storm clouds of the morning long gone. Hebron Municipal had one long concrete runway and we soon located the windsock. The place had a deserted air with not an aircraft anywhere in sight, and no cars by the cluster of buildings which included some shiny new hangars!

In fact the only sign of activity was a single individual who appeared to be carrying out some kind of war dance at the side of the runway. Thinking he might have been flying a radio-controlled model, I made a low pass along the runway, which he totally ignored. After landing, we passed close to the intersection, still unable to attract his attention. We could now see that the war dance was nothing more exciting than his waving a small rotary mower over the grass at the side of the runway.

We taxied up to the pumps and wearily climbed out into the baking heat and an air of utter emptiness. The heat shimmered up from the expanse of glaring white concrete, even under the wing, which was the only shade to be had anywhere. In the strange quiet after switching off the engine, not a sound was to be heard. We had flown for 2¼ hours, and Brian was having difficulty in standing upright after this latest confinement in the rear seat. Loueen's iced orange juice from Topeka had long since gone, and we had borne the last half hour on the promise of a long cool drink when we landed. Alas, the office was also locked and empty. Returning to the Champ, the grass-cutter looked a long hot walk away, and we thought we would wait a few minutes to see if he would come over.

The nearest airfield in the direction we were going was 54 miles distant and we had insufficient fuel for that. The only possible alternative was Fairbury, now 22 miles behind us, and on the very limit of our range. Hebron was one of the airfields that had returned my questionnaire, and thus should have been expecting us on the 27th July, non-radio; they said nothing about being closed, in fact they had offered to try and obtain some 80-octane fuel for us!

Eventually, the grass-cutter tired of his activities and drove his pick-up towards us and then, to our horror, straight on past, turning out of sight behind the office! We rushed over and found him just locking away the mower and discovered the awful truth that the airfield was closed on Sundays! Airfields don't close on *Sundays*! At home this is the day that most people try and get some flying in!

Nevertheless, he was very helpful and although he was only there in a voluntary capacity, eventually found a key to let us into the shade of the office. The reason he had not noticed us in the circuit or when we landed was that he was wearing ear-protectors. We were most relieved to find a toilet in the building and cooling liquid refreshment, even though it was straight out of a tap. After much searching, the key to the pumps was found and at last, a life-giving brew was gurgling into the tank and another emergency was behind us. With profuse thanks for his help, we quickly got under way.

Despite the heat, the airfield elevation of 1,465 ft and our now full tank, we had no difficulty in climbing out. Passing close by the neat little town of Hebron, nestling peacefully amongst the trees on the Little Blue

River, its white-painted church spire showed up conspicuously. We were soon back over the Trail, feeling somewhat more awake than when we had left it! The route continued a further 45 miles along the picturesque river valley until, just south of Hastings, the river angled away to the south and the Trail continued north-west.

Here it crossed 32-mile Creek, near the site of Elm Creek Stage Station, and started to climb up over the low, arid sand-hills that separate the Platte and Little Blue river valleys. And here, in our continuous quest for ruts, we found our first real sign of the Trail since leaving Rock Creek *[Fig. 23]*. What was more, in circling to photograph the first ruts, we saw, running parallel and some 100 yd to the east of them, a beautiful set of deep ruts, furrowing through a muddy water hole in a dried-up creek bed *[Fig. 24]*. While the main route appeared to run along the crest of a ridge, the secondary tracks diverted to the water hole and rejoined further along. They looked much like those we had seen at Rock Creek, obviously old and deep, and now grassed over.

That was really the last we saw of Trail features that day. Somehow we missed the prominent grave of Susan Hail. Perhaps because we had seen nothing at any of the other grave sites marked on my map, and were near the end of a long, tiring flight, we were not as alert as we needed to be! Maybe also, as with the emigrants as they breasted the last hill, we were all eyes for the broad Platte River.

What we saw would have been a very different sight to that which greeted the earlier travellers. Then the river bed would have been very much wider, often quoted as over a mile in width and "too thick to drink," in some years full of fast-flowing water to a depth of 3 or 4 feet, and in others just a twisted skein of channels through sand banks and islands. Trees grew on some of the islands even then, but the plain and the banks of the river would have been completely clear.

Now, the water level is much lower, due no doubt to upstream irrigation schemes. The river is now little more than a series of widely-separated, narrow channels, weaving among numerous large islands, so thick with trees as to give the impression of a broad strip of woodland. Now, trees grow also in profusion on the banks, there being no herds of buffalo to keep them in check!

Although we had missed the Susan Hail grave, in approaching Lowell we caught site of a concrete marker, shining so brightly in the sun that we simply had to divert the necessary half mile from the Trail route to look at it. It was to the south of the Trail, and on closer examination looked to have a giant, grey stone riding boot on top of it. There was nothing marked on the map at this point, and tantalisingly, we just could not read the wording on the base, even though we made several very low, slow passes. Now we were very near Kearney so maybe my friend there, Ritch Rundstrom, might know of it.

Back on the Trail route, near the site of Valley Stage Station *[Fig. 26]*, I swung well clear of an 1,160 ft-high aerial mast, which towered above us. It was not so much its height that created a menace for us as the near invisible guy lines which radiated out from it for a considerable distance! Approaching Fort Kearny we could see the course of an old branch of the Burlington Northern RR, now ploughed over, showing as a dark streak through the vegetation. It ran east along the south bank of the Platte, from the rail bridge which is still standing, near the site where north side traffic from Council Bluffs forded the river for Fort Kearny *[Fig. 27]*.

Just ahead was the site of the old Fort, now a State Park, beautifully maintained, with a restored adobe blacksmith's shop and defensive palisade. Built to protect the emigrant route and never the scene of any fighting, it served its purpose well from the time it was built in 1848 to its demise in 1871. The Fort site was our last landmark for the day, and after circling it to take photographs, we flew north for Kearney airport.

Although we were expected at Kearney, no one would have known when. We kept our eyes skinned as we flew a wide circuit looking for a windsock, while Brian tried unsuccessfully to raise them on our radio. A passing WW2 B-25 Mitchell bomber seemed not at all out of place; the airport had been built during the war as an operational training base for B-17 Fortress crews, some of the original hangars still being in use.

There was nothing in the circuit, so I picked the nearest stretch of into-wind runway and landed, turning off where the taxyway joined at the threshold. Ahead stretched seemingly miles of glaring white concrete. At least in taxying in, there are the airport buildings to aim at and one is not so likely to get lost in the acres of concrete as when trying to find the runway to take off from! It was 5.40 in the afternoon when we landed, giving a flight time on this leg of 1 hr 30 min against the estimated 1:32, making a total for the day of six hours.

We were greeted by Ritch and introduced to the airport manager, who had arranged hangarage for us overnight. After filling up with fuel and oil and tucking up the Champ for the night, we lingered to photograph a beautiful red Stinson Reliant. This was a resident and was pushed out for a spot of local flying, and meanwhile a passing Waco cabin biplane landed to refuel. Such activity we had not seen since leaving Sky Manor!

Ritch drove us back to his home, and although it seemed later than expected, it was another two hours before the ground crew arrived at half past nine, hot and tired and with much to tell us. Over an excellent dinner of prime Western steak and corn-on-the-cob, washed down with Californian wine, we all caught up with each other's activities and made plans for the morrow. Initially, they had tried to locate Trail features, and successfully visited St. Mary's Mission, the Red Vermillion Vieux bridge, and Alcove Spring. After that, they had to drive as fast as possible to have any hope of getting to Kearney that night, frustrated several times by major diversions and road works.

Somehow, the Rundstroms managed to fit us all in, with much shuffling around of bedrooms by their ever-patient children. It was well into the wee small hours before we settled down, not that any members of our party had any difficulty in getting to sleep that night!

But if we had found it a tiring day, it would have been nothing like the corresponding journey the Whitmans made in 1836. They had left Liberty (opposite Independence) on May 3rd, and I estimated they passed through the Kearney area on May 31st: 29 days to get as far as we had come in one!

They had been late in arriving at Council Bluffs, where they were due to meet up with the fur traders' caravan which they were to accompany to the Rendezvous in the Rockies. The caravan had left without them and they had made desperate attempts to catch up, finally doing so after a week or so of hard driving of their cattle and wagons. In that time, they had made innumerable dangerous river crossings, and had become almost hardened travellers. And still they had worse to come!

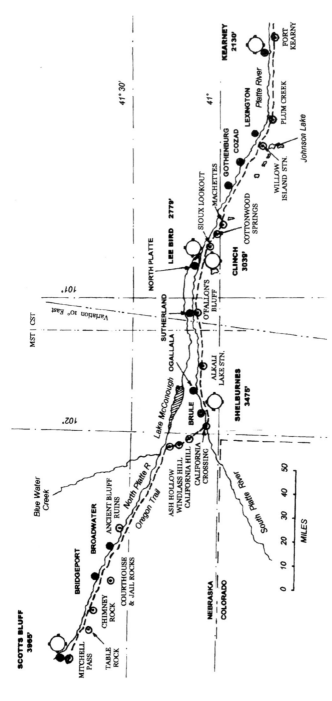

86

CHAPTER 9

DAY 2:
TO SCOTTS BLUFF

Although we managed a fairly early arrival at the airport, it still took an interminable time to get away. Ritch kept a Piper Cub at the field and had arranged to fly out with us beyond Fort Kearny, to see us safely on our way. George was to accompany him and take some air-to-air pictures of us actually flying over the Trail. Ritch had his Cub out on the tarmac, warming up and ready to go, with George in the front seat, while we were still trying to stow everything aboard the Champ!

At Kearney's 2,130 ft altitude, the early morning air was bright and crisp, though a stiff breeze was blowing from the west – the sort of dawning that inspired song-writers to lyrics like "Oh! what a beautiful morning." But the sun was already climbing high when at 08.40 we flew off the airport's great empty expanse of concrete and headed south. Apart from Ritch's Cub we had the sky to ourselves.

We joined the Trail route where we had left it the day before, where State Highway 10 crosses the Platte. Near the bridge is the site of another ranch of which there is no longer any trace. Indelicately known as Dirty Woman Ranch, it was built on the outskirts of the first town in the area, short-lived Central City. The ranch was the only building remaining of the original town, after the nefarious Kearney City (or Dobytown, abbreviated from Adobe Town) later sprang up closer to the western boundary of the Fort. Of neither 'City' is there now any vestige, the modern city of Kearney being located 3 miles to the north on the other side of the river.

We swung west along the south side of the river, heading for a privately-owned airfield, Shelburne's, near Ogallala. The Platte River was paralleled by the Trail route for the next hundred miles to the city of North Platte, which is located at the junction of its North and South branches. Along this stretch, eighteen sites were marked on the map, of which only Fort Kearny, Fort McPherson and Sioux Lookout retained any elements to be seen today in their original settings. Most were sites of road ranches, stage and Pony Express stations, only loosely associated with the Oregon Trail in its later phases. The stage stations were spaced at approximately 10 to 15-mile intervals for the purpose of changing teams and, less frequently, drivers.

The Platte River valley stretched straight ahead into the distance, running due west, flat as the proverbial pancake. It was so wide and flat that it looked more like a plain than a valley, bounded by low sand-hills on each side. The floor of the valley was green and fertile while the hills bore a coating of coarse, arid, sun-scorched hay-grass, probably looking much as they did when the Whitmans came through 150 years earlier.

Winding through the middle of the valley plain were the tangled skeins of the main channels of the river, marked more by the presence of the dark green foliage of trees than by visible water.

Along the north bank of the river ran the famed Union Pacific Railroad, accompanied for much of the time by Interstate 80 (which could not make up its mind as to which bank it preferred). The sand-hills merely presaged the onset to north and south of the rolling plains, which disappeared uniformly into the distance on all sides to a flat, barely defined horizon. But if it sounds boring, it wasn't. There wasn't time to be bored as we sought signs of either the Trail or any of the marked sites.

Seven miles beyond Fort Kearny Park we circled over the site of the first stage station west of the Fort, identified on Greg Franzwa's maps as Platte Station. We saw nothing for our pains, which in view of the uncertainty of the precise location of many of these sites is not surprising. Merrill Mattes, perhaps the prime authority on the Platte River area, in his book "The Great Platte River Road," gives the Platte Station site location as 12 miles from Fort Kearny, and other sites are equally contentious! At this point, Ritch and George waved farewell and swung back to Kearney – George's business was now in getting the ground crew under way again.

And so we continued for the next 20 miles – an easy, pleasant progress along the river at 500 ft altitude, the sun warming up all the time but not yet hot enough to be uncomfortable. The wind was stiffening but not turbulent, navigation was easy with the regular mile-grid of roads and close proximity of the river, and the remote control camera appeared to be behaving itself. Although we searched diligently, we found no ruts over this stretch and no evidence of building foundations at the marked points.

Our first positive location, 35 miles from Fort Kearny, was at Plum Creek, where a small wagon train, trailing the main emigration, was attacked by Indians in August 1864. Their campsite of the night before, on the banks of a small stream some three miles to the east, could be picked out very easily, though the site of the massacre was fairly meaningless, at the edge of what is now a featureless field. The 11 victims are reputedly buried in a small, well-tended cemetery nearby, adjacent to the Trail [Fig. 28]. But if that sounds horrific, it has to be said that many, many more than that number would have died in the same area due to cholera!

From Plum Creek the river course, now confined to fewer and more prominent channels, turned north-west as far as North Platte, with the Trail following it. Upriver, the valley had been gradually narrowing, and the sand-hills at either side almost imperceptibly rising, so that it was looking a little more like a valley than a plain. A string of small towns was located on the north side while beneath us, on the south, the only buildings were of farms and the like, leaving us to follow the main route of the Trail without diversion.

Prominent on our left, on the high plain, was a series of man-made lakes. The largest, Johnson Lake, boasts an electricity power station, though its elevation is only several hundred feet higher than the river. High enough that, when travelling the same region by car, I had seen no sign of the reservoir hidden in the low hills. Of much greater interest was the first sign of anything that looked like the Trail since leaving the Little Blue River – and we nearly missed it!

We had been looking for the Willow Island Pony Express and Stage Station, some five miles west of Lexington (and nowhere near the small community of Willow Island). Fixing its position relative to Johnson Lake and a single gravel road, that headed towards the Platte before it made a 90 deg turn west, I suddenly caught sight of a barely perceptible trace through a field of green corn *[Fig. 29]*. It curved off north-westwards from the right turn below and was so faint that I wondered if I saw it only in my imagination – sometimes when looking hard for something you want to see, wishful thinking takes over! After flying along it for about a mile, I circled for a good look back at it, and the sight was quite breathtaking.

With the early sun behind us the trace had been difficult to see, but as we turned and looked upsun a broad dark line stood out very clearly. It was as if the vegetation grew more sparsely so that shadows cast by the still-low sun showed markedly darker in the undergrowth. We circled a number of times to take a better look – such excitement was still rare enough to want to make the most of it!

Of the Willow Island Station (sometimes referred to as Mullally's) there was now no sign, the original log cabin being moved in 1938 to the City Park in Cozad (where it can be seen to this day).

On past Gothenburg (where we kept a sharp lookout for Batman) we saw our first Trail marker of the day near the site of the Machettes' Trading Post. Now there is no sign of the buildings, but a log cabin was taken from the site in 1931 and re-erected at Gothenburg as a Pony Express building.

Six miles further on we spotted another marker at Cottonwood Springs, one of the more famous of the Pony Express and Stagecoach Stations. Located by the side of Cottonwood Creek, it boasted not only the usual cottonwoods but also cedar trees, which were highly valued for building construction. Circling the area we looked for some evidence of either the stage station or the adjacent Fort McPherson, the latter nestling at the base of the sand-hills. There are farm buildings near the site but nothing else, unlike the nearby Fort McPherson Cemetery. Here there are long rows of white crosses, laid out in military precision. The graves include those of the 30 US Army victims of the Grattan Massacre, which took place in 1854 some 250 miles west near Fort Laramie.

From here on, there was much more to see. Three miles west is Box Elder Canyon (site of another stage station) and four miles beyond that a spot now known as Sioux Lookout. A 16 ft-high statue of a Sioux warrior marks the point known by the pioneers as Point Lookout, the highest hilltop for miles. Some 300 ft above the Platte valley, it afforded a commanding view of the Trail for as far as the eye could discern in each direction. Behind stretch miles of deep gulleys and canyons. Here, any number of warriors could remain out of sight, until summoned by a lookout, to carry out a surprise attack on a ripe target.

Here seemed an ideal location to exercise our ciné-camera, with a focal point of interest and more scenic appeal than anything we had seen earlier. Unfortunately, the weather now took an interest in our activities, throwing a few clouds our way and rustling up noticeable turbulence to go with the increasing strength of the wind. The result was that we spent more time than intended trying to get some good shots of the Point.

This was the first and last time I tried a full sideslip while anyone was filming through the open side window. The idea was to yaw the aircraft sideways to the right, with the left wing lowered so that Brian could shoot at a straighter angle. Unfortunately the wind pressure, built up through the now forward-facing open window, was enough to burst open the makeshift, agricultural catch securing the door on the opposite side, which let go with a bang.

Suddenly all was noise and commotion; there was a battering blast of air as the door flew open, a great fluttering of paper and an agonized shout from behind. Quickly straightening up and looking back, it was to see Brian frantically grabbing at a cloud of whirling loose papers and flapping maps, the camera now forgotten. I reached back to help close the door after Brian hauled in seemingly yards of unfolded, escaping map (the standard US Sectional Aero Chart is five feet long!).

That took a few minutes while Brian smoothed his ruffled feathers and counted the cost. We got away with it very lightly, but somewhere near Sioux Lookout lies Brian's copy of the day's Route Sheet and some loose papers which would cost me many hours study back home in England and some doubt about my conclusions! These were the sheets on which Brian had made notes about where we had taken photographs.

Back on the Trail for another two miles, then a diversion to fly over the famous Forks of the Platte, the confluence of the North and South Platte Rivers. Even from the air, the exact point is difficult to discern as there are so many minor branches and wooded islands to confuse the scene. Here we also had to be watchful as we neared the North Platte, Lee Bird Airport with its 8,000 ft runway. Its Airport Directory entry for 'Airlines' quoted 'Frontier' which conjured up visions of medium-sized jets. We were unable to raise the airport on our radio but everything pointed to its use by commercial airliners so we kept a respectful distance.

North Platte is a sizable city, probably the biggest we had seen since leaving Topeka, located between the two branches of the Platte. The Trail lay on the south side of the South Platte and the next point to look for was the site of the Cold Springs Pony Express Station, immediately south of the city. As I circled the site, looking for traces, Brian called from the back that we could have trouble reaching Shelburne's airfield. With the increasing strength of the wind, and the time we had spent over places such as Sioux Lookout, we were well behind schedule. A quick glance at Brian's figures showed that he was right – if the wind increased any more we would not make it to Ogallala without refuelling.

But where should we land? Neither of us favoured dropping in at a large commercial airport, such as Lee Bird looked to be, without talking to the tower first (that outlook would change later!). Brian favoured somewhere closer than our planned alternate so we picked the nearest whose symbol on the chart showed that fuel was available. This turned out to be Clinch, which boasted a single dirt runway of 2,725 ft length. Despite the airfield height of 3,039 ft and the rising air temperature, it seemed ample for our needs. Besides, Clinch's Airport Directory description also showed a Frontier 'Airlines' entry so, if good enough for them it should be for us (though the visualised medium-sized jets had now shrunk to light feeder twins).

My chart showed the field located to the east of Highway 83, opposite a large reservoir and on top of the sand-hills to the south of the river, and thus easy to find. Mistake number one! We flew south along the highway, scanning the open ground to our left and expecting sizable hangars and buildings to stand out clearly – as they always had up to now. But by the time we reached the southern end of the reservoir and were obviously well south of the field we had to admit we had missed it. Making a large half-circle we flew back paralleling the highway but now a mile east of it. And still we failed to spot an airfield. Thoroughly puzzled by now I started to climb for a better view, when Brian shouted that he had seen an aircraft on the ground.

We circled over the spot, and sure enough there it was – an uncovered skeleton of a machine standing near a small house. Then we spotted another, about 100 yards away in front of a barn. But still no adjacent runway! Finally, the sight of a dull orange windsock, at the end of what looked at first to be a twin-rutted farm track, about a quarter of a mile from the house, convinced us that the track was the runway. Circling low over the house we looked for any sign of life. There was none! But now the fuel gauge was pretty insistent – it was here or Lee Bird.

Making a low inspection run along the 'runway' showed the windsock streaming nearly horizontal and at angle of about 45 deg to it – this could be interesting. If nothing else it would be good practice for what was yet to come. Small weeds were growing between the ruts, with bigger ones at each side, and beyond those, memory tells me there were tall crops like maize, or perhaps weeds on top of low banks. On final approach, crabbing into wind, we appeared to be dropping faster than usual, calling for a long burst of throttle to counter it. Despite the wind we were travelling fairly fast as I kicked the Champ straight for touchdown and it tried its usual trick of darting to the right when landing at too high a ground speed. This time I was ready for it and helped by the wind strength and the dirt surface held it straight, despite a slight downhill slope. At least the latter would be helpful for take-off!

On the ground there was no sign of the buildings until we reached the end of the runway. Then by turning left we could see them at the end of a cart track between two fields. Taxying down the track, we came to a yard in front of the buildings with two red-painted fuel pumps at one side which looked as if they had not worked in years. Never mind, the smarter one of the two was marked '80 octane.' Switching off, we climbed wearily out into what seemed more like some deserted Hollywood movie farmyard set than a live, working airfield! Walking round and shouting produced no sign of life. Whatever possessed Frontier Airlines to operate into here we wondered?

A tour of inspection showed a line of lockup hangars with an Aeronca parked outside. The uncovered airframe we had seen from the air was behind a fence in what would have been the garden of the house, had it been cared for. Surprisingly, the aircraft turned out to be a wrecked Cessna 150 with the aluminium skinning stripped off the wings. On the far side of the house was a door which led into a dusty, untidy room obviously used as an office and, joy of joys, there at last were signs of life.

We came face to face with a tall, thin, stooped character straight out of the Beverley Hillbillies, whose weather-beaten, wrinkled face and silvery grey hair gave more than a hint to his age. We expressed our relief at finding him and asked if he had any fuel to sell us. "Yup" was the only response, and that took a moment or two before it came. No doubt many years of open-cockpit aviating had robbed him of much of his hearing, as conversation was very hard to maintain, but we did find out that he and his brother ran the airfield and that they had been in flying all their lives. What a tale he would have if only he could be persuaded to tell it! But here was the archetype of the laconic, poker-faced Westerner; telling him we were from England and that we were trying to fly over the Oregon Trail produced not a flicker of interest: perhaps he had not heard what we said?

Never mind, there were more pressing matters, like: "Where was the gents, er toilet, er lavatory, oh heck! – the bathroom?"

"If ya want th'john, it's out back."

We all went round to the pumps, which was a very protracted business. I guess that at his age, if I last that long, I will also move that slowly, but right then, we really needed a little more speed.

Leaving Brian to investigate the 'john' situation I helped fill up – the 80-octane pump on further investigation was rusted up. Although the glass over the dial of the other pump was broken, at least it worked, and eventually we had persuaded 10 gallons to enter our tank. I found myself hoping fervently that all ten gallons were pure Avgas, not diluted with water (we need not have feared – they weren't). Leaving our host to go back to the office, I wandered round the corner to see how Brian was getting on, and met him coming back, frustrated. Of the 'john' there was no sign. He had followed instructions up to a point, but when he found himself heading out into a field, came back.

We tried again and found two wooden one-holers, side-by-side, so far away from the buildings that it was no wonder Brian gave up, especially as he had no idea that they were what he was looking for! By the time we got back to the office our friend was sitting at the desk with a little book in front of him. When asked how much we owed him, the final shock was yet to come.

Ten of anything puts a nought on the end of the price for one, or moves the decimal place over by one if it is in cents. But now the reason for the little book became clear; it was a book of tables, and we had to wait a good five minutes while he peered shortsightedly for the right page, the right row and the right column before he could tell us how much! He would brook no interruption from us when we tried to explain how to calculate the total. But we could bear him no grudge, only be grateful that we had come across such a timeless character in such a timeless setting. And no disrespect intended, Mr Clinch!

Fortunately, this was the point at which we switched from CST (Central Summer Time) to MST (Mountain Summer Time), so the hour and a half we spent there looked like one hour less when we reset our watches. The Champ started readily, as usual, and we set out on our cross-country drive to the end of the runway. Sitting there, it seemed a whole lot shorter than when we arrived. What was more, the wind had swung round so that if anything it was more down the runway than up it. After agonizing over it for a moment or two, we decided that downhill was better than uphill, despite the wind change. Fortunately, when we got to the far end and turned, the wind had swung back in our favour.

Take-off was quite laboured, which we put down to the rough dirt and weed surface, but the Champ showed a similar reluctance to climb out at the usual rate; perhaps the heat was getting to it already? Pulling the mixture control fully out seemed to have no marked effect, but it made me feel better, so I left it out and there it stayed until we reached Oregon!

Swinging round to overfly the house we felt most honoured to find that the old man had come out to see us off. We gave him a farewell wave despite the fact that the old rogue had charged us 5 cents more per gallon than the highest we paid anywhere else! But it was a priceless and ageless experience, one that neither of us would have missed! So who had the last laugh?

Back on the Trail route, we found nothing more of note until we reached O'Fallon's Bluff, 18 miles west. At this point, the South Platte ran close to a high sandy ridge, an ideal spot in the early days for an Indian ambush of anyone travelling along the river bank. Here in 1856 the newly-appointed Secretary of Utah, travelling to take up his post in Salt Lake City, was killed, together with his companions, by a party of Cheyenne. To avoid this danger spot, the main Trail routed up over the top of the ridge, and the deep rut swales ascending the gentle slope are there to this day *[Fig. 31]*. It all looks pretty innocuous now, with the Interstate 80 sweeping through where no doubt ran one of the river's many channels. A rest stop at this spot shows visitors where the Trail ran, with sets of wagon-wheel iron tyres placed upright at several points *[Fig. 32]* to lend scale.

It was difficult now to visualize the herds of millions of buffalo which in this area once darkened the plains for miles. They not only provided food and clothing for Indians and travellers alike but added more hazards to the emigrants' lives, with their pollution of the rivers where they watered and their terrifying stampedes. The noise when they were on the run could be heard as continuous thunder from ten miles distant, and nothing could stand in their way – wagons, animals and men would be pounded into the dust.

All along this stretch of the river, ranches were built and destroyed in the warring years of the late 1850s and '60s but little if anything remains to be seen now. Not until we were four miles past the little town of Paxton, itself located at one of the widely used fording points of the river, did we see any further evidence of the Trail. At a point almost a mile south of the main river channel we saw faint ruts by a dirt road, and three miles beyond that, a trace in the vegetation.

The latter was interesting in that we only noticed it because a very dark streak of lush green grass, through a rather arid meadow, showed the winding course of an old water channel. This led to a small lake now collecting drainage from the adjacent highway, possibly at one time that giving its name to the nearby Alkali Lake Pony Express and Stage Station *[Fig. 34]*. Skirting south of the watercourse was a faint trace of slightly darker grass and very shallow ruts, which we would not otherwise have seen. Confirmation that this was a very old track came when we saw that it headed diagonally under the highway and could be seen for a short distance on the other side.

We were now approaching Ogallala, one of the principal cattle-drive centres once the Union Pacific Railroad had thrust this far west. The wind strength was still increasing and our ground speed was down to a little over 50 mph, so we decided we would stop to refuel at Shelburne's as arranged. This was a smooth grass field with a single 3,000 ft runway, well-mown with clean, well-kept buildings, used as a crop-spraying base by the Shelburne family. Rod Shelburne was on hand to greet us, having replied enthusiastically to my questionnaire. He was most interested in what we were up to and was not too upset at finding us in a Champ and not the two old biplanes he had been expecting.

Rod gave us some good advice about local weather conditions, and about hot and high flying. He warned us to be on a constant lookout for storm clouds, which could form up very quickly, rush about at 60 mph, and were definitely not to be tangled with. Two weeks earlier, some cattle in the area had been killed by hailstones! The weather now was very clear and very hot, too hot for him to do any spraying as the droplets dry out too quickly – most of his work at this time of the year was done very early in the cold air of dawn. He filled us up with Mogas, found us something cool to drink and would not hear of taking any payment.

It was a pleasure to taxy out on the smooth, mown surface, with windsocks where we could see them easily. Despite a strong, turbulent crosswind, take-off was no problem and the Champ climbed out reasonably well. Airfield elevation was 3,475 ft and temperature in the nineties; if the Champ continued to behave like this we should have no problems.

Rejoining the Trail, we turned west towards the town of Brule and almost immediately became aware of a pungent smell resembling that of a farmyard dung heap. The source was soon identified as lines of immense cattle enclosures – the cattle drive stockyards perhaps, or feed lots? These were still in use for fattening up cattle before shipping, and though the population in each was well thinned out, there must still have been many thousands of both black and brown & white cattle. The ground looked to be bare earth, of an unusual shade of brown, and the cattle were mostly clustered round feeding and drinking troughs. No grass, no shade from the unrelenting sun – one felt rather sorry for them!

But soon we were passing Brule and eagerly searching for the site of the famous California Crossing of the South Platte [Fig. 35], the main ford for those crossing the South Platte en route for Ash Hollow. As with many of the landmarks along the Trail, there seems some confusion over the name of this crossing, it also being variously identified as the Lower California Crossing (a modern terminology), Old California Crossing, Upper Crossing, Upper Ford, Kearny's Ford, Beauvais' Crossing, Laramie

Crossing and Ash Hollow Crossing! Whatever it was called, the only evidence of it today lies on the north bank, the river bed constantly changing and rechannelling. The best we could do was to relate to adjacent features and say: "It was about here."

Whereas now the river consists of several insignificant main channels and a number of minor streams meandering between broad sandbanks and cottonwood-covered islands, it was not always thus. In emigrant times, the river was many hundreds of yards wide (sometimes referred to as two miles wide!), very fast-flowing and, depending on the snows of the previous winter, either easily fordable or so deep that the wagons had to be floated across. Even when it was fordable, it was a back-breaking task to get a wagon train across, and emigrants' diaries note that it took three-quarters of an hour for a single crossing, and of taking three days to get the whole train across. The banks could be four feet deep and the river bed included treacherous quicksands!

Beyond the crossing, the Trail ascended the steep and long California Hill [Fig. 36] to cross a 12 mile-wide plateau separating the North and South Platte Rivers, before continuing along the left bank of the North Platte. The ruts left by the wagons as they were pushed and pulled up the hill are easily visible still. But once over the uplands, we found it difficult to pinpoint the route. Although my map showed a number of roads, they did not always fit, and the tracks I was following may or may not have been the Trail. Whatever they were, they led us to the top of Windlass Hill, the steep drop that took the wagons down into Ash Hollow. Along the crest of the ridge which terminated in the hill, the Trail stood out clearly, the twin ruts winding across the uneven terrain to give as level a track as possible [Fig. 37]. This was the best preserved section of the Trail we had seen to date.

On the ground, it is not clear why the wagons had been taken down such a steep and difficult hill, when there appeared to be lesser slopes elsewhere. From the air it could be seen that the easier ones led to more difficult gullies further down, though a better route would have been westward round the back of Ash Hollow, as some early travellers discovered. Windlass Hill was not known as such in the Covered Wagon days, though most diaries speak of the dreadful difficulties they had in getting down "the terrifyingly steep hill," or even "the perpendicular hill." Now, there are deeply eroded gullies where the iron-rimmed wheels cut through the turf, the rain having washed away the loose undersoil. To lend scale to the scene, the State Park has provided a shelter in the form of wagon hoops and a white wagon cover – very evocative.

From Windlass Hill we flew over Ash Hollow, the Trail following the east bank of Ash Hollow Creek for three miles, almost to where it runs into the North Platte. This is a pleasant, sylvan glade, aptly named for its beautiful trees (though these were mostly cedars). It runs through a steep-sided gorge of whitish rock outcrops and must have seemed a heavenly refuge after the weeks without respite across the open plains. A small cemetery provided another sort of refuge, the earliest grave being that of 18-year-old Rachel Pattison, who was buried here on June 18th, 1849.

And then it was back to the Platte, the North fork this time, which would accompany us all the way to Casper, 250 miles west. The route we were following was along the south bank, and we were expecting to see ruts where the Trail ran through flat meadow land four or five miles on. They were there all right, crossing a large field where the Trail took a direct route across a wide curve of the river, now a mile away. On the opposite side of the river, Blue Water Creek wound up into the sand-hills, from this distance showing no sign of the infamous Battle of Blue Water in 1855 between the US Army and the Brule and Oglala Sioux Indians, some six miles along the creek. Here, some 500 soldiers and 250 Indians were involved.

There were more ruts, including some unmarked ones, along the stretch of river near the small town of Oshkosh. Ironic that we should be so close to the latter. One of the highlights originally planned for our return flight had been a visit to Oshkosh, where the EAA Annual Fly-In is the Mecca of all light aviation enthusiasts. But that Oshkosh was 750 miles to the north-east, up in Wisconsin, and we would have needed to fly in there the previous day!

Beyond Ash Hollow, the scene had been gradually changing. Now the sand-hills were occasionally replaced by craggy rock formations, the shapes of which sometimes reminded those emigrants who had journeyed from Britain of the ruined castles of their homeland. One such landmark to the north of the river was named Ancient Bluff Ruins, and with a vivid imagination one could see why. Near here is a marker, dedicated to Narcissa Whitman, whose party travelled along the north bank in June 1836. We continued over the south bank, and found more unmarked ruts some five miles west.

Now to the south-west could be seen a distant line of hills, still no more than 1,000 ft higher than the river valley, but they were closing in. Suddenly I realised that the rocky crags that were protruding from the rolling plain some ten miles ahead could only be the famous Courthouse and Jail Rocks! It was not difficult to understand the excitement felt by the emigrants as they spied these mighty rocks for the first time – just a little of it rubbed off in the cabin of the Champ! When we first saw them, the smaller Jail Rock was lost in the massive bulk of Courthouse, but as we came abreast of them, the angle changed and Jail could be seen as a separate stack to the east.

We followed the Trail as far as Bridgeport then, emulating the early travellers, detoured south four miles to gaze in awe at the Rocks at close quarters *[Fig. 38]*. The emigrants had climbed and carved their names in the buff-coloured, soft Brule clay base or sandstone layers; we just circled and filmed them. When here in 1985 I too had climbed to the top, but could find no sign of old name carvings (there are a few remaining, but these are near the base of the south face).

The heat was now getting to us and Brian had difficulty in holding the ciné-camera steady in the turbulent conditions, the strong wind adding to the air disturbance by curling over the crags as we swept round. They stood in glorious isolation, towering perhaps 300 ft above the surrounding grassland. Courthouse is elongated, and stepped like the famous Pyramid at Sakkara. On the long, north side, the rock faces had crumbled at the centre into steep, grass-covered slopes, but elsewhere they were near vertical, the creamy-coloured sandstone gleaming in the sun.

An added attraction on Jail Rock was an enormous eagle's eyrie, inaccessibly high on the vertical north face; we kept a wary eye open for the big birds as they have been known to attack small aircraft! At least this time we would not have to worry about rattlesnakes. No, I didn't believe it either when there on foot, but I covered the fastest hundred yards of my life after stepping on a 3 ft-long brown-green snake, without stopping to ask whether it was rattled or not!

What made these Rocks so notable was not just their sheer size or even their shape so much as their being the first that the emigrants had encountered in some 500 miles of travel from Independence, and that they stand in glorious isolation. They are in fact the detached, eastern extremity of the Wildcat Hills, a string of cliffs that extend 30 miles west to Gering Valley and Scotts Bluff, marking the edge of a higher tableland.

From above Courthouse Rock could be seen Chimney Rock, perhaps the most noted landmark on the Oregon Trail, just 14 miles west. We were more fortunate than the emigrants, who would typically first spot it in that crystal-clear atmosphere some 25-30 miles away, and then have one or two full day's drives to reach it. Little wonder that excitement ran high in the columns! Resisting the temptation to fly straight to it we rejoined the Trail route near Bridgeport, and were rewarded by sighting more unmarked ruts near an old spring site (Facus Springs).

But soon we were diverting a mile and half south to Chimney Rock *[Fig. 39]*. This stands alone on the rolling plain like an enormous inverted funnel, the northernmost extremity of a long ridge extending several miles from the Wildcat Hills. As with all of the rocky features in the area it consists of a soft Brule clay base with successive layers of sandstone, clay and volcanic ash. The top of the spire is quoted as being 325 ft above the surrounding grassland and is now 15-20 ft shorter than it was 150 years ago, erosion and man taking their toll (it is rumoured that soldiers with a cannon used it for target practice and succeeded in knocking off some of that footage).

Though perhaps not as impressive as many of the taller and more slender pinnacles, such as those in Monument Valley, it is more attractive, with a greater variety of colours. The base is corrugated with ridges and gulleys, and the underlying buff alternates with dark shadows and light grey overlays, dotted with green bushes and patches of lesser vegetation. Flying round and over, this effect is heightened by the variation in sunlight, from bright light to deep shadow. We lingered long in the vicinity, though not as low as I would have liked, the heat now having a deleterious effect on the Champ's ability to climb and manoeuvre at low level. Nevertheless, this viewing more than made up for the bitter disappointment felt a year earlier, when I saw it only from the overlook maintained by the Nebraska State Historical Society on the ½ mile-distant road. Time did not then permit me to explore on foot to the base of the Rock.

Seven miles beyond Chimney Rock was a whole series of named rocks of differing shapes – the massive Castle Rock, flat-topped Table Rock, the castellated Steamboat Rock, Coyote Rock and Roundtop. But most impressive of all was the huge bulk of Scotts Bluff, looming 12 miles beyond, extending north from the Wildcat Hills to the very edge of the North Platte, almost blocking the way west.

We decided to call it a day, leaving aerial exploration of Scotts Bluff to the following day, when we would feel fresh and the morning air would be cool and less turbulent. Having the sun in the east would also make for better light for filming the approach to Mitchell Pass. By now we had been flying on and off for almost six hours in quite trying conditions, so at 15.45 we joined the circuit (or 'pattern') at Scottsbluff County Airport.

Brian tried unsuccessfully to raise the airport Tower on the radio, but we knew they were expecting us, and there was no question in this wind which runway to land on. Again, as at Clinch, the Champ dropped faster than expected on the approach, confirming that we were running into a Density Altitude problem. Airport elevation here is just under 4,000 ft and temperature was still in the nineties – it was beginning to bite! What with the strong wind and the loss of height, a fair amount of power had to be kept on nearly all the way in. Even then, in holding off to save too fast a touchdown, the Champ dropped hard onto the runway and threatened to dart off to one side. At least this time, although we used up the full 150 ft width of the 8,000 ft runway, we stayed on it; things were looking up!

Once down, with the engine ticking over as we taxied in, Brian was able to make contact on the radio, and we got our taxying and parking instructions. We tied the aircraft down in the lee of the airport buildings, and the wind was strong enough for us to be thankful that the tie-downs were chains and not the usual nylon ropes. As usual, at such a large airport, refuelling arrangements were very slick, and while Brian hauled much of the gear into the reception lounge, I attended to fuel and oil top-ups.

All was cool and quiet in the lounge. We booked in, paid the $3 tie-down charge and fuel bills and found out about local motels. After reserving three rooms at the least expensive of the motels which provided courtesy car service, all we had to do was relax and wait. Which was when we met the by-now almost inevitable reporter, as polite, informed and interested as had been all the others up to now. Brian put this period to good use and promptly fell asleep!

It was a long drive from the airport to the motel, but our young driver kept us amused with his experiences in learning to fly, and we learned that he volunteered to provide the airport pick-up service off his own bat. Enterprising, as we would not otherwise have been staying at the Parks Motel. After dumping our gear in our rooms we went exploring for a restaurant. Fortunately there was one just a block away, and we decided to have a meal there and then rather than wait for the ground crew to arrive. By now even Brian was beginning to get used to the idea of eating a hearty breakfast in the morning and having nothing more than Granny's Country Cookies until we could get a dinner in the evening.

Our ground crew arrived just after Brian and I finished, at around 7.00 pm. Despite a long day of driving, they had found time to have a look at the tourist attractions in Ogallala, climb Windlass Hill and visit Ash Hollow Museum. They also went to the tiny Ash Hollow Cemetery for silent homage at the Rachel Pattison grave.

Over their meal we discussed the next day's program and mutually decided that George and Brian should swap places. George weighed 20 precious pounds less than Brian – the equivalent of three gallons of fuel! That could be an essential saving at tomorrow's higher elevations if the temperatures then were the same as today's. We were due to fly over South Pass (elevation 7,550 ft) and refuel at a remote spot in the desert, the small Webster airstrip (elevation 6,594 ft). Brian welcomed the opportunity to give his aching back a change of posture in the more comfortable car seats, and George was keen to get airborne again.

What of the Whitmans? They would probably have been overnighting on the north bank of the river, above Scotts Bluff, on June 11th. They made Fort Laramie on June 13th, averaging 22 miles per day from the Forks of the Platte. Near the latter, on June 3rd, they had encountered their first buffalo, even then, in 1836, driven far west of the areas in which they were originally found by the first white explorers. The party was still enjoying good health, though Eliza Spalding was finding difficulty in keeping down the greasy buffalo meat, which formed their staple diet from then until they reached the Rockies.

Fig. 29. Looking NW towards Willow Island Station on the south bank of the Platte River, nearly opposite Lexington. Nothing much notable until we looked back, up-sun, to see a very distinct trace.

Fig. 30. This shows the trace seen up-sun, where the sun's bright morning light threw dark shadows more visible through the thinly-spaced vegetation growing in the path of the old, now-cultivated, way. This is right where the Oregon Trail is charted (or is it the course of the old Burlington Railroad, though the curve looked a little too sharp for that?). In Fig. 29 the trace is paralleled by a white line added to the right of the trace.

Fig. 31. O'Fallon's Bluff, near Sutherland, Nebraska. A rest stop on the I-80 is located adjacent to a wonderful set of rut swales (here marked by an adjacent dotted line), with a concrete path and viewing area. They have even set in the ruts a number of wagon wheel iron rims (marked by arrows).

Fig. 32. Seen from the ground, the wheel rims lend a ghostly scale to the scene, and add a magic air of authenticity. Perhaps nowhere prior to this point can the isolation and vastness seen by the pioneers be more readily visualized by modern travellers.

Fig. 33. Typical of occasional trace sightings in agricultural areas in Nebraska is this one, extending NW from a waterhole. No ruts were marked on the maps at this point but the trace lay exactly where the Trail route was given.

Fig. 34. A trace clearly seen from the air, where the Trail was crossed by I-80 just past the site of the Alkali Lake Stage Station, near Roscoe. There was nothing at all to be seen from the ground!

Fig. 35. Lower California Crossing of the South Platte River, in August reduced to several minor skeins and streams, trickling through the silver sandy bed. The south bank is at the top, whilst at lower right is a small, tree-covered island.

Fig. 36. Having forded the river, the wagon trains were faced with a long, steep slog up California Hill, seen here looking west-north-west. Highway 30 runs across the middle foreground and the Trail would have ascended from centre right.

Fig. 37. Approaching Windlass Hill, looking north-west. The dotted line parallels the Trail route, marked with some fine ruts to the very top of Windlass Hill indicated by the LH arrow. The right arrow points to a white speck which is a canvas wagon cover erected over an information board at the foot of the hill.

Fig. 38. Courthouse (centre) and Jail (right) Rocks, located some four miles SE of the Trail, here seen looking to the west. Pumpkin Creek is in the lower left corner.

Fig. 39. Chimney Rock, perhaps the most famous landmark on the Oregon Trail, and one eagerly looked for by both past and present users. Awe-inspiring no matter from where it is seen. In this case looking north, with Highway 92 just visible top right.

Fig. 40. Looking NW through Mitchell Pass, along Highway 92. The building complex in the foreground is the very fine Oregon Trail Museum. The footpath between it and the road follows the course of the Trail.

Fig. 41. Looking NW over North Bluff at Scotts Bluff, towering 700 feet above the road. At lower left and at left centre is a footpath following the route of the Oregon Trail, ending at Jackson Campsite. At top right is a tunnel carrying the road to the carpark at the top.

Fig. 42. This shot looking NNE, to the west of North Bluff, shows the tortuous, deep ravines which made the Mitchell Pass more difficult than the longer Robidoux Pass. The North Platte River is across the top and the Bluff west face at upper right. The Trail route is not easy to pick out but there are prominent ruts just below left centre.

Fig. 43. Robidoux Pass, looking west. The site of Robidoux's first trading post is near the trees at top left. Water from an adjacent spring has furrowed a deep ravine right across the valley floor that effectively blocked the passage of the wagons along the flat ground, forcing them up the slope to above the spring. The rutted Trail route can be seen as a dark line running from the trees to rejoin the road to the top of the Pass at the right.

Fig. 44. The top of Robidoux Pass, looking north-west, where the Trail continues roughly in that direction, and the modern road hairpins round to the south. Note the steep ravine on the right.

Fig. 45. A fine set of rut swales going NW up from the Henry Hill Grave site, from lower right to top left. The North Platte River bank is just visible in the upper right corner. This is located SW of the town of Henry WY, and some five miles SE of Torrington.

Fig. 46. Fort Laramie, built in 1849 to replace Fort John, nestling in the bend of the Laramie River, looking NW, with the North Platte at top right. The adobe Fort John, which replaced Fort William in 1841, was at the left (south) side of the rectangular parade ground, but the exact location of the wooden Fort William (1834) is not known.

Fig. 47. Register Cliff at Guernsey, a great, near-vertical cliff of white sandstone, where the wagons were funnelled between its foot and the south bank of the North Platte (marked by the trees in the lower right corner). The white arrow points to the approximate location of the names seen below.

Fig. 48. Typical of the names carved on rocks throughout the length of the Trail route, but nowhere perhaps more accessible.

Fig. 49. Guernsey Ruts, just west from Register Cliff. Here there was no passage between the sandstone outcrops and a loop of the river: the wagons had to be taken over the top. The arrow points to Deep Rut Hill (see Fig. 50).

Fig. 50. A round figure of 100,000 wagons left a poignant and awesome reminder of their passage! Imagine the sights and sounds at the height of the emigration, if you can!

Fig. 51. Casper WY looking SE. Fort Caspar site and the location of the Platte Bridge are marked in white.

Fig. 52. Emigrant Gap, marked by parallel white lines just left of and above centre. Poison Spider Road is marked by an adjacent dotted line. Viewed looking south-west. The Oregon Trail roughly followed the road from lower left, continuing to upper centre.

CHAPTER 10
DAY 3:
TO CASPER

As with most previous days, our plans for an early morning start were thwarted by the tiredness from which we were all now suffering. Consequently, we were not finished packing until nearly seven and it needed two hours to get breakfast, drive out to the airport and have the aircraft readied for the day. As George would be flying for the first time over the Trail, there was much for him to acquaint himself with, in the way of stowing equipment and arranging everything to hand. Additionally, he had the recalcitrant radio to handle, and George disliked microphones and headphones as much as I.

Because on the previous day we had been able to talk to the Tower while taxying, we did not telephone them from Reception. Instead, we got ourselves installed and the engine started, whilst George, with Brian's instructions ringing in his ears, tried to establish communication. Meanwhile I turned the aircraft ready to taxy out. But the radio obstinately refused to co-operate, and remained silent. George cajoled, pleaded and finally swore at it, told the Tower what we were doing and then gave up. We set off on the mile-long trek to the far end of the runway, watching to see if the tower flashed a red at us while George sorted out his navigation – maps, route sheet, compass deviation, variation and wind factors in case I suddenly needed to know what heading to fly, etc.

After we had gone some distance, I looked back to check how far we had come, and was intrigued to see a police patrol car driving towards us from the distant airport buildings, red and blue lights flashing. As we neared the end of the runway in use, I noticed that the car was now right behind us, though not making any threatening moves. Puzzled, I stopped in case it was us he wanted to talk to. It was. It seemed that George's transmission had not been picked up by the tower, and they sent the local policeman to ask our intentions. He was able to talk to them on his walkie-talkie and convey our genuine apologies for causing them so much concern. We parted company on friendly terms, he wishing us good luck!

As promised we got a green for taxying, but nothing from then on. After several minutes at the holding point, we taxied out onto the runway having established that there was nothing on the approach. Still no green, but no red either! In the end we went, and got off at 9.02 MST into a freshening wind under a clear blue sky.

Heading south-west, we made straight for that great gash in the bluffs, Mitchell Pass *[Fig. 40]*. The ensuing 15 minutes were magic, as we circled round and round, and up and over the great crags of Scotts Bluff

101

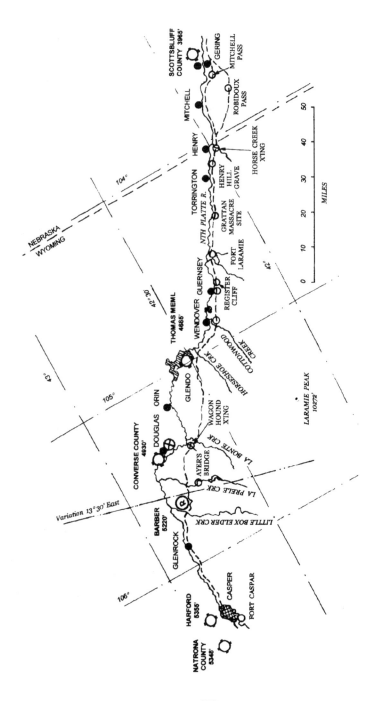

and the nearby Dome Rock; flying over the hard-won road, built under Roosevelt's WPA (Works Progress Administration) land-work scheme of the Depression years, as it snaked up from the eastern side of the cliff and through three rock tunnels *[Fig. 41]* to the car parks on the very summit; diving down beneath the 700 ft peak of the North Bluff to fly through the pass; following the tracks of the Oregon Trail as they zigzagged through and over gullies and dry stream beds; roughly paralleling the smooth, flat highway, at first close to it and then 300-400 yards distant; winging round the west side to the north *[Fig. 42]*, observing the disruptive pattern of ridges and ravines which make up the 'badlands' between the base of the bluffs and the river. It was the latter's impassability that sent early travellers on a five-mile detour to the south through Robidoux Pass.

We could willingly have played tag with the trails and the tops for much longer, but had to tear ourselves away to get on with our self-appointed task. Back then to where we had turned away from the Trail the day before, to follow it through and beyond Robidoux Pass. Initially, over the cultivated ground south of Gering (on the south bank of the river, opposite the city of Scottsbluff), there was no sign of the Trail. But as we approached the foot of the Wildcat Hills and crossed the grassy plain beyond Carter Canyon, there were well-defined ruts, on and off, for three miles.

When I had visited the site on foot the year before, I had stood high on the hillside above the plain, and wondered why the route had made a great dog-leg to the south. Flying in from the east, the ruts could be seen to skirt what might have been boggy ground, and then angle back towards a spring site at the foot of the hills. They could not proceed due west because a gully, some 15 feet deep, crossed the plain at right angles to their path. We thought we could see clear ruts on a shorter course than that shown on the maps, but there looked to be many poorly-defined tracks all going in the same general direction.

This area is steeped in history of the early days of the explorers, fur traders and pioneers, with two successive trading posts operated by Joseph Robidoux and two by the American Fur Co (the second known as Fort John after their earlier post of that name was sold to the US Army and renamed Fort Laramie). No doubt the emigrants made many minor variations of routes over the years, depending on which of the posts they were visiting.

All the tracks converged on the spring site, at the only point at which the transverse gulch could be crossed, and from there, one well-defined trail led to the Pass *[Fig. 43]*. It crossed the modern gravel road just below the summit, no higher up than it need be to follow another east-west ravine *[Fig. 44]*, down the slope and out onto the plain, finally clear of the Wildcat Hills.

From there we were over featureless, open ground, with the Trail following the course of the dried-up Owl Creek for 12 miles to Horse Creek. Here, in 1851, 10,000 Indians of 12 nations, including Arapaho, Cheyenne, Crow, Shoshone and Sioux, met and agreed the Great Fort Laramie Treaty, which for a few short years brought peace to the area. Of this, of course, we saw no remaining sign, but four miles further along, as we crossed the border from Nebraska into Wyoming, we could see several tracks ascending a long, low hill *[Fig. 45]* opposite the small community of Henry. We kept a lookout for five emigrant graves, all invisible to us on this trip. Not so in earlier times; indeed in 1850 one reporter counted 500 graves along the North Platte before reaching Fort Laramie, mostly victims of cholera.

Ahead was a picturesque stretch of the river, a broad main channel replacing the earlier untidy skein of streams, with the normally sandy brown water reflecting the cobalt blue of the sky. It meandered through a shallow, wooded, fertile valley, with contrasting whitish sandbanks, dark green trees and lush green grass. Soon we were looking for the monument commemorating the Grattan Massacre, on the plain above the bluffs overlooking the river.

This was where, in 1853, an emigrant's lost cow started a far-reaching chain of events. First it cost the lives of a respected Indian Chief as well as the young and inexperienced 2nd.Lieutenant Grattan, his interpreter and 29 soldiers; it culminated in the breaking of the Fort Laramie Treaty and renewed fighting and destruction that continued intermittently for the next twenty years. The cow wandered into a camp of hungry Indians where it was killed and eaten, and Grattan was sent to reclaim it. When he failed to do that, he opened fire with a cannon and the soldiers loosed off their muzzle-loaders; before they could reload, all were killed by the Indians. By such mistakes is history made!

Fort Laramie *[Fig. 46]*, perhaps the best-known of all the forts along the Oregon Trail, lay nine miles to the north-west. It is located on the north bank of the Laramie River, a mile upstream from Laramie's Fork, where that river empties into the North Platte. The winding course of the Laramie, coiling westwards across the tawny plain, was marked in dark green by the trees which grew thickly on each bank. Now a National Monument, the Fort was conspicuous amongst the surrounding, hay-brown sand-hills by its grass green parade ground, encircling gravel road and the white-painted, two-storey timber building known as Old Bedlam. The latter is the beautifully restored Officers' Quarters which stands in a row of restored buildings of wooden, adobe or stone construction. But anything less like a fort is difficult to imagine.

Always popularly known as Fort Laramie, the earliest fort on the site was literally christened (in champagne) Fort William, when it was built in 1834 by William Sublette. This was a stockaded, defendable trading post for the fur traders, which changed owners several times over the years. Unfortunately, the cottonwood logs from which it was built quickly rotted, and by 1841 a new trading post was built nearby, and named Fort John. This was an adobe-walled fort but was little longer-lasting than its predecessor. Bought by the Government in 1849, the fort was in such a bad shape that, again, new buildings were started, the military establishment being known as Fort Laramie. Old Fort John had crumbled away entirely by the early sixties and Fort Laramie was abandoned as a military post in 1890.

No mention of this area would be complete without reference to the Deadwood Stage, which in 1876-87 ran between Cheyenne and Deadwood in the Black Hills of Dakota (not to be confused with the Black Hills which lay ahead, in Wyoming). The Concord coaches crossed the Platte on an iron bridge built by the Army in 1867 (closed now but still there) and stopped at the Fort before crossing the Laramie on their way south. The old road to Cheyenne can still be seen running roughly parallel with the Laramie River.

For the emigrants, Fort Laramie marked the end of the Plains; from here on they would never lack sight of mountainous country either distant or too close for comfort. For us it meant the end of the old familiar mile-square grid pattern of roads which, through Kansas and Nebraska, had made navigation so simple. No longer would we be able to rely on the roads pointing north and west, and if we lost the Trail or muddled important navigation features, we would have to rely on that rather imprecise compass.

We circled several times over the old fort before rejoining the Platte. Next point of note was to be Mexican Hill above the south bank of a great loop in the river, and ruts approaching it. Here the wagons descended to river level from the low, rolling plateau separating the Laramie and Platte river valleys. We saw a trace through the vegetation there and spotted ruts a mile and a half beyond, leading us straight to Register Cliff.

Where the river valleys and creeks cut through the undulations of the tablelands, outcrops of soft whitish limestone are often visible. We had seen these along the North Platte from below Fort Laramie, where occasional steep bluffs above the valley and the looping course of the river had forced the trailblazers to stay on the plain. But they were able to descend to the river at Mexican Hill and travel alongside it as far as the modern town of Guernsey, passing a 50 ft-high vertical cliff on the way. As we flew past the latter *[Fig. 47]* I, like earlier travellers reminded of scenes from their homeland, likened it (on a miniature scale) to perhaps the most famous landmark of England, the white cliffs of Dover.

Here they camped and had time to etch their names *[Fig. 48]* – a register of who had got this far for those yet to come. Rut swales across a narrow stretch of meadow land in front of the short straight cliff testify to aerial visitors as to their passage, but not so poignantly as the names they carved in the rock face do for those on the ground. At least from the air we gained a good overview of the overall route of the Trail and the shape of Register Cliff.

Beyond the cliff, the Trail route could be seen ascending another shallow slope before winding across a rock-scarred ridge *[Fig. 49]*. There was no easy way round it for those who had passed in front of Register Cliff, the ridge ending abruptly at the very edge of a branch of the river. The main channel swept in a great loop well away from the ridge, but from the air it was evident that the land within the loop was cut off by the branch to form an island, which would have called for two river crossings to get round the ridge.

Great grooved channels, in places an incredible three feet deep, were worn in the rock by the iron-rimmed wheels and axle-trees of nearly a hundred thousand wagons, and the iron-shod hooves of the oxen that pulled them *[Fig. 50]*. One after another, like lemmings, each followed in the tracks of the one before. In this, the narrowest bottleneck of any along the Oregon Trail, is irrefutable evidence of their passage which must rank, in terms of human toil, with any wonders of the ancient world.

From Guernsey, the Trail pulled a mile or two away from the river and up into the hills for the first time since leaving Independence. To the north lies the bulk of Haystack Ridge, elevation 5,656 ft, but only 1,250 ft above Guernsey. But 18 miles to the west, from the Black Hills (named for the trees which mantled their slopes) looms the grey outline of Laramie Peak, at 10,272 ft looking every inch a real mountain. Popular belief amongst the emigrants was that this peak, visible in clear weather from Scotts Bluff, was in the Rockies, but they had many weary miles to go before those majestic snow-capped mountains would brighten their horizon.

The Trail route formed the basis of a gravel road for much of the way to and just beyond Old Bitter Cottonwood Pony Express Station on Cottonwood Creek. At this point the road bumped over a level crossing of the Colorado & Southern RR just south-west of the tiny, isolated community of Wendover. Two great lines of stationary wagons and trucks marked the location of the railroad long before we could have seen the tracks. From here, the Trail crossed open, hilly country and could be followed at times only by the tracks that mark it. On the right lay a reservoir in Guernsey State Park and ahead a much larger one at Glendo, both from damming the North Platte.

There were some fine unmarked ruts to be seen approaching Cassa and again just past Red (Twin) Springs though we saw no sign of the springs. That there were so many miles of ruts on this cross-country section was perhaps a measure of how little cultivation was carried out in the area, and how difficult was access to it. At several points where the route was indistinct, we had to circle while we tried to locate the next set of ruts to follow.

Suddenly, we woke to the fact that all this circling over the Fort, Register Cliff, Guernsey Ruts and now this part of the Trail had taken its toll of time, which meant fuel. It was obvious that in spending nearly 2½ hours to cover less than 90 miles we would get no further than our first alternate, Converse County Airport at Douglas, and in the wind conditions now prevailing, would be hard-pressed to do even that!

I had not really wanted to divert to Douglas unless absolutely necessary, as it lay six miles off our route. So when George, having thumbed through our Airport Directory, announced that the Thomas Memorial airfield at Glendo, just a few miles ahead, supplied 80-octane fuel, it needed no persuasion to land there instead. It boasted a 4,000 ft dirt runway which seemed ample for the airfield height of 4,665 ft, the only problem being that the runway was at roughly 60 degrees to the now obviously strong wind that was blowing from the south-west. Ominously, the directory entry made no mention of hours open.

At Horseshoe Creek, the Trail recrossed the US Highway 26, near the site of the Lower Horseshoe Stage Station, but we turned right to follow the road to Glendo. The intention was to rejoin the main Trail at this point after refuelling.

From the chart, it appeared as if the airfield was almost wholly situated in the reservoir. Fortunately this turned out not to be the case. Even more fortunately, there was a second, very short but rougher runway (at 700-800 ft length, perhaps considered not worth showing either in the Jeppesen or AOPA airport directories), dead in line with the windsock. This was discovered in the course of making a low, crabbing, inspection run up the main runway.

So I turned out over the water and made a low, flat approach. It was not actually intended to be particularly low, but what with the wind strength and the combination of hot and high, it needed full throttle to maintain height and make any progress towards the shore – this was no place to touch down short of the field! The short runway was even rougher on close acquaintance than it looked from the air, but the Champ took it all in its stride, to the relief of both George and I.

It needed almost full power to keep the Champ moving over the rough grass, and it felt more like autocross than taxying as we headed towards a line of small lock-up hangars. After 2½ hours flying we were both a little stiff so, on finding no one around, were not too upset at the prospect of going in search of someone who would refuel us. After all, something similar had happened on at least two occasions in the past.

After 30 minutes trotting up and down, visiting the several trailer homes on the airfield and finding no sign of life other than waking up some pretty vicious-sounding dogs, the only contact we had made with the human species was that of a young teenager. He was carrying out target practice, with a fearsome, modern hunting bow, at a house a quarter of a mile down the road. He was unable to suggest any course of activity other than to walk up to the mile-distant Glendo where we just might find some one who could help.

It was now past midday and getting very hot, and the thought of a two-mile, half-hour hike with the possibility of nothing at the end of it overcame my previous objections to landing at Douglas. Apart from that, I wasn't too sure now that I would like taking off in the considerable crosswind with the extra weight of fuel on board. It was obvious that it would be no use attempting to take off from the into-wind runway, especially as it pointed straight at the side of a steep hill. The long one didn't look much more promising, heading as it did up a shallow slope, but at least, in turning into wind after becoming airborne, we would not have to go out over the lake!

The biggest problem of course was whether we had enough fuel left to reach Douglas safely and legally. Allowing five minutes circuit time for take-off and landing, and another 25 minutes to cover 25 miles at a ground speed of 60 mph: total 30 minutes. Time already flown, 2 hours 30 minutes. Total time on landing, three hours. Theoretical maximum endurance was also three hours, which we had never proved, our longest flight time being 30 minutes less. The saving grace was that our fuel consumption figures to date had been 3½ gal per hour compared with the theoretical figure of 4 gal per hour. That would give an endurance of 3 hours 20 minutes. "Let's go!"

Starting our run from beyond the end of the runway, we got off reasonably well, but climb rate tended to be not much greater than that of the rising ground. The Champ was probably no higher than 30 ft as we turned over the end of the field and headed into wind. Initially I had ideas of following the Trail route, as it would have been little longer than the shortest bee-line. Unfortunately there was a hill between us and it that the Champ showed no inclination to fly over. By now I had learned that, in these conditions and in this aeroplane, if there was a hill in the way it was sometimes better to shrug one's shoulders and go round rather than try to go over it. Emigrant diaries indicated they did the same!

Thus, we unintentionally followed US Highway 26 and one of the alternate trail routes (quoted by Irene Paden as the original route of the Trail) as far as the small town of Orin. Here we crossed the North Platte and another alternate, the Chiles' Road, where it swung in from the east. We had been climbing steadily if unspectacularly ever since take-off, and were now about 500 ft higher. Unfortunately, the ground was also climbing so we were still only about 250 ft above it.

And so we progressed, still following the US 26. To our right stretched the great rolling expanse of the Thunder Basin Grassland and to the left, the Black Hills in the Medicine Bow National Forest. When we passed an aerial mast marking the highest point between Glendo and Douglas, we had gained nearly 1,000 ft, but the ground was still only 250 ft below. Over the brow of the hill, I heaved a sigh of relief. It was all downhill now to the 4 miles-distant town of Douglas, and we should arrive with height in hand over the 4,876 ft altitude of the airfield.

Now I was very concerned about the fuel state. The fuel gauge had long since stopped registering, but then it was never a very reliable instrument at the lower end of the scale. What was of greater concern was that all of this leg had been flown at full throttle, and we could have been using fuel at a much higher rate than allowed for in my calculations. There could be no hanging about round the airfield; we would have to go straight in.

As we overflew the field and searched unsuccessfully for a windsock, I saw something else – the very last thing we could have expected. At first I simply could not believe that at each end of the most beautiful asphalt runway I had ever seen was a very prominent, white X. Runway out of use: dangerous to land: GO AWAY! Well, with an unknown amount of fuel left and no sign of the secondary dirt runway, it could be even more dangerous not to land there. Without further ado I circled to make a low pass along the runway to see what catastrophic dangers it had in store for us. This seemed a good occasion on which to play it by the book!

Apart from heavy cables hung some 12 ft high across the approach end of the runway, with a cluster of strange-looking huts and enclosures close in at each side, there was nothing that should cause us any problems – the surface looked perfect. Of course, what I forgot in the excitement, was that in making a low, slow pass, I should lose all my hard-won height and speed which, at this altitude and temperature, would be difficult to regain. That was not in the book!

Beyond the end of the runway, the hill that we had just flown over loomed menacingly. At barely 50 ft we staggered round the circuit, trying to pick up both speed and altitude and gaining very little of either. Once again, it was a question of dodging round anything that looked high, like overhead cables or rising ground, and keeping well clear of any buildings – that would not be a good way to drop in unannounced! Fortunately there was a fairly clear path and very soon the ground was dropping again to the river. As we lined up with the runway after the tightest possible turn in, the reason for the buildings and cables suddenly became clear: the airfield had been converted to a drag strip!

Chopping the power as we crossed the boundary fence, we crabbed in against a vicious crosswind, under the cables strung across the runway, and settled in to a tail-high touchdown between the enclosures, the black tyre burns on the asphalt streaking away before us. We had stopped before we reached the first intersection and I swung off there in case anyone else was tempted to do the same thing. Switching off, we sat there for a moment or two, hardly able to believe that we were down safely.

The first thing to establish was how much fuel was left. At last, there was a reason for using that broken stick that I had been so tempted to throw away at Sky Manor. Sure enough, it was just long enough to reach the bottom of the tank from below the filler, and miraculously, it showed there was still over a gallon left. Not bad; three hours flying on less than eleven gallons!

At that point, a pick-up truck drew up alongside and a white-stetsoned figure enquired if we were OK. If we needed fuel he would fetch us some, but why had we not landed at the airfield? It transpired that a new airfield, recently opened, had been built out of town just three miles along the river to the north, and he pointed out a white roof visible in a dip in the hills. At three miles distance, the gallon of fuel we had left would be ample, though there would be little margin for error. It would be better to take off light from here, with its mess of surrounding buildings and crisscrossing cables, and the 90 deg crosswind. I had already experienced after the inspection run how reluctant the Champ was to climb out in this heat and we could expect no help from the wind. The runway at the new airfield was longer and the surrounding land more clear, which would offer a better chance to gain height in peace.

But now a new problem threatened. Our visitor observed that a black and white patrol car was headed in our direction, and as there was nothing more he could do for us, he departed. At first, our policeman was very stiff and formal, and I had visions of being spreadeagled over the engine cowling while he frisked us both. But after inspecting endless documents – passports, driving licence, pilot's licence, aircraft ownership registration, bill of sale etc, and reporting his finds over his car radio, he became more friendly.

He was very concerned over whether we now had enough fuel to get to the new airport and would have arranged for someone to send some over for us. Problem was, that would have taken a lot of time to organise. I still have to chuckle at the look on his face as we tried to convince him by means of our broken stick that we had sufficient! In the end we asked him to notify the airport that we were coming in and to give us a clear run in if anything else was about, and that seemed to satisfy him.

Take-off was no problem, and picking up speed in the ground effect along the 5,000 ft long runway gave us a better climb out than on my previous low pass. Even so, we were unable to get high enough to be able to pick out the new airfield until we had flown several increasingly worrying miles. There was absolutely no room for error, so it was a great relief to suddenly spot it almost under our nose. There were two runways, one with 6,700 ft of asphalt and the other, almost dead into wind as shown by a 'tee,' with a dirt surface. A half circuit brought us in line with the latter, and we landed less than ten minutes after take-off – the shortest cross-country I have ever made!

This airfield was very new and not quite finished. It was also almost deserted, very hot on the baking expanse of concrete near the airport buildings. Neither did it offer any refreshment other than the interminable can of fizz, though that was very welcome. What we did find, on looking again at our charts, was that the later one showed both the new airfield and the old one with a cross through it. As luck would have it, George had the new one, and I the older.

By now the wind strength was increasing to the point where we had to tie down again whilst refuelling. It presented us with a problem unexpected in an aircraft fitted with wheel brakes (though familiar in our unbraked, tailskid biplanes). With the wind blowing really hard from the right, the Champ absolutely refused to turn left, despite full left rudder, left brake hard on, and wide-open throttle. Other than have George get out to haul the wingtip round, the only direction it would turn was to the right. So that was the way we went, weathercocking rapidly into wind to get it swinging, and then kept it going round until it was pointing in the desired direction – turning through 270 deg for a right-angled turn! It must have looked amusing to anyone watching!

Take-off was from the dirt runway, which was chosen for its being downhill and into wind in preference to the extra length of its asphalt neighbour. My intention was to fly a short way back down the Trail so that we could take in the interesting area around La Bonte Creek and Wagon Hound Creek, but the Champ had other ideas. With a full load of fuel, slightly higher airfield elevation at 4,930 ft and even higher temperature, climb rate when more than 50 ft above the ground was almost imperceptible. This was the first occasion on which I had to resort to using the wind flow over the hills to gain altitude, learning as we went.

South of the airfield the ground fell away, which at first helped considerably, but by the time we crossed the lowest point, over the US 26 Highway, we had no more than 300 ft clear. Ahead lay ground rising progressively all the way to where the Trail route lay. For the next 15 minutes we fought a prolonged battle with the wind, which swept down from the heights ahead and curled over a quite low but wide ridge blocking our path. Again and again I would gain height at one point only to lose it all, and sometimes more at another, with the ever present fear that we would get trapped in one of the canyons in air descending faster than we could climb.

Round and round we went, cautiously seeking rising currents, noticing features which gave us lift and those where we lost height. It was a deadly game of patience and I was learning all the time, building on that slight experience gained at home on the dummy run over the Black Mountains in Wales. Gradually we worked up to sufficient altitude to cross that miserable little ridge and then found more ahead, with networks of valleys and canyons. But at least now we could gain height from the upcurrents on the windward side of the ridges – a form of powered slope-soaring!

From now on, until we reached lower ground, there would be no more flying at 500 ft above the Trail. If we didn't take the opportunity to climb when we could, we might find it impossible to do so later on when we needed to. Height in hand meant safety, and in these hot and high conditions I felt unhappy unless there was at least 1,000 ft clearance to act as a buffer against the wayward down-currents encountered over the ridges in this strong wind. Later on, that figure would have to be increased first to 1,500 ft and then to 2,000 ft as the ground level and temperature rose beneath us.

But now at last we were back over the main Trail route, though we had never been more than seven miles from it. We rejoined it where the Bozeman Trail branched off to the north-west. Almost immediately we found a very clear track marked as rutted on the map, and followed it into a broad valley to the south of Table Mountain, a long high ridge whose top inched above us. Looking ahead, it was difficult to understand why the Trail should be heading into what appeared to be a dead-end valley when there was a much easier-looking route along the North Platte (as Chiles had discovered later). The answer of course was time and distance – the route here arced across a great loop of the river.

Fortunately, as we neared the head of the valley, we could see how the wagons went through a natural exit in the north-west corner where Prele Creek ran down from what is now La Prele Reservoir. To our left was the natural phenomenon known as Ayre's Bridge, a huge slab of rock bridging the stream, though we saw nothing of it from our height. The creek followed a winding gorge, not visible until we were nearly on top of it. Here, we thankfully followed the Trail, our height at this point being only a couple of hundred feet above the ridge which had initially threatened to block us in. The rising currents which took us safely through the gorge now curled over the ridge, and I watched with dismay the altimeter slowly unwinding as we flew over the descending foothills to the river plain.

As we left the valley, we were about 1,500 ft above the level of the North Platte, but the altimeter remorselessly unwound, no matter what I did to counter it, until we were down to 700 ft. The big question was, would the descending currents of air from the hills force us down into a layer of warm air similar to that which had held us captive for so long at Douglas? We needed to stay in the cool air and away from the down draughts to retain control.

Watching the altimeter, willing it to stop unwinding, I held my breath as it seemed to do just that. Almost unbelievably, the Champ started to climb again, very gradually, until we reached 1,300 ft when, again for no apparent reason we encountered another downdraught. This took us back to 1,100 ft before relinquishing its hold and this time I just kept on climbing until we were 2,000 ft above the river. Not till then did I feel that it was safe to throttle back to cruising revs for the first time since leaving Glendo.

Meanwhile, though fairly well preoccupied with our battle for height, we had spotted a small private airstrip, Barber, near the Little Box Elder Creek massacre site. Here, on July 12th 1864, a small wagon train was attacked by 250 Oglala Sioux Indians. All but four of the men were killed and a mother and daughter were taken captive. The child, Mary Kelly, ran away but was killed next day. She was buried here with three of the men who died. Her mother was returned unharmed by Blackfoot Indians after five months captivity.

We were now too high to pick out small objects such as Trail Markers or grave markers on the ground, but rutted sections of the Trail still stood out well. We spotted these along the south bank of the Platte, from opposite a large processing plant with enormous, 500 ft-high chimneys (which at that point were still rather too close for comfort), almost into the small town of Glenrock. From there on we saw no more evidence of the Trail although the rails of the Chicago and Northwestern Railway (not Railroad!) seem to have been laid over or alongside the Trail route for much of the way into Casper.

We had originally scheduled to use Harford airfield when landing at Casper, both because it had a dirt runway (more suitable for our tailskid biplanes) and also to shorten a long leg, being eight miles east of the main airport, Natrona County International. Having refuelled at Douglas, neither of these factors were now applicable, in fact it was more important to shorten the next leg west. What was more, Natrona offered four runway directions to choose from, of between 7,600 and 10,600 ft length; enough even in this heat to get our Champ airborne and well clear. George made an attempt to raise the Tower on our radio, but that had definitely died on him.

Overflying Natrona at 2,000 ft, it looked vast, with its main, 2 miles-long runway pointing roughly south-west. It also looked deserted. With two pairs of now wide-awake eyes keeping a very sharp lookout for any other traffic, particularly big jets coming in on long finals, I throttled back and circled left to lose height and line up on the into-wind runway. It was not easy to be certain which that was, as the windsock, horizontal in the gale that was now blowing, was swinging from side to side through roughly 60 deg, so I took the nearest.

From the height at which we started the let-down, it should have been no problem to get into an 8,680 ft runway without opening the throttle again, but the wind was so strong that I found full throttle was necessary through the last 500 ft. Even then it looked doubtful at one point as to whether we would actually get into the field, as at low level we ran into the old problem of losing height in the heat.

We made it and had stopped before we got to the first taxiway turn-off. Now it needed almost full power to make headway into wind, with the added danger of being blown over as we turned across it to taxy to the terminal buildings. We were delighted to be met by a Follow-Me car with a very helpful young man who offered to hold our wingtip if necessary. It wasn't, but the Champ felt very unstable. By now it seemed obvious that we would progress no further that day, what with the wind strength making it questionable as to whether we could reach our next refuelling stop, and the extent by which we had fallen behind schedule.

When we reached the terminal area I asked if hangarage was available as I thought it unwise to leave the Champ tied down outside. It was, but they were unable to open the hangar doors in the wind, now reported as being 40 mph gusting to 50 mph. If we tied down now, they would put the aircraft in the hangar as soon as the wind dropped sufficiently to open the doors, which it was expected to do by the evening. As to getting it out in the morning, there would be someone there to do that by six o'clock. There were willing hands to help us tie down (it took three of us to hold the aircraft and another to attach the tie-down chains) and to refuel. Incredibly, no charge was made for any of this, other than fuel!

Our day was made on discovering from a delightful young lady in Reception that there was an airport courtesy car available for us (the first of a number that we came across), also free of charge. This is a great American institution, unthinkable at UK airports, whereby one or more old cars are left for use by visiting pilots to drive into town, to return next morning. What a godsend when the airport is six miles out of town – it also gave us an opportunity to visit Fort Caspar [Fig. 51] and find somewhere to eat. We booked a room by phone at the local Motel 6, only one in case the ground party missed us at this unscheduled stop, and left a message for them at the desk. Thank you, Natrona, for such an efficient, friendly and helpful service!

Due to some intelligent reasoning by Brian, who from first-hand experience recognised that the hot, high and windy conditions could so easily halt our progress, our ground crew got our message. They had a good day, easier in terms of distance than any since leaving New Jersey. There was time to visit Scotts Bluff visitor centre and museum, and drive to the top; call in at Fort Laramie; stop at Register Cliff to goggle at the names carved there; walk through the mind-boggling Guernsey Ruts and take in the atmosphere that goes with that place. They booked in at the motel and were leaving for a meal just as we returned from ours.

Whilst I was disappointed at the loss of the day during which we were to fly over the Sublette Cut-Off and visit the site of the 1836 Rendezvous at Daniel, I recognised that it was probably a blessing in disguise. It gave all of us a chance to recuperate a little and be more ready for what was to come. It also gave me a chance to contact a sergeant from the Fremont County Sheriff's Office, who had offered to meet us at our next stop, Jeffrey City. We arranged to meet the next morning at the airstrip at around 09.30. He had not been available to meet us today so we would have missed him, and that would have been a great loss!

The Whitmans had reached the Casper area on 26th June, after a week's rest at Fort Laramie. As with the bulk of later travellers, west of Fort Laramie they left the North Platte to cut across the rugged, barren region amongst the foothills of the Black Hills, in order to save precious miles. They finally crossed the river, for the last time, probably at the point where the original Mormon Ferry operated in 1849, near what is now the eastern end of modern Casper City. Too deep to ford in 1836, the river had to be crossed in boats.

They stayed there a day whilst the Fur Company men constructed 'bum boats,' similar to, but much larger than the coracles used in Ireland and Wales. These were made by stretching oiled buffalo hides over willow hoops, leaving them to bake hard and taut in the sun, The party was in good health apart from Eliza Spalding, who was feeling sick and debilitated from the unvarying diet of buffalo meat.

What a reflection on man's avarice that buffalo meat is now a rare delicacy!

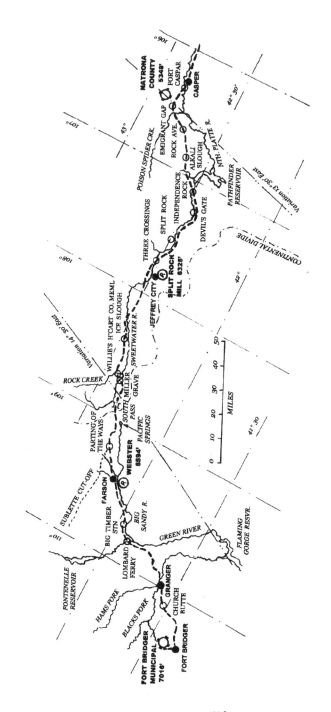

116

CHAPTER 11

DAY 4:
TO FORT BRIDGER

Experience the previous year, when driving across the desert from Casper over South Pass to Farson, had shown that it was essential to have a good meal before setting out, there being nowhere to eat between the two. If that applied on the ground then it was that much more necessary to do the same when flying to the sort of isolated airstrips we were proposing to use on this stage. So we accepted an enforced delay in getting a good breakfast, somewhat stoically, despite the two hours difference between time of rising and getting to the airport at 7.30!

When we arrived at Natrona County, we found that they had been as good as their word, the Champ snoozing snugly in the corner of a cavernous hangar. Willing hands soon had the doors open and the Champ wheeled outside. A barely-stirring windsock showed how much the wind had dropped, though in the short time it took to be ready to depart, a 10 mph breeze had sprung up. The air was crisp and cool, the sun shone from a cloudless blue sky and visibility seemed limited only by one's own perception. "Oh! what a beautiful morning . . ."

This time we made no attempt to use the radio, leaving it with the ground crew to save a little weight. Phoning the tower, we were told to taxy out and watch for their lights. They gave us a green to taxy, but then seemed to lose interest in us, as we sat at the end of the runway for a good five minutes waiting for another. In the end, with nothing in sight, we went without – George, still watching the tower in case they gave us a red, reported that he saw a green just as we got airborne!

As we were not certain of obtaining fuel at Jeffrey City, we took the precaution of filling up two 3-gallon fuel containers with precious 80-octane Avgas. Stowing them in the back of the Champ added another 40 lb of weight in the wrong place but, for all we knew, they could save us being stuck there for hours waiting for the ground crew to arrive. There were no complaints from the forgiving Champ when we took off from the 8,679 ft runway 25, it still being cool enough at 8.00 am to cause no problems in getting airborne from Casper's elevation of 5,348 ft.

It seemed to take ages to clear the airport boundaries, heading into a steadily increasing wind. Climbing hard (all of 200 ft per minute!) we were at about 1,000 ft as we swung across the end of the two-miles-long main runway 21, heading back towards Casper City. Circling over the City, we easily picked out the west-bound Poison Spider Road which is named after the north bank route of the Oregon Trail. This was also the road our ground crew would take out of Casper and we looked in vain for any sign of their big white estate car. Heading west over the arid brown grass expanse we were Oregon-bound again!

After zigzagging round an enormous vehicle park, miles from anywhere, the route swung south-west through a winding pass in a low ridge (Emigrant Gap Ridge) and out across an expanse of sand and sage desert [Fig. 52]. Dark green trees dotted the upper slopes of the ridge, the first we had seen for many tens of miles.

Beyond the ridge the land looked a promising pale green, with patches of cultivation, darker traces of creeks and the blue waters of irrigation canals. But the green was a sage green and the desert no less a desert for all its greenery. Protruding here and there were brown ridges with white rocky outcrops, while to the south rose Bessemer Mountain and the red earth scars of Red Buttes, a well known landmark on the Trail.

We passed a pond on our left which I identified tentatively as Poison Spring, but there followed a number of small lakes and ponds, with no counterparts on my map, and the pattern of creeks, tracks and roads was as confusing from the air as I had found it on the ground. As on that earlier occasion we somehow found the right road, confirmed by its winding descent through the barren Rock Avenue *[Fig. 53]*. Perhaps the emigrants found it no less confusing and equally stumbled on the right trail in much the same manner?

In Trail days this area mixed marsh with sandy desert, the waters in the marsh gathering in poisonous alkali ponds and creeks, which killed animals and men alike who were crazed enough to drink from them. Names given by the early travellers on this road often reflected the severity of the barren countryside through which they passed. What tragedy, I wondered, drove some unfortunate to give the name Poison Spring Creek to the ugly gash that crossed the road at the foot of Rock Avenue?

Ahead, the way stretched relentlessly across the dips and rises of the foothills of the Rattlesnake Range, to the flat plains of the confluence of the Sweetwater and North Platte Rivers. In the distance, the Green Mountains stretched mistily blue on the horizon. Where the Trail crossed Rattlesnake, the pioneers called the long uphill pull Prospect Hill, though the prospect looks a pretty grim one. At least it must have been softened by Willow Spring nestling at the foot, the first drinkable water they would have encountered after leaving Casper, 25 tough miles behind them.

Willow Spring was marked by verdant green grass, an attractive blue pond, a clump of small, dark green trees and an old ramshackle log cabin. There was even a little knot of brown and white cattle – a veritable oasis in a desolate waste.

The dirt road we were following is named Oregon Trail Road and for nearly thirty miles coincides roughly with the cart tracks of the pioneers.

Soon we were nearing yet another Horse Creek [Fig. 54], where the Trail route continues straight on but the dirt track turns left onto a new road taking traffic south to Highway 220. Here, when driving a hire car, I had to leave the Trail because the route is too rough for a normal road vehicle, but now we were able to follow the clear ruts all the way to Independence Rock.

After crossing the main highway, the aptly-named, dumpy little Steamboat Rock stood out from the flat plain, guiding us on. But, despite eagerly seeking sight of the famous Independence Rock, so large when seen from the ground, it was not until we had passed the Pathfinder Reservoir, formed by damming the North Platte, that we spotted it. Then it looked for all the world like an insignificant grey slug.

Everything was a little different to what I had expected – the reservoir was marked more by wide shores of light-coloured sand than by any great stretch of water. A dark green line showed the looping course of the Sweetwater as it meandered into the reservoir, little more than a stream in comparison with rivers such as the North Platte. Independence Rock was dwarfed by the 1,000 ft higher bulk of the nearby Sentinel Range and the distant blue line of the 10,000 ft-high Ferris Mountains. It lay in a uniform carpet of dull straw and sage, the eye being consistently drawn instead to the jewel that was Lake Piaya, just in front of it.

Little Lake Piaya drew attention first by the bright cobalt blue of its waters which, as we approached, gradually changed through turquoise to viridian green when overhead. The water's edge was circled by a brilliant white rim, perhaps of soda – beautiful to look at but dangerous to touch!

Independence Rock [Fig. 55] marked for the emigrants a significant and joyous achievement, being regarded, erroneously, as the halfway mark. If they made it on the Fourth of July so much the better and they would celebrate both, in traditional style with music and dancing, the ladies trotting out their carefully-hoarded Sunday best. A touch of that feeling permeated the cabin of the Aeronca, as we cavorted light-heartedly up and over and round the 300 ft-high rock.

In the mid-morning light, the grey looked darker than I had remembered it from the year before, and we searched unsuccessfully for some sign of the hundreds of names I had seen when clambering over it. Pulling up over the top it also became obvious that the sun was already heating the air, the temperature combining with the 6,000 ft altitude to reduce the Champ's already miserable climb rate even further. Enough! On to more serious things!

Five miles along the Sweetwater brought us more excitement at Devil's Gate, a dramatic 370 ft-high, near-vertical cleft in a ridge, through which the river flowed [Fig. 56]. But the human tide could not emulate it, the gap being too narrow to allow passage for the wagons. Fortunately for them, there was an easy way round, calling for a very small detour, and they were soon back alongside the Sweetwater on the other side of the ridge. Here again, we took full advantage of the Champ's handling to drop down and skim over the top, just above the gap, looking down into and filming the awesome chasm. It was also a popular diversion for the fitter elements of the emigrants' trains to climb to the top and look over the edge – I must say I preferred to do it with a pair of wings to hold me up!

We had lost a lot of height in making that low pass and wasted no more time in trying to climb back up for another. Instead, we flew along the foot of the Sweetwater Rocks hills, seeking Martin's Cove. There was nothing to identify it other than the curve of the hills and the presence of a dead-end track. Here occurred perhaps the greatest of all the many disasters associated with the Oregon Trail.

In order to speed the intake of settlers for Salt Lake City, the Mormons had successfully recruited large numbers of the poorer people in hard-hit areas in England, and also in Scandinavia. Unable to afford the cost of outfitting large wagon trains, these emigrants walked, pushing and pulling handcarts, from Council Bluffs to Salt Lake City. Five persons to a handcart, carrying a total of 100 lb each of provisions and clothing! In 1856, three groups set out, the first two getting through with no major problems. The third, starting late, encountered early snows and suffered dreadfully. Captain Edwards' Company of 376 men, women and children lost 145 of their number in freezing conditions here in November, the survivors being met by rescuers from Salt Lake City.

Ahead, the Trail bore on, at times quite clearly rutted, running alongside the Sweetwater for 20 miles, past another well-known landmark, Split Rock, with its Vee-shaped cleft at the peak. Most of the landmarks proved easy to spot, the names proving very descriptive, as with the next, Castle Rock. Here the river was following the base of a rocky ridge, sometimes through quite narrow defiles between high outcrops. Where this happened, the Trail had either to leave the river or cross it, and over the next 30 miles crossed it eight times.

From Castle Rock, the route diverted south of the river for a short distance before rejoining it at Three Crossings. There was a Stage Station here, and after tracing the route back and forth across the river and round the ridges, we wondered how the Stage passengers viewed the ride. The main route, after crossing the winding loops of the Sweetwater, took the wagons along the bed of the river where it ran through a rocky canyon, now deep water above a beaver dam *[Fig. 57]*. The alternative was known as the Deep Sand Route – which speaks for itself!

The map showed that it was time to look for our first refuelling stop, at the small community serving the uranium mines at Jeffrey City. Here were mine workings above the broad, soda-encrusted shore of a beautiful pea-green lake. As we swung south away from Three Crossings and across the Deep Sand route, we could see the single 4,580 ft long, dirt runway of Split Rock Mill airstrip dead ahead *[Fig. 58]*. The airfield elevation of 6,325 ft was higher than any we had landed at, but so far so good, despite the sun's heat now seeming as great as anything yet encountered.

Losing height to make an inspection run along the runway, we saw a police truck and the white-stetsoned figure of Sgt. Dee Darnell waiting for us at the threshold. We saw something else as well – a group of five or six deer grazing halfway along the 100 ft wide strip. Well, I had often chased sheep off a grass runway at home but this was indeed something else.

They showed no inclination to move as we approached at 50 ft up, so opening the throttle wide I dived at them and spent an exhilarating few seconds chasing them well away. Could they run? Not only run but zigzag in such a way that it took all the manoeuvrability the Champ could muster to stay with them as they tried to head back towards the strip. They seemed to glide rather than run, their little black and white tails bobbing to disprove this. Their horns were quite unlike any I had seen before outside of a zoo, sticking up like twin prongs. With a sudden flash of comprehension I yelled to George: "They're pronghorns!"

All this chasing around had reduced our speed somewhat and taken us half a mile away from the strip. Circling round to line up with the runway saw us headed downwind towards a small cluster of buildings with attendant poles and lines, but at first the Champ refused to climb higher than 20 ft. How embarrassing in front of an invited and official audience!

Attempts to pull the nose up to climb increased the drag of the wings and just resulted in loss of speed, any initial gain in height soon being lost! Lowering the nose to gain speed also meant loss of height until the speed had built up. We looked for anything that would help reduce drag, but there was not a lot to be done other than closing the windows and concentrating on keeping the ball of the slip indicator centred (did I really hear Bill Smela growling in my ear: "Kick the ball!"?). Watching the ground ahead, and the air speed indicator for the slightest loss resulting from juggling the controls, demanded equal attention. The now very hot and high conditions called for a careful balance of lift and drag against the available engine power – speed and height against climb. I learned a lot, fast, in that circuit!

Making a larger circle steered us clear of the buildings but it was a long time before the Champ started to regain lost speed and was gradually coaxed back up to 50 ft! Fortunately there was sufficient descending ground to get us back in line with the runway and just enough height to make a respectable approach. This was no time for the usual three-point landing. This time it would have to be a 'wheeler,' keeping the tail high in order to retain rudder control for as long as possible, as the touchdown would occur at a fairly high speed. In these conditions the difference between stalling speed and maximum speed was minimal! Fortunately I was ready for the sudden dart to the right and was braking hard on the left before a swing developed. My watch showed the time as 9.50, nearly two hours of flying.

As we taxied back over the rough surface, Dee came out to meet us and helped to swing us off the runway to a sheltered spot. He proved to be a jovial giant, the type who is good to count on as a friend but not one to meet if on the wrong side of the law!

We soon confirmed our needs, mainly to empty the six gallons we had brought with us into the tank and to obtain another two gallons to top up with. Anything left in the container we would take with us. Dee readily offered to run us down to the filling station for the extra two gallons and then to take us out to a local cave he knew, where there were a number of Indian pictographs. I was concerned about the increase in temperature as the morning wore on into noon, both here and at our next stop, but Dee reckoned that it had already peaked and would get no worse. Bowing to his local knowledge we happily agreed to go with him to see the pictographs.

So we all climbed into his very fully equipped 4WD truck. A couple of pump-action shotguns, in a rack alongside my seat in the back, served as a grim reminder that he was the sole representative of the law over a very considerable area. But it seemed that the locals were on the whole a very law-abiding lot, any troubles being mainly confined to payday activities from some of the miners. Even that would soon cease, as the mine was in the process of closing down.

The cave proved to be quite close and as it was on private land we called in to meet the owner and obtain permission to visit it. That needed no detour as we had to go through the owner's farm to get there. The pictographs were certainly worth visiting and for both George and I were the first we had ever seen. Without Dee we would never have found them, even had we known they were there, and they were little known outside a few locals. Dee had apparently come across them when he was a boy riding the range on horseback.

After that he insisted on us visiting his home for a long cool drink, an offer we accepted with alacrity. Maybe he was right that it was not getting any hotter, but I could have easily been persuaded otherwise! Dee was also something of a collector of local art, so when he invited anyone to see his etchings it was just that!

Back at the airstrip, George and I had a little discussion about the conditions. The strip was slightly uphill, but the wind, strong enough to move the Champ while we had been away, was straight down it. The temperature had been up in the nineties when we arrived, but Dee was still insistent that it was no hotter now. We had taken on only another two gallons of fuel so would be about 15 lb heavier, but the weight distribution was better now that we had emptied the six gallons from the containers in the back into the fuel tank at the front!

I felt fairly certain that if we could work up enough speed close to the ground we would have no problem in getting up, Then it would be just a matter of patience to gain height, as we had seen on the circuit before we landed. The runway was long enough to allow us to abort the take-off if we failed to climb away by the time we reached the halfway point. We agreed to give it a try.

Our stop had cost us two hours, so it was just before midday that we taxied out. The pronghorns had not come back and we had a clear run. From the pilot's seat, the runway looked to be much more of a slope than it had from outside, and the ground beyond continued up to the eight miles distant, 2,000 ft higher ridge of Oil Field Mountain. It would pay me to turn downwind as soon as we had sufficient height, to avoid any wind curl-over from that ridge.

At full throttle, the Champ moved off much as usual, and we quickly gained enough speed to get off the ground. There I held it to just skim the surface and obtain maximum benefit from ground effect (at very low level the air is squeezed between the ground and the wings, increasing the air pressure and giving more lift). We picked up speed until it settled at about 75 mph (probably the true air speed, corrected for temperature and altitude, was about 90 mph) at which I felt we could zoom up without too much loss. But at about thirty feet, the Champ lost momentum and started mushing back down. Dropping the nose picked up speed and halted most of that sinking feeling, but the aircraft settled lower and lower, even though close to maximum speed.

There wasn't a lot I could do, except to keep going, the end of the runway disappearing under the nose before I realised it would be better to be back on the ground! This time, there was no question of checking the descent at 20 ft and climbing away from there. It needed as much speed as we could get, quickly, so I dived off most of that precious height to get the speed back up to about 75 indicated, and even then the aircraft just kept on settling down. Fortunately it stopped doing that just as I was certain we were about to touch down in the rough. At something like five or six feet above the ground we were back in ground effect and miraculously the dear old Champ maintained height at that.

After surviving the first half minute of this it seemed we could perhaps keep going indefinitely as long as nothing got in the way. Abandoning all hope of circling back over the strip to give Dee a farewell wave, I cautiously nosed away from the slope, heading west and towards lower ground. Fortunately, although the surface was very stony and much too rough to land on safely, it was fairly level.

We kept going like this for about seven or eight miles, gradually edging down the slope towards US Highway 287. Suddenly, in heading out over a steep drop, we were flying in free air again, possibly a combination of reduced weight from burning off fuel and the slightly lower altitude. Whatever it was, the Champ started to climb and we gradually worked back up into cool air at 1,500 ft (i.e. about 8,000 ft a.s.l.!). At this altitude it even proved possible to ease back on the throttle to drop the engine revs 100 rpm to the recommended maximum, and still maintain height.

It was time to start thinking about where we were, as the Trail route diverged from the highway a little way west of Jeffrey City. The landscape below was almost entirely featureless. US Highway 287 stretched straight to the west, with just a slight curve to the left where we joined it, followed by an equal angle back to the right four miles ahead. Otherwise, the ground was an almost uniform sandy brown with an overtone of sage green. On each side, at a distance of six or seven miles, ran a long ridge of hills, striated with folds and gullies and dry creeks. The winding course of the Sweetwater was slanting away from us to our right, marked as usual by a deep green band of lush grass. Not much to go on but knowing how long we had been flying and thus approximately how far we had flown, it was enough.

The next landmarks were Ice Spring and Ice Slough, but I knew from looking for these on the ground (and finding no evidence of ice), that there would be little to see from our altitude! At least, Ice Slough Creek *[Fig. 59]* showed by its attendant verdant green stripe both where it, and the Oregon Trail route, crossed the highway, and the latter forked away before heading off north-west in the distance.

Ice Slough was one of the wonders of the old Trail in that, at the height of summer, travellers reported finding sheets of clear ice 18 in below the surface of the peat bog. Alas, that is no longer the case. But what, one wonders, made anyone go and dig several feet down in a peat bog to look for ice?

At this point, the car driver following the Trail has to keep to the highway in a great loop that takes him 25 miles to the north. We could see the fork where the Trail and a rough track coincide in heading into the wilderness. Here, if anywhere, one gets a real feeling for the vastness of the wasteland that the immigrants crossed, and the utter desolation that entirely surrounded them. In the early days they were 250 miles beyond the last slight signs of their own civilisation, with another 150 miles to go to the next, and even that was only a couple of mud hovels. Indeed, even these days, there is a 50-mile stretch before the Trail crosses another road.

Soon we were back over the Sweetwater River, where it swung round to a south-westerly course that would take it nearly to South Pass. There were a few landmarks to look for along this section, but the landscape of ridges, slopes and gullies was dominated by the broad, snaking, green swathe through which ran the river.

The Trail route was not always obvious, with conflicting tracks occasionally confusing the picture, but the main features came up where expected. Sixth, Seventh and Eighth crossings of the Sweetwater, St. Mary's Stage Station site, Silver Creek Reservoir off to the right, and the silver sandy track of the Trail where it ran along the crests of ridges and crossed the infamous, boulder-strewn Rocky Ridge. A string of three small lakes, reflecting the cobalt blue of the sky, marked the point where the Trail descended to the relatively level McClean Meadows.

I had wondered why the Trail so often followed a precarious, undulating path along the tricky spine of the ridges, but now it suddenly dawned on me that the numerous gullies and creeks, taking the run-off waters into the river, presented an even greater hazard. All along the banks, the creeks dropped into the main channel. Driving a wagon along the river where it ran through this tangled confusion of ridges would have demanded an endless succession of crossings of sometimes impossibly deep creeks and ravines.

The Trail gradually swung away north of the river, parallelling Strawberry Creek *[Fig. 60]* and under a dusty, dirt road that I had driven over the year before, looking for James G. Willie's Handcart Company Memorial *[Fig. 61]*. If ever a place warranted a more descriptive title than the repetitive Rock Creek, this must be it – Heartbreak Halt springs to mind. Identified on the air charts as a cemetery, a simple rock and stone slab marks the site. Here a large number of Mormon emigrants, without shelter, warm clothing and food, shrugged off the cares of the world, forgot the trials and tribulations they had endured to get this far, and huddled together for the merciful release of sleep; here they froze to death in the early snows of October 1856. After all the promises of a new life, the appalling discomforts of the Atlantic crossing, and the dreadful hardships of the overland journeys, what a God-forsaken desolate place – and what desperate circumstances – in which to die!

From here the Trail swung back south-west to rejoin the Sweetwater, and to all intents and purposes disappeared under a multitude of tracks that were quite unlike my chart *[Fig. 62]*. We crossed the Sweetwater again and flew along a broad flat valley that led to South Pass. Twin Mounds, two little light-coloured cones, suddenly materialised almost under our nose as I was beginning to think we had missed them and then, quickly, we were over South Pass. We had seen the last of old faithful Sweetwater.

Circling over the Pass, I only knew where it was because I could identify the two stone markers that I had seen on a previous visit by car. One marks the Oregon Trail at South Pass on the Great Divide. The other

[Fig. 63] records the fact that Narcissa Whitman and Eliza Hart Spalding were the first white women to cross the Pass, on July 4th 1836.

Here was the Great Divide, or Continental Divide, which had been running parallel to our route, but about 15 miles south of it, ever since we left Devil's Gate. Here was the point at which the emigrants' long uphill slog from the Missouri changed to an equally long downhill slope (with major and minor ups and downs en route) to the end of the Trail at Oregon City. This, at 7,550 ft altitude, was one of the highest points along the Trail.

This invisible line runs down the chain of mountains which constitute the Rockies, all the way from Canada to Mexico. On one side of the Divide, all the streams and rivers run down to the Pacific, and on the other, to the Gulf.

When the Whitmans passed this way, the Great Divide marked something else, in a way more significant for them. When they crossed this Pass they were turning their backs on the United States Territory and entering Oregon. This was disputed land, the subject of a short-lived war between Britain and the United States in 1812, the outcome of which, in 1836, had still not been finally resolved!

But for us, in our little low-powered Champ, it meant that we had crossed what some people predicted would be the biggest obstacle we would face. In fact, but for the altimeter showing a reading of 9,000 ft as we crossed the Pass, it seemed little different to much that had gone before. True, we had been forced to fly at 1,500 ft above the ground instead of the preferred 500 ft, but at that height the Champ was behaving perfectly normally.

Twelve miles to our right, the 10,404 ft Granite Peak marked the end of the Wind River Range, which stretched more than a hundred miles north-west to the Teton Wilderness Area, with a highest point of 13,804 ft. Eight miles to our left was Continental Peak which, at 8,612 ft, reached a mere 1,000 ft above the plain. South Pass was certainly not the rocky track between towering snow-capped mountains of popular imagination, but a 20-miles wide, flat, sage plain. The gradient either side of the Pass was so gentle that travellers could never be certain when they had crossed it!

Just a few miles beyond the Divide the Trail turned south-west, past Pacific Springs, where the emigrants had their first taste of water that flowed to the Pacific. That it looked, smelt and tasted no different was neither here nor there, it was where it was going that counted! We found an unmarked lake here instead of a small spring. Here also we found a main road again, Highway 28, which would accompany us on and off to our next stop at Farson.

Now we were looking out for the Dry Sandy River, which certainly lived up to its name. It stood out from the sage desert like a bright, white, wiggly chalk line. We had a clear pointer as to where the Trail branched away from the highway, opposite the end of the large Hay Meadow Reservoir. From there it made a lazy "S" past a prominent rocky outcrop, known as Plume Rocks, to cross the Dry Sandy. It ran along the north bank, roughly parallel with the Highway but some three miles from it; far enough away to look the way it must have done to the emigrants.

We soon came to the "Parting of the Ways," where anyone taking the tough, cross-desert Sublette cut-off parted company with those following the less hazardous, but 53-miles-longer, main route to Fort Bridger. The main Trail still headed south-west while the cut-off made a bee-line for the west – it needed to, as those using it would see no water for almost fifty miles after crossing the Big Sandy! Both trails were still clear cut.

It was a straightforward jaunt along the Dry Sandy, then along the Little Sandy where the two came together, finally leaving the Trail route at Farson. The latter was a little huddle of several houses, a café and a filling station at the point where Highway 28 joined US Highway 187. It was also the point where the Trail crossed the Big Sandy, just above the confluence of the Big and Little Sandy Rivers. This tiny hamlet only served to emphasise the vastness of the surrounding wasteland – it was the first such we had seen since leaving Jeffrey City, 93 miles to the east.

Two miles south along US 187 is Webster airfield. According to the book, it had a 4,500 ft long dirt runway and a much shorter turf runway just ten degrees off it – to all intents and purposes a single runway strip. Sure enough, there was a dirt runway marked by a small yellow windsock and nothing else. The threshold was just beyond a gate in the wire fence running alongside the highway and, as at Clinch, the runway looked to be no more than a twin-rutted track. Except that this had taller weeds growing between and in the ruts and was almost indistinguishable from some sections of the Oregon Trail!

Making a wide circuit while we lost height, I watched for a gap in the road traffic. That was not difficult, with just one vehicle travelling in each direction, a mile or so distant. On the way round, I opened up to see whether we could still climb away if an overshoot proved necessary and, to my relief, it appeared to do so more easily than at Jeffrey City. Perhaps the temperature was lower here?

Landing was no problem, again adopting a tail-high technique. Swinging round at about halfway along the strip, we taxied back, the prop chopping down those weeds we had missed on the way in! Trying to turn round under power to park off the strip proved impossible as the sand was so soft in places that the tailwheel just dug itself in. Climbing out to manhandle the aircraft round, with the engine switched off and no cooling slipstream, proved how wrong I was about the temperature – it seemed even hotter here! Time down, 13.43: time in air, 1 hour 55 minutes.

We still had approximately 1½ gallons of fuel in a container, so the first thing was to empty this into the tank. Then I planned to take the two containers to the road and see if I could hitch a lift to Farson, or walk if not. George agreed to stay with the aircraft; we could not risk losing those precious Leica cameras and had no desire to lug them about with us!

Before I had gone a few steps, a battered yellow pick-up truck stopped on the road opposite the end of the strip and the driver waved. Needing no second bidding I hurried through the gate and climbed aboard. It seemed he had seen us fly over the filling station at Farson, where he worked, and reasoned that we would need fuel. So what else than to get out the truck and come and pick us up? Such was typical American hospitality, though the cynical would say it was merely an eye for business. One thing was sure, we would not have been going anywhere else to get our gas!

Having filled our containers, with leaded fuel on local advice, the driver obligingly drove me back down to the airstrip, accompanied by two cans of rapidly-warming drink. From him I learnt that the airstrip was named after the owner, that there was another strip closer to 'town,' and that nowadays it was a rare occurrence to see an aircraft fly in.

George had already topped up the oil when I got back, and while we were emptying the fuel containers into the tank we had a couple of visitors – one man (Tim) and his dog. Tim turned out to be the local Deputy State Fire Marshal, off-duty and just passing, and very curious to see what a little yellow Aeronca was doing, landing out in the wilds.

By the time we were ready to go it was nearly three o'clock and still very hot indeed. We pondered at length over what to do next. Conditions were obviously little different to what they had been at Split Rock Mill. We were perhaps fifteen pounds lighter from carrying less oil and petrol, and the ground was level instead of sloping uphill; but the ground elevation at 6,594 ft was 270 ft higher than before and the temperature seemed higher also. There was a good case for stopping here and getting off early in the morning!

Against that was the fact that our next stop, at Fort Bridger, was even higher, at 7,016 ft, and I now felt that the only way we would get off the ground there, other than dropping off George, would be to take off at crack of dawn. At least the Champ had demonstrated that it would keep flying in ground effect at Jeffrey City, and that last circuit before landing had seemed to indicate that it was performing better here. Perhaps the final, unspoken thoughts of both of us were that it was a barren, desolate place to stay overnight, especially if we missed our ground crew on the road.

Tim gave us a hand to pull the Champ round in line with the runway and stayed to watch us leave. The engine started easily as usual and produced full rpm. Time to go! The runway stretched ahead, looking like no other runway I have ever seen, though the 'tween ruts weeds were now a little shorter than when we arrived. At full throttle we heaved up out of the sand and waddled up to the runway, gaining speed rapidly once we were on firmer ground with the tail up.

As before, we got airborne quickly and I held her down until the A.S.I. settled at 75 mph before pulling up into a gentle climb, trying not to lose too much speed in the process. As before, we got up to around thirty feet and again mushed slowly back down, the controls feeling soggy and slack, indicating the verge of a stall.

By the time I had regained flying speed by putting the nose down, as before, the end of the strip flashed past and we were slowly settling in ground effect. There the similarity ended: instead of maintaining height at five or six feet it continued inexorably to sink, very slowly, giving time to reflect on what would happen if the wheels touched! At this point I was doing a Yuri Geller job, talking to the Champ: "Come on, old girl, you can do it, you can do it, just keep going . . ."!

There came a point where I knew she was about to touch down, and waited breathlessly for it to happen. With power off (we would have to cut the switches immediately we touched down) and no slipstream over the rudder the Champ could not be trusted to run true on the smoothest tarmac at anything much over 55 mph, and at the speed we were travelling, the left brake would not hold her straight.

But we were over a flat, open, sandy plain, dotted with small rocks and stones, clumps of coarse grass and sage brush, and criss-crossed with shallow gullies. Fortunately, the sage was only ankle high, and before we started cropping that with the propeller (which would have slowed us more) or the wheels ploughed through the clumps, the Champ miraculously stopped her descent. She must have heard me – I have always thought that much-loved old aeroplanes look after fools like me!

For what seemed an age, neither of us could believe that she was not going to touch at any moment. Long moments passed, and she kept going. Instead of looking for the best place to point at for the inevitable touch of the wheels, bracing ourselves for the tearing, tumbling, crashing cartwheel that would surely follow, we were able to look further ahead for the best course to steer to ensure we kept airborne.

There could not have been more than a foot between the wheels and the ground, and now it was essential to make sure that nothing higher than that got in the way. To our left was slightly rising ground, so the first thing was to edge away to the right, applying very little rudder and no aileron to minimise drag. We crossed, or flew for short distances along, rutted tracks and then were faced with a major obstacle, a comparatively deep stream bed with a trickle of water at the bottom. The creek was probably no more than two feet deep and perhaps forty feet wide, and it twisted and turned too much for us to fly along it, threatening to turn sharply across in front of us.

There was nothing for it, we had to cross it and choose the point at which to do so. Eventually, there was a spot where the banks looked shallow enough to venture out across, and we did so safely. At this point I had no idea at all where we were, in what direction we were headed, or what stream we may have just crossed. Looking at either the map or the compass was not on. I tried to visualise the map I had drawn of this area, but my mind refused to register on a map. At this stage I dared not take my eyes off the terrain ahead for a moment – it was as if the slightest relaxation could lead to contact with the too-close ground below. I had the throttle lever rammed fully open against the stops, to prevent it moving fractionally closed and costing us a few vital rpm.

Running through my mind was the thought that if we were unable to climb away from the surface, even if we did not run into something that we could neither get round or over, we would eventually run out of fuel and be forced to do three hours later what we were trying hard not to now. What was more, if we survived the ensuing crash we would have no idea where we were! Not a happy thought. Something had to be done!

George suddenly spotted a blacktop road over to our right, which we were running roughly parallel to. If we could get to that perhaps we could pick up a thermal from the hot surface and gain height that way; if nothing else, if we had to touch down somewhere it would be better on that smooth surface than the rough desert floor below us. Irrational thinking on both scores, but we were clutching at straws now. George confirmed there were no poles and power or telephone lines running alongside the road, so I edged towards it. There was another gully to cross before we reached it, but I was beginning to gain confidence and to get a feel for this strange sort of flying, and crossed that also.

At this point the road ran a foot or so above the desert, carefully levelled to iron out the undulations, so we had another little bank to surmount. By careful experiment I had found that the Champ could be induced to hop up shallow banks without much loss of speed, and would settle back into that foot-high flight again. There was no sign of traffic in either direction, as far as we could see, but at closer quarters, another hazard presented itself. On our side of the road and a dozen or so feet from it, snow-depth poles, about five feet tall, were spaced at regular intervals. A flat slalom to the right took us between a pair of poles and a quick hop saw us safely above the road!

Alas! there were no thermals to be found above the road, and neither should we have expected any. If anything we might have expected a down-draught, though with a long soak in the sun there was probably virtually no vertical movement of air at all over the road. The other hope, that of being able to land on the road was dashed with the realization of just how fast we were travelling over its surface. On each side, the ground shelved away, and we also saw that as well as the snow markers on the left there were poles, possibly carrying telephone lines, just off the road to the right. Touchdown on the road could be just as catastrophic as on the open ground, once a swing started!

We now seemed to be flying up a very slight incline, with some sort of mast off to the right, but the Champ still kept going. Somewhere along this stretch the poles and lines, not happy with being on the right side of the road, decided to cross over to the left. We could see them across the road way up ahead. There was no question of what to to do – the Champ was very definitely not going to hop that high, so we just carried on underneath!

Over the brow of the rise, the road could be seen stretching away into the distance, running almost straight for several miles, still with no vehicles in sight. How long would our luck hold like this? And how long should we continue flying in this direction? For some reason, I was convinced we were heading north but still dare not take my eyes off the road long enough to look at either map or compass to verify that. After some minutes of this, the road curved through ninety degrees to the right, following a creek on our left, and then gradually swung back to the left again, over a distance of about three miles [Fig. 64]. And here we saw something else – way off in the distance was the unmistakable outline of a large tanker, driving towards us!

Now what? I have often mused over what that driver must have thought when he finally realised that there was an aircraft flying towards him, one foot up, in the middle of his road, and showing no inclination to climb or turn away. He did what any sane person would do in the circumstances – pulled off to the side of the road and stopped. I wished I could have done the same, but as it was, at the last possible moment, I dodged off to the opposite side, down the incline, past the tanker, and back up over the road, surprised to find at the end of it that we were still flying. I wonder how many free drinks the driver has had on telling his version of it – if any one will believe him!

Several miles further and the road again curved round to the right and kept going. In the middle of the bend a dirt road branched off to the left and I followed it, reasoning that as I could not land on the road, and it was not giving any extra lift, we might as well head back west. In any case, the ground between the two roads seemed to be dropping lower so I abandoned the dirt road for the lower ground.

Now we were heading towards another river and there were other dry creek beds running towards it. Approaching the river we dropped down over a five-foot-high bank while that on the far side looked to be about four feet high, a veritable vertical cliff face! Swinging left to follow the wide, flat, rocky bed of the river, mostly high and dry above a central channel of water, we saw ahead several islands covered with greenery and low bushes blocking the way *[Fig. 65]*. At which point, the far bank looked low enough to climb, and gingerly raising the nose resulted in a short-lived zoom that took us over it. Although, so far, the Champ still refused to stay up out of ground effect, it no longer felt as if balanced on a knife edge and the gap between wheels and ground now seemed more like two feet. Such luxury!

Ahead was another bank, but this time, as we soared up over it, something else came into view. There was a cluster of farm buildings and some sort of cultivation ahead with a man driving a tractor in a field. Perhaps there would be one of those large irrigated circles of wheat that all the farms we had seen to date went in for?

Trying again and again to coax the Champ into a climb finally worked, and we gained about twenty feet before having to lower the nose. Repeating the exercise several times as we approached the farm gained us about fifty feet. And there was the great golden yellow expanse we were looking for. How I blessed that farmer for his industry here in the desert, miles from anywhere. There was a satisfying bump as we crossed the circular field of wheat, which could only be a thermal, a giant bubble of warm air rising.

The Champ quickly gained tens of feet all on its own, enough to encourage me to use the ailerons for the first time since take-off to make a tight circle. We still flew out over the edge of the disc, but now a hundred feet higher, enough to risk making a tight turn to get back over it. Again, a satisfying, telltale bump as we crossed the edge, this time aiming at the rim of the disc, in order to circle within it. At last I was able to look at my watch, hung up next to the compass, for the first time since leaving Webster – we had been flying in ground effect for 26 minutes. They must rank as the longest and most worrying 26 minutes of my life!

We were flying again! Round and round over that magic field of wheat, sometimes bumping out of the thermal and having to seek it out again in order to keep climbing. Gradually, we worked up to about 750 ft, then temporarily lost the thermal and started to sink again. Frantic searching and another satisfying bump took us back within it and this way we progressed up to 1,300 ft. The next time we lost the thermal, the Champ maintained height and it was time to move on!

But where? We were totally lost. Still under the firm impression that we had been flying north or north-west for nearly half an hour, I felt it was pointless looking at the narrow strip on my Oregon Trail roller map. Roughly north of us lay a shimmering expanse of water, and a long, straight road ran roughly south-east past the farm. George looked in vain for some recognisable feature on the Sectional chart, unfortunately looking north of Webster at my suggestion. Webster being on the edge of the chart meant that he had turned the map over, so losing the very features which would have shown us where we were.

Used by now to seeing large expanses of water that were not shown on our air charts, we accepted the fact that we could not locate the large lake to the north. Maybe we had circled round and the river was the Big Sandy and the lake the Big Sandy Reservoir, though that did not really ring true. Starting on this comparatively short leg with a little less than a full tank, we had flown for nearly half an hour, probably in the wrong direction, and spent a lot of time gaining height. It was imperative to be heading towards an airfield and not milling about over the desert!

Turning south-west over a junction in the road that ran past the farm, we followed another road which steadily deteriorated into a track leading seemingly nowhere. Still slowly climbing, with one or two anxious moments in which the Champ started to lose height again, we eventually got up to about 2,000 ft a.g.l. at which level there were no further worries about maintaining height. After what seemed a lifetime flying over almost totally featureless desert, we could see two separate sets of chimney stacks in the distance, one straight ahead, the other to the south.

Looking at the chart, we could have been anywhere, but the best bet seemed to be to fly due south until we came across our old friend Interstate I-80, which ran from Rock Springs past Fort Bridger. Providing we had not gone too far west we would then only need to turn right and it would lead us in. If we could at least reach that wide dual carriageway before running out of fuel it would give a better chance of making an emergency landing!

Turning towards the southerly stacks we soon came across a railway leading south-easterly towards another distant complex of buildings. There was also a junction of two rivers, a main road and another railway. If we failed to identify that lot, we might as well give up now!

It suddenly became clear, as we circled over the scattered sprawl of industrial buildings, mobile homes and empty plots, that this was the small town of Granger, and we were miraculously back over the Trail! Rolling my chart on to the new position, we sought, found and photographed the Ham's Fork Crossing *[Fig. 66]* and the confluence of Ham's Fork and Black's Fork of the Green River. Things were back to normal again!

Approaching Granger, we had flown over the site of the Fur Trappers' Mountain Rendezvous of 1834, on slightly rising ground above Ham's Fork valley. There was nothing notable about the location, other than that the flat, marshy ground through which both rivers meandered was green in comparison with the sandy, arid plain over which we had been flying.

Nearing Church Butte, the ground below was patterned by a herring-bone labyrinth of serpentine creeks and streams, dark green against the sage and sand desert. Further out, the sage was thicker, so that great areas were a dull, uniform, light sage green, and over all, the scattered dark shadows of late-afternoon cu-nimbus clouds superimposed their own moving, disruptive display. Quite attractive in a wild sort of way, viewed from above, though it must have been anything but, at ground level and 2 mph, when the emigrants passed this way!

The Trail trace was clearly marked by its own narrow green line, angled clear of the worst of the creeks as it swung round the low rocky outcrop of Moss Agate Knoll, south of Granger, and arched back south-west close to Church Butte. This is a high, gaunt, steep rocky ridge, standing dark grey against a bed of light sand, looking more forbidding than any other major landmark along the Trail *[Fig. 67]*.

From Church Butte, the Trail ran along the east bank of Black's Fork, past a small jumble of rocks, yet another of those desert registers, Name Rock. Interstate I-80 swung in from our left and ran alongside the Trail for a short distance, before heading off north of Fort Bridger and the Trail. There was no more to see of the Trail on the run in to the site of old Fort Bridger, and little to see of the latter. We turned over the scattered buildings of the Fort site and headed for the Municipal Airport, three miles to the north, up in the hills above the town.

Circling high over the airport, there was no sign of activity. Wise now to the ways of airport owners in siting their windsocks, we soon spotted one and decided to land on the main runway, which was fairly well into wind. With an airfield elevation of 7,016 ft, and in the still-prevailing heat, experience indicated there would be little hope of correcting an undershoot or of carrying out an overshoot if I didn't judge the rate of descent correctly as we neared the ground. It had to be right first time.

With 5,000 ft of runway, there was not much excuse for not getting it right, and we settled, tail-high, onto the smooth black tarmac, countering the anticipated swing before it developed. With 60 lb of fuel burnt off (plus a pint or two of perspiration from George and myself in that first half hour), the touchdown speed into a wind that was now holding the windsock out straight (perhaps 25 mph) was quite manageable. Time down, 16.40: time in the air, 1 hour 40 minutes, and it seemed like twice that long!

The pumps were deserted as we taxied up and switched off, and both of us sat for a minute or two, feeling pretty relieved at being there, still hardly able to believe that our luck had held out. We filled up, met the airport owner and arranged to hangar the Champ overnight. He showed us proudly round his shiny new hangar, which he explained he had erected himself from a kit of materials! As a flying school operator he used Cessna 172s, the more normal 150s having insufficient performance. We could believe him on that point!

He arranged for his very young helper to give us a lift down to the town, and showed us the complex control sequence for operating the three-section, up-and-over hangar doors if we arrived in the morning before he was about. He advised us to leave before the sun was up, but I hoped to do some filming en route to our next stop, and thought we could make it OK at first light. That of course depended on us meeting up with our ground crew, who possibly might not make it. So we arranged for the young man to look out for us on his way to work in the morning, in case we needed a lift.

The unmade road from the airport, past the local town rubbish tip, was incredibly bumpy. Combined with the seemingly springless state of the ancient pick-up truck and the youthful exuberance of its driver, it gave us an interesting ride. We were thankful enough for the lift not to have minded if it had been an ox-drawn cart!

After booking in at the motel, there was time for a quick look round the grounds of Fort Bridger before the sun set, but of course, nothing was open so we were unable to look inside the buildings. The oldest surviving remnant is a tottering section of dry-stone wall, built by the Mormons after buying the place from Jim Bridger, now shored up and protected from the rain by a roof. Many of the later buildings used by the military have been renovated and are in good shape but, as usual with these ex-trading establishments, they look nothing like the popular conception of a fort.

In the peace and quiet of the motel room, we had another look at the maps to try and fathom out where we had been. The first river we had crossed had to be the Big Sandy, and the road we had been flying over led to the Seedskadee Wildlife Refuge on the Green River. The big river we flew along before seeing the ranch was the Green and we had joined it near the old Lombard Ferry site. In seeking the lowest ground to fly over, we had emulated the wagon trains and to my astonishment had incidentally followed the Oregon Trail almost exactly, despite being totally lost at the time! We had never been more than five miles from the route!

A very weary team arrived after we had returned from the fort and, over dinner, recounted their experiences. They had found Poison Spider Road but, at a crucial point after passing through Emigrant Gap, missed a left turn. Not realising they had missed it until it was too late to turn back, they took every subsequent left turn, but even so, finished up forty miles north of the main road past Independence Rock. For 100 miles, they travelled on dirt roads and saw nothing but desert, occasional deer and a danger sign that said "DO NOT ENTER – RADIO ACTIVE AREA!" Frustrated – yes. Downhearted – no!

When the Whitmans left South Pass on Independence Day in 1836, they headed north-west to the Rendezvous, held that year at Fort

Bonneville, another meagre trading post near the present town of Daniel, Wyoming. From there, having switched from the American Fur Company caravan to a group of Hudson's Bay Company fur traders, they crossed the Wyoming Range Mountains, and rejoined the main route of the Oregon Trail at Smith's Creek on the Bear River. They were there late in July, and Narcissa's diary notes weather conditions similar to ours – very hot and dry.

Meanwhile, we got to bed relatively early after deciding the next day's plans. We had to be at the airfield for first light, so would have breakfast at Soda Springs and take the rest of the day off. A restful day would do all of us good!

Fig. 53. Rock Avenue looking NW. Although damaged by pipeline builders, it stands out clearly in this view; the new road follows the Trail route as it S-bends from upper right, down the ridge.

Fig. 54. Alkali Slough location is marked by the white arrow. The black arrow points to McCleary Reservoir. The pipeline lies almost exactly over the Trail route. Viewed looking SW. Fish Creek runs parallel to the Trail at left, joining Horse Creek at top.

Fig. 55. Independence Rock, looking NE, towards Lake Piaya. The Oregon Trail lies under the road running diagonally from top RH, and the Sweetwater River meanders down from the same corner to pass this side of the Rock. Highway 220 is at extreme top left.

Fig. 56. Devil's Gate looking NE, with the Sweetwater just visible from top centre right, wandering through the gorge at the foot of the 370 ft high, near-vertical face. One branch of the Trail skirted round to the right from in front of the buildings seen at top right.

Fig. 57. The last two crossings of the Sweetwater at 3-Crossings, looking NW. The lower dotted line is to the right of the Trail ruts on the north bank. The middle crossing (R.-L.) is marked by the R. arrow, which also points to a beaver dam (a tiny white spot), and the left arrow to the last crossing (L.-R.). The Trail route continues west, marked by the adjacent upper dotted line.

Fig. 58. Approaching Jeffrey City and the old uranium mines, looking due north. The dotted line is just above the Deep Sand Route (the tracks are clearly visible on the original photo). The unbroken line marks Highway 287, and the arrow points to the airstrip, seen looking straight up the dirt runway.

Fig. 59. Ice Slough, where it is crossed by Highway 287 some ten miles west of Jeffrey City WY, looking south-west. The Trail route came in from the lower left, crossing diagonally to upper right. Here, even in the height of summer in Trail days, pure, clear ice could be found by digging a foot or so down through the tundra.

Fig. 60. Strawberry Creek looking SW. The Creek is on the north side of the 7,925 ft high Rocky Ridge, and the Trail lies under the white dirt road paralleling the creek. The road makes a lazy S-curve before crossing Rock Creek at the top right corner.

Fig. 61. Willie's Handcart Company Memorial, 100 yds south of the bridge over Rock Creek, marks 'Journey's End' for most of the Company, who died here in the early snows of 1856. On the horizon is Granite Peak of the Wind River Range – the Rockies!

Fig. 62. Miller Grave site on Slaughterhouse Gulch, looking WSW towards South Pass. Burnt Ranch off to the left and the Lander Road just below the dotted line. The Sweetwater runs across the top.

Fig. 63. Our flight was to celebrate the sesquicentennial of the Whitman's journey in 1836, as marked here at South Pass.

Fig. 64. The Farson Road (just above the white line marker) runs straight and flat if slightly downhill, across the Big Bend of the Big Sandy river, towards Big Timber Station site (marked by the arrow). Here the Champ was flying in ground effect at a height of 18 inches! The Oregon Trail runs to Big Timber just beyond the Farson Road.

Fig. 65. The Green River looking WNW, with Horse Shoe Bend at left top. The Lombard Ferry site, and the irrigated disc of crops which gave us the thermals that enabled us to climb to cooler air, are just off the bottom of the picture, while the Kenney Cutoff Trail (seen as a thin white line) follows the right bank above the loops in the river.

Fig. 66. Hams Fork Crossing at Granger WY looking WSW. The Union Pacific Railroad to Salt Lake runs across top right, and helped us pinpoint our location after our low-level escapade.

Fig. 67. A deeply-rutted section of the Trail runs from bottom left to coincide with the highway at Church Butte, looking SW. Note the misleading sections of buried pipeline visible here, which if not so straight and regular could easily be mistaken for Trail traces.

CHAPTER 12
DAY 5:
TO SODA SPRINGS

Up at 05.00 and groping around in the pre-dawn half light, we made it up the winding dirt track to the airport by six o'clock. All was still and quiet, the wind obviously waiting for the sun to get up before it stirred itself. Here there was no equivalent of the dawn chorus of birdsong that we would have heard at home, but to make up for that there was a breathless quality in the crisp, cool air. It was as if time and the world were poised, waiting on tiptoe for the first shafts of sunlight to slant over the eastern hills. We even found ourselves talking in muted tones, as if we had no right to disturb the silence.

There was no sign of the owner being up and about, so we carefully opened the complex, motorised hanger doors, bearing in mind the warning that we could wreck the whole lot if we got it wrong! It took us a good half hour to get the aircraft out, close the doors and load everything on board. Jean and Sonia had come with us in order to take the car back, and they waited to see us away.

The sun had sneaked up while we were busy, so that all about us was either bathed in its brittle golden light or lingering in exaggeratedly long, dark shadows. There was the promise of another glorious day with not a cloud in the sky, and a gentle breeze was shaking the windsock into wakefulness. As usual, the engine purred into life at the second swing, its quiet, even beat amplified and sent barking back from the hangar walls. The quiet was finally destroyed when we ran up to full power, the tranquillity gone, and the day begun.

We took off on the main runway, the Champ running true on the smooth black surface. Climb was positive but slow and by the time we had completed a wide circuit to wave goodbye to the girls, we had only gained 300 ft. Even that seemed like a blessing compared with our experiences of the previous day! Circling back over Fort Bridger we took some pictures in the early morning light, every visible building having a golden, east-facing wall, and every black shadow shaping a hundred feet or more along the ground.

From Fort Bridger, our route headed north, back past the airport, now three miles to the right. Ahead, we were faced with a veritable wilderness in which there were, again, large areas without roads, railways, rivers or lakes from which to check position. So we used the leg from Fort Bridger past the airport to establish the compass error and confirmed that here the variation just cancelled out the deviation, the compass actually reading true when we were flying north!

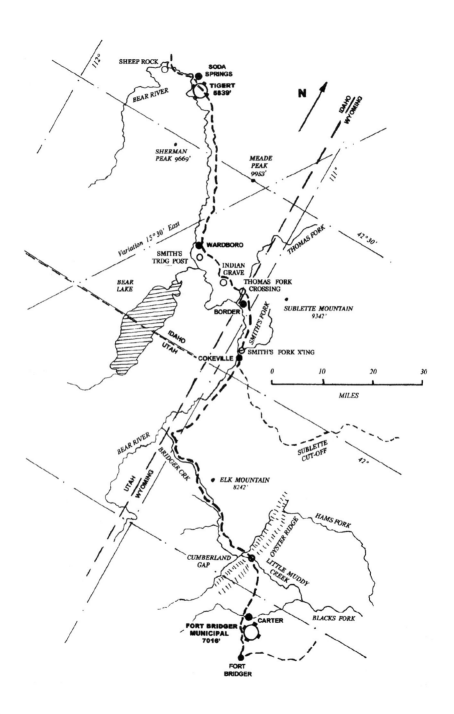

There was a tangle of farm tracks below as we approached the Union Pacific Railroad that ran from beyond Granger to Salt Lake City; this was the same line that had helped locate our position the day before. According to my chart we should expect to see a small huddle of buildings at Carter, a mile and a half to the east of where the Trail crossed the lines. Up-sun, peering into the golden glare, we could see nothing. Eventually, by circling, we could just make out a few buildings, and used those to estimate the position to cross the railroad.

From there, rutted tracks ran more or less where we expected them to, heading north, so we followed them for some eight miles to Little Muddy Creek, where they turned west along the south bank. And then we came to one of the most magnificent sights we had seen – the die-straight spine of Oyster Ridge, running north as far into the distance as we could see.

What made it look so fantastic was the startling contrast between the brilliantly lit eastern slopes and the long, black shadows thrown far over the flat ground to the west [Fig. 68]. Adding to the effect were several minor ridges running in parallel in front of the main one. It is doubtful if the effect could be so dramatic at any other time except sunset, when the lighting would be reversed. It would certainly not be apparent in driving along US Highway 189 which runs along the western foot of the ridge.

Little Muddy Creek – and the Trail – ran straight through a very convenient break in the ridge known as Cumberland Gap (no connection with the well-known, similarly named counterpart in the East, through the Appalachians). Beyond the Gap we came across a reservoir that was marked on none of our maps, which lent a degree of confusion to the picture for a while, until we decided to ignore it (if in doubt, leave it out!). The Trail followed the creek, on and off, for the next fifteen miles, to the head of the valley, before crossing a ridge of over 7,500 ft altitude to pick up Bridger Creek.

This is a most beautiful stretch of country with its grassy slopes, parkland valleys and high hills, so enhanced on this occasion by the early morning sun. We circled to film the scenery and the view up-sun behind us was quite breathtaking. A great area of low-lying mist, which seemed to have formed between us and Oyster Ridge after we had passed over, caught the early sun's rays, and became a vast silver lake. Out of this lake the blue-grey, shadowy shapes of ridges and hills rose in succession, beyond and beyond, until lost in the distance. Such compensation for our early start!

Below us, rutted tracks ran both by the sides of streams and along the crests of ridges. It was not easy to determine which would have been easier to follow in a wagon: the ridge-top tracks with their steep climbs and descents to and from the top, or the twisting trails hopping over creeks joining the main streams. Perhaps in dry weather, the lower trails would have been best, with their easy access to water for the animals, but in wet seasons, the high roads may have been easier. Apart from a corral noted on the air chart, we saw little evidence of farming or ranching in the area, so there was a good chance that the tracks were all made or used at the time the Trail went through.

The hills are part of the Bear River Divide; on our right was Elk Mountain, whose foothills marked the highest point of the Trail. Ahead, the Trail circled 180 deg round Sillam Ridge, following Bridger Creek as it descended into Bear River Valley. Along one stretch of the creek, Trail ruts appeared on the 'wrong' side compared with what was shown on the maps; in fact it looked unlikely that they could have been located on the 'right' side because of the slopes down to the creek!

Now the Trail ran north along the Bear River, across Smith's Fork, where the Whitmans, descending from their crossing of the Wyoming Range mountains, rejoined the Oregon Trail, near present-day Cokeville. Ahead rose the tree-clad slopes of 9,342 ft-high Sublette Mountain, in front of which the river, road, railroad and Trail swung west to cross the border into Idaho at Border Junction. Here the Trail left the valley after crossing Thomas' Fork, climbing the 300 ft-high ridge near Border Summit to avoid looping seven extra miles along the Bear River. There were rut swales parallelling the new highway, but the low eastern light was not best angled to show them up.

As the main highway descended back towards the Bear River, it swung round the base of a high mound, at the foot of which is marked on the map "Indian Grave." Though we could see no evidence of any sort of grave marker, there were ruts both sides of the highway, none being marked on the map at this point. The brilliant sunlight and long dark shadows made this ridge, and the pass through it, another unforgettable sight *[Fig. 69]*.

Rejoining the Bear valley again at Wardboro, we had another 30 miles to fly along the river to take us to our destination at Soda Springs, with no Trail landmarks to watch for. We saw no sign of ruts, either marked or unmarked, along this section. The mountains rose more steeply on either side of the valley, Meade Peak at 9,953 ft on our right, and Sherman Peak at 9,669 ft on our left. The valley was grass-green but the hill slopes were the usual hay brown.

The wind had risen as the morning wore on, and now blew at 45 deg to the runway at Soda Springs Tigert Airport. The into-wind runway seemed to have a slight downhill slope, which did not help in slowing us down. Tigert is still high, at 5,839 ft, and the temperature was rising rapidly, and we knew all about it as we touched down. Despite a tail-high landing, the Champ, stalling on at about 70 mph, immediately careered off to the right and down among a weed-strewn jumble of sand, stones and small rocks. Miraculously, with left brake full on and the rudder hard over to the left, she came back onto the runway and behaved herself from there on, as if nothing had happened!

On inspection afterwards, nothing seemed to have been damaged, the only evidence of the mad plunge into the rough being a small bunch of purple flowers trapped between the brake lever and backplate of the right wheel; these I later thoughtfully presented to my wife. As on several other occasions when the Champ had displayed my deficiencies for all the world to see, the world had not been looking. In fact, at that time, 8.40, the world might still have been asleep.

We soon found a charming young lady, with several children and a bouncing young puppy, who lived in a mobile home on the airfield. She looked after things during the day while her husband was away on other municipal work. We saw to our delight that there was a fuel pump marked 80-octane, but no way could we make her believe that it was the right fuel for the Champ. She said she had been instructed not to let anyone have it without some sort of certificate to say that it was OK to use it for the aircraft. Unbelievable!

Eventually, we got it sorted out after she had rung the fuel company rep. Apparently it was Mogas, not 80-octane, and she was unaware of the difference. Rather than press it any further, we decided to fill up with fuel from a local filling station, which was considerably cheaper, needed no certificate and worked just as well! It was something to do with avoiding liability for serving the wrong type of fuel, as Mogas is reckoned to have such a high volatility as to cause vapour locks in the fuel lines. The Champ had not heard about that, and never suffered from vapour locks, even in the hottest temperatures, no matter how long the fuel had stood soaking up the heat!

We were out of luck for a courtesy car – there was one but it had a flat tyre (tire) and no replacement. The woman offered us a lift when she went shopping later, but it was such a beautiful morning that we were happy to walk the half-mile into town. We soon tracked down a restaurant/motel and enjoyed a leisurely breakfast at around ten o'clock, returning to our room to have a snooze until the others found us.

It was around 3.00 pm that they put in an appearance, and for the first time since leaving Philadelphia, we had an opportunity to go sightseeing together. They had also had an easy day, visiting the old fort site before leaving. It was enjoyable walking round the town, even though Soda Springs had a slightly sad air about it. Typical of many small, out-of-the-way towns in the west, it had been hard hit by a decline in local industry and farming. Many of the younger people had moved on, and half of the shops were closed or closing.

Despite indifferent signposting we found Hooper's Spring, the one remaining major spring that can be seen, on the northern outskirts, now sheltering under a broad canopy in an attractive little municipal park.

The authorities have done a very good job of preserving and making available to the public a most important part of local history. But one felt they could have done more to help encourage visitors to what could be a major tourist attraction.

A stopover at the springs was one of the highlights of the Trail days, the iron-laden, effervescent water, when sugar was added, making a pleasant forerunner of 'pop.' We tried the water and found it quite pleasant, even without sugar. While we there, an American couple arrived, the lady's appearance taking us straight back to the 19th century – blonde hair piled high, black choker, black off-the-shoulder blouse, black and red-patterned, calf-length, flared skirt and high, buttoned, black ankle boots. It all went together very well!

Of the hundred or more springs originally to be found in this area, Steamboat Spring was perhaps the most famous, puffing like a steam engine and sending up a four-foot-high spout of water every ten seconds or so. Alas, this is now under the waters of Soda Point Reservoir, as are most of the others. The authorities in the town have done their best to replace it, with a man-made and controlled geyser that spouts every hour – when the wind is in the right direction. Needless to say, having waited nearly half an hour, the wind swung into the wrong quarter and the geyser merely bubbled. The reason for taking account of the wind direction was that the sulphurous water killed off any grass and other vegetation on which it fell!

An extra treat that evening was a 45-mile jaunt out to the small neighbouring town of Preston to see a rodeo. This was obviously a star attraction for families from miles around, as it was well-crowded, with a small fairground thrown in for good measure. There was a beautiful red sunset that evening, the air was warm and the atmosphere a happy one with everyone obviously enjoying themselves. We got back to the motel at around midnight, but the next day would be another short one, distance-wise.

We finally crossed the Whitmans' path both in location and calendar time, they having passed through Soda Springs exactly 150 years earlier, to the day! They too had found the weather very hot, and Marcus and Narcissa had ridden ten miles off their route in order to visit the springs together. Marcus was in need of some diversion, having worked abnormally hard to keep his wagon going in the face of opposition from other members of the party, who viewed it as a needless hindrance to their progress.

It had tipped over twice on the steep mountain sides, got stuck in a creek and finally broke the front axle cross-tree, probably when going over Border Summit (though it was not named as such at that time). Despite being sick and suffering from rheumatism as a result of spending so much time in the water when crossing rivers and creeks, Whitman converted the wagon to a two-wheeled cart with the front wheels lashed to it.

Narcissa was having her share of troubles at this time, noting in her diary entry for July 31st: "Nearly sick of excessive fatigue yesterday." She did not mention that she would have been about six weeks pregnant! Not exactly the best basis for another month of travelling, mostly riding sidesaddle, over the roughest country imaginable in the extreme heat of summer.

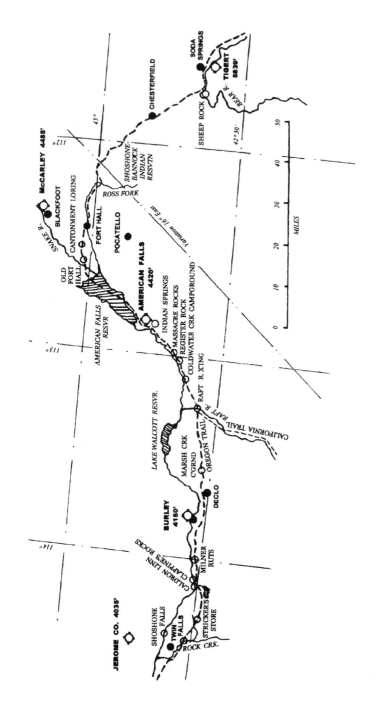

144

CHAPTER 13

DAY 6:
TO JEROME

We had two legs to fly this day, so decided not to miss breakfast. Consequently, though we were up at 05.30, it was nearly 07.00 before we got out to the airport, Jean and Renie coming out with us to take the car back.

It seemed a good idea to get them to shoot some ciné film of our start-up and taxy, and of all occasions to do so, the Champ decided for the first time to act like a temperamental prima donna. The engine refused to start and needed a couple of dozen swings to get it going! But it then ran up to full power with no further problem. Just to let us know who was boss!

We were not sure that Jean thought the filming such a good idea – shots of us taxying out necessitated her running to catch us at the end of the runway, after shooting, so that we could take the camera with us!

Conditions were much the same as they had been the day before, cool, clear, calm and cloudless. The sun had been up for an hour, but was still casting long dark shadows. We decided to take off up the slope rather than down towards the town, the breeze being fairly neutral. It was just as well that we headed away from the town as the Champ struggled slowly for height, taking ages to gain enough to clear power lines and trees about half a mile beyond the end of the runway. Renie said afterwards that it didn't look to them as if we would!

Circling back over the airport, we had climbed to perhaps 400 ft as we flew west along the shore of Soda Point Reservoir. The still, barely rippled surface of the waters showed no tell-tale disturbance to indicate that the 40 ft deep Steamboat Spring was blowing, which it does roughly every ten seconds. We must have passed over just before another puff was due; at the speed we were flying we would cover roughly 1,000 ft in the ten seconds, so could easily have missed one.

On our left was a 1,400 ft-high wooded ridge, the northern end of the mighty Wasatch Range of mountains which, at their highest point, tower 6,000 ft above Salt Lake City, more than a hundred miles to the south. At the western end of the reservoir, the Bear River does a U-turn south, round Sheep Rock (also known as Soda Point) which marks the end of the ridge. Nearby is thought to be the site of another Indian massacre on the banks of the Bear.

More importantly, this is where the Hudspeth Cut-off to California starts. In the 1849 Gold Rush, time was of the essence. Hudspeth, by heading due west through the Bannock Mountains, saved a great 40-mile northward loop to Fort Hall, rejoining the California Trail along the Raft

River, 90 miles west. Just after the Hudspeth route left the main trail, where the latter swung north west, it passed the curious Alexander Crater. This is a single, small, cinder cone, perhaps 50 ft high, marking some ancient volcanic activity; the surrounding ploughed fields, from which it protrudes like an angry black boil, show the same dark slate grey, lava-based soil.

After circling the Crater, we followed the Trail north-west along a valley between the Portneuf Range and the Blackfoot Mountains, finding faint evidence of ruts at the foot of the Soda Springs Hills as we left. There were more ruts, not marked, on the approach to Chesterfield, near the Portneuf Reservoir. And from here, we flew out over the Fort Hall Indian Reservation, leaving behind the familiar grid pattern of roads.

Fortunately for our Trail-following ambitions, we almost immediately picked out clear ruts showing the route of the Trail – just as well, as there was little else to fix our position! These, the best of any we had seen, led us fifteen miles unerringly through the bare brown hills, swinging gradually round to head due west on the approach to old Fort Hall site. Here, perhaps more than in any other area we flew over, we came closest to viewing the country as it would have looked in emigrant days, with no roads or criss-crossing telegraph and power lines, no ploughed-over ground or herds of white-faced brown cattle, and no trees! Just a pair of deep ruts winding lonely round the desolate contours, progressing ever westward.

Just before we left the Reservation, we came across a stretch of really magnificent, deep, grassed-over ruts, sweeping round the foothills near a puny little stream, Ross Fork. A branch line of the Union Pacific Railroad, descending from mine workings in the mountains, together with a country road, wound alongside the stream, but the Trail looped south of them all, steering clear of marshy-looking ground in between [Fig. 70].

Here was another variance of the Trail ruts with the route shown on the maps. According to the latter, the Trail lay on the right of the railroad whereas we saw them clearly on the left. What was more, it looked as if the ground contours would have been more difficult on the right side of the tracks, which seemed to corroborate our findings.

All too soon, we were nearing signs of civilisation again as we crossed a major north-south, dual-carriageway trunk road, Interstate 15, followed by a railroad and highway at the town of Fort Hall. The Trail followed a minor east-west road at the outskirts [Fig. 71], heading into a 12-mile-long by 5-mile-wide wedge of swampland between the Snake River and one of its tributaries, Clear Creek. The air chart showed the ground between the two as entirely waterlogged, but in fact there were obvious areas of dry ground with snaking, looping watercourses intertwining across the whole area. Having read several accounts of the difficulty experienced by previous searchers for the site, I for one hardly thought we would be lucky enough to find it.

We were following a road to start with, but expected to have to look for rutted tracks to lead us to the site, the map showing the road bending away from the site when about two miles distant. Instead, the newly-gravelled road kept going almost to the point where the site was thought to be [Fig. 72]. It ended in a turning circle close to the main course of the Snake, with a footpath leading 100 yards west along the bank. We circled over the end of the road, excitement now at fever pitch to have found the site.

There were numerous clumps of small willows and bushes and we just could not see whether these concealed the small stone monument marking the site, which was erected in 1916. As far as we could tell, the new road coincided with the Trail all the way from where it left the old road. There seemed little doubt that this was the site of the old Fort (confirmed on a later visit by car, in 1988, with an Indian guide from the Agency, when we viewed and photographed the marker [Fig. 73]).

A short distance ahead the Snake River, and the Trail with it, was swallowed by the waters of the American Falls Reservoir, the green swampland just melting into the blue. For the next ten miles, any Trail ruts would be invisible to our eyes, as would the site of the nearby Adobes Stage Station. This was built using material from the Fort after the latter was abandoned in 1855, and the ruins were reputedly still visible after the reservoir flooded them.

It seems that even old Ezra Meeker, a young Trail traveller in 1852, who later went round the Trail marking important landmarks, mistook the Adobes for the Fort site when he erected a marker there in 1906. It was not until ten years later that he changed his mind, fortunately for posterity, discovering the site where, fortuitously, it can now still be reached above the flood level!

Perhaps old Nathanial Wyeth knew a little more than he is generally credited with in choosing the site of his Fort Hall trading post when he built it in 1834. How much longer the site will survive is questionable, as it was originally reportedly half a mile from the Snake; now it is almost on the banks of the river, which changes its course with every major flood.

Between Fort Hall and the confluence of the Snake and Portneuf Rivers was an area dreaded by travellers. Here they found a dangerous marshland, infested with clouds of mosquitoes, horse-fly, deer-fly, hornets and the rest, which allowed no respite from their biting and stinging for human and animal alike. Diary entries mentioned swarms so thick as to be scarcely able to see, with cattle being driven nearly mad and bolting.

Here, Eliza Spalding, with the Whitman party in 1836, was thrown from her horse when it stepped on a hornets' nest, and dragged across the ground as it bolted with her foot caught in the stirrup. Amazingly, she quickly recovered and continued on horseback with the main party! Riding sidesaddle in such country it was amazing that more such accidents did not happen to the two women in the party!

We flew down the southern shore of the reservoir to the American Falls Airport, the intense blue of the wide waters reflecting the clear blue sky above. The early morning sun lit the golden wheat fields and picked out in deep shadow the low cliffs along the shore. The eastern face of any small, isolated, light-coloured building shone brightly in the sun – visible for perhaps thirty miles – while occasional vehicles moving along the roads glittered and flashed like jewels. Just as well that we were flying west with the sun behind us!

There was little activity on the ground at the airport as we flew round, engaged in the usual search for a windsock. There was a single, 4,000 ft long runway, parallel with Interstate 86, and a little cluster of buildings halfway along, one of the hangars sporting a limp windsock. A crop-duster landed as we circled so we followed him in. George picked this occasion to film the landing, aiming the ciné-camera over my shoulder. If ever there was a recipe for a disastrous arrival, this was it, but fortunately the Champ behaved herself and we made a smooth and straight touchdown.

It was 9 o'clock as we taxied up to the pumps and switched off. Following correspondence with the airport manager, I was expecting to find someone about, but the place was not merely deserted, it had a 'dead' look about it! For a municipal airport, open from 8.00 am to 5.00 pm, to have no one in sight at this time suggested that something was sadly amiss. There were no cars around and the Flight Office was empty. We needed fuel, but with no one to operate the pumps they might as well not have been there.

Several houses alongside the airport buildings at first appeared deserted but eventually a woman appeared in one of the gardens to water the plants. She knew very little about what was happening, but commented that the place seemed to have been shut down, there having been no activity in recent times.

We returned to the Flight Office to see if there might be a telephone, and found the office open. Here was immediate confirmation of what had been suggested: the previous occupants had pulled out, leaving a few odd documents and old magazines about, the usual clutter of someone moving out. There were the expected charts on the walls, some old notices of nearby Flying Meetings etc., but most thought-provoking was a chart showing how to work out equivalent (Density) altitudes for given temperatures and airfield (Pressure) altitudes. As the air temperature

148

rises, its pressure drops, so that an aircraft acts as if it were operating at a higher altitude, the thinner air requiring the aircraft to fly faster to provide sufficient lift to remain airborne.

Perhaps, had we seen such a chart before we took off at Farson, we would not have done so – working out the density altitude for Farson at 100 deg (which was the temperature given in the weather reports that night), gave a figure of over 10,000 ft. No self-respecting 65 hp Champ could be expected to take off, at full load plus, at that altitude!

A new arrival on the scene parked his car and we thought that perhaps he was something to do with the airport. Alas no, he was just out for a drive, but he did know that the local authorities had pulled out of the airport a few weeks earlier!

This was evidence of the growing concern by airport owners over the need to cover themselves with enormous indemnity insurance against third party claims from users. Indemnity mania was growing in the States, as we had seen ourselves in trying to satisfy our sponsor's fears; even leading aircraft manufacturers such as Piper and Cessna had been frightened into total withdrawal from the light aircraft market in view of some of the illogical and stupid claims awarded against them by the American courts. As is so often the case, the greed of a tiny minority can ruin an idyllic existence for a vast majority!

Meanwhile, we were stuck for fuel. Another crop-duster had taken off, and there appeared to be some life at the western end of the runway, on the opposite side. We started up and taxied down there, and found an FBO (Fixed Base Operator – a company offering flying services from their own or a public airport) operating cropdusters as well as school and charter operations. The pleasant and helpful young blonde in the office produced someone who would supply us with the 80-octane fuel we needed, found us some very welcome coffee and agreed to us using the phone before we left, in order to tell Jerome, our next stop, that we were coming.

Unfortunately, we seemed to have acquired a jinx – not only had the municipal airport closed down just before we arrived, but now the man who had the key to the fuel supply was out with the crop-dusting ground crew. When he returned, he insisted on starting up the fuel tanker and driving it the few yards to where the Champ was parked, rather than have us wheel the Champ to the tanker in the by-now very warm sun. The tanker had other ideas, and refused to start until we feared that it would run its battery down.

When, eventually, it was positioned alongside the Champ, our problems seemed over as petrol gurgled into the tank. But then the sight glass bubbled and went empty, and the supply of fuel dried up after less than a gallon had registered!

"No problem!" said our enthusiastic helper. "I can refill the tanker from the fixed pumps."

There seemed to be some obscure but definite reason why the tanker could be refilled from the pumps but the Champ not, so we shrugged our shoulders and smiled hopefully.

With the tanker positioned near the pumps, fuel was soon flowing into its tanks. But the word must have got around as, once more, the gurgling stopped almost as soon as it started. After a series of assaults on a filter assembly, reputed to have caused this sort of problem before, produced no tangible results, our man went off, looking for the resident expert who would quickly deal with this if only he could be found.

He was soon run to earth in the depths of the workshop, and came out and dismantled the filter assembly. Despite which, when assembled, it still refused to function. In the end, we did what we should have done at the first sign of failure – we filled up with Mogas – but not until after another search was required to produce the keeper of the appropriate key! In all fairness it has to be said that they were not geared up for a public service, this being a new imposition after the Municipal authorities pulled out!

At last, and with a mixed quantity of petrol in the tank, we phoned Jerome and were off after almost two hours on the ground. But now the wind had got up and the temperature had soared.

The wind direction and strength forced us to take off towards the town. The temperature decreed that, even from American Falls' comparatively low altitude of 4,420 ft, climb rate was miserably low. This caused some anxious moments aboard as we steered round the outskirts of the town, with its fearsome mish-mash of overhead lines and cables, out over the lake, before gaining sufficient height to circle back over the airfield and head west.

From the dam at the western end of the reservoir, the Trail route ran along the south bank of the Snake, and did so for the next 150 miles, with occasional inland diversions along rivers and creeks that dropped into the river gorge. At first, the river ran between cliff-like banks, some 40 ft below ground level, but later it was to drop into a wide gorge more than ten times that depth.

Our first target was to locate the site of Indian Springs, but not knowing what to look for, we were fooled into thinking it was surrounded by a group of trees. The picture we took of this clump of trees later revealed that it was several hundred yards west of where the spring site should be. What sometimes confused us was when major roadworks had changed the pattern of roads on our charts. The other factor was that State highways were sometimes difficult to distinguish from private ranch roads, etc.

But there was no mistaking the next site, of Massacre Rocks, where there is a fine National Parks Interpretive Centre *[Fig. 74]*. Near here, in August 1862, a train of eleven wagons was attacked and destroyed by Snake Indians, losing three men, with a man and a woman wounded and all the livestock stolen. Another wagon train was attacked and successfully made a run for Massacre Rocks, a defensible position. Two more trains had joined them that night, bringing in the wagons and survivors of the first train, and yet another train caught them up next morning.

The five wagon trains now mustered a force of thirty men to try and retrieve the live stock. They caught and unsuccessfully attacked the Indians, losing at least two more men. Apparently six men were buried here and several more were missing, while the woman died two days later. Despite this being one of the few well-documented "massacres," there remains confusion over exactly how many lives were lost here.

A little way along the road was another Register Rock, this time a great boulder, covered with now barely legible names and protected by a roof and a wire fence. Here also is one of those well-laid out rest centres that the Americans make such a good job of, with toilets ('bathrooms' in the local idiom, with no baths!) and picnic tables – a little green oasis amongst the barren brown hills, where our ground crew enjoyed a picnic meal.

The Snake was now broad and beautifully blue, looking more like a winding lake than a river as we came upon Tule Island *[Fig. 75]*. A few miles beyond the island, the Trail headed inland, to cross the Raft River, four miles above where it emptied into the Snake. This detour was necessary as the Raft plunged down to the Snake through a deep gorge, and the crossing point was the first upstream at which it was possible for wagons to be taken up the steep west bank.

At this point, the Oregon-bound emigrants continued west and those for California struck off south *[Fig. 76]*. What scenes of heartbreak must have been witnessed here as friends and families who had endured together the worst imaginable hardships and dangers split up, knowing they were unlikely ever to meet again.

When visiting the site by road the previous year I had seen no evidence of the trails when viewing it from the east, and really expected nothing more on this occasion. So it was a great thrill to find that clear ruts could be seen leading off in both directions – exactly as shown in Franzwa's maps. What was more, the Oregon Trail ruts continued unerringly west across the scrub desert *[Fig. 77]*; as on a number of earlier occasions, they came to our rescue in an area completely devoid of the usual features by which an aviator would fix his position!

After nine miles the ruts petered out just before crossing the big Interstate I-80N Highway. They resumed briefly as we approached the old Marsh Creek camp-ground site, with rather more evidence visible than shown on the maps, extending almost into the small community of Declo. The winding course of Marsh Creek was well marked by green vegetation as it meandered into the Snake, which we soon rejoined at Milner Lake. Here the waters of the Snake are backed up twenty miles above the Milner Dam, filling the gorge so that the lake looks more like a very wide river than a reservoir!

A great irrigated bite out of the desert shows up as a green and gold chequer-board, cultivated and well-settled all the way along the Snake Gorge into Twin Falls. Now we were back to the old, familiar, one-mile grid pattern of roads surrounding the busy little town of Burley and could expect to see nothing more of the Trail until past Twin Falls, other than a short stretch of ruts near the Milner Dam.

The Milner ruts were disappointing after what we had seen before Marsh Creek, and we had to look hard to spot the straight section through the uncultivated ground left between the lake and the Union Pacific Railroad. Below the dam, the once-mighty Snake was reduced to a pathetic stream trickling along the bottom of the deep gorge, the waters instead channelled away in the blue irrigation canals radiating out from the lake.

When Bill Kee had taken us to visit the dam some years earlier, Renie and I had watched fascinated as a squadron of common terns demonstrated their fish-catching skills, with their folded-winged dives into the little pool below the dam. Now as we flew over, I drew quiet satisfaction in knowing what the little white specks circling the pool were, and that they were almost certainly descendants of those we had seen before!

On that visit with Bill, I had wanted to visit the sites of Clappine's Rocks and Caldron Linn, five or six miles below the dam. Bill, a near-lifelong resident of the area, had thought that it was not possible to get to them by road, but I had not forgotten them. On another occasion I had actually reached the south rim of the gorge to look down-river at Caldron Linn, but so far upstream as to gain little idea of what it looked like. Now, at last, there should be nothing to stop us seeing both sites.

Explorer William Price Hunt, leading John Jacob Astor's expedition to the Pacific, had in 1811 been cruising down the river in two canoes. Until, that is, they reached a foaming water chute at which one of the canoes was lost, and Antoine Clappine drowned. From then on they wisely abandoned boating on the treacherous white waters of the Snake. Of Clappine's Rocks, nothing we could identify as such was visible from above, along a stretch of water full of rocks and rapids. But Caldron Linn [Fig. 78] was another matter altogether.

It was so named because a series of falls churned the water into a raging cauldron, 'linn' being an old Scottish word for a pool below a waterfall. Here the river made a pronounced S-bend, before plunging down three or more steep cataracts between vertical rock faces – a gorge within a gorge. Even the trickle of water which today is all that is spared to the Snake at this point, rushes white and foaming through the cleft. What it must have looked like when the river was at full flood we can only tell now from old photographs taken before the dam was built.

We circled round and round, absorbing the scene. Bright blue and tumbling white water, white-scoured rocks in the river bed, the cliff faces on the north side a funereal volcanic black and those on the south a mix of light greys; elsewhere, greens of every hue from verdant grass patches to the darks of trees and bushes. Even the water varied from cobalt blue to sombre viridian as we swung from down-sun to up-sun. Something else I was particularly pleased to note from my bird's eye view was that tracks led down to the river bed from the northern rim – this helped enormously in making a visit at water level two years later!

Again the Trail struck away south from the river, round 300 ft-high Hansen Butte, to approach Rock Creek, where later travellers found the first trading post west of Fort Hall. Built of hewn logs in 1863 by one James Bascom it was sold in 1876 to Herman Stricker, hence its identity now as Stricker's Store [Figs. 80 & 81]. It was one of a number of buildings erected at about the same time, including houses, a saloon, eating house, overnight rooms for stage passengers and of course a stage station of the Ben Holladay Line (later bought by Wells Fargo). There was also a Pony Express station here. Of all these, only the store and its outhouses remain, now preserved as the first buildings erected in Idaho.

The Trail was reputed to pass the front door of the store and, from the air, several traces could be seen criss-crossing areas now fenced into paddocks and corrals.

The detour south along Rock Creek was necessary to find a crossing point as, where the creek emptied into the Snake, the gorge was 500 ft deep, and Rock Creek dropped down through its own deep ravine. The crossing point was five miles south of the river, on the outskirts of the city of Twin Falls, and even there entailed a considerable incline into and out of the creek [Fig. 79].

And here we left the Trail for the day, turning north over the ravine carrying Rock Creek into the great gorge of the Snake four miles below the Perrine Girder Bridge [Fig. 83]. The gorge is at it greatest depth at this point, the half-mile-long road bridge being 500 ft above the river. We circled to indulge in a little photography, marvelling at what mighty forces of nature had carved this great gash through the plateau millions of years before.

Either side of the gorge, the land is virtually flat, and from just a short distance away, at ground level, there is no indication of the existence of the chasm at all. Emigrants' diaries recorded that they could hear the roar of the water over the falls from three miles away – they would be very disappointed today! The Snake drops 212 ft at Shoshone Falls, three miles upstream of the bridge, and 186 ft at Twin Falls (not the City of that name), three miles further up *[Fig. 82]*. Both falls are mere shadows of their former glory during the summer months, Twin Falls being reduced to a single trickle as a result of hydro-electric and irrigation projects. Even so, we could see the mighty Shoshone Falls, seemingly in fine fettle, as we crossed the river.

But for now, we had to hurry on to Jerome County Airport. Eight miles north along Highway 93, over hay-covered lava beds, across the broad band of Interstate 80N, and the main east-west, 5,000 ft long runway lay dead ahead. Nothing in sight in the air, the windsock almost in line with runway 26, and a little knot of people near the pumps – they were expecting us!

It was again very hot and I was most conscious of the poor rate of climb when we left American Falls. Although Jerome was lower, at 4,035 ft, the higher temperature would offset that. Once again, there could be no question of getting it wrong and having to go for an under- or over-shoot – with my old pilot friend Bill Kee, and former USAF pilot Ralph Peters in his official capacity of Mayor of Jerome, waiting to greet us, this was one landing that had better be a 'greaser.' Old NC2979E must have heard my prayers!

Our reception party was augmented by a local reporter and photographer who wanted to know all about us and what we were doing. Time passed in a blur while we talked and fuelled and unloaded the Champ. A local pilot, Forrest Hymas, had been there to welcome us in and generously offered us space in his private hangar, there being no other hangarage available. This we gratefully accepted even though it meant leaving his Bonanza tied down outside. If we had a freak hailstorm that night (extremely unlikely) it could rip our fabric to shreds but, most likely, leave his metal-skinned aircraft unharmed. As an antique vehicle and memorabilia collector Forrest thought that the Champ would feel at home amongst the collection he showed us in the hangar!

After riding into Twin Falls to pick up Bill's wife Beulah, we were taken to Ralph Peters' house, meeting more local celebrities. Our ground crew had arrived via the local Police Station, escorted to the Mayor's house by the Chief of Police! From there we all went to pick up a renowned local historian and OCTA Member, Virginia Ricketts, who was to show us some of the features of the early days on the North Side (of the Snake – most attention is given elsewhere to South Side activities!). It was great meeting her and her husband (Claire) after so often reading her local history articles in the newspaper cuttings sent to me by Bill.

Eventually, after viewing some very good ruts on the North Alternate of the Oregon Trail *[Fig. 84]*, we headed back to the Hymas household for an evening barbecue. What a spread that was, an old emigrant wagon forming the focal point with all the goodies displayed on the tailboard beneath the overhanging white canvas cover. Brian and Sonia were to enjoy the Hymas' hospitality overnight, George and Jean stayed at the Peters' house, and Renie and I with Bill and Beulah in Twin Falls. Our visit to Jerome was certainly a memorable one!

Meanwhile, at Twin Falls, the Kees and the Bretts had a lot of catching up to do. At 1.30 am we finally decided the talking would have to give way to sleeping!

It was months before we discovered how brave Beulah had been in not showing or letting on that she had recently had bad news from the hospital about her health. It says so much of her that the memories of our last meeting were happy ones: tragically, she died less than six months later.

And how were the Whitmans faring as they passed this point? There are no diary entries to identify when they were in the Twin Falls area, but Narcissa mentions passing the Indian salmon fishing grounds on August 12th at the end of the day, having travelled 25 miles. The Salmon Falls are 20 miles beyond Rock Creek Crossing, which would have been a good place to camp, so we could assume that they were there on August 11th, having stayed overnight at Fort Hall on August 3rd, and passed American Falls on August 5th.

The ladies were having a difficult time, both diarists making references to excessively hot, tedious marches over dry, parched earth and sage desert – difficult to equate in these days to the vast green area of Magic Valley obtained by irrigating the desert. Neither diary mentions Twin Falls or Shoshone Falls, perhaps not surprisingly as the Trail passed five miles south of the Snake at both points. With the falls deep in the gorge they may not even have been within earshot at that distance.

One thing all members of the party would have known for sure: the estimated remaining distance to Fort Walla Walla was less than 400 miles, and that would have helped keep flagging spirits high.

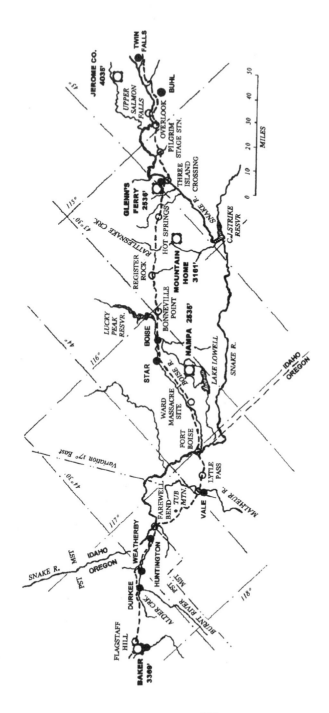

CHAPTER 14
DAY 7:
OREGON AT LAST!

Despite our late night we were up early at 05.30, had a quick bite of toast, and arrived at the airport by 06.30. It was another beautifully clear morning, the distant hills brushed with a pale, pastel-coloured wash in the pre-dawn light. When the sun appeared, anything bathed in its brilliant golden light made an unnatural contrast with the long, deep shadows it cast. This of course, was particularly so with the Champ; its bright yellow colour scheme had me searching feverishly for my sunglasses!

The Champ was already out of the hangar when we arrived *[Fig. 85]*, both Mayor Peters and Forrest Hymas lending a hand to push it up to the tarmac. Forrest was to accompany us for a short way in his Bonanza, and Brian and Sonia were going with him. Renie needed no second bidding to join them!

We took off at 07.35, and headed straight back to Rock Creek, on the way looking out for the North Alternate tracks we had walked along the previous evening. Forrest was coping well in matching his Bonanza's lowest speed with the Champ's highest speed, needing a fair degree of flap to stay with us. He soon tired of this precarious balance and darted around us like a swift, first on the left then on the right, sometimes above and then below, but always at a safe distance. As we swung west along the Trail route, the Bonanza gave a final wing waggle and turned back.

Over the cultivated fields, there was no sign at all of the Trail, a feature we had noted wherever it had traversed desert areas since reclaimed by irrigation. Near Stricker's Store, in springtime, traces had been seen at ground level across vegetation, when the growing crops were young, but at the height of summer we could see nothing. After fifteen miles along the Snake, just past the small town of Buhl, the irrigation and the fields finally petered out, and we were back over the desert.

The Snake Gorge was a constant attraction as we flew down it, the river gradually growing in volume as the irrigation water found its way back. Although still not as powerful as in years gone by, the river rippled white over the fearsome rock bed at Kanaka Rapids – the now-exposed white rocks showed how vicious the Snake would have been at this point when at full flood.

From here the river swung north in a broad arc past Banbury Springs, of which we saw nothing, and again past Thousand Springs, of which only a few now remain. The vertical cliff of the north face of the gorge sprouts miniature waterfalls from underground streams, these being few in number now as a result of the irrigation schemes. "He that giveth on the one hand, taketh away with the other," or something like that!

Beyond Thousand Springs is the Upper Salmon Falls, a popular fishing spot for the Indians before they were settled elsewhere. These falls, as with so many others, now dammed for a hydro-electric power station, mark the highest point of the Snake to which the salmon travel to spawn – one of those unbelievable miracles of nature which provided a vital food source, in the middle of the desert, for those who lived there. When the Whitmans passed through here, they too enjoyed fresh salmon as a present from the leader of the Hudson's Bay Company they were travelling with.

Once again the Trail swung away from the river, climbing up into the barren hills which bordered the Snake Gorge. At one point, where a new road loops round in a great hairpin, giving a fine overlook over the Falls, the old Trail ruts can be seen cutting across the apex of the bend *[Fig. 86]*, with protective banks created by the road-builders. All other traces of the Trail along this section appear to have been obliterated in building the new road.

Although there had been several sections of the Trail marked as rutted on the map, we had seen nothing other than the short strip at the Overlook. But now the Trail struck out twenty miles across the desert to Glenns Ferry, cutting off two great loops of the river and remote from any modern roads. As we had now come to expect, this meant there should be ruts to lead the way. And there were *[Fig. 87]*. In fact there would be fine ruts for more than two thirds of the way for the next 170 miles, almost into Boise, and most of it far from roads and across sage desert.

First they led us past the darkly-shadowed Pilgrim Stage Station site, curving round the butte and down into and up out of the dried-up Big Pilgrim Gulch. Idiotically, the words of an old childhood song intruded and refused to go away: "She'll be coming round the mountain when she comes . . ." The sound of my singing, clamorous above the roar of the engine, startled George from his reverie. "No, George, there's nothing wrong – I was just singing!"

As we circled the site, I wondered: was this the Pilgrim Springs where Naomi Sager is thought to have died in September, 1844, leaving orphaned her seven children (one a Trail-born babe of a few months)? There was no sign of the clumps of bushes I had come to associate with springs, but the local topography could have changed drastically in the intervening years, or they could simply have been hidden in the deep shadow. The Sager saga was another well-documented, tragic tale of emigrant hardship, with Henry Sager dying near the Lombard Ferry site on the Green River, where we had been lost and discovered that helpful thermal.

The Sager children's fate was inextricably mixed up with the Whitmans at Walla Walla, who had taken them in until they were old enough to fend for themselves. They had all suffered at the infamous Whitman Massacre of 1847, both Whitmans being butchered and the two older Sager children, both boys, shot and killed at the hands of Cayuse Indians. One of the five girls was ill at the time and died, while the remaining four were taken hostage by the Indians and later released.

The Trail showed us the way to the hills overlooking the famous Three-Island Crossing of the Snake, across Black Mesa and past Deadman Canyon. From the air, the relationship of the three islands was clear [Fig. 88], whereas gazing across the river from the State Park on the north bank the previous year, I had been unable to make any sense of it at all. It is doubtful if the configuration of the islands has remained unchanged over the years since a great flood occurred in 1866, and that probably altered the former layout out of all recognition.

Comparing what one can see now with what that renowned artist of the Trail, William H. Jackson, painted, reputedly from sketches made on the spot in 1866, almost the only thing they have in common is that there are three islands! The southernmost island in both cases is the widest, but whereas it was also the longest as seen by Jackson, the centre island is now by far the longest. Of the eastern tip of the southern island as Jackson saw it, only half-submerged sandbanks now remain.

What is particularly interesting is that several pronounced swales can be seen on both southern and central islands. These indicate that heavy traffic proceeded not only as Jackson shows, from the western to eastern tips of the southern island, but similarly from west to east of the central island. Although the shores of the islands may have been washed away in places and added to by deposits in others, the surface of the ground is probably unchanged. Certainly, no other wheeled traffic can be envisaged!

On the southern island, three and possibly four separate routes can be clearly seen, and two on the central island [Fig. 89]. The pity is that, owing to erosion, it is not possible to see the points at which the wagons were brought ashore or entered the water. Trail traces can be seen through cultivation along the south bank of the river, opposite the southern island, but again, no water entry point. On the north bank we could see nothing at all – hardly surprising as they emerged from the river where they could, and that was usually where the current had taken them!

Over on the north side of the river, the Trail followed the bank round the present Glenns Ferry Airport (more of that anon) and under the tracks of the Union Pacific and the I-84. Slowly it climbed 1,500 ft up into the east/west range of the Bennett Hills, past Hot Springs in which Narcissa Whitman recorded that she boiled dried salmon in five minutes.

This stretch must rank amongst the worst of the whole journey, and today looks very much as it must have done then, if you can shut your eyes to the power transmission lines! We used them though, to good effect, to give us important checks on position.

Here again, the ruts were mostly in an excellent state, and with their age-softened outlines could easily be distinguished from more modern tracks [Fig. 90]. The latter were mostly to be seen running alongside the power lines which often parallelled or crossed the Trail. Few, other than the maintenance men who looked after the lines, would want to drive across such a desolate landscape!

From Hot Springs we had a power line to follow most of the way into Boise, the next landmark being an Oregon Trail marker near the site of the old Rattlesnake Stage Station on Rattlesnake Creek. From there the power lines paralleled the Trail just over a quarter of a mile to the right, gradually moving further away as the Trail curved left to cross Canyon Creek where the canyon walls dropped to creek level. There was water in the creek and a couple of ranch houses, together with trees – a veritable oasis in the desert! The Trail ran under the road where it crossed the creek, and angled off north at a bend in the road, the swales being evident for a short distance beyond. They reappeared further on as they headed back to cross the power lines again.

An isolated outcrop of rocks [Fig. 91] close to the power lines, with the Trail ruts winding round the base, seemed a likely candidate for the title Register Rock shown on the map, though of course we could see no confirming name carvings!

Of the next landmark, Bonneville Point (also referred to as Emigrant Point), high above the city of Boise, there was however no doubt. A spur road leads to the Point, where a covered stone marker has been erected. In 1832 Captain Bonneville led an exploratory party here, having crossed miles of dry desert over the Indian trails which later became the Oregon Trail. Members of the party, seeing cooling cottonwood and willow trees lining the distant, heat-hazed river (called the Big Wood River by Narcissa Whitman), reputedly shouted in French: "The woods, the woods, see the woods." The French word for 'wood' is 'bois' and Bonneville named the river 'Rivière Boisée,' perpetuated now of course in the name given to Idaho's State Capital, Boise (pronounced 'Boycee').

Lucky Peak rears 3,000 ft above the city and lends its name to a breathtakingly beautiful reservoir, formed high up in the hills by damming the Boise River. With our eyes glued to the Trail and the immediate surroundings, we were taken by surprise at the sight of the intense blue of the waters, set amongst the barren straw-coloured hills like a scintillating sapphire. It looked almost unreal, as if an artist had painted a dream vision, an impression heightened by the fact that, from just a few miles away, the lake could no longer be seen.

But now we were in danger of infringing the Special Rules, Terminal Control Area surrounding the International Gowen Air Terminal at Boise, if we continued following the Trail round the north of the city. Without radio we dare not land at such a busy international airport, so decided to divert to Nampa, on the south side of the city. This was just about on the safe limit of our range, the light breeze which had sprung up preventing us having a look to see if we could land at Glider. Joe Turteling had a very interesting collection of aircraft at his private field there when I had visited it a few years earlier, but this had since been auctioned off. Sadly, an enquiring letter to the owner had evoked no reply.

A helpful railway line led us straight to the airfield at Nampa, where the single runway lay conveniently into wind. We landed smoothly at 10.00, 2 hrs 25 mins after take-off. Taxying up to the airport buildings, we found that, as so often was the case with such rural airfields, it was a base for a very active crop-dusting outfit. We had to wait in line while a thirsty 'duster took on what seemed like hundreds of gallons of fuel. While we eventually satisfied the Champ's thirst, there was nothing to fill our needs for a substantial breakfast. We finally got away at 11 o'clock after an hour on the ground, part of which was spent looking round the serried ranks of aircraft tied down in the open.

By now the sun was busily warming everything to an oven-like temperature and, although Nampa was only just over 2,500 ft altitude, the Champ was reluctant to climb, and we had to circle carefully, avoiding high-flying power lines and the like. This sort of activity had been bad enough over the desert areas in which we had encountered it before, but over the rural, tree-dotted countryside we were flying across now, it was positively worrying, not helped any by the turbulence we encountered at this level. As usual, the Champ eventually tired of low-flying and agreed to climb up to a safer altitude.

We rejoined the Trail route at Star, on the Boise River, the Trail following the river all the way to where it runs into the Snake. The map showed only one short section of ruts in all this 30-mile stretch of extensive cultivation, and although we looked carefully at some tracks around Canyon Hill, could not be certain that these were the ones shown on the map. As expected, there was nothing to see at the Ward Massacre site, though this was easy to pinpoint from the railroad and the grid network of roads. This had been a particularly nasty attack on a small wagon train in 1854, when 18 to 20 people were reputedly tortured to death.

The river flowed through a great flat plain, the extent of the irrigation works shown by the vast chequerboard of green and golden fields that stretched northwards to the horizon and ahead to beyond the Snake River. It had not always been like this, being lumped in by early travellers with the rest of the desert between Fort Hall and Fort Snake (an early name for Fort Boise) as "dreary, rough and barren"!

Just below the confluence of the Boise and Snake rivers *[Fig. 92]* are a number of islands which formed the Snake River Crossing near the Hudson's Bay Company's Fort Boise. There is now nothing at all remaining of the fort, and some controversy over its exact site. When visiting it by car we had found the marker erected to show where it is thought the site was located, but had found it impossible to visualise the configuration of the tree-covered islands and channels *[Fig. 93]* – water seemed to flow everywhere! The stone pillar marker *[Fig. 94]* is topped by a red-painted lion's (or beaver's?) head and carries a painting of the Hudson's Bay Company's 'Red Duster'-based house flag (the 'Red Duster' is the name commonly used for the British Mercantile flag – all-red with a small Union Jack in the top left corner).

Circling over the site at 500 ft, we could pick out the red-topped marker, but more importantly, could now see its relationship with the islands. The main channel of the Snake flows round the westmost and largest of the islands, over three-quarters of a mile west of the broad waterway facing the fort site! No wonder I could make no sense of it at ground level.

For me, the site is an enigma. If Narcissa Whitman knew her facts when she made her diary notes, the courses of the Boise and Snake Rivers have changed almost beyond recognition at their confluence. She mentioned Fort Snake (which preceded the Hudson's Bay Fort Boise) as being sited on the Big Wood River (her name for the Boise River) six miles from its mouth. When crossing the Snake, she noted that they travelled a short way from the Fort and crossed the Snake by two islands. That can only mean that the mouth of the Boise river was then about six miles from the two islands in the Snake, otherwise the Fort could hardly have been "a short way" from the Snake.

Comparing what could be seen from the air, with a map of the area, a possible solution presented itself. There is a narrow eastern channel of the Snake which extends six miles north of the Fort site, merging briefly with the main course of the river at two points, creating two enormous islands where it cuts across two loops of the Snake. If that eastern channel had at one time not made those two contacts with the main channel, but had been the course of the Boise River, it would all fit exactly with Narcissa's description!

Could the rivers have changed that much over the period? Well, there was a major flood of the Snake in 1853 which washed away the adobe walls of the fort. There was another in 1866 which was thought to have changed the configuration of Three Island Crossing, and the effects must have been felt, and even magnified, at all points downstream of there. An analogy can be drawn to drastic changes made to the course of the

Missouri in its flood years which are well documented. Well, it's an interesting thought . . .

Circling over the point where the Trail is mapped as crossing the Snake, it looked as if there were traces crossing a neck of land at the southern tip of the biggest island, just where they should be. As at Three Island Crossing, the channels appeared to have changed course sufficiently for the traces to no longer point to the best points of entry and egress. Time was pressing, so reluctantly we turned our backs on this fascinating area and pressed on. Into Oregon, at last!

From the west bank, the Trail route passed through a heavily-cultivated area and we saw no more traces of the Trail until we passed over the section which climbs up from Cow Hollow to Lytle or Keeney Pass [Fig. 95]. Here the ruts were first on the right of the road, then on the left, leaving very clear eroded swales just beyond an interpretive centre. Then on past Vale, over the Malheur River with its attendant Hot Springs, and up into the wild rolling hills, barren and, at first sight, featureless. If ever there was an occasion where some good ruts were needed, to show us the way, it would be here!

In fact, it proved easier than we expected. Dry Gulch, now not so dry, pointed the way after leaving the main road, rail and river complex along Willow Creek. From there, the Trail ruts branched briefly back east, up into the hills along Alkali Gulch, before turning north past Tub Mountain. At 3,447 ft, this was not much of a mountain, rising only 1,200 ft above the Snake at Fort Boise, but from our low altitude it had cut off our view of Farewell Bend of the Snake.

We followed the ruts over the variegated sand and sage-scrub hills, large areas of sage mantling the upper slopes to make a dull, dark patchwork against the straw-coloured valleys. Up-sun the sage patches were olive green, darkened by shadow; down-sun, a drab, green-tinged, earthy brown, all the colours drifting into a uniform, misty, blue-grey as the hills merged with the horizon. Interspersed here and there were chalky streaks of bare sand and rock, and the green pencil lines of creeks and streams; on closer inspection, these hills were anything but feature-less, and attractive in a wild sort of way. But I was jolly glad not to be walking over them in the heat we could now feel, even in the aircraft.

Beyond Tub Mountain, the ruts pointed us to the strange-looking Love Reservoir, its unsavoury green waters ringed with the white shores which I had come to associate with alkali lakes. Ahead was the broad, azure blue sweep of the Snake as it curved west to meet us – in following the Trail we had, as the emigrants did before us, cut off a great 30-mile loop of the river. At one point it had been twenty miles distant, and now it rejoined our route briefly and finally at Farewell Bend. An appropriately named spot, where the emigrants saw their last of a river which had been a grudging companion on and off for the previous 300 miles [Fig. 96].

We approached the Snake at the site of the Olds Ferry, looking in vain for the ruts reputed to remain on the slope down to the river. The river looks magnificent here as it winds through the hills, being about half a mile in width at the bend. It is difficult to grasp the size of it, there being little to lend scale to the scene – one solitary speedboat helped, its minuscule white wake being almost lost in the wide expanse of blue water.

The Trail continued a few more miles over similar terrain to Huntington, though here there was no trace of it. Huntington looked to be a once-important railroad town, with goods sidings and several massive trains of wagons and trucks. It lay on the Burnt River (a name that takes some understanding), which the Trail follows for the next twenty miles. And now, the emigrants were headed for the dreaded Blue Mountains, their 9,000 ft peaks looking more like real mountains than the Rockies, from land which was only 2,200 ft a.s.l.

Although the Trail rose to no more than 4,000 ft ahead, we were now encountering turbulent and difficult conditions, flying towards rising ground with a stiff breeze curling over the top, and with warm air that encouraged the Champ to stay close to the ground. We had stayed too close too long, and were now having problems in persuading the plane to climb faster than the ground. This necessitated circling round Huntington to gain height before we ventured up over the canyons along the Burnt River and Alder Creek.

The hills sloped quite steeply down into the canyon, and some early travellers reported problems with animals occasionally unable to keep to their feet. It was certainly no place in which to carry out a forced landing so we kept above the level of the adjacent hills wherever possible. Only where the Trail route struck away from the valley bottom did we see any tracks through the hills, notably just past Lime (where, perhaps, the small industrial plant we could see produces lime?).

Another great loop round Gold Hill had no ruts, but it looked as if the gravel road here was laid over the Trail. The route shown on the maps, half a mile to the right of the road, looked most unlikely – who would take their wagons up a steep incline when a flat route could be taken round the hill?

What the emigrants could not have known as they struggled through this inhospitable area was that they were literally walking over gold. Not the golden hay-grass but gold as in mines! Looking down on the unpromising terrain, this geological ignoramus wondered what possessed anyone to put a spade into the matted, dead grass to see if any gold lay beneath.

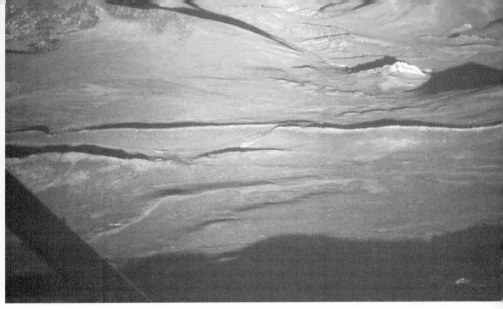

Fig. 68. A low sun at dawn casts striking shadows at Cumberland Gap in the Oyster Ridge, where the Little Muddy Creek and the Oregon Trail wend a winding passage through. Looking west, this is some 20 miles NNE of Fort Bridger, with the Bear River and Idaho border 30 miles to the west.

Fig. 69. Similar shadows throw a sharp relief at Indian Grave (just west of Border Summit ID), as Highway 30 sweeps round from the south-east (top left). A track from Sheep Creek Reservoir joins the Highway at bottom right, and the Trail route runs close to it from centre left.

Fig. 70. Deep Trail ruts follow the foot of a hill, away from possible marshy ground, along the nearby Ross Fork Creek between Basin and Fort Hall in the Indian Reservation. The Union Pacific RR (Gay Branch) and a road run side by side adjacent to the creek across the lower right corner.

Fig. 71. A dusty white gravel road runs past Cantonment Loring site, across the loops of the Snake River and over the Trail route, to the Fort Hall site. This view is looking SW towards the American Falls Reservoir, across the top of the picture.

Fig. 72. The gravel road (from upper left) ends in a turning bay at the Fort Hall site, close to the Snake. The Fort monument (see below) is just to the right of the turning bay. South is at the top and McTucker Island at the bottom. 28 years on from the Haines Survey of 1958, it is difficult to find any features that now coincide with the map that accompanied that survey.

Fig. 73. The Fort Hall Monument as seen in 1988, when the author and his wife were taken to the site by a guide from the Fort Hall Museum. This is facing NW and the turning bay is to the right.

Fig. 74. Massacre Rocks State Park ID, on the right between the I-86 and the Snake River. Looking south-west, towards Register Rock at the very top of the picture. The I-86 runs over the Oregon Trail route and the Rocks from which the site takes its name suffered at the hands of the road-builders.

Fig. 75. Cold Water Campground site at centre left. Looking west towards Tule Island on the Snake. Opposite the island, on the north bank, are a number of irrigation discs, roughly 1/2-mile in diameter, a common feature in the west and easily seen from the highest-flying jet airliners.

Fig. 76. The Raft River Crossing, at the apex of the bend, the first point south of the Snake where the west bank was low enough to haul wagons up. This is where the Oregon and California Trails finally parted, as indicated by the adjacent dotted lines, the vertical (west) to Oregon and the horizontal (south) to California.

Fig. 77. A section of the Oregon Trail ruts that extend eight miles across uncultivated range land between the Raft River Crossing and the I-84.

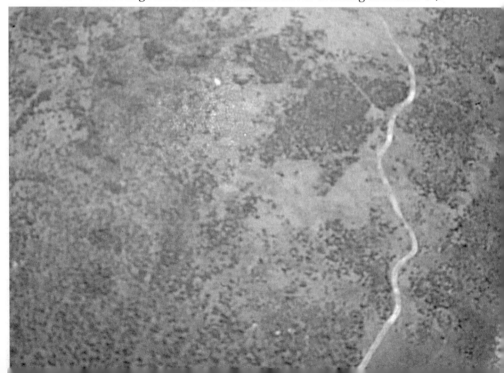

Fig. 78. Caldron Linn on the Snake, near Murtaugh ID, looking NW. High and almost dry in modern summers, but a savage, boiling torrent when the Astorians party met disaster here in 1811, the mighty Snake being channelled through a narrow defile. A beautiful and wild spot, yet accessible by a road down the northern bank.

Fig. 79. Rock Creek Crossing, on the outskirts of Twin Falls city where, as at the Raft River, the crossing point was five miles south of the Snake. Rock Creek winds north-west from lower left to upper right. The crossing point was this side of the road bridge.

Fig. 80. Stricker Store, the first building in Idaho, dating from 1863, located a few yards south of Rock Creek across the top. An Oregon Trail marker can be seen just to the left of the building.

Fig. 81. The well-preserved log building is protected by a false roof, with a sunken storehouse (one of two) to the right. The front of the building is at the other end, facing the old Trail road.

Fig. 82. The Snake Gorge at Twin Falls looking south-east. The Falls are hidden by the near wall of the gorge, but the visitors' overlook is just visible. Locals quote the Gorge depth as 500 ft at this point. Tracks of the North Alternate Trail are to the left.

Fig. 83. Perrine Bridge over the Snake near Twin Falls city, looking east. The Shoshone and Twin Falls are respectively 3 and 5 miles upstream from here. The zigzag wagon road up the cliff side dates from the turn of the century. Rock Creek empties into the Snake four miles below in a gorge just as deep.

Fig. 84. Well-known local (Jerome) historians and OCTA members Claire and Virginia Ricketts, and Bill and Beulah Kee, took the six of us to view and walk here in the tracks of the North Alternate Trail near the Perrine Bridge. It is apparent from this to see why at times the ruts show up so well when viewed from the air.

Fig. 85. Another Jerome enthusiast, Forrest Hymas, gave up his hangar to provide overnight cover for the "Champ," his Bonanza seen here with the "Champ" in dawn silhouette. We had just wheeled out the "Champ" but the Bonanza had stayed outside!

Fig. 86. One of several Overlook sites on the Snake River, this one is just north of Miller Island (off top left), looking south. Highway US 30 generally overlays the Trail, except for a short section of deep ruts cutting across the bend at the left. These are well-preserved, protected from the road-builders' machinery by a prominent bank erected to their left.

Fig. 87. The Oregon Trail crossing Deer Gulch, west of Big Pilgrim Gulch, from lower left to upper right. Deep in the sage desert, south of the Snake River, these ruts are as good as they come, anywhere.

Fig. 88. Three Island Crossing of the Snake, looking east, with the very fine Interpretive Centre located approximately one third of the way across the top from the left. Glenns Ferry Airport is just off top left. When the Whitmans crossed here in 1836, Narcissa referred to it in her diary as the Two Island Ford, the third island being created in floods later in that century.

Fig. 89. The ruts on the two southernmost islands must be the most unsullied by 20th Century users and give very clear evidence of changes to the shape of the islands due to subsequent flooding.

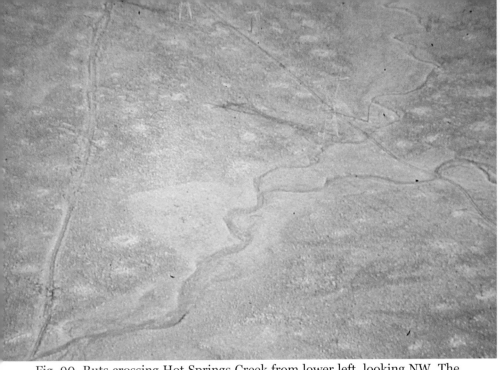

Fig. 90. Ruts crossing Hot Springs Creek from lower left, looking NW. The tall pylons of the Idaho Power Company power lines, accompanied by their service road, march across from the right.

Fig. 91. Trail ruts climb the slope from Ditto Creek to wind through the outcrops of Register Rock, meeting the ever-present power lines. Miles and miles of pristine ruts pointed the way from the Snake River to Bonneville Point and Boise.

Fig. 92. Nowadays the Boise River joins the Snake near the site of old Fort Boise (marked by an arrow), but in 1836 N. Whitman recorded the Fort as being "six miles up from the mouth," which suggests that both rivers have been changed by heavy flooding since then.

Fig. 93. Close-up of the site of Fort Boise, with a 'lion-headed' monument at centre of the picture, just to the rear of the trailer.

Fig. 94. The monument erected by local historians to mark the site of Fort Boise. As the Fort was a Hudson's Bay Trading Post, the Hudson's Bay Flag is displayed prominently. Though in print as 'lion-headed' the author thought it was intended to represent a beaver's head, painted a reddish brown, the skins of the beaver being the prime reason for the HBC presence.

Fig. 95. Lytle Pass, six miles south-east of Vale, Oregon. Also known as Keeney Pass. An interpretive turnout is at upper left centre; here are located a number of information tablets about the Trail and typical wagons and their contents. Several sets of ruts and swales (to the left of the road) are easily accessed from the turnout. This photo was taken on a hand-held camera and shows interior reflections on the aircraft windows.

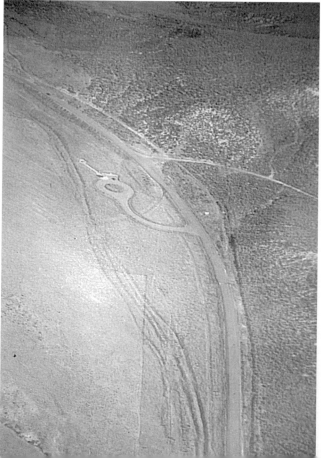

Fig. 96. Farewell Bend on the Snake, where the travellers saw the last of the river. Ruts descend from lower left to the Olds Ferry site (by the trees on the right). Farewell Bend State Park is located by the trees at the apex of the bend.

Fig. 97. The Oregon Trail, snaking across Virtue Flat and its myriad gold mines, from bottom left past Flagstaff Hill (upper centre). Looking NW over Baker Valley and Baldock Slough (white area at upper right beyond the 4,170 ft high Baldock Hill). The dark area is Missouri Flat, 800 ft below.

Fig. 98. Approaching the top of Ladd Canyon Hill from the south, overlooking Grande Ronde valley some 1,300 ft below. The approximate Trail route is marked by the white dotted line, crossing the prominent oil and gas buried pipelines before plunging down the hillside.

Fig. 99. Ladd Canyon Hill looking SE, along the I-84, with a safety rest centre just before the bend, where there are the remains of a Stage Station. The dotted line shows an approximation of the Trail route down the hill, as defined by John W. Evans in his book *"Powerful Rocky."*

Further along the canyon, the small town of Durkee marked the point at which the Burnt River Canyon joined Durkee Valley; here Alder Creek, which collected the waters from the myriad small creeks higher up, ran into Burnt River. The Trail ran along the bottom of the valley for another seven miles, without trace, before striking up into the hills. Although the map showed ruts present along the next seven miles we saw none until we crossed Virtue Flat at the top of the hills above Baker.

On Virtue Flat was another collection of active gold mines, with names like Friday, Gray Eagle and Hidden Treasure Mine. Here also were more marked ruts and this time we saw them quite clearly, leading us round Flagstaff Hill, 300 ft above the swampy Missouri Flat and Baldock Slough [Fig. 97]. Though the lower flats now look an untidy mess, with weed-dappled, abandoned, once-cultivated areas showing great patches of bare earth or sand, they and Baker Valley were earlier regarded as a place of great beauty. This impression would have been heightened by seeing so much greenery around the Powder River and its many tributaries, after journeying so far over the arid brown hills.

Here grew the famed Lone Pine, which afforded early travellers shade and kindling, but suffered the indignity of being laid flat in the autumn of 1843 at the hands of some unknown, hungry and cold emigrants. Between Baldock Slough and our old friend Interstate 80N was sited our immediate objective, Baker Municipal Airport, sleeping peacefully in the sun.

As usual, we could not at first see a windsock. At least we were saved the prospect of circling round and round over the field till we spotted one by a solitary aircraft landing, which showed us the active runway. Time down 13.03, which converted to 12.03 as we were now on PST (Pacific Summer Time); time in the air, 2 hours. On the ground the airfield looked fairly deserted at first, with acres and acres of lonely concrete. We soon had the Champ refilled, oiled, unloaded and tied down. Meanwhile, we phoned the appropriately-named "The Oregon Trail Motel," whose manager cheerfully agreed to come out and pick us up straight away. Breakfast at last!

There was time to walk around the attractive old town of Baker, visit its charming museum, saunter through the park and watch an open-air wedding party in progress (it was a Saturday), and toss stones in the little Powder River from a bridge. What was more, we found an excellent example of that great American institution, the ice cream parlour – "Charley's" to be exact – and in enjoying a well-earned, high-heaped, exotic ice cream sundae, discovered that Charlie was serving us personally, and was a fellow pilot. He owned a rare Bellanca Cruiser, but no amount of scheming by any of us could find a way for him to get us out to his airstrip to show us his plane. Pity!

At six o'clock, our now rather weary ground crew arrived, having started out late. They had all congregated at Ralph Peters' house for breakfast, and discovered that he was a 'rock hound.' They soon found that this had nothing to do with any form of music or dancing, as Ralph had a fantastic collection of rare stones and rocks, and they could not resist his offer to show them. By coincidence, Baker Museum had a rare collection of rocks which I had seen that afternoon, and we were all full of stories about how fascinating each collection had been, especially as both included fluorescent rocks lit by ultra-violet light.

For a change, we all had an early night – there was much sleep to catch up on!

The Whitmans had stayed in "Lone Tree Valley" on August 26th, having taken two weeks to get here from where we left them at Upper Salmon Falls, near Jerome. Their journey had been a hard one, with the Missionaries' horses and cattle so tired and worn that they had to split from the main party the day before they reached the valley. The Whitmans travelled on, light, with the Hudson's Bay men, leaving the main party to continue at a slower pace. They had abandoned their two-wheeled cart at Fort Snake, intending to return for it after they had established their Mission. In this beautiful, peaceful valley, the end of their journey must have seemed very near, and Oregon was already living up to its promises!

CHAPTER 15
DAY 8:
TO WALLA WALLA

Brian was to resume his place in the rear seat for the next two days, having now recovered from back-seat backache. This coincided, we thought, with having left behind us the problems associated with high temperatures and high altitude airfields. How wrong one can be!

But to start with, taking off from Baker at 09.15 gave no hint of later troubles, the Champ climbing cheerfully away from the 3,369 ft high airfield. Brian's extra weight and the additional radio equipment, which seemed to accumulate round him whenever he flew, made little difference – at this early hour. We set off over the Trail at our intended low altitude of 500 ft a.g.l., with nothing between us and Walla Walla higher than 4,200 ft.

The morning light no longer helped to reveal the trail with its deep shadows – over those cultivated fields at that time of year, no trace showed. Not even a stretch shown as rutted, across uncultivated meadow land, alongside Baldock Slough. In fact we saw no more ruts until we came to Ladd Canyon, 25 miles further on. Meanwhile, the trail continued along Baker Valley, where the little Powder River circumscribed a great 180 deg northern loop from Baker round Magpie Peak to the small town of North Powder, before arching back east towards the distant Snake. The little Thief Valley Reservoir to our right, above the Lower Powder Valley, helped confirm position in an area criss-crossed by small rivers and creeks.

There were various short rutted sections marked where the trail ran alongside I-80N, but we saw none of them. But at least we recognised the old building marked as 15-mile House, presumably an old Stage Station, on the approach to Ladd Canyon. Here we realised how much the wind had got up since we took off; in trying to out-climb the rising ground, our forward speed was reduced and the wind pulled it back even further, to the point where we were being overtaken by almost everything on the road, including large trucks!

Ladd Canyon proved to be a real eye-catcher, with its long haul up from the south *[Fig. 98]* and the incredibly steep (for wagons) drop into the Grande Ronde Valley. We could see the far-off valley floor beyond and below the rim of the surrounding hills, the perception of distance heightened by the difference in size and density of colour of the trees on the brow of the hill and those down in the valley.

A buried pipeline, heading straight up and over the hill, distracted the eye from the curving ruts of the trail, which swept to the right before looping back, always seeking the smoothest and gentlest descent. But there was no avoiding the steep 1,000-ft drop completely, reckoned to be

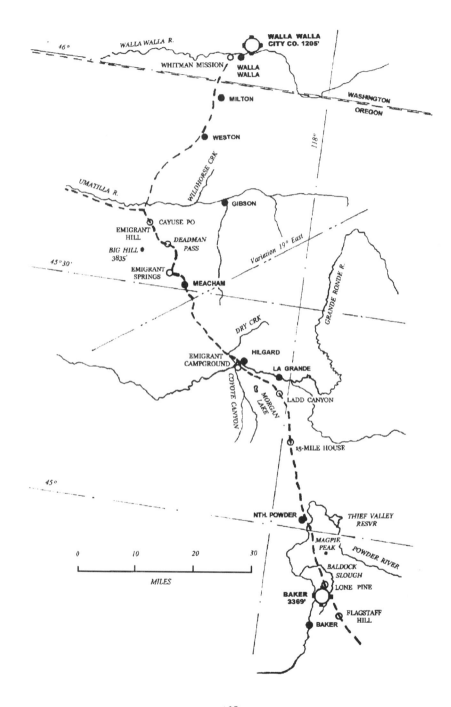

46°

WALLA WALLA R.

WALLA WALLA
CITY CO. 1205'

WHITMAN MISSION

WALLA
WALLA

WASHINGTON

OREGON

● MILTON

118°

● WESTON

WILDHORSE CRK

UMATILLA R.

● GIBSON

CAYUSE PO

EMIGRANT
HILL

DEADMAN
PASS

Variation 19° East

45°30'

BIG HILL ●
3835'

EMIGRANT
SPRINGS

MEACHAM

GRANDE RONDE R.

DRY CRK

EMIGRANT
CAMPGROUND

HILGARD

LA GRANDE

COYOTE CANYON

MORGAN
LAKE

LADD CANYON

15-MILE HOUSE

45°

NTH. POWDER

THIEF VALLEY
RESVR

MAGPIE
PEAK ●

POWDER RIVER

0   10   20   30

BALDOCK
SLOUGH

MILES

BAKER
3369'

LONE PINE

FLAGSTAFF
HILL

● BAKER

one of the worst along the trail *[Fig. 99]*. Certainly, Windlass Hill, so far back now as to seem a hazy memory of months ago, was nothing compared to this monster. The only point in its favour was that at this stage, all the survivors were old hands, more able here to take it in their stride.

Before us stretched a near circular, flat plain, some twenty miles across and ringed on all sides by mountains. The valley floor is irrigated by the Grande Ronde River, and widely cultivated, but in emigrant days it was an eagerly-looked-for, beautiful green pasture, dotted with tall trees.

We should have had no problems in finding the trail route out of La Grande – the trail ran along the southern outskirts of the town before following a creek up into the hills. But somehow we missed the creek, got muddled up with several roads leading up the side of the hills, were confused by two white circular domes, and were distracted by the big white letters LG on the hillside. There was no real excuse for being confused by the latter, as the practice is common to every city which boasts a college and a hillside for the students to daub the initials on! Here also we were being buffeted once more by turbulent air spilling over the hills from the west.

Eventually, having circled round and round, partly to climb up out of the turbulence before venturing over the hills, but mainly to obtain a positive fix, we found the point at which the trail ascends the hill, aided by the twin wooden poles and cables of a power transmission line. It must have seemed a steep ascent for the wagoners, but once up, there was a rolling parkland plateau, enhanced now by the blue waters of Morgan and Twin Lakes *[Fig. 100]*. It was an attractive landscape, despite the straw colouring of the grass, broken up now by the deep greens of groups of conifers.

According to the map, we should have seen a 6-mile stretch of good ruts, but they were not easy to spot, as the sun was shining along the tracks thus throwing little in the way of shadows. However, we found some, more or less as marked, so were reasonably happy that we were on course *[Fig. 101]*. This was confirmed by their leading us down Lower Coyote Canyon to Hilgard Junction *[Fig. 102]*. Suddenly there was a great profusion of navigational features to assure us we were on course – the usual three 'r's, river, rail and road, with a main fork in the road and the river, and the railroad sweeping up the right fork.

On the opposite side of the road was the site of Emigrant Campground, and a track curving up to the top of a ridge, where it ran along the crest for several miles before dropping down to cross Dry Creek. From that point on, we had only to follow the ruts, ever upwards, for another sixteen miles to Emigrant Springs, with short breaks at Strickland Flat and Meacham. This was one of the most beautiful stretches of the trail, as it wound up the wooded slopes, through the heart of the Blue Mountains. In our hot little craft, we could imagine, if not actually smell, the glorious fresh scent of the pine woods. Conifers can be boring in unbroken expanse, but here the beauty of the trees was enhanced by the varied patches of straw-coloured grass. In the spring, when the grass is emerald green, it must be a wondrous sight.

Beyond Emigrant Springs, the trail lay under I-80N as it made a great sweeping curve from north-east to west, entering the Umatilla Indian Reservation and heading through Deadman Pass *[Fig. 103]*. The latter's 3,615 ft elevation afforded a grand view over the great flat plain 2,000 ft below, which extended north west to the Columbia River and north to the 30 miles-distant Walla Walla Mission of the Whitmans. From our lofty seat above the Pass, we could see the trail ruts curving round between Big Hill and Kanine Ridge before heading off down Emigrant Hill.

There was the usual herringbone pattern of creeks and ridges dropping down from the plateau – Doe, Moonshine and Coonskin Creeks, to name a few of those that emptied into the Umatilla River. Tracks ran down the crests of several ridges from Deadman Pass, one, following a buried gas pipeline, being that designated as the Oregon Trail. Probably the others were used by the wagons at various times, especially in the early days when many of the trains went via the Whitman Mission.

Unused after 1847, when the Whitman Massacre closed the Mission, no one apparently now knows the route followed to Walla Walla. The plain is so flat that possibly the only features to dictate the route were the river crossings, though all of these were minor in comparison with what had gone before. So we had no trail route to follow, as a result of which we actually got lost!

This came about because my roller map showed only the trail route, through Pendleton, so we were dependent on the Sectional Air Chart. We knew we had only to follow the rail, road and river complex up past Weston and Milton to Walla Walla and, thinking that with only 30 miles to go, we were home and dry, got careless. So careless that we followed the wrong river!

As we dropped down along Emigrant Hill towards the Umatilla, we were busy with filming and trying to pick out which of the tracks were those of the trail. In particular, close to the river was a large field with so unusual a pattern of crop rotation that we got carried away in discussion over what it was all about *[Fig. 104]*. Coming to the river, I turned right and followed it, comfortable in the knowledge that the river, railway and road all conformed to what was shown on the Sectional chart, and that in less than 30 minutes we would be circling over the Rendezvous site.

We had descended to below the height of the hills behind us and thought no more of it. That is until, suddenly, I was aware that we were flying up a very picturesque canyon *[Fig 105]*, whose steeply sloping sides ran down to a very narrow, wooded defile through which the rail, river and road ran. In the bottom of the valley there was nowhere to make an emergency landing in the unlikely event that one should be necessary. The fact that we were now below the hilltops on either side did not at first ring any warning bells, so firm was the belief that we would, at any moment, emerge at the end of the canyon over a flat plain.

Nevertheless, I opened up to full power and started to climb. At first, all that happened was that we stopped dropping any further below the tops, which were perhaps 50 feet above us. It soon became obvious that it needed a determined attempt if we were to climb up out of the canyon; the last thing I wanted was to get caught in the curl over of air and forced down to the bottom. There was little enough room up at the top to circle – down there, it would be impossible. The worrying thing now was that something was amiss with our navigation as we should not have been heading back into higher ground.

The Champ was now displaying all its old reluctance to climb in hot and high conditions, despite our comparatively low altitude of 3,000 ft a.s.l., the wind curling over the northern rim of the canyon no doubt adding to our troubles. Edging over to the southern rim made a difference. Slowly we started to gain on the high ground, and at last were out of the clutches of the downdraughts. But when we came to a fork in the canyon, which demanded a decision as to which way to turn, we were still not high enough to fly out over the hill tops.

Circling over the fork we could see that the railroad followed the right branch, but the road went to the left. That settled it, we could not be at Weston, so where the heck were we and how the devil did we go wrong? After what seemed an agonising age, Brian announced that the compass heading I gave him for the right fork translated into 190 deg True. Suddenly, it all clicked. We were circling over Gibson, having followed the Umatilla instead of Wildhorse Creek. Now we were nine miles south of where we should be with growing concern about fuel consumption. We could not afford to go on circling for height on full power, for too long, otherwise we would find ourselves eating into our safety reserve.

Patiently, the Champ was coaxed up, gaining more over the south side than we lost over the north, until we had sufficient height to cross the north rim. There was little enough in hand as we set out on an unbelievable compass heading of 290 deg to fly north, but at least once clear of the turbulence over the canyon we were able to climb well clear of the ground. Soon we flew over two more canyons and at last a major road. This unfortunately was east/west and we needed to go north-west. Reluctantly we left it and carried on north, until we came across another canyon with a road and river heading in the right direction.

The canyon floor was a bright green gash through the straw-brown hills, the latter quickly giving way to a cultivated plateau. The canyon continued, meeting another also with a road and river, and soon we were over Milton, and our problems seemed over. But the Champ had not quite finished with its playful pranks for the day!

On phoning our contacts in Walla Walla, to tell them we would arrive that morning, we were invited to circle low over the Rendezvous site to let them know we had arrived. Few pilots need any second bidding at such a request, and it seemed a good opportunity to take some airborne shots of the gathering. There was no problem in picking out the site, west of Walla Walla, with its rows of white teepees and grass arena within a half-circle of museum buildings. We dropped down to 500 ft above the ground to fly over and round the site, and then found that although we were now down to just over 1,200 ft a.s.l. the Champ would still not climb!

We made two very brief circuits over the site, waving to a surprisingly small number of people visible there – only afterwards did we discover that nearly everyone was attending a Commemorative Church Service. We scuttled off to the south, with our tails between our legs at the Champ's refusal to perform, well clear of the town, to circle round to the north-east. That was where the airport lay, but unfortunately nearly 500 ft higher than the Rendezvous site, so we were at just about the same elevation as the airfield. This was ridiculous – if we failed to climb we would be unable to get up to the airfield! This was like our arrival at Jeffrey City all over again, but instead of open desert we had to steer clear of small communities, farm buildings and power lines in a rural area!

It was now very hot and I recalled having a similar problem once before at home in England. On just one occasion, in the Jackaroo when it was fully loaded and the temperature was abnormally high, I had been unable to climb above 50 feet after taking off. Then a wide circuit over flat farm land in Norfolk saw us gradually climb away.

The Champ relented and gave us another 50 feet, and that was enough. I could hear Brian in the back talking to his radio but whether he got the response he was looking for I never found out – at that point the airfield appeared dead ahead, filling our view from side to side. With nothing else in sight, we crept over the airfield boundary and found runway 25 stretching out before us. Although the wind was at almost 90 deg to the runway it was now so light as to be no problem and we thankfully touched down to a respectable landing as soon as the throttle was closed.

The Champ stopped before we reached the first taxyway intersection which took us quite quickly to the tie-down area. There, a well-built chap in an orange shirt seemed to be expecting us, and showed us where to tie down [Fig. 106]. He introduced himself as Jim, and said he was to act as our escort for the day and would drive us out to the Rendezvous site as soon as we were ready. This was service with a big friendly grin!

We had touched down at 11.20 after just over two hours flying, on what would have been the shortest leg over the trail, had we not got lost along the Umatilla! After the usual business of refilling the Champ and removing all our sundry bits and pieces, Jim took us out to the Rendezvous site. There we found that our ground crew had arrived, just after we had flown over, had been enthusiastically received and were now looking round the display while waiting for us to arrive.

As so often in such cases, the day's events passed in a whirl of introductions, friendly faces and interesting activities laid on at the Rendezvous. We met genuine, modern, skin-clad counterparts of the Mountain Men of old, who tuck themselves away from civilisation for most of the year, producing crafted goods to sell or barter at the now Annual Rendezvous. Here also were Indians from the local reservation, with deerskin-clad, attractive young squaws indulging in smoke-pole races. In these, each had to remove the two smoke poles of a teepee and race with them to the far end of the arena and back, before replacing them in the teepee. This of course attracted much verbal and flag-waving encouragement. All exciting stuff!

There was much to see: old reconstructed log buildings from far and wide, recreating an early settlement, with schoolhouse, church, railway booking office, jailhouse and shops, the latter stocked with period items. There were permanent single-storey buildings housing items of local interest, perhaps the most eyecatching being an exhibit of an early mule-hauled combine harvester. There were 31 mules in the team, represented by a single leader and five rows of six realistic, wooden animals; imagine the job of harnessing all that many mules and keeping control of them!

We wandered round rows of stalls, reminiscent of those to be found at a village fête at home. The atmosphere was much the same, friendly, happy people enjoying themselves – the difference here being that the sun was shining and it was if anything too hot. On such an occasion at home it would be pouring with rain!

From the Rendezvous we went on to visit the Mission site, beautifully kept by the National Park Service *[Fig. 107]*. There was a small museum and visitor centre and the grounds retained the layout of the old Walla Walla Mission at Waiilatpu (pronounced 'Wy-ee-la-poo,' an Indian name meaning 'the place of the rye grass'). Around the well-kept lawns and shady willow trees there was an aura of peace and tranquillity. On the nearby ridge, the tall monument to the Whitmans looked down on the site, a constant reminder of both the triumph and the tragedy that had been perpetuated on this spot.

The evening was rounded off by a barbecue, arranged for us by the Park Superintendent and his family and some local people who had provided the initial contact. We were introduced to a local speciality, sweet onions, which none of us had ever come across before. So, if you wish to try sweet onions, Walla Walla is the place to go!

Here, of course, the Whitmans reached their ultimate goal. As there was nothing here for them on their arrival, they stayed at the Hudson's Bay Company trading post, Fort Walla Walla, for five days from Sept. 1st to the 6th. They departed for Fort Vancouver, by row-boat down the Columbia, then a rough ride in comparison with the smooth waters of the river as it is today. There the men were to obtain supplies, and materials necessary to build the first log cabin, while the women waited for it be made habitable for the winter.

The Whitmans successfully set up their Mission at Waiilatpu, and two others, one near present-day Lewiston and the other near what is now Spokane, having been joined by two more Missionaries and their wives in 1838. Narcissa's baby was born in March, but tragedy struck when the little girl was two years old and she drowned in the nearby river. In addition to bringing religion to the Cayuse Indians, Whitman's Mission performed an unofficial but essential function, as a haven for the weary and sometimes near starving emigrants on the Oregon Trail.

Unhappily, the Trail brought not only emigrants to take the Indian's land; they brought with them disease and illness against which the natives had no natural immunity, and which took their lives on a grand scale. To make matters even worse, medicines administered successfully to the emigrants failed to help the Indians, so that they feared that Dr. Whitman was denying them the help they so desperately needed. It was almost inevitable that in the end the Indians took their revenge on the unfortunate Whitmans in the infamous Massacre of 1847.

CHAPTER 16
DAY 9:
TO END-OF-TRAIL, OREGON CITY

After the previous day's tantrums by the Champ, we decided to revert to an early start for our last day over the Trail. After today, we would be able to fly higher and the heat would be not quite such a problem to us, so later starts would be more acceptable. Following a late night we decided to forego breakfast for a few minutes more sleep, and got out to the airport before seven.

It was another beautiful, cloudless morning, and already warm when we took off at 07.25, but the Champ behaved herself and we had no problems in climbing out. We headed south, back to the Umatilla River, but there was to be no repeat of the previous day's nonsense in the canyons of the Blue Mountains – this time we would fly west along the river, away from the foothills!

We rejoined the Trail route near where we had left it, following the south bank of the river past Mission to Pendleton, looking for but not positively identifying the Umatilla Crossing. We saw no sign of the Trail until ten miles west of Pendleton, when a short trace appeared unexpectedly on an unmarked section; other marked sections were either invisible to us or had been ploughed up. But at Echo Meadows, we located the marked Umatilla Crossing and more unmarked swales over fallow, previously ploughed land. This was just beyond an area remarkable for its succession of disc irrigations – we counted over twenty of them fitted neatly into a great triangular wedge of land.

Ahead lay the Boardman Bombing Range, an area of sage and sand desert, where we could anticipate trouble in obtaining the precise position fixes that would be necessary if we were not to stray into the airspace over the Range! As it happened, once we had crossed Butter Creek, we had intermittent swales and Trail ruts to lead us most of the way. What we found very surprising here was the extent of cultivation and irrigation that had taken place in an area we expected to find deserted.

The first seven miles beyond Butter Creek were the most difficult as, over this stretch, there was nothing with which to fix our position other than the tracks. Had they not been the Trail route, but some other ranch roads, we could have finished miles off course as for this sort of work our compass was almost useless. As it was, a shallow, wide, dry creek, marked as Sand Hollow on the maps, came into view as expected. What were not expected were yet more irrigation discs, with the subsequent loss of more Trail ruts.

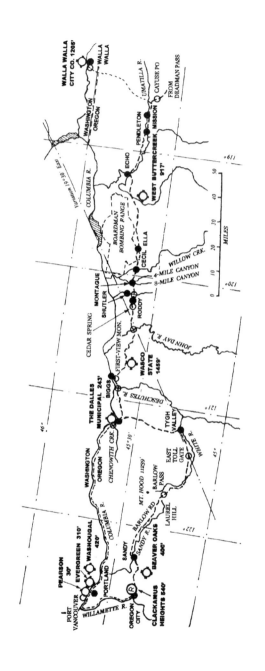

After another four miles of featureless land, a road with a tee-junction gave us a fix, though the nearby Cayuse War Battlefield looked no different to any other stretch of the desert. Another mile, and a power line marked the boundary of the old area of the Bombing Range, since cut off by a new demarcation. Up to the power lines, the eager-beaver ranchers had cultivated the soil, but beyond was original sage scrub. There was no sign of aerial activity though we could see several small bomb craters to the north of our track – we will assume that the aim of the Navy pilots and bomb aimers was too good for their bombs to hit the Trail itself!

Upper Well Spring lay just outside the old Range boundary, the ruts heading straight for it, before turning west again and paralleling the boundary road. As we approached a spot marked on the map as Ella (where we expected to find a small hamlet and discovered just one ranch house and a pair of trees!), the ruts which ran close to the road were accompanied by a trace meandering through the vegetation, several hundred yards to the north *[Fig. 108]*. The latter was as shown on the map, so what were the others?

By now the wind had awakened and our progress over the ground was noticeably slower than when we started. Although we had initially made good time, it was beginning to look as if we might not be able to reach The Dalles without refuelling. The question was, where else to go? We had already passed our alternate at West Buttercreek before we realised how strong the wind had become. Fortunately, the question was quickly answered – Wasco State Airport was right on track, and being shown as having a hard surface runway might be open for fuel. It was also getting warmer and the Champ was rocking and bumping in sympathy with quite noticeable turbulence.

With the decision to land at Wasco, we could concentrate again on picking out the Trail. It swung south-west across the gravel road we had been following, and from there we saw no further off-road trace of it for another eight miles, any rutted sections on the way having been ploughed up. At yet another Willow Creek, the identity of which was settled for us by a north/south railway and the small community of Cecil, there was a beautiful stretch of ruts. They wound up into the hills until they were completely eliminated by a ploughed field *[Fig. 109]*. Right in the middle of the field was a small island of unploughed ground, probably too rough to cultivate, and the ruts could be seen continuing across that too before disappearing once more under the plough.

Then there was little to fix our position other than the creeks and the ranch road, but Four-mile and Eight-mile Canyons appeared as expected *[Fig. 110]*, as did State Highway 19 as it passed through the almost non-existent community of Shutler. There were intermittent stretches of ruts across here, some very clear.

We had not seen any Historic Markers for a long time, so it was most heartening to come across a large roadside sign by Shutler Creek, which we thought must have been the Weatherford Historical Monument marked on the map. Then suddenly there was a mass of landmarks, the best being our old friend the Union Pacific, as it swept regally through the long curving Alkali Canyon. The road and the Trail route accompanied the railway through the canyon until the latter curved south at Cedar Spring.

All the way through the canyon, to where a new road led up to a great sprawling lime quarry and plant, on top of the hill at Roddy, the Trail showed as a clear trace to the north of the main road *[Fig. 111]*. It was on higher ground, no doubt to keep clear of any marshy effects of the creek wandering through the valley bottom. Beyond Roddy, the trace disappeared under first one road, then another, as far as Cedar Spring. The spring site showed as a lone clump of trees at the point where the Trail branched west, up a draw descending into the main canyon.

Then we were off again over featureless scrub-covered hills for six miles to the next valley, where ran the John Day River, named after a member of the 1812 Astorians who reputedly went mad during the return to the East. We followed a gravelled track down to the river, where none was shown on my map, other than the route of the Trail *[Fig. 112]*. Then south along the east bank of the river, where an industrious farmer had cultivated some broad strips along each side. Another grey gravel road snaked down from the hills to the McDonald Ford, where the Trail crossed the river.

From the Ford, the Trail climbed back up into the bare hills, but from here on we saw no more ruts – those marked on the maps were ploughed over. We gave up the search when abreast of Wasco, as time and the fuel gauge, now bobbing on the 'Empty' mark, were insistent that if we did not soon get down voluntarily we would be down involuntarily!

It needed a two-mile detour to locate the small town of Wasco, the first real town we had seen since leaving Echo an hour and a half earlier. The airfield had a single, 2,700 ft long tarmac runway, parallel to a good highway that led into the half-mile distant town. The runway was near the crest of a rise, and sloped downhill into wind, now obviously very strong as shown by the horizontal state of the windsock by the hangar. That helped us to slow down easily on the slope (which ended in a huddle of buildings!), and in fact was strong enough to cause us a little concern as to where was the best place to park. Time down, 10.05: time in the air, 2 hours 40 minutes.

There was no one in sight as we swung round in the lee of the hangar, near the pumps. This was a scene all too familiar, as at Penn Yan, West Penn, Kindelberger, Hebron, Clinch, Glendo, Farson and American Falls. The place was absolutely dead, though there was a crop-duster by the hangar and another up the hill at the end of the runway. As Rod Shelburne had told us, it was no good dusting when either the temperature or the wind is too high – here both together were obviously too much!

There were several houses near the hangar, but either no one was in or they didn't want to let on that they were. There was no traffic on the road, so it was going to be a long hoof down to the town, carrying our two empty 3-gallon containers. We didn't dare take a chance on leaving the two Leica cameras, so the fixed one came off its mounting and we carried them both down with us.

It was very hot and even the crickets seemed to have taken a break, almost the only sound to be heard being the blustering of the wind. The road down to town, though only half a mile to the centre, seemed much longer, with the bright sun glaring back off the concrete. When we got to the crossroads in the town, it was still deserted, but at least we could walk in the dark, cooler, shadows of the buildings lining the main street. This was a feature of several towns we had seen in Oregon, unlike many others in the West that had seemed to spring up along a single main road and where the low buildings were all set far back from the roadside.

At the crossroads we had a choice – downhill to the left or uphill any other way! We could see no filling station in any direction so opted for the easy way out. Fortunately, at the bottom of the hill was a garage with pumps, but no attendant! Wasco was beginning to take on the air of a ghost town! We poked around in the workshop and finally ran someone to earth – not only the garage man who was willing to fill up our containers but also the local representative of the law, complete with armoury! The latter offered to run us out to the airstrip and return a funnel loaned us by the garage. Suddenly, all was light and life!

We quickly filled up, though the wilful wind managed to deposit some of our fuel outside the tank despite the use of the funnel. Our friendly sheriff saw us off and we were blown by the wind back up the runway to the top of the slope. After a stop of only 40 minutes, we were back in the air after the briefest possible run into wind. Here again, after eagerly leaping off the ground, the Champ demonstrated how much it loved old Mother Earth by its reluctance to climb away. Same old problem, even though now we were only 1,500 feet above sea level!

At least it was mostly downhill to The Dalles and the Champ could be coaxed up again without too much worry. Our next landmark was Spanish Hollow, possibly an old Stage Station site in a shallow canyon of that name, and the Trail was shown as rutted, leading down into and up out of the Hollow. There was a rutted track across a wheat field, and a gravel track nearby, either of which could have been the Trail route leading into Spanish Hollow, but nothing showing on the far side, now fully cultivated.

What was perhaps more exciting was our recognition of Mount Hood, its snow white peak gleaming in the sun and looking much closer than the fifty miles that separated us. To the north-west could be seen the white peak of Mount Adam 60 miles away, whilst to the south was the 80-miles-distant and smaller peak of Mount Jefferson. It would have been near here that many emigrants would also have caught their first real view of Mount Hood, and what joy that must have engendered. For most of them, it meant that the end of the overland Trail was only a day or so away!

Soon, too, would they have their first sight of the majestic Columbia River, which would come as they breasted the last hill before the river, near the small community of Biggs. The trail they left as they approached that point showed up well, though we had difficulty in keeping our eyes off the magnificent sweep of the river as it channelled either side of Miller Island. There was a long road bridge, typical of many over the broad rivers of the west, with long approach ramps and a short, high, girder section near midspan. The south shore of the river (it would not seem right to call something of these proportions a mere bank!) was dominated by towering crags, and the Trail route wound down past the present-day First View Monument [Fig. 113].

The map showed a section of ruts running alongside the main highway, and sure enough, there it was, high above the road, running along a low cliff top. Further on, where the road makers ate into the cliff, the Trail disappeared, and we saw no more of it until it climbed the hills west of the Deschutes River.

We circled several times over Biggs, awed by the sheer size of the river, only the minute road vehicles and railway goods wagons lending scale to the scene. In both directions the picture presented was a study in straw and earth browns, deep black shadows cast by the cliffs, and the incredible, intense blues of water and sky. There was little in the way of obvious cultivation on either side, and it was not difficult to visualise the scene as the emigrants would have viewed it. On so vast a canvas, the man-made additions were almost lost when viewed from our lofty perch.

Opposite Miller Island, the Deschutes River runs into the Columbia, and must have presented quite a tricky task for the wagons to cross [Fig 114]. At least for most, it was the last river to cross! No mean river in its own right, it is but a stream in comparison with its mighty neighbour. Even so, and despite the dams which restrain its flow, it still manages to run white over a rocky bed just a little way up from the crossing point.

Having crossed, the wagons and their tiring oxen were faced with an uphill drag as long and steep as any undertaken to this point; the difference was that the end was now almost in sight. Just over this last range of hills lay the small town of The Dalles, where most of the weary travellers embarked on log rafts for the journey down river. But first, for us, there were more ruts to look for as we crossed the last hills, with The Dalles now clearly in sight.

The Trail route into Petersburg, in the hills above The Dalles, was shown as rutted, but we saw no sign of such, just the usual grey gravel track, no doubt laid over the Trail road *[Fig. 115]*. And from there, the Trail made an incredible U-turn back south east, seeking an easier way down than following Fifteen Mile Creek. It led us back south-west, over cultivated fields, where the only evidence of a Trail was another grey road.

At last, our route headed straight down into The Dalles, and we swung west along the Columbia, high over the town, to the mouth of Chenowith Creek *[Fig. 116]*. Here the wagons were embarked on the rafts, to head downstream amongst the rocks and rapids, now long since covered by the higher level of water. We circled back over the town, trying to pick out landmarks like the old Courthouse, End of the Trail Monument, and Pulpit Rock, but soon gave up, not having a sufficiently detailed street plan to do that.

What we did not need a map to identify were the impressive road bridge, The Dalles Dam and the huge lock giving access to Celilo Lake and the upper reaches of the Columbia. Then it was on to The Dalles Municipal Airport on the north of the river. As we approached, a swarm of what looked to be large insects over the airfield, turned out to be menacing-looking, drab green helicopters, milling about in great profusion and confusion. We made a wide circuit in the hope that they would sort themselves out and settle before we landed, which they eventually did.

Meanwhile, Brian was twiddling his knobs and talking to his radio again, with little success. There was nothing airborne other than the helicopters, and the last had dropped down out of sight as we lined up with the 5,000 ft Runway 27. At least this airfield had a more civilised elevation than any we had previously used, an English-style 243 feet above sea level!

The wind low down was now so strong that it needed full throttle to get anywhere, and it was only when we were about to touch down that I could chop the throttle and let the Champ settle. We soon stopped but it needed a long burst of full power to prevent being blown backwards by the wind – as a measure of its strength we had taken 40 minutes to fly the 25 miles from Wasco to The Dalles and circle over the town! Then we were faced with a long, long, tail-high taxy to the turn-off. That was OK, but in trying to turn to head to the terminal, the wind threatened to blow the Champ over.

Brian leapt out and hung on to the upwind wing struts as we taxied slowly in, and then held the wing, while I got out and chained the Champ down. It needed three of us (with a welcome extra pair of hands from a friendly onlooker) to tame her tantrums. The stick was waggling around like a spoon stirring a Christmas pudding, and had to be tied back by one of our bungee straps. She didn't like it and sat there with a scowl on her face and one wing very low, pulling sideways on the chains *[Fig. 117]*. We had a long wait while the helicopters refuelled, and dare not otherwise leave the aircraft unattended. And we had an important date with some food and drink – or so we thought!

The airport buildings had been practically taken over by the military invasion; on closer acquaintance the green combat-suited soldiers turned out to be a National Guard unit on exercise, a friendly and lively bunch of young men, with a few young women thrown in for good measure! They had, however sadly depleted the contents of the food machine and the coffee pot.

The machine-served food turned out to be the usual collection of sticky bars or fruit and nut cases, fortunately with just enough of that old stand-by "Grannies Country Cookies" to prevent Brian expiring from total starvation. We soon had a fresh pot of coffee bubbling and found comfortable chairs to relax in while we watched the swarm depart.

I needed to try and telephone our sole contact in Vancouver WA, where we were to spend the night. Having stuffed the 'food' dispenser with most of our small change, there was first the usual hurdle to get over of finding a supply of sufficient quarters and dimes. After a suitable interval, in which a number of total strangers were successfully accosted for small change, the terrifying task of battling with the telephone system could be put off no longer. It came as no surprise to find that, having finally tamed the beast, the chap I wanted to talk to was not there, and all I could do was to leave a message that we should be at Evergreen Airport that afternoon.

It was roughly 120 miles to Evergreen, following the Barlow Road, and we should have done that easily in one hop, in around two hours. Taking off at around 13.00, and allowing for the increased wind strength, we should have been down well before 16.00 – in any case, we had insufficient fuel for it to take any longer! That was the ETA I left for Art (a fellow de Havilland Moth Club member), in the hope that he would be there to meet us.

We took off at 13.10, into a wind of slightly less strength than it had been when we landed. Climbing laboriously out over the Columbia to the west of The Dalles, we headed back over the town to locate the start of the Barlow Road. As we turned, the view west, where the river bends, was breathtaking in its beauty *[Fig. 118]*.

There, the hills were coated with trees and the grass was mostly a glorious green, the first we had seen since leaving Walla Walla. Downstream, the water was low enough to reveal silver-sanded strands and shores on both sides of the river, contrasting delicately with the glorious blue of the water. The hills and the river merged in the distance in a heat-hazy blue grey, foretelling the advance of big-city haze from distant Portland.

But for now, we were headed south, with growing excitement at the prospect of a close-in view of Mount Hood. The Barlow Road had been hacked out of the forest, and scrambled precariously over a 4,000 ft-high saddle at the foot of Mount Hood. Despite the incredible difficulties of hauling wagons over the mountains, many emigrants preferred to pay a toll to Barlow rather than face the extortionate costs imposed by the river men.

The reduced volume of traffic using the Barlow road meant that there was little prospect of finding any ruts, the only ones shown on the map being a short stretch through the Barlow Pass. Even so, we followed the Trail route as accurately as possible in the hope of seeing something that others may have missed.

We had difficulty at first in finding landmarks, but had located the Trail route by the time we were two miles from the Columbia, and then kept with it pretty well all the way. As the map suggested, there was little evidence remaining of the Trail, most of the southbound section to the Tygh Grade being under cultivation. There was no mistaking the tortuous descent from the Tygh Ridge *[Fig. 119]*, too steep for tractors to plough, though we could not tell whether the tracks which could be seen at various points were those of the Barlow Road.

On the far side of the valley, the Trail climbed a steep escarpment to cross a plateau leading to the Smock Prairie, a well cultivated plain at the foot of the Cascade Mountains. Of the East Toll Gate site, at the foot of the climb up to Barlow Pass, we saw nothing, the road from there on winding up through a dense forest. All we could gain from the air was an appreciation of what a stupendous task Barlow had taken on in cutting a way through here. It was difficult to be certain even that we were above the right road, and the gradients which might help a traveller on the ground pick out Little Laurel Hill were invisible to us.

Soon we came to a sizable river, running alongside the road, with another road branching left to cross it – it had to be the White River. Ahead, our road swung north and then followed a curving valley to the north-west *[Fig. 120]*. At the head of the valley lay the Barlow Pass, at the very foot of Mount Hood, which reared majestically to its snow-capped 11,239 ft peak, 7,000 feet above. But the Pass was not yet for us. At that time I was unaware of the exact elevation of the Pass, knowing only the heights of the surrounding ridges as over 5,000 feet. And the Champ was struggling to make even that 5,000 feet.

We had already found a marked reluctance to climb as the ground below rose from 250 feet to 2,000 feet at Smock Prairie. From our experiences in Wyoming, around Douglas and Casper, I determined not to cross the ridges unless I had at least 2,000 feet clear of the tops. With the strength of the wind blowing towards us over the ridges, even that might not be sufficient for our precarious rate of climb to keep us in safe air. As we followed the White River north and crossed the 4,000 ft contour lines, our climb rate hovered around zero, with the altimeter showing just over 5,000 feet!

This was crisis point, with a clear choice – either climb, or give up and go back! The Champ was doing her best, bless her. Nose up and climbing, with no hint of hovering on the stall, which had been the hallmark of those desperate minutes at Douglas and Farson, it was clear we were in a considerable downdraught. The wind was curling down over the ridges ahead, pinning the Champ down and buffeting us badly to boot.

I beat back and forth in the hope of finding calmer or even rising air, and eventually found it over some clearings in the trees on top of a shallow ridge to the south. Where the trees had been felled, the ground was yellow with sun-burned grass, so we had both a slight reversal of the air flow as it blew up the slope, plus the thermal effects from the dried grass. Barely perceptibly at first, the altimeter needle edged upward, occasionally slipping back as I strayed too far. After circling round and round for more than fifteen minutes, we had gained 2,000 feet and I felt it safe to set out for the forbidding, tree-covered ridges at the foot of Mount Hood.

In fact the Champ continued to climb as we approached the mountain, now that we were in cooler, calmer air, above the turbulence. Below us, the road wound round to the head of the valley, crossed Barlow Pass and headed down a westbound valley towards Oregon City. The wind had forced us to fly too high to be able to identify any ruts or other trail traces at Barlow Pass, almost the only point where our map showed known ruts to be. My guess was that they were, in any case, hidden by the all-enveloping trees.

We were literally not out of the woods yet, as any failure of our game little engine would have had us searching frantically for somewhere to make an emergency landing. That I knew, as I had one eye unsuccessfully open for possible clearings big enough to land in, whilst taking in the sheer, incredible beauty of the scene with the other.

At first, it was difficult to gain any appreciation of the size of the mountain, until we realised that a tiny rectangle scratched in the snow on the southern slopes was in fact a skiing slope, high above a ski centre. A string of cable pylons stretched up the slope connecting the two, and a large number of cars in the car park suggested there was active skiing in progress as we watched. At two miles distance, there was no way we were going to pick out any skiers, but at least it helped to add scale.

The mountain naturally dominated the scene, drawing our eyes to its attractively patterned grey and white bulk, again and again [Fig. 121].

The snow was glaringly, glistening white in the bright sun, enhanced by the backdrop formed by the solid, clear blue of the sky. And all around its grey rock base, the deep valleys were cloaked with conifers, the sides positively dripping with shaded, dark green trees. We circled for longer perhaps than we should have done, unable to tear ourselves away.

Another surprise awaited us, just down from the Pass – up here in the mountains, seemingly remote from civilisation, we came across a full-blooded, motorway-style flyover, where State Highway 35 joined US 26! Could there ever really be sufficient traffic up here to warrant that?

There was no problem in picking out the course of the Trail, as it wound down from the Pass *[Figs. 122 & 123]*, following roughly the course of the Sandy River as far as the small town of Sandy. From there, we were over increasingly built-up areas, with many navigational features to fix our position with accuracy. Suddenly, the Willamette River lay ahead, and we were circling over Oregon City *[Fig. 124]*.

Here at last was the goal that we, and all those hundreds of thousands before us, had been seeking. It was impossible, in that moment, not to sense a tiny thread of kinship with those that had gone before. We, too, had experienced our moments of anxiety and danger, of tiredness, and even hunger and thirst, in arriving at this exalted spot, though ours were but fleeting fragments, as minute in comparison with theirs as was the time that had elapsed since starting out.

The river was broader than I had anticipated, and the direction, from which those coming upriver on their primitive log rafts would have arrived, looked all wrong, curving in from the north-west. In fact we could see that the course of the river maintained that direction until it disappeared from sight in the haze, miles to the west of Portland. The Falls of the Willamette, which would have marked the end of navigation in the early days, are now so insignificant as to be difficult to spot.

The Barlow Road terminated where those coming upriver would have landed, near the spot now occupied by the End of the Trail Monument. Though we could see the site, there was nothing we could pick out in detail, and the whole area was now just part of a small modern town, with motorway flyovers, shops, warehouses and chimneys. All too soon, in anti-climax, it was all over.

Or was it? We located and circled over the small private airfield of Clackamus Heights that I had tried to get clearance to land at (it proved impossible to obtain the owner's name and address in the time available), and decided against taking a chance and landing there without permission. It looked far too small for our overloaded Champ in the heat that we could still feel, situated as it was in a built-up area, with no room for treetop height gadding about if I had to overshoot.

Now, we had another concern. Our low ground speed, due to the wind strength and our circling for height, meant that we had taken more time than we had allowed. There was insufficient fuel left to safely make a low level flight around Portland with its International Airport. Brian was unable to make contact on the radio, and we had no desire to go blundering around their Control Zone without it, so there was no alternative but to backtrack to one of several airfields we had spotted on the way in.

At least, we now had the wind behind us, though it seemed to have dropped considerably (is that not always the way?). The fuel state was now getting to be a problem. We had done a lot of full-throttle work, and the gauge, in its pessimistic way, was declaring that if there was fuel in the tank it was not aware of it! We decided to land at the first field we saw, regardless.

This turned out to be Beaver Oaks, with a nice little mown grass runway – such luxury! It looked deserted, but this was no time to go swanning around searching for another, so we went in. The field was quite short, at 1,700 feet, but should have been ample for the Champ, despite the significant crosswind. The buildings and some parked aircraft were at the far end of the strip, so I let it run on a little, instead of making my normal over-the-hedge approach. I should have known better!

At a critical point the Champ decided it was 'pranks' time again. When I applied the left brake to correct a swing to the right, which started to develop as we approached the parked aircraft, nothing happened! There was insufficient room to correct the swing by opening the throttle and using the slipstream to blast us round to the left – that way we would have speeded up and charged into something else. Neither was there room to use the right brake to ground-loop to the right! We both sat there and watched with bated breath as we swung closer and closer to an expensive-looking Cessna, finally missing it by little more than a foot.

Nothing seemed visibly wrong with the brake to suggest why it should suddenly have stopped working. Operating the foot pedal moved the hub brake lever, but of course we were unable to tell from that whether it was actually doing anything. Certainly, the left brake had seen a great deal of use in correcting the almost inevitable swing to the right which developed to a greater or lesser degree on almost every landing. Our next arrival could also be an interesting one if we could not fix the brake beforehand. While we were looking at it, the owner of the field arrived in a small Cessna, and made us welcome, offering to fill us up from a private supply.

There was nothing he could do to help us with the brake, but on hearing that we were going into Evergreen Airport, he suggested that we could get it fixed there easily enough. As for landing there, the runways were pretty wide and long, with no close-in obstructions.

Beaver Oaks was very much like the similarly named Beaver Valley field at Kindelberger, a small private field, almost totally dedicated to parachuting, using a DHC Beaver. There was a roomy Clubhouse, full of trophies and interesting knick-knacks, and a cold drinks machine. With one thing and another, over an hour elapsed before we could tear ourselves away!

By now, we had come to recognise that taking off in a heavily-loaded Champ, in anything approaching high temperatures, almost irrespective of airfield elevation, was an interesting exercise. That from Beaver Oaks proved no exception! A still strong crosswind did nothing to help, neither did a row of cables in the next field, strung across the take-off path! Fortunately, there was a succession of open fields beyond, which provided room for our long, flat climb out.

Time had simply flown, and now it was already nearly an hour past our ETA at Evergreen – I just hoped Art would wait for us there. After corresponding over several months, I was keen to meet him and see his Tiger Moth, and any other interesting machines there might be around. We still had over thirty miles to go, which would take us another thirty minutes at best.

There were no more hills to fly over, and the plateau rose little above the 400 feet altitude of Beaver Oaks, before terminating abruptly in 500 ft-high cliffs marking the Columbia River Gorge. Crossing the river over Reed Island we turned north-west, looking for Washougal airfield which would give us a good fix for Evergreen. We were still very concerned about the possibility of infringing any traffic rules at Portland International and wanted to be able to go straight into Evergreen, right first time.

At Washougal we turned west and were soon flying low over houses and trees which tended to block our sighting of Evergreen. And then suddenly, there it was, just to our left. No activity that we could see, and we had a choice of runways. There was a windsock on top of a hangar which showed the wind still brisk, but at this point seemingly now blowing from the north-west. There was a grass runway, more into wind than the main one, and the element of left-side crosswind on the tail might help counteract that right swing, which the brakes would be powerless to stop.

Still nothing in the circuit, and no one taking off, so we dropped in over the hangars and touched down on the grass, running between a line of small hangars on our left and trees on the right. I kept the tail up as long as possible, but then when it dropped, despite the crosswind, she started off to the right. The left-hand brake was still not working! Fortunately, the ground was rough enough to slow her down quickly, before the swing developed, and then we were stopped, still facing more or less the right way.

We taxied back and tacked ourselves on the end of one of several long lines of tied-down aircraft. Leaving Brian to tie down the aircraft, I set off for the flight office, to see if I could contact Art. Alas, he had gone, and though I tried phoning him at home could get no answer. As for repairing the brake, there was a hangar just up from the office where a Jenny (Curtiss JN-4 WW1 trainer) lived, and they should be able to fix us up there!

Sure enough, there was a hangar with a Jenny lurking darkly in the back, in beautiful condition and authentic Army colours and markings. The owner (also the owner of the airport) was not there, but I was assured he would be, first thing in the morning, and would try and get us under way as early as possible. Meanwhile, Brian had discovered why the brake was not working. The multi-strand brake cable was reduced to just one strand, all the others having worn through!

Apart from the Jenny, there were many interesting aircraft based at Evergreen, most of them unfortunately locked in their hangars. A rare (to us) Waco UPF-7 WW2 trainer was outside where we could see it, and the lines of tied-down machines included a good cross-section of all the popular aircraft in use in the States since the thirties.

We were fortunate in being offered a lift to the nearest motel by one of the airfield regular onlookers. When he heard us asking about transport and motels, he offered to help straight away. This was in contrast to the cold, unhelpful and almost contemptuous reception we had received in the flight office, which was noticeable in being so very untypical of any of the other airfields we had visited. Fortunately, it did not extend to the owner, for when we met him the following morning, he could not have been more helpful.

When our ground crew caught up with us in the evening, we heard they had enjoyed a very full day. The scenic routes along the Columbia must rate as one of the most beautiful riverside drives in the world, and they were full of it. The highlight had been a visit to the 600 feet high Multnomah Falls. This day they had clocked up a total of 4,000 miles – some going in only 13 days, and all on the wrong side of the road! That averaged just over 300 miles every day, and as there was to be another long trip the next day, they would then have kept that up for a fortnight!

We decided to move on to Bandon the next day, and take a day's rest there – we were all very much in need of one. Such a pity there was not time to spare to drive over to Oregon City and view from the ground what we had seen from the air. But if we were in need of a rest, imagine what the emigrants would have felt like when they arrived here – weary, half-starved, cold, counting their losses in material goods and, worst of all for many, in loved ones buried on the way. But they would have been supremely jubilant and relieved at having made it. Even we felt a little of that – and tomorrow, the Pacific!

Fig. 100. Looking south from the head of Wilson Canyon (bottom) to Morgan Lake (upper right), some 1,300 ft above La Grande. The main Trail route (white dotted line) tops the hill at centre left, above the head of Deal Canyon, running to lower right. The arrows point to probable campgrounds, the left one used by John G. Glenn in 1852.

Fig. 101. Looking WSW across the top of Wilson Canyon. Trail ruts run across the flat ground from lower left before making the perilous descent into Hilgard Junction. An immigrant grave site at the extreme right edge is believed to be that of Emily Doane.

Fig. 102. Looking NW over Hilgard Junction, where the I-84 and Union Pacific Railroad follow the Grande Ronde river from bottom right. The railroad turns right up Five Points Creek, and the Oregon Trail (lower left) descends from above Little Coyote Canyon to cross the river, before ascending again from the Junction to top left.

Fig. 103. Deadman Pass with Kanine Ridge across the centre. The dotted line shows the Trail route from crossing the I-84 to where it drops down to the Umatilla River.

Fig. 104. Looking NW over Cayuse (upper centre) and the Umatilla Valley where the wagons left the Blue Mountains. Until 1848 they followed Moonshine Creek (centre left) to Cayuse, turning either west, or NE if calling at the Whitman Mission at Walla Walla. After the Whitman massacre the main route turned at the 'Cayuse Post Office' (arrowed).

Fig. 105. Looking east up the Umatilla Gorge, where wind curling over the north rim pinned us down in the valley, causing concern until a northerly fork at the end led us into a gorge where the wind blew along the valley with no curl-over effects, so that we were able to climb out.

Fig. 106. The Champ relaxes from her labours in the heat at Walla Walla. Jim, our Indian guide for the day, listens sympathetically while the author explains why we made only one circuit over the Rendezvous before disappearing behind the surrounding trees!

Fig. 107. The green and peaceful Mission site at Walla Walla as it is today. The Blue Mountains, down which the immigrants brought their wagons, dominate the horizon.

Fig. 108. Trail trace (right of centre) at Ella, perhaps the most exciting discovery whilst exiting the US Navy Boardman Bombing Range. We expected to find a small town, but Ella turned out to be the clump of trees and farm at top centre!

Fig. 109. Just as exciting were these ruts up the hill out of Willow Creek. Irrecoverable damage done by farming is clear to see. Once dug over, the ruts disappear, only those in the rough ground at centre showing the curving course.

Fig. 110. A clear rut trail approaching Montague, ten miles SE of Arlington. Hickland Butte is at top left and this section lies between Fourmile Canyon and Eightmile Canyon.

Fig. 111. A lime plant (upper right) above the canyon at Roddy, and the Union Pacific Railroad on the left, provide positive location for this stretch of ruts just to the right of the railroad and the old dirt highway.

Fig. 112. Approaching the McDonald Ford (off bottom left) of the John Day River, the Oregon Trail winds down the hill from upper right. Looking north-west.

Fig. 113. When the Columbia River was sighted near present-day Biggs, for most the end was also almost in sight. First View Monument is at lower left by the trees, and the Trail sweeps down above the white disc to run along the foot of the cliffs above the roads, the ruts still visible over this section.

Fig. 114. The confluence of the Deschutes and Columbia rivers, Miller Island at lower right. The Trail forded the Deschutes, then climbed the slope, splitting as shown by the dotted lines; ruts on the right fork are still visible.

Fig. 115. The Dalles Dam on the Columbia from above Petersburg and Fifteenmile Creek. The Trail entered at bottom right, looping back to lower centre to cross the ridge before dropping into The Dalles at top left.

Fig. 116. Chenowith Creek at the west end of The Dalles, where the wagons were embarked on log rafts for the trip down the Columbia and up the Willamette to their final destination, Oregon City. Others went over the Barlow Road.

Fig. 117. The "Champ" forcibly restrained at The Dalles Municipal Airport from going off and doing its own thing. Perhaps the 45 mph wind had something to do with that!

Fig. 118. Taking off from The Dalles, looking west up one of the world's most glorious waterways. The Columbia still seems able to bite, judging from the white water in the left channel round Rocky Island, though with low water levels this may just be a sandbank.

Fig. 119. The Barlow Road ran along Tygh Ridge from centre right, down the very steep Tygh Grade, across the swampy valley floor and straight up the escarpment opposite. If they thought this was bad, they hadn't "seen nuthin' yet."

Fig. 120 (above). Approaching Mt. Hood (at top left) from the SE we were prevented from climbing above the ridge off to the left by winds curling over it, until we spotted a large clearing in the trees (centre) which provided warm rising air that lifted us clear. The White River, alongside which is the Barlow Road, runs along the bottom of the valley on the left.

Fig. 121 (right). Mount Hood peak rises in all its magnificence to 11,239 ft, still some 2,000 ft above us as we crossed the ridge. The deep blue sky contrasts spectacularly against the snow-covered ski-slopes – this in August!
(Photo Brian Hargrave)

Fig. 122. Over the top by Barlow Pass, unseen in the carpet of trees, and on west over the Barlow Road switchbacking along the valley bottom, at the base of Tom, Dick & Harry Mountain. Dripping with trees and no place to suffer a power failure!

Fig. 123. Overlooking Laurel Hill, where the wagons were let down successive 45-degree inclines of 240 ft and 60 ft!

Fig. 124. Oregon City at last, end of the long, long Trail for the emigrants, but not for us. Looking west from the Barlow Road over the Willamette river, those coming in from the Columbia would have sailed up from the right, all aiming for the Land Registry Office at top left of the large central grassy area.

Fig. 125. Our Trail-end was the Hudson's Bay Co. Trading Post at Fort Vancouver. Chief Factor of the HBC Trading Post was Dr McLaughlin, seen by many as the Founding Father of Oregon, whose rebuilt house within the stockade is shown here (also at the top of Fig. 126).

Fig. 126. Shot on take-off from the adjacent airfield, this shows the replica stockade and defensive tower. Now a National Parks site, it is intended to recreate the Fort in full.

Fig. 127. Heading for the Pacific coast meant crossing the Coastal range of mountains – again, as with the Cascades, covered with a wall-to-wall carpet of trees. The clouds are over the coast, and the old US Navy Airship base at Tillamook is top left.

Fig. 128. Running south down the coast with a 45 mph tailwind, Newport and its airfield quickly came into sight, though intermittently through a low-lying bank of cloud.

CHAPTER 17

THE BEAUTIFUL PACIFIC

George was to accompany me on this last westbound leg, it being an old ambition of his to fly into Bandon Airport, as being the only right way to visit our mutual friends there. So he and I were out early for breakfast, for there was work to do before we could get going. Jean came out to the airport with us and left us on the doorstep – which was unfortunate, as we realised almost as soon as she drove off that we had not brought our toolkit with us. Not only that but, at that time in the morning, we were discovering that temperature-wise, Oregon is not all that it might be. We needed our warm, woolly jumpers while we worked outside on the aircraft!

A telephone call to the motel soon brought both, and the offending brake cable was quickly removed, in the process of which, George established why the cable had worn through. The outer conduit lay at the wrong angle where it was clamped to the undercarriage leg, so that the inner cable rubbed against the rough lip. By slackening the clamp and changing the angle, we hoped to overcome that.

Meanwhile we found the airfield owner in his hangar, and he readily agreed to provide the cable and ferrules so that I could make up a new cable. He showed me how to use his swaging tool to fix the ferrules, and in the end charged us only $1.50 – that must be the cheapest replacement brake cable anywhere! While there, we talked about the Jenny and the fact that I had worked with the Shuttleworth Collection (a well-known museum of aircraft dating from 1909 to WW 2, mostly in flying condition) back in England. He volunteered the information that he was now well into his seventies, and that his wife, of similar age, flew with him in air displays and still went wing-walking on the Jenny!

By 10.00 we were ready to go. It was still quite chilly, with a light breeze, the sky half full of banks of low cloud and the distant hills lost in mist. We decided to call into Pearson airfield in order to visit the replica Fort Vancouver, built partly within the airfield boundary – perhaps while there, the weather conditions would improve. As it was, they were not good enough for us to fly over the Coastal Range of mountains, which lay between us and the coast.

It was only six miles to Pearson, on the west side of Vancouver. To get there we had to skirt the Portland control zone, keeping our height down to 1,000 feet. The single tarmac runway lay parallel to the north shore of the Columbia, pointing straight at a large bridge over the river, with a quay and a shipping terminal alongside. A steep approach was called for, down over the bridge, leaving an impression of grey girders and tall lamp standards clutching at us as we sideslipped in.

After just ten minutes in the air, we had landed at Pearson, and quickly found our way to the Fort *[Figs. 125 & 126]*. This was really the end of our Oregon Trail flight, coinciding with the end of the Whitmans' journey west. The American Missionaries (and many other emigrants) had found Dr McLoughlin, the British Hudson's Bay Factor at the Fort, helpful and accommodating to his visitors.

We found his current American counterparts no less so to these British visitors, and the sight of a large Union Jack fluttering at the masthead inside the stockade brought just a tiny lump to the throat! A little bit of old British Colonial history, so carefully restored, so far from home. At least, we got the impression that the new owners were proud of the connection, and we felt our forefathers had left it in good hands!

By the time we were ready to leave, the early morning haze and low cloud were beginning to disperse in the now warm sun. The wind had risen to around 25 mph and swung right round so that we had to take off in the opposite direction, out over the bridge. Climbing laboriously out, despite George's lighter weight, no radio and now without the heavy roller map and mounting, we headed north-west, into wind and over open country, while we gained height. From here on, we had no strict schedule and no set route – we would just be following our noses.

Once clear of Portland, we climbed to clear the 3,500 ft-high hills that lay between us and the coast, crossing first the broad Columbia, then the Willamette, the latter looking almost as wide at this point. That it could accommodate large ocean-going boats was demonstrated by the presence of a number of cargo ships, anchored nearly a hundred miles from the sea. South stretched the wide Willamette Valley, the Eldorado of the toiling pioneers. This was what they had risked their all for, a great flat, fertile chequerboard of cultivated fields, streams and green woods, one of the most fertile agricultural areas in the United States.

The cloud base, though well broken, was still low enough to cause anxiety about clearing the first range of hills, but opened up before we reached them. Our landmarks came up as expected, and soon we were in relatively clear air and climbing for 4,000 ft to cross the main range. The wind was increasing and swinging more northerly, so that we had to crab into wind to hold our course to Tillamook. An old wartime airship base, this was chosen as an easily recognisable landmark, approached from a low crossing point over the mountains.

Visibility was improving all the time, and the clouds were down to about three eighths cover, their shadows dappling the forested hillsides as we flew over the mountains *[Fig. 127]*. Another unbroken carpet of trees! And more buffeting from the wind as it curled over the hills. But ahead, long before we got to them, we could pick out the enormous airship sheds, looking so familiar to our eyes, accustomed to seeing the corresponding sheds at RAF Cardington on the circuit at our home base of Old Warden.

We could also see fog banks and low clouds over the coast, where we had expected to find the blue Pacific! Past Tillamook we were faced with an enormous white cloud, whose top was at only 2,000 ft. Thick white fog blanketed the shore and extended solidly out to the western horizon – were we not to see the Pacific after all? Well, at least there was a little clear stretch to the north, the water showing blue in front of the fog.

Circling above the cloud, which we guessed was hanging over Cape Lookout, we were amazed to notice that the fog bank extended south in a dead straight line, as far as the eye could see, and just off the shore for much of the way. As the coast line wavered in and out so the edge of the fog bank hung over the land or way out to sea.

Where the water was visible below, it was a beautiful cobalt blue, lighter as it washed onto the beach, deepening to ultramarine out to sea. The now very strong wind was whipping up the surf in short, curving white lines of breakers. White horses speckled the blue and where the sun caught the ripples it sparkled back. Occasional short-lived, thin, white wisps of low cloud dappled the surface with darker blue shadows. And all along the shore, a broad stripe of silver sand gleamed in the bright sun, offset by a darker brown tidemark of wet sand on one side and the edge of the dark green woods on the other. Heady stuff!

Turning south, we flew down the coast, one of those unforgettable flights which make such treasured memories. No matter that the wind was now blowing at some 40 mph, even if it was going to shorten the flight time. At least we had no worries about having sufficient fuel to get us to Bandon. What was of far more concern, was whether that and other airfields along the coast would be clear of the fog bank when we arrived overhead!

Out to sea, the fog extended down to the water from about 2,000 feet. Along the edge of the fog bank, little puffs of low cloud occasionally detached themselves before dissipating. Inland, visibility, as usual with such wind strength, was as clear as a bell. Would Bandon be clear of the fog, and if not, was there an airfield within reach which would be? We decided that we would land at Newport, or the next open field after that, if Newport lay under the fog. Then, with plenty of fuel on board, we could easily find an alternate to Bandon if necessary.

On past Cape Kiwanda, one of the prime beauty spots along the whole of this stretch of coast, with the blunt bulk of Haystack Rock standing proud on a mat of foaming white breakers. Here we had watched hang gliders when visiting by car several years earlier, but there were no gliders today! Lincoln City was clear, but aptly-named Cape Foulweather was lost under the cloud and fog-bank, as it had been on my previous visit. Yaquina Head, a few miles to the south was just clear, and beyond that Yaquina Bay, at the mouth of which was Newport.

As Newport town came into view, we could see that it would be touch-and-go as to whether the airfield, on the headland on the opposite side of the bay, would be in the clear or not *[Fig. 128]*. The cloud hung over the shore and partly obscured the town, and then we spotted the airfield – just! Fog and very low cloud was scudding over the runway as we flew overhead; it would be best to land here if we could as the airfields further south might be completely covered. Fortunately, as we lined up with the runway, the clouds seemed to roll back a little; with the throttle wide open, in order to make progress against the bucketing wind, we dropped down onto the runway. Time down, 13.42; time in air, 1 hour 35 minutes; a short leg for a change!

Once down, the Champ slowed in no time at all, so that we could turn off at the first intersection; here the fog was rolling through the trees and the wind was threatening to turn us over. Fortunately, the terminal area was sheltered by a wood, but even so George had to hold onto the wing as we taxied in. After refuelling, the Champ was tied down while we went in search of refreshment. The forecast gave a wind-speed of 25 knots, but it was patently gusting well in excess of that locally, with the madly dancing windsock threatening to detach itself from the pole.

The food facilities at Newport proved no better than at any other small airfield, so lunch was a can of 'Coke' and some of Granny's Cookies. We phoned through to Bandon Airport and established that there was no fog there as yet, but the fog bank was just off shore, and threatening. Meanwhile, at Newport, although the fog was still rolling through the trees to the west of the taxyway, the runway had stayed in the clear all the time we were there. Amazingly enough, any wisps of cloud that strayed overhead dissipated immediately, almost as if there was an invisible barrier.

Take-off was a piece of cake, once we had survived the crosswind turns along the perimeter track and at the end of the runway. The Champ was off literally in a matter of yards. I held her down to a few feet above the runway to build up speed, then let her climb, and she had kited us up to 750 feet before we turned above the end of the airfield. No left-hand circuits today – they would have taken us straight into the cloud that was rushing menacingly past off our left wingtip, so a tight right turn took us back south parallel with the runway.

Now the ground, over which we had seemed almost to hover as we took off, raced past. Running downwind along the shore, occasionally we skimmed over the cloud bank; against the wispy cloud-tops our speed seemed normal, but the occasional glimpses of ground through the ragged edges showed it whipping past at a most un-Champlike rate, and demonstrated how fast the clouds were moving.

Mostly, the coast was in the clear and we watched fascinated as it slid beneath. There are many beautiful bays where the numerous rivers and creeks emptied into the sea, great irregular winding stretches of calm blue water, contrasting vividly with the angry white lines of surf tearing at the edge of the ocean as it dashed against the seashore. Waldport, Florence, Woahink Lake (of fond memory where I managed several exciting circuits of dual instruction in a floatplane, years before), Reedsport, North Bend, Coos Bay, and finally, Bandon.

Bandon – where the Coquille River wends its wooded way to the sea, conveyed way out beyond the surf by twin breakwaters; Bandon, with its sand and surf, cliffs and rocks and legends – Face Rock, which Indian folklore avers was a beautiful but wayward princess, transformed with her pet kittens into rocks when she disobeyed her parent's wishes and played in the sea with her pets. Alas, the facial profile of the rock, visible from the shore, can not be seen from the air. Worse, as we approached, it seemed from a distance as if nothing at all would be seen of it from the air – the whole lot looked to be hidden under the fog bank!

We circled over the town and found that the cloud was just clear of the south beach, with the offshore rocks on the very edge of the fog bank, sometimes clear, sometimes obscured. At least, it meant that the airfield would be in the clear. Before landing, we had to go and look for our friends' house and let them know by circling over it that we were in the area. How different familiar features sometimes appear from the air! At first we could not identify the area where the Mazons lived, and then when we did, had great difficulty in picking out their plot. All to no avail, no one was home, or if they were they did not come out!

When we landed at Bandon, the wind was straight down the runway, and nothing like as gusty or strong as it had been at Newport. Time down, 15.55; time in air, 1 hour 35 minutes (again). By the time we had refuelled and tied the aircraft down, George and Evelyn Mazon arrived, followed by a reporter and photographer. Seemingly, interest still abounds in Oregon about the Oregon Trail and its travellers, even modern ones!

Our ground crew caught up with us a couple of hours later, after a very enjoyable drive down the coast, following in our wake from Lincoln City. What a joyful reunion that was for old friends, and first meetings for new ones. We all slept well that night (almost too well) with, for the first time since leaving New Jersey, no compunction for an early rising the next morning! We had a whole blissful day to spend in bountiful Bandon before making our way back East!

PART 3: THE WAY BACK

CHAPTER 18

A FOND FAREWELL

There was to be no flying on our day off – the weather saw to that. Visions of taking all the members of our party in turn, and perhaps our hosts, for a pleasant flight along the coast to, say, Cape Blanco (the westernmost point in the contiguous United States), Port Orford or Humbug Mountain, were blown away by the continuing wind and washed out by drizzle and low cloud. No sense in taking people up in such poor conditions that the weather knocks the fun out of it!

All too soon came the day of departure, Thursday 7th August. The weather charts showed good sunny conditions inland, but on the coast fog and low cloud still persisted from the previous two days. At least the wind had dropped. As the morning progressed, there was a noticeable lightening of the sky to the east, followed quickly by a thin strip of clear sky showing above the distant hills. If only we could take off and stay clear of clouds, it would be worth flying towards that clearing sky, to see if conditions would continue to improve.

Initial plans had been to fly north east to Corvallis, the highest point in crossing the Coastal Range then being only 2,800 ft high. After refuelling, the intention was to head east for a 4,800 ft-high gap in the Cascades between Mount Jefferson and Mount Washington, before turning south-east for an overnight stop at Bend. A slightly shorter, more direct route would have taken us across the much higher Three Sisters Wilderness Area, but we dared not plan on that in case the clouds covered the peaks, or the temperature rose too high and stopped us climbing. Brian was to fly the Champ back to Salt Lake City and we had to bear his extra weight in mind!

The weather forced us to change our plans rather than take a chance on going north-east, where the clouds were pretty solid, and finding no way through or over the Coastal Range. That thin strip of clear sky to the east was our best bet, providing the cloud base over Bandon was high enough for us to get clear. Brian got off at 10.40, with no problems at Bandon's near-sea-level elevation and in a quite chilly temperature. Circling back over the field at 700 feet, we waved goodbye to the Mazons, who had come to see us off, and headed for the clearest patch of sky!

The local cloud base was just over 1,000 feet, with visibility to the east quite good but poor in every other direction. The small town of Coquille soon came into view to the left, giving us a good fix before setting out to cross the fairly featureless Coastals. The cloud base lifted as we went east, so that the 2,000 ft-high hills gave us no problems.

The hills were shrouded in mist [Fig. 129] and, in crossing the Range, perhaps half a dozen could be seen to each side, rising above the fog-filled valleys. The closest were clear enough to reveal the solid, sombre blanket of trees covering the slopes. Behind, the next stood out starkly, uniformly, grey against the lighter grey of the one beyond, and so on, successive hills extending ever more faintly into the distance till they merged into the grey of the clouds.

An eastbound road crossing the hills pointed the way to the Interstate Highway 5. The latter's dual carriageways would lead us north along the Willamette Valley, between the Coastal and Cascade Ranges, to pick up our original route from Corvallis. We planned to land at Hobby, a small airfield to the south of Eugene but, with the wind now behind us, made such good time that we decided to go on to Lebanon. Visibility was gradually improving all the time, though the Cascades looked as mistily dark and mysterious as the hills we had just crossed.

At Lebanon, the sun was just breaking through the thin overcast above. Landing at Lebanon State Airport at 12.45 gave us an air time of just over two hours, not bad for a distance of 165 miles – hooray for following winds! On taxying up to the terminal buildings there were no fuel pumps to be seen, but there was at least one of those enormous tankers which seem to live on even the smallest airfields.

We seemed to be objects of much idle curiosity as we parked by the tanker, but no one came out to serve us, which was most unusual. There was an air of almost amused detachment when I approached a small group of bystanders to ask about fuel. "Sorry, no can do – ask in the office if they will let you have some." What was all this then – 'let' us have some? Most operators fall over themselves to sell their fuel!

In the office there were several uniformed men and a girl sitting about nattering, and the reaction to the question as to whether any fuel was available was much the same: "Ask the guy on the phone.' No other information was volunteered, and they lost interest in us after that. Eventually the 'guy' on the phone finished his conversation, and asked what we wanted. One would have thought we had asked for a gold mine – the negative answer could not have been much less emphatic. But at least he explained what it is was all about!

Whereas virtually every other full-time airfield visited had been a base for cropdusters, these people were operating borate bombers (or something similar) for fire-fighting. There had apparently been a large number of forest fires recently, and fuel was getting short. They could not spare any for mere joyriders, not even a gallon, and would we please go somewhere else. When pressed, they suggested possibly Albany might be able to help, but not Corvallis, another fire-fighting base.

The only problem was that Albany was on the next chart, which we had left with the car crew in the interests of weight saving! Taking a bearing and distance from their wall charts we decided to fly blind (as far as having a chart was concerned) to the 10 mile distant Albany. Located on a great bend of the Willamette River and alongside the I-5, it seemed that even with our funny compass it would be impossible to miss. But it did leave a nasty gut feeling flying in a strange area without a map! There could be no question of missing the airfield and spending time searching for it with our low fuel state!

The bearing was 321 degrees, minus 4 degrees correction for wind drift, minus 19 degrees for variation, minus 36 degrees compass deviation. Fly on a compass reading of 262 degrees for Albany?. Unbelievable – flying 60 degrees off course in a light breeze takes some swallowing, especially with no map to check against! In the event, Brian flew along the railway tracks to the I-5 then turned north and kept going until the airfield turned up under our nose. Railroads and highways are far more reliable than 'Mickey Mouse' compasses – usually!

Already a broad river, the Willamette at Albany was used for storing great rafts of logs for processing at a large lumber mill *[Fig. 130]*. It was a good spot for a lumber town, with river, rail and road serving transportation demands over the years. The airport, in direct contrast to Lebanon, was a friendly little place. They had fuel enough for us, and more Granny's Cookies to keep Brian happy. Something else, which we had not seen before, was a motel in the airport grounds, with a taxyway leading up to tie-downs at the front door; what a pity we had not planned to stay there overnight! That would have impressed the ground crew! What does one call a motel on an airfield – an aerotel?

From Albany, the sun again shone from a clear blue sky, and snowy peaks could be seen rising out of the haze over the Cascades. This was a beautiful stretch of country, well-wooded, intertwined with rivers and dotted with blue lakes. The foothills gave way to higher mountains as Brian climbed to 8,000 ft to clear the 4,817 ft high Santiam Pass. Here for the first time, it really felt as if we were flying amongst the mountains, unlike the Barlow Road, where Mount Hood stood in glorious isolation.

Conditions here were much more favourable for mountain flying, the wind being behind us, carrying us up the slopes well clear of the dangerous curl over of the eastern slopes. On the long approach from the west, there was plenty of time to gain the height needed, and we crossed the Cascades in smooth, clean air. Although our fire-fighting friends at Lebanon had mentioned numerous forest fires, mercifully there were none to be seen – they had obviously done a good job!

In crossing the Santiam Pass, there were the magnificent peaks of Mount Jefferson on our left *[Fig. 131]* and Mount Washington on our right, the latter dwarfed by the triple crowns of the more southerly Three Sisters *[Fig. 132]*. Stretching away in a long line to the southern horizon, beyond the Sisters, were more distant, snowy peaks. Way off to the north, the 65 mile distant Mount Hood could be clearly seen, its snow cap now yellowed by the intervening haze. 10,500 ft-high Jefferson, so sharp and clear with its large patches of snow, seemed just a few miles away – in fact it was sixteen. Between us lay the gaunt outlines of Three-Fingered Jack, the lower slopes covered with trees and large areas of bright green grass: a scene of breathtaking, awe-inspiring beauty.

Once beyond the Pass, the giant conical mound of Black Butte could be seen ahead, and then behind that, the town and airfield of Bend, with the small cone of Pilot Butte showing clearly above the northern end of the town. Having been helped over the mountains by a tail wind, we were surprised to find that at the airport, the wind had swung north, exactly in line with the single north/south runway. We never ceased to be amazed at how much the prevailing wind could vary over quite short distances.

At Bend there was, as usual, no problem with transport to a motel. After booking in to one by phone, the manager cheerfully agreed to pick us up, but took a surprisingly long time to arrive. It transpired that having double-booked us, he felt obliged to find us another motel and still came out to drive us in! Our ground crew caught up as Brian and I finished our dinner. Their ride over the two mountain ranges had taken them to one of the most beautiful lakes in Oregon, Crater Lake, and they were full of it!

That evening we drove to the top of Pilot Butte, to watch a most memorable, glorious sunset. The golden sky turned to red as the sun dropped reluctantly behind the Cascade Mountains, the skyline etched sharp and clear. All those local peaks we had identified earlier from the air now stood starkly silhouetted on the western horizon, while down below the black bulk of the mountains gave way to a twinkling fairyland of lights from the town of Bend.

There was a long desert crossing ahead of us the next day, and an early start was called for to beat the heat! A favourable thing about navigation over the American desert is that one is almost certainly going to the same places as do the few roads. Today was no exception, long straight stretches of highway leading us all the way into Burns. How can there be so much nothingness? Mile after mile after mile of it! Brian flew at around 3,000 feet above ground and had no problem with the heat. With a good tailwind we made a fast time (for a Champ) into Burns, and were soon down on its vast expanse of glaring white concrete.

As with several other airfields we had visited, Burns was run by a charming young lady, all on her own. She operated the radio (which we did not!), answered the phone, filled up the tanks, fixed the coffee, swept out the flight office, and provided a not inconsiderable improvement to the decor! Thank heaven for little girls!

A local pilot came in and chatted. He warned of considerable smoke haze as a result of forest fires, and was surprised to find that we had just arrived from Bend without having being troubled by them. According to the weather forecast, there was very thick haze from fires in eastern

Oregon. Meanwhile, the sun was still beating down from a clear blue sky and visibility was unlimited.

Brian noticed the heat when we took off: the Champ was reminding us of how little she liked 'hot and high' when near the ground. The ground elevation of Burns was 4,144 feet, and it was now really hot, the Champ's climb out suffering accordingly. Brian circled out low over wheat or hay fields, adjacent to the airport, slowly gaining height in the thermals. American farmers are nothing if not inventive in the patterns they make in their fields! One looked for all the world like an enormous, irregular, brown and hay-gold chequerboard. It took me a long time to fathom out how it was done, and even now I am only guessing that it was made by a combine harvester of some sort, dropping the unwanted chaff at regular intervals.

Our route, due east, took us over the awe-inspiring Owyhee Range – 65 miles of nothing but a continuing succession of herringbone-patterned ridges and creeks, starting with Stinking Water Creek (fortunately we were by then high enough not to know whether the name was aptly applied or not!) and the Malheur River. After that there were a few solitary tracks and minor roads, but nothing of any note to provide a positive position fix until we crossed the Owyhee Reservoir. Brian flew by our error-ridden compass over a scene of utter desolation – dry creeks, dull brown hills and scrub, stretching in every direction to the limits of visibility. For once, I gained comfort from the presence of the little Emergency Locater Transmitter, sitting in the back beside me, and hoped that it would not be needed there!

Conditions were by no means ideal for the Champ. Although we were not bothered by wayward air currents from the wind curling over the hills, the thermal activity more than made up for that. At one point, at being tossed in a violent updraught, Brian drew my attention to the altimeter as the hands wound rapidly round – gaining a thousand feet in probably no more than ten seconds, then losing fifteen hundred feet almost as quickly.

At the Owyhee reservoir, we finally came across signs of civilisation. A few power boats, tugging water skiers and drawing their curving white wakes across the incredible blue waters, marked a popular water resort. A small marina, with lines of moored craft, was tucked away under the vertical cliffs of the gorge which the reservoir now half filled, and a solitary white gravelled track winding into the hills showed how people reached this haven in the desert.

Shortly after the reservoir disappeared behind us we were back over the Snake River, and heading south-east to Glenns Ferry for our overnight stop. Glenns Ferry airfield was dry (of fuel) and right on the limit of our range, so we landed at Mountain Home to top up, despite the now very strong wind blowing at thirty degrees to the runway. Brian made a good landing but found the Champ quite a handful on the ground in the wind.

Mountain Home's expanse of baking white concrete looked deserted at first, but I found a solitary occupant relaxing in the cool comfort of the flight office, who came out and refuelled us. Here, we switched back to Mountain Time, losing a precious hour in the process.

At Glenns Ferry an unwelcome sight awaited us in the form of a wrecked Cessna 172, being dismantled by the unhappy owner. Jim told us that he had been flying back home to California, and late in the evening had run into 60 mph headwinds (no doubt related to those we had encountered on the coast). He had first run out of daylight, then fuel, and felt he had been misled by the air traffic controllers; with his wife and two of his three small children on board he had tried to find Glenns Ferry in the stormy dark and almost made it. Having left him in the lurch, Lady Luck came to his rescue at the last moment, finding a clear patch for him to drop into and enabling him and his family to walk away from his blind 'arrival.' The price paid was the total write-off of his uninsured pride and joy – it could have been much higher!

Jim had his whole family with him and was trying to dismantle the aircraft and load it on a trailer, virtually single-handed. His very patient wife was only able to give limited help as she had to keep an eye on her young and energetic children, including a new baby. So we felt privileged to be of real assistance – a chance to pay back to one American just a little of what our party had received from so many of his countrymen. After helping to remove the wings, there was no more to be done until he had finished stripping out the avionics equipment, so we tied the Champ down and looked for some way to get to the town to book into a motel.

Apart from a couple of small, dilapidated tee hangars, the airfield consisted of a windsock and a dirt runway, the minimum necessary to allow visitors to the adjacent Three Island Crossing State Park and Museum to arrive by air. So, no phone and no alternative but to start walking to the mile-distant town. Matters could have been worse; it seemed that the local town council, who own the airfield, were thinking of closing it. They feared the possibility of enormous claims being made on them, if anyone landing there put a wheel in a gopher hole and wrote themselves off. Similar cases had proved negligence against the airfield owners and won enormous sums in costs and damages! They could afford neither the insurance against such claims, nor pay anyone to fill in the holes faster than the gophers could make them!

Fortunately, almost as soon as we started walking along the road, we were offered a lift from someone who lived near the airfield. First, he took us to his home for a most welcome cooling drink and slice of water melon. There he showed us his collection of local Indian arrow heads and Stone Age flints (and demonstrated his patiently-acquired skills at flint-knapping), and then drove us into town to book a motel for the night. Western hospitality again! After that he ran us back to the airfield, and joined in with helping Jim load up his trailer.

Several other locals turned up, having seen us land, and also gave a hand. Suddenly, there were enough people about to get the whole shooting match loaded precariously on the trailer for the long drive back to California that night. Having hired the trailer for a couple of days, it had to be back in the morning. Jim seemed a nice guy and his determination deserved to be rewarded – alas it was not to be. Meeting him later than night, in the town, he told us he had sold the wrecked airframe locally for its scrap value, having decided that nothing was worth salvaging.

After seeing Jim off from the airfield, our ground party turned up, and we all drove back into town for a slap-up meal. There was just one place to eat, in a little diner which was obviously the focal point for many of the local inhabitants, where all the local gossip was exchanged and old friends met – the equivalent of an old English pub! Here we enjoyed a rough, tough, but genial, Western atmosphere, complete with sheriff, handguns and stetsons, both for dinner and, next morning, breakfast.

We tried a spot of movie-making early in the morning, in order to get some shots of the Champ taking off and landing. That meant making a circuit and landing back on before setting off for Salt Lake City. The film shows just how marginal the Champ's performance was under such hot and high conditions; when watching it now I find myself willing it up as it oh! so slowly gains height after take-off!

Landing at Burley on the next leg after passing very close to Jerome, we resisted the temptation to drop in and look up our friends there again; the final leg to Salt Lake City would be a little marginal, even from Burley, with anything but a tailwind, and we really could not spare the time for another landing to refuel. As it happened the wind remained very light, which did nothing to reduce the soaring temperature. The sun seared down from a clear sky, though distant haze formed as the day wore on.

At Burley, after taxying in, we could hardly believe the large notice which read "Cut-price 80-octane gas – $1 per gallon." At a little over half the price everyone else was charging there had to be a catch? But no, it meant what it said and much more. We climbed out of the Champ into a time-warp! The operator turned out to be a real old-timer, who might have been anything over 75, wearing one of those old-fashioned, large, flat, cloth caps, complete with button top, seen only in old Hollywood movies of the twenties!

He was working on old fabric-covered aircraft, keeping his skills and himself alive, on what was now little more than a self-financing hobby, meeting folks who would be attracted by his "cheap gas" sign. We stayed

201

an hour, and could cheerfully have made it many more, just nattering over a common interest, but the clock indicated otherwise.

The temperature was still inching upward, and it did our morale no good at all to see how marginal were the take-offs of several other, higher-powered, more modern aircraft. The take-off was perhaps the worst Brian had been faced with, the flight path taking us over a maze of tall lamp standards and cranes. But the Champ staggered clear, and after a little precarious low-level threading between high-flying obstacles, was soon gaining altitude for the flight across the Sawtooth Mountains.

En route we passed close below the beetling brow of 9,385 ft high Black Pine Peak, following Interstate Highway 80N as it climbed the pass between Black Pine and the Deer Creek Mountains. Our flight path took us round the northern shores of the Great Salt Lake, the latter appearing as a shimmering white line in the heat haze. Distant peaks could be seen rising out of the mist, appearing at first to be mountains to the south of the lake. They turned out later to be those on Promontory Point, halfway along the lake – the southern shore was lost in the haze some 70 miles away!

Ahead could be seen the mighty Wasatch Range of mountains which flank the east shore of the lake like a line of cliffs, while below was evidence of the Mormon style of agriculture. As a change from the usual 100-plus acre fields we had become accustomed to, we now saw an irregular patchwork more reminiscent of those at home. Here, irrigation tended to be by self-drive pipes which trundle back and forth across rectangular fields; there were very few of those that rotate to form the great irrigation discs which are such a noticeable feature of the landscape elsewhere.

As we swung south round the north-eastern tip of the lake, the shining white line grew into a great expanse of salt flats, with a heat-hazed silver stripe showing where lay the 15-miles-distant water! Drawing closer, we could see that some of the white salt beds split into great squares of thin pastel hues of blue, green, yellow and pink – somebody was making a buck or two out there!

Where the Bear River ran into the lake was a great untidy marsh, the result of the myriad channels of fresh water snaking into the salt waters of the lake, creating a weird landscape of swirling patterns and colours. Mostly the latter were varying shades of dirty greens, from milky to deep olive, interspersed by yellow sand and white salt beds, like nothing I have ever seen before: nature in the raw, looking like some ghastly school chemistry lab experiment on a nightmarish scale!

But if the primeval marsh was fascinating, the Wasatch Mountains were sublime! Towering grey granite cliffs, steep rocky slopes and green grassy tops, studded with conifers, 5,000 feet above the flat farm land

and townships nestling at the foot. Beyond could be seen range after range, reaching up to snow-capped, 13,000 ft-high peaks.

And then the lake itself. The waters were of constantly varying hues, depending where you looked. Close in shore, blue where they were enclosed for water sports, or viridian green outside the enclosures, or patchy muddy green where floods now covered agricultural land. In the distance, hilly islands rose from their reflections in the tranquil hazy blue lake. Somewhere out there in the haze were the Salt Flats where boyhood heroes risked their lives to bring home for Britain the world land speed records: inspiring names such as Henry Segrave, Malcolm Campbell, George Eyston and Goldie Gardner.

Over extensive areas of flooding, power line pylons stood ankle deep where roads headed out, under the water, to distant huddles of water-logged farm buildings and small communities *[Fig. 133]*. Telephone poles and occasional lines of forlorn trees marked the routes of the unseen roads, and the pylons marched out across the water to Antelope Island and beyond. What amount of man's minor works had nature so lightly brushed aside – what heartbreak stories lay soggy beneath the surface?

Our destination was Skypark at Bountiful, just outside Salt Lake City, and here we found sufficient aerial activity to not have to search too long for a windsock. With perhaps several hundred aircraft tied down in long rows there was plenty to interest us while waiting for our crew to arrive, which they did half an hour after we had completed our usual post-landing chores. Again we found people were interested in what we had been up to with the usual warmth of feeling about the Champ: like the Tiger Moth back home the Champ attracted instant friends!

We enjoyed a day and a half of being ordinary tourists in Salt Lake City; with perhaps a better appreciation and understanding than most visitors of what the magnificent memorial to the handcart emigrants stood for. Having seen so much of the Oregon/Mormon Trail country, and especially the sites of their greatest tribulations, how could it be otherwise?

Standing before the statues, memories came flooding back: my journey along the north bank of the Platte the previous year, when I stood on the banks of 'small' rivers such as the Elkhorn and Loup and wondered how the footsore emigrants could contemplate the primitive crossings; Rebecca Winters' wagon-tyre grave in the shadow of Scotts Bluffs; the desert wilderness on the run-in to Independence Rock; Martin's Cove near Devil's Gate; Willie's Handcart Memorial in the middle of nowhere; the silent stones brooding over the great surge of human hope that had trundled through South Pass; the Lombard Ferry over the Green River. That stopped my train of thought, when I recalled our own near-disaster at that point!

Our stay in Salt Lake City was both happy and slightly sad. Here George and I were to say goodbye to Brian and our ever patient wives, who had provided such a valuable measure of support throughout (and what was more, they were still talking to each other despite being cooped up together in close confines for four weeks!!). We two would soon find out just how valuable had been their contribution, in the course of the next two weeks, when we had to do without them!

Our last night together was a time of anxiously deciding what we could do without, and what we simply had to have with us – and then cutting the latter in half, not once but several times until we had reached the bare minimum! We had a bag of clothes and the two Narco radios sent on to await us at Gerry Schwam's place in Philadelphia – at least we would have a change of clothing when we got back. The Leicas were carefully packed and despatched back to Leitz. Our faithful 'tank,' which had never even hinted at letting us down in the course of over 6,000 miles of motoring, was returned to the car-hire firm after dropping George and myself at Skypark the following morning.

The end of one era and the beginning of another!

Fig. 129. Homeward-bound from the Oregon port of Bandon meant re-crossing the Coastal Range, this time shrouded in grey mist and cloud, but still beautiful for all that.

Fig. 130. By the time we reached Albany the sun shone, lighting up the log rafts waiting their turn at the sawmills.

Fig. 131. Perhaps the most thrilling, yet humbling, sights were on the return crossing of the Cascades, when a whole range of glorious peaks, mostly snow-topped, could be seen stretching to north and south. One of the lesser ones was Three-Fingered Jack (7,841 ft) with the 16-miles distant Mt. Jefferson at 10,497 ft towering beyond it.

Fig. 132. To the south lay Mt. Washington (7,794 ft) and, beyond, the magnificent Three Sisters: North (10,094 ft), with Middle (10,047 ft) partially hiding the more distant South Sister (10,358 ft).

Fig. 133. End of the road for Brian and our wives was Salt Lake City, and parting was a wrench after a hectic four weeks together. We approached from the north, with Antelope Island and the gradually rising waters of the Great Salt Lake on our right.

Fig. 134. Returning north, now just George and the author, with the towering Warsatch Range now on our right, and a friendly red Luscombe from Skypark to wave us farewell.

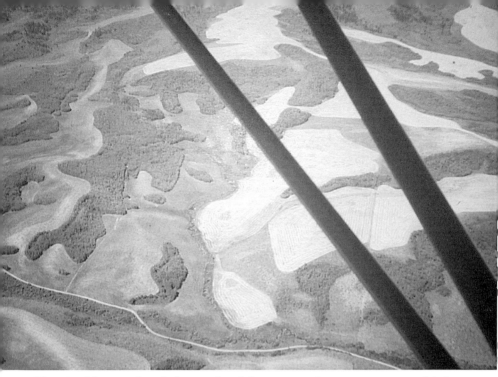

Fig. 135. Many and varied were the sights we saw, but we never ceased to be amazed at the wonderful patterns created by the agricultural activities of the hillside farmers such as here, near Inkom in southern Idaho.

Fig. 136. Though a pretty mundane subject, we were always grateful for that great American institution, the Airport Courtesy Car. This one was at St. Anthony ID, far from the town and any taxis, and saved us a long slog!

Fig. 137. South Pass of the Rockies was flat, but the next one we tried, Raynolds on the Montana/Idaho border, was anything but, with a snow-storm thrown in for good measure. Looking east over an unnamed 11,300 ft ridge to Yellowstone National Park. Here we climbed to 12,000 ft.

Fig. 138. No comfort to the west with Black Butte rising to 10,545 ft. But what satisfaction we felt at the end!

Fig. 139. The mountains seemed to stretch all around us, but the way ahead was clear – for a while. Little did we know that lurking to the north of Gallatin Peak (11,015ft) was a thunderstorm that tried to stop us landing at Gallatin Airport at Bozeman – luckily without success!

Fig. 140. After crossing the Rockies at Bozeman Pass, the route south-east took us up the Little Bighorn River past Custer Battlefield National Monument (lower centre).

Fig. 141. After racing into Sheridan County Airport WY to land before the snowstorm ahead got there, we found that it had already passed through, going the other way! Sitting on the apron is a rare bird, a Martin 4-0-4 airliner dating back to the late forties, almost as old as our "Champ"!

Fig. 142. Our last real mountains, in the Black Hills of Dakota, Harney Peak (7,242 ft) and Mount Rushmore, where the cloud-base threatened to sit on the tops to block our way but fortunately never quite made it.

Fig. 143. Circling the Rushmore National Monument we were very aware of the downdraughts curling over the top, which threatened to drag us into the trees. Sitting at a safe height it was a while before we spotted the heads, marked here by a black frame – looking west.

Fig. 144. No wonder they are called the Badlands: any landing here would be bound to be bad!

CHAPTER 19
A WITCH'S BREW

Freed of all daily schedules, our next target was to arrive at Blakesburg for the Antique Airplane Association's Fly-In, by no later than Thursday, three days hence. Bearing in mind the problems in taking off from airfields higher than 5,000 feet in the heat of the day, we decided to fly north to cross the Rockies between Bozeman and Billings, in Montana. Hopefully, the air would be cooler that far north, and it would in any case be an interesting flight up through the mountains, following the old Lewis & Clark Trail for a few miles.

Our ground crew took us out to the airfield for the last time, and we set about stowing our now minimal gear. Each of us had one shoulder bag, a sleeping bag, a camera, and a flight bag with charts etc. Shared between us was a carrier bag of essentials like raisins, mints, fruit, cartons of fruit juice, film cassettes, etc and that little red Pizza Hut water container we had been given at Topeka. Finally there were the two empty 3-gallon plastic containers for fuel.

Apart from my flight bag and the water container, which stowed away in the front with me, it was all packed in round George, filling completely the space between shelf and roof. The official maximum permitted load on the back parcel shelf was 20 lb, so it was perhaps just as well that we were never able to weigh what we actually stowed on it (we calculated that it weighed 19.999 lb); the Champ flew it all, and "where ignorance is bliss . . ."!

One of the most attractive aircraft on the line at Skypark was a beautiful red Luscombe Silvaire *[Fig. 134]*, a neat little all-metal contemporary of the Champ, albeit higher-powered and better equipped. The owner had talked to us when we arrived, and he was there again to see us off. He said he would like to fly out a little way with us, and was left in no doubt that nothing would please us more! After final farewells to our wives, we got off the ground at just after ten o'clock.

Conditions were fine, as one would expect, the sky blue, the sun shining and what little wind there was behind us. The only fly in the ointment was that already it was very warm, and obviously going to become very much hotter. We took off OK but the long slow climb out told its own story. We turned to cross over the terminal area to give a final wave to our ground crew and then set off north. The Luscombe soon caught up, flew in close formation and cavorted around us for a while, finally departing home with a friendly wing waggle. Thank you, Red!

We climbed slowly to 7,500 ft to give ample height over the hills ahead and retraced our route of the previous Saturday as far as Tremonton, then followed the Little Malad River along a long narrow valley. This took us into the Bannock Mountains, among 9,000 ft peaks, along another long valley to Inkom [*Fig. 135*] and then out over the plains to cross the Oregon Trail near Fort Hall; could it really have been only twelve days previously that we flew over here on our outward journey? The map roll of the Oregon Trail was now on its way back to England, but knowing roughly where to look, we were able to pick out the ruts quite easily, despite flying very much higher than before.

Our immediate destination was the small town of Blackfoot, for fuel and to obtain maps for the next section of our route. These had been out of stock at Skypark, and we could not take a chance on running out of map! Alas, there were none in stock at Blackfoot either, so we had to arrange to land at the tower-controlled Fanning Airport at Idaho Falls. They gave us instructions over the phone to watch for a light, and to come straight in on Runway 16 if we saw none – how sensible and down-to-earth the American air traffic controllers are! Any self-respecting controller at an airport in England, with 9,000 ft and 5,000 ft runways, would be so bursting with self-importance and power that he would not hear of anyone landing without radio!

Taking off from McCarley Field at Blackfoot was quite exciting; there was still sufficient wind to need to use Runway 36, and this headed out over the town. As was to be expected, the Champ got off easily enough but was most reluctant to climb. Skirting right round the built-up area, keeping over the lowest ground until enough height had been gained to climb away, took ten minutes flying before we could set course!

At Idaho Falls, there were no lights from the tower so I landed as instructed, despite considerable misgivings over the wind direction – it did not seem possible that in a distance of 25 miles, the wind could have swung completely round. In fact it had not moved that much, but was across rather than along both runways, the directions given keeping us off the main runway and, in the lee of a line of trees, with a slight into-wind component.

Turning off the runway, we could see a large red-painted hangar, about a quarter of a mile ahead, with large, white Gothic script lettering announcing "The Red Baron." This turned out to be the home of a famous racing P-51 Mustang of that name. We had an interesting conversation with the owner, who had written off the Mustang but planned to rebuild another. He now flew an F-104 Starfighter, also named the "Red Baron," the world's fastest privately-owned aircraft!

He sold us the maps needed and checked on the availability of Saint Anthony for us, there being some doubt as to whether it was still operational. And then walked all the way to the pumps in the now blistering heat to sell us just $1.77-worth of 'gas,' which was all that could be squeezed into the Champ. I just hoped he really did want to see our little plane. We also rang the tower to arrange to use the long runway, hoping to benefit from thermals off the glaring white concrete. Control said they would give us a green when it was OK to roll.

They gave us a flashing green to taxy to the end of the runway, but then seemed to forget we were there. We sat and sat at the end of the vast expanse of concrete, the runway disappearing into the shimmering heat haze over the brow of a slight rise. In the end, with the oil temperature approaching the red mark, I decided to go, George keeping a sharp lookout for a red light in case they had not simply forgotten us – he reported seeing a green just as the tail came up! I held the Champ down to gain maximum speed before climbing away; we had reached all of 150 feet by the time the end of the runway passed beneath us. At least this time the Champ was still climbing and we had heaved ourselves up out of the blanket of hot air at ground level!

Since rejoining the Snake River valley near Fort Hall, we had been flying over a populated, loosely-farmed area, with occasional large towns, but north of Idaho Falls our route was again reaching out towards the wilderness. The highway looked not quite as broad, the traffic had lessened and the farming was less intensive. Now we had only to follow the dead straight stretch of railway which would lead us directly to the airfield at Saint Anthony. It was hot and soporific in the cabin, but the sight of the long, newly-black, asphalt runway beneath jerked me into wakefulness.

Taxying up to the cluster of buildings at the north end of the runway, the place looked deserted. A vast yellow and black Grumman Agcat dwarfed us as we scuttled past looking for the pumps. The hangar, with more Agcats, was deserted, as was the flight office. But I finally ran the sole occupant to earth, making coffee in a little room off one end of the office. Here was yet another airfield crewed only by a young lady, as pleasant as had been all the others we had encountered.

But she was brighter than the others, handing over the keys to the pump for us to help ourselves, trusting us to tell her how much fuel had been put in. She had some good news – the airport courtesy car was available for the night; the bad news was that it would cost seven dollars for the insurance! It was just as well we took it though, as we had covered more miles than either of us would have cared to walk with our gear by the time it was back at the airport in the morning!

Saint Anthony was a pleasant western town, with Henry's Fork of the Snake running through the green, well-watered park which served as a memorial to the explorer Andrew Henry, his name being immortalised in several natural features in the area. That night we dined in a restaurant, every inch of whose walls was covered by cattle brands; try as we might we could discover no two of the many hundreds displayed to be the same!

Next morning, there was a change in the weather – an overcast, rain-filled sky, puddles underfoot, and a forecast of little improvement. On the way to the airfield, the clouds started to break; if they would lift enough for us to fly it might still be possible to have a go at getting over the Rockies. They did, and at 07.45 we taxied out! Despite the cooler air, Saint Anthony's 5,000 ft elevation made for the usual slow climb out, the Champ staggering disconcertingly close to some tall trees beyond the runway – it did not exactly augur well for what was to come!

Ahead lay the Rocky Mountains, grey and menacing under a blanket of clouds and mist, blocking our way like a brooding watchdog. Though they had hardly bared their teeth at South Pass, here they looked like the real thing! First we had to cross a 6,000 ft-high ridge, where the road could be seen climbing through a wide carpet of trees. The wind was on our nose and would be curling down over the top of the ridge; without several thousand feet in hand as we approached, the Champ could be forced down into those trees. Here was where my lack of experience in mountain and bush flying began to tell; a mountain flyer would have known more accurately the safety limits and may not have wasted so much time gaining height.

Beyond the ridge the ground dropped away briefly, but I carried on climbing; I wanted as much height as possible before venturing between those peaks! Our track wound round 10,196 ft high Mount Jefferson (yes, another one), followed a minor road past Henrys Lake, over Raysnolds Pass and along the Madison River Valley in descending to Ennis Lake. On our left were the mountains of the Gravelly Range and on the right those of the Madison Range, terminating in the 11,000 ft-high Gallatin Peak. Our route had again taken us across the Continental Divide, which also formed the State boundary between Idaho and Montana at this point.

I had encouraged the Champ to keep climbing, to see just how high she would go, and also to obtain a better view across the mountains. In the cool air, she kept on up to 12,000 feet, a full-power, nose-up, balancing act, trembling on the brink of a stall. We had to work for it, the Champ and I, but it was worth it. At that height, it was like sitting on top of the world, hundreds of feet above the very highest mountains around us. They stretched in every direction, range after range, as far as the eye could see.

Initially, we had been flying under threatening, black cumulus, whose shadows rendered the adjacent peaks dark and evil-looking, reminding me so much of Wagner's "Ride of the Valkyries" that I burst into a da-diddy-da-da rendition which had George wondering if there was anything wrong with the engine! But to the east, the clouds had given way to clear skies. Bright sunlight lit up the 60-miles-distant mountains of the Absaroka Range on the far side of Yellowstone Park, and reflected off the waters of Yellowstone Lake *[Fig. 137]*.

Despite its threats, the big black cloud did no more than toss a few snowflakes at us in passing, though we could see a thick white veil draped over an adjacent peak, suggesting that it was snowing hard down there. We were soon out from under it into bright sunshine, and could only marvel at the scenery around us. Ahead, the grey stone faces of the Madison Peaks shone brightly in the sun above the dappled, grassy green slopes, dotted with the dark forms of conifers *[Fig. 138]*. On our left, where the clouds still prevailed, the dark craggy outlines of aptly-named Black Butte groped crookedly for the sky *[Fig. 139]*.

Below us, the floor of the valley was the usual scrub land with occasional meadows and irrigation discs; those farmers never give up, not even high in the Rockies! We could see where someone had carved out some strip fields over the undulating slopes, and the intricate patterns and whorls created by ploughing round the high ground left shapes any abstract artist would be proud of!

As we emerged from the mountains, the Madison River dropped down from Ennis Lake between the walls of a steep gorge, finding a tortuous way through the ridge closing off the valley. Here we were to turn north-east for Gallatin, but between us and the airfield lay a great menacing black cu-nimbus cloud, towering high above us. Below the blackest part, a grey blanket extended down to the ground, and as we watched, several flashes of blue lightning arced down. There was no future in taking on that beast, we would have to run before it. But which way to run?

We never did learn to anticipate accurately which way the storm clouds would go; they never seemed to follow prevailing wind patterns. By heading at the centre of the cloud for several minutes, it looked to be approaching from our right. So we diverted westwards to Three Forks, thinking it would pass safely behind us. Three Forks might prove an interesting place to visit, being one of the better-known landmarks on the Lewis & Clark Trail. But after another five minutes the storm appeared to be moving the same way, and now looked like getting to Three Forks first!

Back towards Gallatin, and once headed east again we looked to be clear of our troubles. Only to find another, initially quite small, dirty grey cloud approaching fast. The cloud base was at our level and connected to the ground by a vertical swathe of grey interspersed by an occasional blue flash. Taking early avoiding action kept us clear not only of it, but also Gallatin, to which the thing now seemed to have taken a fancy, hovering lovingly above the airfield.

Circling just off to one side, willing it to move on before we ran out of fuel, we were occasionally drawn into the turbulence which stretched for a surprising distance from the ragged edges of the cloud. Then the Champ would be rolled and tossed about, completely ignoring my control movements until she escaped from the invisible threat. Behind the cloud, in clear air, a string of new, puffy little grey horrors was forming up, and I began to wonder whether the air would ever be clear of them.

After an eternity, the main cloud loosed its grip on Gallatin and edged westwards, looking for fresh fields to conquer, while the airfield's glistening wet runways came back into view. Which way to approach it? I had been certain that the wind which blew us through the Rockies had been a south-westerly, but there was no doubt that the clouds were scudding north-west – could it be that different at ground level?

Circling round to the north, looking in vain for a windsock, I became aware of another little grey-black beast approaching from the east: that settled it. I scurried in quickly to an approach on Runway 30 to see what it was like at low level; I could always do an overshoot if the wind turned out to be unfavourable. In lining up with the runway, we could at last see a windsock. It was threatening to tear itself off its mast, and swinging violently from one side to the other, but at least it was mostly pointing towards us. We should just have to try and touch down at mid-swing!

The actual touchdown was something of an anticlimax: the wind went all quiet, and the Champ ran true, so that we were able to turn off at the first intersection and scuttle away to the terminal area. A sudden gust nearly wrenched off the Champ's door as we opened it, but after that last abortive attempt to do us some actual bodily harm, the wind seemed to lose interest, and we were able to tie down for refuelling. An enormous tanker rushed out to fill us up, but as quickly retreated when we said we wanted 80-octane! Another then drove up from the firm next door and deposited nine gallons of the right stuff in our tank.

We had an interesting stop there, in the course of which we were shown a local rebuilding project. This was an original, 1932 vintage, Pietenpol Air Camper – one of the earliest forms of popular, do-it-yourself, home-built aircraft. Meanwhile we kept an eye on the weather, watching the way the thunderheads built up and the direction from which they approached. There was no doubt about it, they formed and moved very rapidly, and it would be best to choose our take-off time very carefully!

To the north was a close range of high mountains, dropping to the Bozeman Pass area which was the way we hoped to escape east from the Rockies. Their peaks wore a continuous mantle of dark grey, white-topped clouds. Occasionally the latter would spill over and drift towards the Pass. At the same time there were little groups of cu-nimbus to the south, and every now and again a more adventurous fellow would detach itself and make a running pass at the airfield before heading west.

Meanwhile the wind was swinging about all over the place. When we finally decided the time was ripe for take-off, it had swung back to a westerly so that our take-off was in the opposite direction to that of landing! At least it was a lot cooler now, and we had no difficulty in getting off Gallatin's 4,500 ft elevation and climbing strongly away – the Champ was now performing more like an aeroplane than a power-assisted sailplane!

On our downwind leg past the airfield I suddenly realised there was a twin-jet airliner, probably a DC-9, moving slowly along the taxyway from the west end of the runway; it could only have come from the runway, and so must have landed just after we took off. My appreciation of American air-traffic controllers went up even more; when they gave us a green light to take off they must have had the DC-9 under control and probably already approaching long finals! At home most controllers would have had hysterics at the thought of a non-radio light aircraft being anywhere near the runway at that time. I recalled being held at Leeds-Bradford in a Tiger Moth, engine running, for over 15 minutes, while a distant Viscount approached and landed.

Though we had chosen to cross Bozeman Pass as the best place to get out of the Rockies, on the basis that it was 1,500 feet lower than South Pass, we might as well not have bothered. The Pass was in a steep-sided, narrow, winding gorge through a 7,700 ft-high ridge, which still left us needing to climb to 9,000 ft before crossing over the ridge. There was no way I would trust our 65 hp to keep us airborne while flying down through the Pass in such a rolling, rumbustious wind. The Champ was in good form though, and took us over the top safely, but not without encountering considerable turbulence.

What proved of more concern, were the storm clouds bunched over the mountains to our left, as far ahead as we could see beyond the Pass. However, they left us in peace, and gradually rolled back northward. That left us to enjoy the scenery below, following the blue Yellowstone River as it meandered between silver strands to Billings, now clear of clouds and with good distant visibility.

We landed at a little airstrip called Oscars, just outside Billings, obviously used mostly by small private aircraft. But the place was nearly deserted and at first we could get no fuel; on ringing the bell of a mobile home-cum-office I upset a chain-tethered Alsatian that tried hard to have me for lunch. Its enraged barking attracted the attention of a Cessna owner who was cleaning his aircraft and came to see what all the commotion was about.

It transpired that the owner was away and had the fuel pump keys with him, but our new-found friend offered to fill us up from a drum he kept in the back of his pick-up truck, which was complete with pump, hose and filter. That turned out to be so low on fuel that the pump would not prime, so he drove us to the nearest filling station to put in six gallons for us, transferring the remainder into our tank as well – he said he wanted to empty out his drum anyway! At least it saved hunting for fillers and filters, and disturbing all our gear in order to get at the deeply-buried containers.

Naturally, as soon as we had finished filling the tank, the airfield owner returned, with the pump keys! He offered to show us a family fairground in the next field, which included local history exhibits, steam engines and agricultural equipment. It sounded interesting but was obviously going to take an hour or two; we were concerned about the latest weather forecast which predicted a front bowling in from the west, bringing severe thunderstorms, so regretfully had to decline. Locally, the wind was still swirling around from the east, so where the winds and the front came together could be a good place not to be!

Until arriving at Billings we had not really decided where to aim at for the night but, in view of the poor forecast, thought it best to head for Sheridan and make up our minds there. At least, if we decided to stay overnight, there were some fellow members of the Fort Phil Kearny/-Bozeman Trail Association whom we might meet. After dog-legging out to Hardin, we could follow the Little Bighorn River most of the way into Sheridan, and that would take us clear of the Bighorn Mountains. It would also take us directly over the site of Custer's Last Stand!

From Oscars, we headed almost due east. This took us out over virtually featureless country, much like the Kansas prairies, so it was a relief to find Hardin coming into view pretty well as expected. There were storms brewing on all sides and the wind was quite variable but we were still in the clear. This was quite a serious decision point. At Hardin, we could land at the nearby Fairgrounds Airport, but once we turned south to Sheridan there were no intermediate airfields. In eighty miles at Champ cruising speed, a lot could happen!

As it happened we were forced to swing south of Hardin due to a storm brewing over the town, and another racing in from behind. To the south, the skies were still clear, but it was obvious that where we were was no good place to remain: either creep into Fairgrounds under the storm or get the hell out of it! We got!

Crossing the Bighorn River and heading for Crow Agency on the Little Bighorn, we got an unexpected fix on the latter by the sight of perhaps a hundred white teepees in and around an arena on the east bank. Whilst goggling at that, we suddenly realised that a mile or so to the south was the Custer Battlefield National Monument *[Fig. 140]*. This was a neat little patch of green, with rows of white crosses laid out in military precision beside shading trees – a well-kept military cemetery that caught the eye first.

Circling round and round we at first wondered what were the dozens of white dots clustered on the side of a ridge a quarter of a mile to the south east of the visitor centre – and then it clicked. They had to be the markers showing where each man fell – this was the actual site of the battle. It was a wild spot, perhaps half a mile to the east of the Little Bighorn, whose course through the brown grass and scrub was well marked by a wide ribbon of verdant grass and trees. The site was on rising ground above the river, exposed on all sides – what a spot in which to die. Whatever the ethics of the events leading up to the battle, a lot of brave men died here – all those markers looked to be contained within a one hundred foot square!

Dipping our wings in silent salute we left the site, and headed south up the broad river valley. Gradually the hills closed in from each side and were not alone in doing so – the front which had been chasing us from Billings tried to cut the corner to nip in front of us before we reached Sheridan and soon there was a counterpart creeping up on us from the east! There was nothing we could do except keep our nose down and head straight for Sheridan in the hope of not becoming trapped between the two.

The Little Bighorn petered out just over the Wyoming border, to be replaced by another river valley, that of the bigger Tongue River running north-east, twenty miles short of the airport. At the same point, the stormy threat from the east also disappeared. One down, one to go, or was it? For now a really ominous, slate-grey, monstrous storm-cloud looked to be racing towards the airfield from the south-west, with a great white sheet of snow or hail hanging down behind it. With throttle wide open and nose down, the A.S.I. was registering just on 100 mph as we tried to beat the storm to it: I had no delusions about what the conditions might be like if it got there first!

Thankfully, as the runways came into sight, though they were glistening wet, the storm was still perhaps a mile away. Surprisingly, a windsock showed that we were flying downwind, which necessitated making a wide circuit to approach from the opposite direction, into the teeth of the storm; we could not take a chance on anything else being in the pattern and meeting us halfway! The first rain spattered the windshield and turbulence rocked the wings violently as we made the last turn onto the approach, and then we were safely down. It was raining very hard as we taxied up to the pumps.

We got out to tie the aircraft down before the storm ripped in, expecting at any moment to be pelted with hailstones. Unbelievably, at that point, the rain stopped and the whole place was bathed in bright sunshine! Looking fearfully towards the south-west, where the storm had been approaching, we saw that a great wall of dark grey cloud across the southern sky stretched up until lost in a white overcast *[Fig. 141]*– it was actually now further away!. There was a brilliant rainbow to the east – evidently someone was getting something nasty but it was not going to happen at Sheridan!

Thinking about it rationally afterwards, it was obvious that the winds were blowing the storm south-east, and far from beating it to the airport, we had been overhauling it! And yet, in the air, both George and I were convinced it was going the other way! In the course of the next few days we improved slightly in estimating where the storms were going, but not much! While refuelling, the tanker operator confirmed that they had just had a heavy downpour but that the main storm had passed south of the airport!

After that, it was not a difficult decision to stay overnight, but the hoped-for contact with the Fort Phil Kearny people did not materialise. There was a courtesy bus that took us to the nearest motel, and by the time we were ready for dinner, another heavy storm was upon us – the decision to stay was obviously the right one! We met a friendly couple from Lake Erie, flying a Cessna 150, who had planned to visit Gallatin that day but had been put off by the weather forecasts; the pilot found it difficult to believe that we had just flown from there in our little old Champ! As I explained, I thought it not unreasonable; far from home on a once-only opportunity and a tight schedule, one has a more impelling urge to keep going than someone able to come back next year. It is not a question of taking more risks, rather one of assessing them in a different light!

We had dinner together and shared some of the biggest pizzas I have ever seen – they must have been 18 inches across! No way were we going to be able to get through even half of them, and the waitress seemed quite surprised that we did not want the remainder wrapped to take with us – we dare not put that much weight in the Champ!

Next morning at 7.00, the weather forecast was of more scattered thunderstorms to the east, while overhead the clouds formed a continuous cover. By the time we took off at 7.50, there was a break through which the sun shone brightly, but to the east, in the direction we were flying, a low overcast and mist gave visibility of about five miles. Several dark grey masses, reaching down to the ground, indicated where there were local small storms in progress. At least they were well scattered and there ought not to have been too much difficulty in dodging them, if the previous day's experience was anything to go by. We were learning fast – only time would tell whether we were learning the right things!

Initially, there were a few features to check course by, but these became fewer and fewer, and we had increasingly to rely on our compass. That became even more questionable after dodging a rather larger storm cloud creeping up from behind! Somehow, the errors of compass, navigation and wind cancelled each other out, and course check points came up as expected. Visibility improved significantly as we flew east and the storms became more isolated, the only problem being that they grew in size, almost as though each was sucking in all the surrounding rubbish to form more obnoxious giants.

Approaching our first refuelling point, Newcastle Mondell, the road leading to it could be seen disappearing into what looked to be a cloudburst, the storm hanging apparently stationary, blocking our way. Another storm cloud was streaking in from our right to join in and it looked unlikely that we would be able to squeeze through the gap between them before they came together. We retreated north behind the main storm, circling and waiting to see which way to go, and hoping that we would not run out of fuel before they moved on. I had no intention of venturing anywhere near the dark grey mass, my mind recalling too many horror stories of the effect of hail stones on fabric, and remembering the violent turbulence we had encountered in the wake of the storms over Gallatin!

Eventually, a gap materialised to the south, and we skirted round the main cloud mass, soon picking out Newcastle Mondell's runway, gleaming wet in the sunshine ahead. As we scuttled past the storm, it shook its skirts at us, rocking our wings in violent gusts, but we were soon safely on the ground, with George hanging on to the wingtips to stop us turning over as we taxied to the pumps. Everywhere was dripping wet, despite the warm sun, which only served to make the storm we had just passed look even blacker. We quickly refuelled, expecting it to burst on us again at any time. Leaving George to make sure that the Champ did nothing to damage itself, I went into the office to settle up.

Surprisingly, by the time I came out, the storm had moved away north west, virtually into the very strong wind! We never did understand exactly what was happening to those storms, as they never seemed to do what you would expect them to!

Our next stop was to be at Kadoka, a tiny town in South Dakota, which just happened to be at about the right distance. With a slight detour from the straight line track to Kadoka our route would take us over Mount Rushmore, in the Black Hills, for a sight of the giant heads carved from the living rock. The adjacent Harney Peak would be the last mountain of any note on our route. It was just past ten when we took off and the air was not yet hot enough to cause any concern, so we did not anticipate any difficulty in clearing the 7,200 ft peaks ahead.

What did affect our climb was the strength of the wind. It was blowing hard from the north-west, and we had to cross a series of ridges, the first of which, just 2,000 feet higher than the airfield, was too close and too high for the Champ to fly straight over. The wind kept pressing us onto the flanks and in the end we had to stand off and circle to gain sufficient height to sail over the eddies. Beyond was another wide valley and more ridges, leading to the first of the peaks.

By now storm clouds were gathering again from the north-west and spreading across the hills. Approaching Harney Peak *[Fig. 142]*, the grey clouds had rolled right across, the general level of the uneven underside of the clouds being about 8,300 feet, but with many dark, lumpy outbreaks bubbling hundreds of feet below and obviously raining or snowing – a real witch's brew. We were climbing very slowly, occasionally bouncing off the cloud base, penetrating wispy entrails, dodging the stormy ones and wondering whether there would be sufficient clearance between the mountains and the clouds to get through without having to resort to escape routes. It was touch and go, with the tree-clad slopes and craggy rocks rising ever nearer.

If our flight across the Rockies had reminded me of the "Ride of the Valkyries," here I found myself rendering Peer Gynt's "Hall of the Mountain Kings"! It fitted the mood exactly, with imaginary trolls hiding in the dark nooks and crannies beneath! Miraculously, although the air became quite turbulent, and occasional flashes of lightning could be seen from some of the blacker bubbles of cloud, conditions stabilised at just acceptable, and we got through.

Then there was a new problem – that of locating Mount Rushmore. Although a good road led north from Custer round the back of Harney Peak we could not go that way because of the cloud. Being forced round the eastern flank of the mountain, at first we could see nothing that matched our expectations. Circling and holding height on the lee side of the mountains was like walking on a tightrope, the Champ on maximum climb just matching the downdraughts, and I was on the point of giving up.

Suddenly, below us was a vast car park and a number of buildings on the side of a mountain, beneath some whitish rocky outcrops. Surely this must be it, but where were the heads? And then there they were, looking much smaller than expected from our height of about 800 feet above. Perhaps I had been spoiled after viewing the gigantic ancient Egyptian statues and temples at Abu Simbel?

The turbulence from the wind curling down over the peaks prevented us going much lower – get caught in one of those down-currents of air and the Champ would be amongst the trees in no time, so there was nothing for it but to stand off and circle as low as we dared. The carvings, even from our height, were impressive and certainly worth the trouble involved in visiting them *[Fig. 143]*.

Next on our list of places to see was the Badlands, our route taking us straight across the National Park. Once clear of the Black Hills, the clouds rolled back and the sun shone, lighting up the weird rock formations that gave the Badlands their name. Here was another entrancing picture, of striated, grey-rock, herringbone-patterned, crinkle-edged ridges, in places standing clear from a brown green plain, in others rising above chalky grey beds etched out below the level of the plain, crisscrossed by dry creeks. It looked for all the world as though someone had spilled acid over the rocks, so that in running down it had eaten away the earth in great irregular patches, leaving it stained here and there in sickly green swamps *[Fig. 144]*.

Kadoka lay on the very edge of the Badlands. With a good following wind we had made better time than expected and could probably have gone on to White River if necessary. We decided to have a look at the airfield and, if there was no sign of life, keep going. Throttling back to lose height for a low pass, I pulled the Carburettor Heat Control knob out, a standard procedure to prevent ice forming in the carburettor while the engine runs slower and cooler. What was not standard was that the knob came away in my hand!

That left us no option but to land there, and quick. The problem was that I could not be sure whether the knob had come away before or after operating the control; if after, the engine would soon run roughly and we would not continue flying for very long. Without waiting to find out, I completed a tight circuit, almost a spiral dive, slipping off height to drop straight in. Time down, 12.15.

There were a couple of fuel pumps, a neat, white-painted, wooden building serving as an office, and several dilapidated hangars, and I taxied hopefully up to the pumps. We might as well not have bothered. On closer inspection, these pumps, with a red and rust finish, had obviously not been used for a very long time! The wooden shack had once been used as a flight office but now served merely as the Clubroom for a golfing club! The airfield was obviously regarded more as a golf course than the municipal airport!

We urgently needed both to fix the carb heat control and obtain some fuel. There was absolutely no sign of life anywhere and it took only a few minutes to conduct a full tour of inspection. There was an abandoned tanker from some long defunct crop dusting outfit, sleeping rustfully in the long grass, an empty hangar, and another without doors, containing several Cessnas. The Clubroom contained a few club notices, some course booking forms, a broken cooker ring and nothing from which to make a drink – not even a water tap! The golf course-cum-airport was about a mile from town and we were obviously on our own.

Our first-aid toolkit contained a screwdriver, pliers and adjustable spanner – at least we could make a start. Off came the cowlings, to reveal that the carb heat control was 'on'; just as well I decided to go straight in! Off came the side upholstery panel and the recessed plate covering the throttle and carb. heat controls *[Fig. 145]*. The control inner cable, of 18 swg piano wire, had pulled out of the die-cast knob (which to our surprise revealed its previous ancestry with 'Chevrolet' cast on it), so we needed to detach the wire from the carburettor and extract it in order to get it brazed back in again. Even if we managed to get the control repaired there would still be a question mark over whether the inner wire could be persuaded to thread through the outer cable, pushing round the bends without snagging on the conduit. At least, the carburettor heat could be reset to 'off' so that we could fly out.

Carrying our two 3-gallon containers and the control wire, we found it quite a pleasant walk into town, though very warm. Crossing the rusted tracks of a long disused railway we walked in an atmosphere of utter silence other than our own chatter. Coming to the main street, one would have thought it was a ghost town, with not a soul in sight. This at lunch time! Passing what had been a garage and a number of empty shops, there was no sound other than the flapping of old bunting and the creaking of swinging signs. The street was pot-holed, with grass growing in cracks, and occasional pieces of paper whirling around in little dust devils. "Good morning, America, how are you?"

Just as we were beginning to despair of finding anything or anybody, a sizable general store proved that there was life in the old town yet. The doors were open and there were people inside! After much discussion, with several locals called in to listen to our story, one kind soul knew where it might prove possible to have our cable fixed. He most generously offered to drive us out there, wait while it was repaired and then take us on to a filling station, before returning us to the airfield. What more could one ask?

The big question was whether the local agricultural repair/handyman would be in his workshop, or away on a job. He was in, but was reluctant to try what was obviously going to be a very tricky repair, fearful of what would happen if it came apart again in the air. We said there was little to lose; if it did not hold it could leave us no worse off than if it was not repaired. That was a line of argument that appealed to him, so he had a go at it, and, as we all knew he would, he made a good job of it (he was that kind of guy). Total cost of repair $1.50 – having paid the same for the broken brake cable at Evergreen it began to look as if this was the standard charge for any repair job on a Champ!

There was nowhere in town to buy a cup of coffee, but we could not bring ourselves to accept our new-found friend's offer to drive us out along the highway to a fast-food restaurant to get one. The other trips were essential but that one was not! While driving around he explained about the way the coming of the new Interstate Highway 90 had taken away all the through traffic and business which had been their way of life, typical of so many remote western towns.

After filling our containers, we were taken back to the airfield, where our helper refused absolutely to accept any payment for all his time and petrol in running us around; what can one say about such people? You cannot even wish that they will break down near you so that you could repay them in kind – all one can do is to be sure to do the same for someone else in similar circumstances!

The cable was soon installed and reset, cowlings and panel replaced and fuel emptied into the tank. Taxying out, we finally saw some people – a couple taking their dog for a run on the golf course, and this extended on to our runway! We rushed to get off before the dog got there, and laboriously climbed out in the heat of the afternoon. Our repair work and refuelling had cost us just less than two and a half hours – we were well pleased with ourselves!

After the long jaunt over the Badlands, it made a pleasant change to see again small farms and the odd trees, though the novelty would soon wear off! Now the roads were settling into the familiar grid pattern, broken mainly by rivers, major highways and railways, the countryside once more reminiscent of the plains of Nebraska.

There was a good stiff breeze behind us, making for a relatively high ground speed, and our original target destination at Winter looked to be easily beaten. Gregory, 25 miles further on, looked to be the best bet, the next on-route stop being Springfield, 80 miles further on. Both crew members were now feeling the effects of long days cramped in the tiny cabin, so we called it a day at Gregory after 5½ hours flying. We lost an hour in crossing the time zone into Central Time, so it was effectively past five o'clock when we landed.

Gregory was another sleepy little one-horse town, but with two major roads close by and an Interstate Highway intersection, was not yet affected by the Interstate blight. A crop-dusting outfit owned the airport and kept it alive. After refuelling and tying down for the night we gratefully accepted a lift, right to the door of a trim little motel on the edge of town. The manager could not have been more helpful, even insisting on giving us free use of his car so that we could drive into town for dinner, while his charming wife drove us out to the airfield in the morning. 'Western hospitality' takes on a new meaning when you are so often on the receiving end!

Next morning, the weather was kind to us, with a high, thin overcast, a good tail wind and for the first time since leaving Saint Anthony, no hint of thunderstorms! We made a leisurely start for what turned out to be a comparatively short flying day, aiming for Sioux City. First landmark was the mighty Missouri, or rather 70-mile-long Lake Francis Case, which was formed by damming the river at Pickstown, near the Nebraska border. Here again we were following the Lewis and Clark Trail, as evidenced by the next reservoir, Lake Lewis and Clark, dammed just above Yankton.

Along a great sweeping curve of the river we saw a feature not noticed before – a series of breakwaters extending at right angles to the inner bank, almost a third of the way across the river, perhaps to prevent the bank being washed away. In other places, the bed of the river showed how much it must be subject to changes, great yellow sandbanks and bars showing clearly through and above the blue waters, and occasional wooded islands separated from the shore by wide channels.

Sioux City, Iowa lies on the Missouri, where the States of South Dakota, Iowa and Nebraska meet, and our destination airfield, Martin (just in Nebraska), was easy to spot. It had a single asphalt runway, and a smaller turf runway at right angles. The latter was straight into wind and I had no hesitation in choosing it. It ran between two lines of trees, with a break in a hedgerow bordering the main runway, to give a good flat approach. Settling in for a nice short landing I realised at the very last moment that there was a wire fence strung across the gap in the hedge and had to open up to get over it – my short landing turned into a slightly longer one than usual! Grass it might have been but very lumpy and bumpy, evidence of the good work of moles or gophers!

Taxying round to the hangars we were met by the operator, who filled us up with 80-octane. He commented that it was unusual to see someone land on that runway these days, there not being too many 'taildraggers' left; we were not sure whether to take it as a compliment or a hint that we were damn fools for doing so! Martin was a good place to be at, with our kind of people and aircraft. This was the first time we saw aircraft stacked in the hangars on their noses, with their tails high in the air, three Piper Cubs being sandwiched together in the space normally taken by one! The Champ and the nature of our flight occasioned favourable comment, and we left with the owner's well wishes ringing in our ears.

Continuing much on the same line as before, we immediately left Nebraska and were headed towards Winterset in Iowa. The strong wind at our low level seemed also to have stretched up to blow away the overcast at high level, the sky now blue with puffy white cumulus clouds. Visibility deteriorated as we progressed east, with haze extending well up from ground level. The wind was still behind us so that the Champ seemed possessed of seven-league boots, with average block speeds up in the nineties. We were flying over small farmsteads, each set in its own mile-square plot, and this was a pattern we were to see for the rest of the day.

Since leaving the mountains we had been flying at heights of between 1,000 ft and 1,500 ft, a nice comfortable altitude, close enough to see anything interesting on the ground below, and high enough to see where we were going. Winterset Madison County Airport turned up where expected, to the north of the small town. It had a long hard runway, slightly downhill from where the buildings were clustered at one end. As usual, we found a friendly and interested group of people, from whom we discovered that a Tiger Moth had landed a week or two previously on the way to or from Oshkosh. You cannot get away from them, Moths get everywhere!

Here again was a familiar problem. The fuel pumps were kept locked and the guy with the keys was not about. No one knew where he was or when he would be back – where had we heard that before? Whilst we were trying to decide how best to get round that one he turned up so all was not lost. Meanwhile, George had taken a welcome break, sinking into the deep and luxurious comfort of the Clubroom seats, enjoying an instant nap.

Ahead of us was more bad weather. Apparently we were close on the heels of a broad front sweeping across the country to the east; the State Fair at Des Moines, just a few miles north of our track, had been washed out with seven inches of rain over the two previous days! Local opinion was that we would run into it before we reached our next stop, Blakesburg, Iowa.

But here the sun was shining, the wind was strongly behind us, though admittedly there was a line of clouds to the east. We took off with light heart on the last leg to that Mecca of antique (vintage) aviation buffs, Antique Field, Blakesburg, where we were to meet George's friends, Frank Evans and Tom Dietrich from Canada.

The further east we flew, the more the clouds closed in and the thicker became the haze, now forming into mist. When only about twenty miles from Blakesburg, it all rolled together to give us about 1-1½ miles visibility. Fortunately, we had a fine big highway to follow, and we knew exactly where we were on it, so that navigation became simply a matter of marking off the side roads as they passed beneath, looking for one which would lead us south straight to Antique Field.

Turning south-west, within four miles of the airfield, we started to keep a sharp lookout for other aircraft. Not until practically in the circuit did we see any, and they were making nice tight circuits round the field – this was our sort of flying. Remembering Jim Morgan's instructions for landing at Independence, we made a low pass over the single grass runway that was in use, then circled back for a landing on Antique's hallowed turf.

There were trees across the approach, but the runway threshold was well clear, sloping up from a low valley and then flattening out to a slight uphill incline. Real green grass, and good old aeroplanes everywhere one looked – what more could one ask? Of course – for a good three-pointer landing in front of such a knowledgeable audience! With our little Union Jacks on fuselage sides and tail we could hardly let the side down, could we? What followed must have been an unremarkable landing, because nobody noticed it; had we bounced or swung or ground-looped, the whole field would have seen it!

We taxied between rows of parked aircraft, like excited schoolboys recognising aircraft we had only seen before on paper, Stearmans, Travel Airs, Birds, a Parks – what a feast for sore eyes! A stetsonned marshal on a tiny motor-cycle materialised to show us where to park, on the end of a line of "Airknockers." George ambled off to borrow some tie-down stakes and ropes, and I to book in.

We had made it to Blakesburg!

CHAPTER 20

ANTIQUE FLY-IN AT BLAKESBURG

Depending on where its owner lives and to what organisation he or she belongs, an old aeroplane may be classified under quite different names: in the UK, roughly speaking, WW1 and earlier are known as 'veteran' aircraft, and post-WW1 to the fifties are 'vintage.' So at home our little Champ would be classed as 'vintage.'

In the USA it is a little more complex, as various organisations have attempted to classify their aircraft more specifically, with conflicting results! But at Antique Field, home of the American Antique Airplane Association (AAA), 'antiques' are anything built prior to 1935, 'classics' are from then until WW2, wartime aircraft are 'warbirds,' and post-war to 1950 are 'neo-classic'! So our Champ was a 'neo-classic,' not that it seemed at all perturbed by such an appellation (neither did it seem particularly modern)!

As for Antique Field, it was created by one of the founders of the AAA, Robert L. Taylor, opening its 1,700 ft grass landing strip to visiting antiques in 1970. It also houses the Airpower Museum which is affiliated to the AAA. More importantly, it is the venue for the annual AAA/APM Fly-In, when hundreds of old aircraft and thousands of antique buffs get together to wallow in nostalgia for a week. There is ample room for camping, but by the time we arrived, many of the campers had been washed out by the heavy rains of the previous two days.

The field was reminiscent of a typical English Summer Fly-In, with waterlogged tents, soaking wet grass, boggy ground and large puddles. Only the aircraft were obviously different; where in England could one see a Stearman C-3R *[Fig. 146]* or a Travel Air, a Stinson Detroiter or a Bird? But at least there was a small gathering of familiar de Havilland types, with a Dragonfly and Tiger Moths joining in with the joy-riding, the latter a continuous feature of the meeting while conditions were flyable.

We soon found our Canadian friends, who this year had been unable for various reasons to fly in, though they normally did so. And from there the flow of good cheer and conviviality never ceased. The camaraderie that exists between pilots knows no international bounds, in fact appears even to be enhanced between those of different nationalities. We were soon offered rides in the Dragonfly and the Tigers and, during the following day, in a Stearman C-3R and a Brunner-Winkle Bird *[Fig. 148]*. More were offered but the weather intervened, tossing in a passing thunderstorm just to remind us of what we had missed!

The trip in the Dragonfly was particularly welcomed, as the example at Blakesburg (ex-G-AEDU) was the only one still flying anywhere in the world; this had spent much of its life in South Africa, been returned to

England, restored to flying condition, then sold again in the USA. Since then, it has been badly damaged and returned to, and restored in, England (and though I little guessed it at the time in Blakesburg, I was to play a significant part in that restoration). Mike Simpson, the Dragonfly pilot, offered me the controls for a little dual flying *[Fig. 147]*, and that was an unexpected bonus – not only to fly in what is widely considered the most aesthetically appealing of any twin-engined biplane ever built, but to actually pilot it as well!

There remains just one other Dragonfly, ex-G-AEDT, and this was auctioned off just over a month later from its home at Boise, returning to the UK for rebuilding. I had previously visited Boise back in 1979, just to see that Dragonfly, which at the time was thought to be the only one left. Unfortunately, it was dismantled and looking very sorry for itself, awaiting possible restoration in the distant future – little did I think then that I would ever fly one!

As for flying in the big Stearman, that was another out-of-this-world sensation. Having read about and seen films of American radial-engined biplanes of the twenties and early thirties, from around the tender and impressionable age of seven or eight (hands up those who remember Tailspin Tommy at the prewar children's Saturday morning cinema matinées), I could hardly believe that I was actually about to experience one first-hand: the sound and the feel of the engine; the rock-steady ride in quite turbulent conditions; the way the big wheels smoothed out the bumps on the grass strip on take-off and landing; the view forward from the big two-seat front cockpit over the cylinder heads; the snugness behind the wide windscreens; the feeling of power and strength and utter dependability of that machine; these are memories that will stay for life! Thank you, Tom Lowe.

That night we went with Frank Evans and Tom Dietrich into the adjacent town of Ottumwa, Frank lending us his car overnight. We all met up for dinner in a restaurant which the Antiquers regard as their own. The graffiti around the walls endorsed that assertion, as did the names of the dishes! Elaine's, as it is known, proudly claims to be the only restaurant in the world where they lock the customers in! Having seen and heard the utter bedlam within, as everyone tries to communicate at full volume with everyone else, we could quite see why!

The next morning, we were belatedly introduced to 'Dellies' – it seemed our education had been sadly lacking in this respect. Short for Delicatessen, we discovered that they served quite adequate breakfasts (and other meals) very cheaply and very quickly. A sort of fast-food bar without waitress service but providing somewhere clean to sit and eat.

We were in a hurry to get back to Antique Field, knowing that many of the aircraft we had barely had time to look at the previous evening would be flying home that day. And there was much to see. The AAA encourages the formation of Aircraft Type Clubs within the Association and of course these were all well represented with very early examples. Most of our day was spent wandering up and down rows and rows of rare and exotic aircraft, some totally unknown to us. Whoever had heard of a Welch OW-8 (unfairly rumoured to be a sort of upside-down Aeronca C-2)? Fortunately the day was warm and mostly sunny till late afternoon, so the ground resembled more a damp meadow to amble through than a swamp to paddle in!

That evening the awards were presented; you name it, they had an award for it – best this, champion that, oldest, youngest, furthest flown, almost as if they intended every one to go away with some little reminder of one of the best shows on earth. It was rumoured that we had won the award for the longest distance flown in, but at the time it was given to someone else – we were later told that was a mistake, that we had won, and the award would be sent on afterwards. I never felt very strongly about it. Although in starting out from Sky Manor and arriving via the Pacific coast we had undoubtedly flown the greatest number of miles, we could not in all honesty say that all that way we were flying to Blakesburg! Just to have attended in our own little aeroplane was honour enough!

The next morning, Saturday, we all returned to the airfield, George and I to fly on to Frank's home base, Guelph, in Canada, while Frank and Tom were to drive back to meet us there. It was touch-and-go who would arrive first! We reckoned to make it there by the following Tuesday evening, after leaving around midday . That would give us a spare day to be used in visiting the United States Air Force Museum at Dayton, Ohio.

There was a sad, last-day air about the place, many of the visitors already having left, and the remainder packing up tents, stowing gear and tidying up behind them. We joined the queue for fuel, filling up with 'neo-classic' 80-octane, knowing that we almost certainly would never attend another Fly-In here. But, the sun was shining, the clouds had rolled away and there were fresh fields to conquer! We took-off at 12.25 and set course for the East!

CHAPTER 21

FLY-DRIVE TO DAYTON AIR FORCE MUSEUM

The next stage of our flight was uneventful, taking us across the mighty Mississippi at Burlington and the Illinois River near Peoria. The latter was a name that conjured up memories of avidly-read passages in Charles Lindbergh's book *"Spirit of St.Louis,"* when he was recounting his experiences of flying the mail to that city in the old DH.4s, even to the presence of thick haze in the area.

The pattern of terrain unrolling below was much as before, small square farmsteads with occasional silos, railways and small towns, each of the latter usually having at least three oval race-tracks, sometimes half a dozen! We had a tailwind which gave us a good ground-speed, and that encouraged us to extend the leg to Bloomington. At 200 miles it was the longest single flight we made. There was also another reason for carrying on to Bloomington.

I had corresponded for a while with Laura, an OCTA member with whom I had journeyed the previous year as far as Devil's Gate and Split Rock. We had arranged to meet when our party landed at Shawnee, but the final details went awry with the change of aircraft and I had been unable to contact her in time to tell her when we would be at Shawnee. She lived at Bloomington, so I thought to phone her while we were there, to explain what had happened.

So much for good intentions. We landed, hot and tired after 2 hours 40 minutes in the air, and after refuelling I tried to phone her. I had a pocketful of quarters and dimes and such, which I thought would be ample for a local call. To my surprise, the operator asked for what seemed a totally outlandish amount, which was far beyond what I had. Attempts to raise that much change failed miserably, and on further acquaintance with the operator, it turned out that I was in the wrong Bloomington.

We were in Illinois, Laura lived in Indiana; there are only two cities of that name and they just had to be in adjacent States! Instead of talking to Laura, the operator and I had a long conversation – seemed she recognised my accent (*"Upstairs, Downstairs"* has a lot to answer for!) and could not get over the fact that she had a real live Englishman on the other end of the phone. We are obviously a rare breed in Bloomington, Illinois! That was the longest free phone call I have ever had and, interesting though it was, it would have been even longer had I not torn myself away! (American accents have much the same effect on locals in off-the-tourist-tracks areas in England!)

What we did find at Bloomington was another air museum, in the shape of a solitary prewar Douglas DC-3, in Ozark Airline colours, parked in the open on the hardstanding. It being a Saturday, there was a group of volunteers manning a small stand and they insisted on showing us around. I never cease to be amazed at the energy and enthusiasm people will put into such a project. Looking after a static DC-3 parked in the open is no small task. Trying to make, and then keep, it airworthy under such conditions takes many deep pockets and a great deal of spare time. Such people deserve all the support they can raise!

Bloomington has a vast expanse of concrete runways and marshalling area, and we were thankful that Air Traffic Control allowed us to take off from a short, into-wind runway that was adjacent to the apron. Even so we kept a very wary eye open for any other aircraft in the circuit, our course being almost exactly in line with the approach to the main runway. But, as usual in the Midwest, the sky was empty!

We planned to stay overnight near Dayton, thinking in our ignorance that it might be possible to fly into Wright-Patterson AFB, the airfield on which the museum is located. We were heading in that general direction, without too much idea of where to stop for the night. If the favourable wind conditions continued we could possibly make it one hop, and at this stage were not unduly worried about time. The countryside passing below was green and pleasant, with a few more trees to break up the landscape. Our track took us over the pretty Wabash River, well-known the world over through a popular song, though fortunately for us the moon was not yet up!

The wind was now easing off and it began to look unlikely that we could count on making it to Anderson, Indiana, selected as a good refuelling stop. George chose Frankfort Municipal as the best alternative, not noticing the small print in the Airport Directory entry that said fuel was available until 5.00 pm! It was 17.58 when we landed, and the place was deserted apart from a small group of sport parachutists on a training session. We asked the instructor if it was possible to obtain any fuel, but there was nothing he could do to help as the man with the fuel key had left. The best he could suggest was to try a small field at Sheridan (yes, another one), which would probably still be open.

Sheridan lay twelve miles south-east, easily located by its single asphalt runway, also with an ominously deserted air. But as it turned out, not too deserted. Taxying up to the pumps, we could see several people in an open hangar – at least here we should get some fuel. When we eventually got them over to the pumps, semi-disinterest turned to almost semi-disbelief when they saw what we had been up to. One remarked to another – about a third who had just left – that he was never about when something really interesting happened. Cor! Did he mean us?

They showed us round the hangar they had been working in, where the finishing touches were being made to a beautiful Rutan Quickie, but by now George and I were getting very concerned about the remaining

227

daylight. On paper, there was still over an hour and a half of daylight remaining, though admittedly it did not really look like it.

We took off at 18.50, with a quick circle over the hangars to give them a farewell wing-waggle, and headed east again. The wind had dropped almost completely, and the sun's big red disc was slowly slipping into the evening mist, now creeping insidiously up on us. If the light lasted as long as expected we should make it easily to Philllipsburg, 15 miles from the Air Museum.

As the minutes ticked away, it became increasingly obvious that something was wrong with our timing and that we were aiming for an airfield too far. George's watch and mine agreed within a minute or two, and local knowledge of sunset time should have been sound. Suddenly, it clicked. Without realising it, we must have slipped over the Time Zone, and had lost an hour in switching from Central to Eastern Time!

At that point, with 30 miles still to go to our first alternate, Baker, the only airfield near Dayton on our track, it became certain that we would run out of light long before reaching it. Fortunately, a private airstrip, Polley, lay right on our track, now almost under our nose, so we would land there. Unfortunately that was easier said than done: too much precious time was spent in an unsuccessful search for it in the poor light, so we really had to find a municipal size airport at least, and quickly!

The private airfield of Polley is shown on four overlapping Sectional charts, subsequent comparison of which perhaps explained why we could not find it. The Chicago map we were then using showed it as west of the town of Lynn, which is where we looked in vain for it, while the adjacent Cincinnati chart indicated that it was a mile and a half south of that town! Now, I would put my money on the latter.

George, peering at the map in the half-light, found a sizable town, Winchester, about ten miles to the north. So, without further hesitation, I turned to follow a road which led towards the adjacent airfield, Randolph County. It would take ten minutes to find it and land: the question now was, would the light last that long?

As in one or two previous similar situations, I noticed that when the light starts to go, it goes very rapidly indeed. One minute it is late evening, and the next it appears to be night-time! After another five agonizingly long minutes it began to look as if we had left it too late even to get to Winchester. The Champ's nose was well down, the engine on maximum power, and we were trading height for speed in an effort to save seconds. The lights of scattered farmsteads and the odd hamlet had been on for a while, and it was by now too dark to read the compass, my watch, or the map (it did not help that we were switching between the extreme edges of two maps). It was now also too dark to look for a field in which to make an emergency landing!

The road could still be seen easily enough, though this eventually swung away from the direct route to the airport and headed towards the town. The airfield was a couple of miles to the east of the town, on another main road, so we had no doubt about finding it even in the half light. The big unknown was what we would find at the airport; if it was one of those that closed at sunset, there would probably be no lights on at all, and that could be awkward.

We soon saw the lights of Winchester ahead and, looking off to the right, suddenly spotted a constantly flashing, bright green light. Could be a neon advertising sign, could be an airport beacon. The flashing resolved itself into a repetitive sequence, but I had already changed course straight towards it anyway. We both heaved a sigh of relief as we flew over the light and recognised airport buildings and runways, and also, joy of joys, saw that the runway lights were switched on.

In the gathering gloom, we searched the sky carefully for any early stars which might have been moving or flashing – signifying another aircraft's navigation lights – in case the runway lights had been switched on for an aircraft on the approach. There were none to be seen, so I went straight in, the first time I had ever made use of runway lights for landing. Without the lights, we would have wasted more time trying to find and line up with the runway, and with every passing second it was getting ever darker. They also made landing easier and I needed all the help available as it was too dark to read the A.S.I. – too slow and we would have stalled in, too fast and the Champ would have ground-looped off to the right as soon as she touched! I silently blessed the caring soul who had followed Al Bowlly's advice when singing with the prewar Ray Noble Orchestra, to "Hang out the stars in Indiana"!

Thankfully, we taxied over to the pumps and switched off, a light in an adjacent office hopefully indicating that someone was about. However a note pinned to the door let it be known that the airfield manager had gone home but if visiting pilots needed anything there was a number to ring. We needed everything – fuel, tie-down or hangar, transport to get us to a motel, and not least, something to eat and drink.

We were in better luck than we deserved; not only was the manager at home and answering the phone, but she would come out straight away and fix us up. Which she did right royally, even finding room for the Champ in a hangar, driving her car between the rows of lock-ups so that we could see to taxy. There was no end to her helpfulness. When we explained that we wished to visit the Air Museum, she told us that we could not fly into Wright-Patterson but suggested we use the airport courtesy car, not only overnight, but to drive there the next day if we intended to stay a second night. After the anxiety of the minutes before finding the airport, we had never been in such need of sympathetic understanding of our problems. Mere words cannot thank such actions enough.

While waiting, we had been puzzled by other flickering lights that could be seen, just above the horizon, towards which occasional cars were headed. When the manager turned up, she explained that they were nothing to do with UFOs, merely the projections on the screen of an outdoor cinema, almost end-on to the airfield. This was the first time that either of us had seen one in operation (for the benefit of American readers I should say that no one in his right mind would build an open-air cinema under England's unpredictable skies!). In driving along the road into town, the screen could be seen in full, though of course we could not hear the sound track.

We found a comfortable motel in Winchester, enjoyed a good dinner and relaxed in that warm afterglow that seems to follow the successful conclusion of a slightly dodgy adventure! All's well that ends well!

The next day, we slept late, and then learnt to cope with the vagaries of our borrowed car. It was one thing to drive it two miles into town, another to take it as far as we did. But it got us into Dayton safely, and back again. We used our air chart as a road map and had no trouble in finding the Air Force Museum. The only problem was that we were late for the Sunday opening hours, and would be faced with a rush to see all that we hoped to see.

The collection of aircraft at Wright-Patterson is absolutely magnificent, and not only aircraft – the reconstruction of an Eighth Air Force flight briefing room and a Nissen hut bar brought back vivid memories of wartime visits to USAAF bases in England. The only complaint I had was about the way that some of the exhibits were shown, especially the very early aircraft: arty-crafty, 'atmosphere' displays, all dark corners and spotlights, roped off and crowded round so that one could see the exhibit from only one angle. To this end, the lighting was sometimes so poor that one could neither see the details beloved by the enthusiast, nor take non-flash photographs.

Having said that, the aircraft shown were beautifully restored, and what a selection of rare birds there was: to mention just a few, these included a Douglas O-46, Curtiss Owl, Boeing P-12E, Curtiss P-6E Hawk, DH.4M mailplane, SE.5E, Martin B-10, Douglas B-18, Grumman J-2F Duck – it is almost invidious to name any of the many!

They finally chased us out at closing time, when we sought refuge in the museum shop. Eventually we were turned out of there, then lingered by the line-up of aircraft displayed outside in the open. After taking one or two more photographs, we decided it would be better to move on as we were exciting the curiosity of a roving patrol car. We could cheerfully have spent another day there, but there was so much elsewhere still to see.

The weather forecast for the next day was quite hopeful, though the weather men were still insistent on throwing in a few isolated thunderstorms to keep us on our toes, with fog as we went east. I felt they were trying too hard to prepare us for our return to England! Started in fog, finish in fog?

CHAPTER 22
SHUFFLE OFF TO BUFFALO

In the morning, after returning our courtesy car to the airport, we walked into what was almost a domestic scene. The manager had several of her offspring with her, helping to wash out and clean up the offices. That she had several young children made her prompt reappearance at the airfield, to help us out when we flew in, all the more remarkable. We were quite sorry to turn our back on this friendly little airport, which proved such a safe haven when we most needed it.

It was pleasantly warm under a clear sky when we took-off at 9.50, and we quickly crossed the State boundary into Ohio. Flying north-east we could see a line of low cumulus tops ahead, and the horizon gradually disappeared until visibility was down to about five miles into the haze. Fortunately, there were sufficient landmarks to keep us on track. Occasionally, we became a little lax in counting off the mile-square sections as they passed below, and then were not sure of the identity of the next town. Invariably a railroad, major highway or river would then appear to confirm our position, and we were rarely more than a mile out.

The flight was entirely uneventful though the wind was quite strong and gusty when we landed at Ashland County, near Mansfield, despite the hazy conditions. This was unlike what we were accustomed to in England, where high winds and fog or mist do not go together.

We were soon refuelled, and took the opportunity to snatch a few quiet minutes on a comfortable settee in the airport office. The general consensus of opinion on the weather was that we were overhauling a wide front, which was moving quite slowly east, currently about 100 miles ahead of us. The fog was expected to thicken as we neared our next destination airport, Erie County, near the shore of Lake Erie.

We had not yet made up our minds where to aim for overnight, as the good folks we had met in Canandaigua had suggested we should look in there on our return. There was also that date we had with Ed Hanley for a Fly-In to Old Rhinebeck, together with Marvin Rapp. I did not think we would be able to make it that far by nightfall if the visibility turned out to be as bad as was being forecast. The best bet would be to wait until we got to Erie County, and make up our minds there after phoning Ed.

It was still warm and sunny when we took off, and the haze remained unchanged at first. Our track took us close to an industrial area, with Cleveland to the north and Akron to the south, and there the haze was consequently thicker. Flying roughly parallel to the shores of the lake, perhaps 20 miles inland, in normal visibility we would have seen the lake quite clearly. Now all that could be seen were the green rolling hills and valleys, with occasional woods and rivers – we could almost have been

Fig. 145. George carrying out running repairs at Kadoka, South Dakota. The rusty pump in the background tells of an abandoned airfield and a ghost town. Even so, help was soon found to repair a broken carb. heat control cable.

Fig. 146. A highlight on the way back was a visit to Antique Field, Blakesburg, Iowa for their Annual Antique Fly-In. What a glorious collection of fascinating aircraft! In this line can be seen two rare Stearman C-3Rs (the nearest of which George and I flew in), and an even more rare British de Havilland DH.90 Dragonfly. *(Photo: G.A. Cull)*

Fig. 147. Fulfilling a long-held ambition, the author takes the controls of the Dragonfly G-AEDU, courtesy of the pilot Mike Simpson. What a delight to fly this most elegant biplane, winner that year of the prestigious Grand Champion Award at Oshkosh. *(Photo: G.A. Cull)*

Fig. 148. Yet another nostalgia flight was in this Lycoming-engined Brunner-Winkle Bird, one of several, flown by father and son on continuous joyrides throughout the meeting. As with the big Stearman, open cockpits, radial engines and large, softly-sprung wheels gave a never-to-be-forgotten flight. *(Photo: G.A. Cull)*

Fig. 149. Leaving the USA for Canada, where more memorable to cross than Niagara Falls? *(Photo: G.A. Cull)*
Fig. 150. *En route* to Ottawa from Toronto, crossing the Canadian Bush. Miles and miles of trees and water and swampland, with the only dry spaces in the trees filled by high-tension power lines!

Fig. 151. The furthest north we reached was Ottawa, to land at Rockcliffe and visit the renowned Canadian National Aeronautical Collection.

Fig. 152. Flying down the mighty Hudson River from Schenectady, to call in at Old Rhinebeck, another Mecca for aviation enthusiasts the world over.

Fig. 153. The approach to Old Rhinebeck – the idea is to touch down well before the track running across the strip, because here the gradient changes from downhill to uphill. The far end of this banana-shaped airfield curves to the right. *(Photo: G.A. Cull)*

Fig. 154. Just one of the attractions at Old Rhinebeck. This full-size replica of a German WWI Albatros D.V fighter flies and dog-fights most weekends in the summer.

Fig. 155. We made it! A dramatic moment for the crew to relish as they flew out over the Atlantic coast at Manasquan NJ. No big deal but it meant the fulfillment of another 'impossible' dream!

Fig. 156 (lower left). The rear seat, with the 'baggage space' filled to the roof with fuel cans, sleeping bags and all our luggage. Note the First Aid box on the seat, fortunately never needed.

Fig. 157 (lower right). Front seat and crowded instrument panel. The empty compass aperture is covered by a 'deviation card' and the cup on the mixture control knob holds vital pilot in-flight sustenance – sultanas.

flying over southern England, only the hedgerows and ancient hamlets were missing.

The leg to Ashland had been a long and tiring 2 hours and 35 minutes, and the next was almost as long. Despite the lowering clouds and late afternoon mist rolling in from the direction of the still-invisible Lake Erie we had no difficulty in finding Erie County. Another apparently deserted airfield, with a short line of aircraft at tie-downs and but a solitary figure working on the grass near the pumps.

The wind was still fairly strong but despite it being at about 60 degrees to the runway, the Champ had learned how to deal with such trifles and gave us no bother. We switched off at the pumps and enquired of the workman about refuelling. He said to wait for the operator to come out and see to us. But precious time was ticking away, and no one came. I needed to phone Ed, to decide whether to aim for Canandaigua or not and in the end walked over to the office to make the call and to see what was happening about the fuel.

Ed had invited us to call him 'collect' wherever we were, in order to make arrangements for meeting up at Old Rhinebeck, and I was relieved not to have to battle with the telephone coin box, the telephone company and the telephone operator. I got straight through to Ed, who advised against going on to Canandaigua that night as the visibility was poor and deteriorating. He was still interested in going to Old Rhinebeck on Sunday, and suggested we call him on the Saturday to confirm arrangements.

Meanwhile we had been filled up, and introduced to the operator's GI bride, who naturally was pleased to hear some English accents about the place. But it was clear the airfield was miles away from any motels, and there was no courtesy car, though the operator generously offered to give us a lift to the nearest motel when he left that evening. We would then be faced with a problem next morning of how to get back out to the airfield. Looking again at the charts, it appeared that the best bet would be to try and find a way over to the lake shore and work our way north along it to Dunkirk, where the sun was shining and there was no fog.

There was a hint of advice against this on account of the weather, and a glance outside suggested it had deteriorated since we had landed. Now the clouds rolling in from the north were thicker and lower, as was the mist which looked likely to thicken into fog before long. If we were going, there was no time to waste, so without further ado we took off, on the old adage that if it was bad when we got up we would come back straight away.

Once up, it could be seen that there was a sufficient gap between the hills and the cloud base, provided conditions did not worsen too rapidly. We set off north over a deep valley with a ridge of hills ahead, the clouds hanging menacingly above them. Beyond the sharply-defined, dark grey crest we could see only cloud and fog. On our right as we passed over the ridge was a deep scar on the north flank where a small river wound its way through a deep gorge; what a pity the sun was not shining to light up what would be an attractive beauty spot in normal conditions.

Suddenly, the cloud layer overhead was breaking up, giving way to blue sky, with corresponding patches of sunlight dappling the ground ahead. In a few more minutes we had broken clear of cloud and mist altogether, flying in bright sunshine towards a great expanse of blue water; a sea which stretched to the far horizon and along the coast in each direction as far as the eye could see. Incredible! Here at last was Lake Erie, spanning a distance, to the opposite shore in Canada, wider than the English Channel; no wonder it looked like an ocean, especially as the far shore was lost in the haze.

Below, the foothills gave way to a broad plain with a major highway and railway near the coast, which was dotted with lake-side houses and small communities. We headed straight for the shore and turned north east to fly along it to Dunkirk. No need for navigation now – all we had to do was wait, and our airfield would swim into view on its own! To the south, where we had just come from, the hills faded into the line of angry black storm clouds hanging above them, and it looked impossible to cross them. If it had been suggested that it was necessary to turn back and fly over them again I would have said: "No can do"!

The coastline was most attractive, with little bays and inlets and narrow sandy beaches, the trees in places growing right down to the water's edge. This was obviously a popular vacation area with numerous boats of all types moored at private jetties or large marinas, while at almost every cove there were car parks, swimming pools, sports facilities and children's beaches, all at this hour relatively deserted.

All too soon, Dunkirk came into sight, with its airport at the north-eastern end. We circled the town and its harbour, and then joined the circuit, following in behind the inevitable Cessna 150 doing a touch-and-go. For the first time, as the aircraft was being refuelled and we were arranging for a motel to send a car out to pick us up, we heard the flat, nasal tones of a New York city accent. No airport courtesy car here either – we were back in the industrious East (no reflections on the fantastic degree of hospitality we were accorded by many generous individuals on that side of the States!).

That evening I took a stroll along the beach which had, as did every other beach visited in the United States, the usual scatter of driftwood, in the form of huge broken branches and even whole trees. The latter were complete with roots torn from the earth, as evidence of the immense power of the storms and gales, somewhere along the 300-400 mile shoreline of Lake Erie!

The good weather continued through the next day, the brisk northerly again blowing down from Canada. With Hurricane Charlie still ramp-aging up the Atlantic coast 300 miles or so to the east, this was to be expected.

We rang Niagara Falls International Airport before leaving Dunkirk, to obtain the necessary clearance for landing without radio. The helpful controller told us to orbit south of the field at low altitude, just outside the boundary and to the east of the runway in use, and to slip in quickly when they showed us a green light.

Continuing the very pleasant flight up the coast, we followed the shore all the way round to Buffalo, over the docks and wharves of the sprawling city, and along the Niagara River, where the waters of the Erie emptied into Lake Ontario. There was great excitement on board when George decided that what had appeared to be smoke, rising from a wooded area off to the north-west, was in fact the perpetual cloud of spray drifting up from the Niagara Falls, some ten miles distant.

We flew alongside the river until it swung away west towards the Falls, while we carried on north to the airport. As we approached, settling down to 300 feet above ground level, and even before starting to circle, a green light was shone at us from the watchful tower. With no delay, we were able to go straight in to land, within five minutes of our ETA, landing so short that the Champ stopped before reaching the runway markers. Turning off on the taxyway, we stopped on the front rank of the visiting aircraft park, to be met almost immediately by a fuel bowser. Efficiency indeed!

The wind was blowing quite hard and we faced the aircraft nose into wind and placed chocks behind the wheels, expecting only a short stay. How wrong can one be? Our first hint of problems to come was when we asked the bowser operator about checking out with the US Customs, as the Airport Directory had indicated that any aliens leaving the US had to clear US Customs first. This caused great confusion, as he thought we were inbound, and said we would have to wait on the tarmac for several hours for the Customs Officer to arrive if we had not previously made arrangements to meet him here.

Everyone we asked said there was no need to clear Customs when leaving, not even if we were aliens, so in the end we gave up trying. The general impression seemed to be that while many people left the States through Niagara Falls, nobody ever came back that way, so the Customs men were never needed there!

In the office we paid for the fuel and, for the first and only time in the whole trip, a landing fee. And then things really started going wrong. We had assumed there would be plenty of information available or know-ledgeable people about to offer advice on what to do to clear Customs in and out. But we drew a complete blank on this vital aspect.

First, the man on the desk knew only one thing, how to collect money! He did not know what the procedures were, either for entry into Canada or to fly round the Falls. We went into the small lounge, where half a dozen people were sitting around in various stages of boredom, establishing quite quickly that none of these knew anything we wanted to know. There was no one else about and we soon realized we were entirely on our own; it did not help that neither of us had ever cleared Customs privately at any airport, anywhere.

We would obviously have to start with a telephone, and fortunately there was a public phone in the lounge. Of course, someone was using that, but the delay gave us a chance to read all the notices on a board located near the phone. There was nothing at all about flying into Canada, but one sheet gave us the required procedure for flying round the Falls.

All sight-seeing helicopters and aircraft had to accurately fly a right-hand circuit round two designated turning points. This was unfortunate for us, as it meant that all our photography would be through the badly scratched, non-opening windows on the starboard side. There were three height bands to observe, the lowest, from 2,000 to 2,200 feet a.s.l., being for use by joyriding helicopters. The middle band, from 2,500 feet to 3,000 feet, was for slow fixed wing aircraft, while the upper band, above 3,200 feet, was for aircraft which cruised at a speed higher than 150 knots. It was difficult to visualize what it would be like flying round there at peak times on a summer weekend!

Our maps showed various airfields as Airports of Entry, and my first thought was to go to the nearest, though there were none on the direct route to our eventual destination, Guelph. What was more, Customs needed several hours notice of our arrival in order to have the Customs post manned. With only 20 minutes flying time between us and the nearest Airport of Entry, including time over the Falls, we would have a lot of time to lose, sitting in the Champ on the tarmac. When I noticed that Guelph, an hour's flying time further on, was shown on the Detroit Sectional as an Airport of Entry, the best solution seemed to be to go straight there, with little loss of time. Very logical, but it turned out to be a vast mistake!

Eventually, the phone became available, and I sought Directory Enquiries' help for the number of the Canadian Customs post at Niagara, in the hope that someone there would know the procedure we should follow. First problem was to raise sufficient quarters and dimes. We built a small pile by turning out our own pockets and gathering in all those from the others present in exchange for dollar bills. We just hoped that in transferring it into the coin box we would not fill the latter as had happened way back in St.Louis!

Armed with the number given us by Directory Enquiries, I went through the usual frustration in getting through because I had not prefixed it 01, Niagara Customs not being of the same area code as the airport. When I did get through, I found that I was talking to US Customs, not Canadian Customs. The somewhat disinterested woman who answered did not know anything about landing in Canada, did not know whom to ask and could not give us the telephone number of their counterparts on the other side of the barrier!

Back to Enquiries, but they could not help either – if someone asked for Customs, it was automatically assumed they wanted US Customs. Back to the chap at the desk in the flight office – surely he must have some idea who to notify, or possess some telephone numbers? He rummaged through the desk drawers pleading 'new to the job,' and eventually unearthed a list of telephone numbers. There was one for Customs, and he carefully wrote it down for me – it was the one I had just rung! Could he find another for Canadian Customs? After another long pause, he found one which professed to be Canadian Customs and gave us that. Success at last!

By now, someone had taken over the phone and was carrying on a lengthy discussion about visiting his mother next weekend and helping her with her new garden layout. While he was describing the shape, position, size and content of every bed of flowers of her very large garden, I began to wonder if we would make it that night. At last he finished and I dialled the number we had been given. A woman answered and listened most attentively while I explained our problem and what we wanted to do, and asked how we should go about it. At the end, she asked in a perfectly charming voice if we should not be speaking to the Customs? When I explained that I thought I was, she said she was a housewife, did not know anything about Customs but had enjoyed our conversation!

Back again to Enquiries, when it transpired that we had been put through to the wrong area code, then back to the operator again, only to discover that there was now insufficient change for the new call. In desperation I explained to the operator that I had been given the wrong number and did this not warrant credit for another call? She sympathetically agreed that it should, and did I want her to put me through to the appropriate office? She was quite deaf to my suggestion that she simply credit me with another call, as had happened on at least one similar occasion elsewhere.

So I next found myself talking to the Refund operator. Although she agreed that a refund was undoubtedly due, it could only be credited to my telephone account; the fact that as a non-resident foreign visitor I had no account made no difference. To add to my growing frustration, I was returned to another operator and tried all over again to get my call put through. Very pleasant she was, but no credit was forthcoming and I soon found myself, willy-nilly, back to the Refund office, with yet another operator. Result, no change, no credit unless I had an account!

So the search began again for sufficient change to make another call, coins being scarcer than gold nuggets on Broadway. By now the desk operator had finished his shift and had been replaced by another, equally ignorant of how to contact Customs at a Canadian airfield, but at least he had some change. At which point a great commotion outside suggested something interesting was happening out there, which George decided to investigate.

It surely was! An unattended aircraft was rolling away on the tarmac, heading towards a row of parked aircraft. A glance outside confirmed the worst: George was in quick pursuit of a bright yellow aircraft disappearing from view behind the tanker! It could only be the Champ up to her tricks again! Dropping everything, I hared off after him just in time to help push the beast back to safer quarters. Apparently the wind had both swung right round and increased in strength, enough to move it off the chocks, now on the wrong side of the wheels, and sail it across the apron!

Once more unto the phone, and of course someone else was on it again; more frustrating delay, which I used to make out our first flight plan. At last, I got through to Canadian Customs, over an hour after making my first attempt. I might just as well not have bothered. Like his US counterparts, he knew nothing about anything I asked of him, and while suggesting that I contact the Customs at the Airport of Entry could give me no telephone numbers to call. Directory Enquiries had no Canadian numbers and there were no airfield numbers available at the airport. Stymied!

At which point I accidentally did the thing I should have done from the start, by contacting Air Traffic Control. I actually rang them to file the Flight Plan. When they heard we were going into Canada, they said if I cared to give them the details over the phone, they would notify Customs at our destination airfield when the Flight Plan was activated. How to activate it? They said they would do that when I radioed instructions to do so, i.e. after taking off and setting course. When they heard we had no radio, they said that would be no problem, they would activate it for us as soon as we took off. They confirmed that Guelph was an Airport of Entry; that there was a Customs Office on the airfield; that I should have no problem in getting a Customs Officer there and if we kept to our flight plan would have no overtime to pay! Fantastic – what more could we ask?

We were not destined to get out of the office as easily as that, though. As I left, the desk operator asked if we were flying the Champ. There was $9.56 to pay for four gallons of fuel and the landing fee. That took another five minutes while I persuaded him that the receipts in my hand related to his book entries – seemingly his predecessor had not made a payment entry in the book!

At long last we loaded the aircraft, started up and received a flashing green from the tower as clearance to taxy out. They had asked us to look out for, and avoid crossing, some newly-painted guide lines along the taxyway. When I reached the intersection where they were supposed to be I could see no sign of them and was confronted with taxyways and runways shooting off in all directions, with none of the usual pointers as to which was which. I beat a hasty retreat to the hold point of the runway we had landed on and turned to look at the tower, waiting the green to go. And waited, and waited and waited.

In the end, I taxied out to the end of the runway after making sure there was nothing on the approach, and lined up, again looking at the tower for a green. Nothing. The tower continued to pretend we were not there, so I revved up and moved off, still waiting for something, green or red, anything! The tower might as well have died for all the notice it took, so I went. George reported that he could see neither green nor red as we took off. Away then to Canada!

First we had to visit Niagara Falls. Taking a wide sweep to the north in order to climb to the requisite 2,500 feet, before entering the tourist merry-go-round, gave us an opportunity to film the scene from a distance out of the open left window. We made four slow circuits of the Falls, with nothing else in our level to bother us, though there were several helicopters below and at least one twin in the band above ours. Of all places at which to happen, my camera lost one of its batteries, and no amount of searching would reveal its hiding place!

The view from the air was superb, and I was able for the first time to gain an appreciation of the layout of the falls and the river above and below them. I had never realised, for instance, that the river made a right-angled turn at the falls *[Fig. 149]*. That made more sense of the film and photographs I had seen previously. What a magnificent spectacle, as we watched the sightseeing boats jockeying for position below the falls, and the helicopters darting about like gadflies.

Round and round we went, intrigued by the plume of mist soaring up from the base of the falls; the sheer volume of solid white water thundering over the rim; the frothing, boiling caldron at the bottom; the turbulence of the water rushing through the gorge below the falls, before finally settling into a fairly placid river, wending its way out over the plain beyond to empty into Lake Ontario. We must have spent perhaps 20 minutes in the area and could cheerfully have stayed longer but time was pressing, and having no wish to be late for Customs at Guelph, reluctantly left the scene.

Flying out west into Ontario, the whole geography of the area unravelled beneath us. There was a great escarpment running parallel to the shore of Lake Ontario, as far as the eye could see, as if the land had split and dropped several hundred feet. Lake Erie lay above the split, the waters running out over Niagara Falls into Lake Ontario below. What a magnificent geography lesson – if only the subject could be taught as clearly at school!

The sun continued to shine, with a few puffy little cumulus scattered about. Our route took us along the shore of the lake, over the industrial city of Hamilton, and on out to Guelph, following a long straight road. Soon the pleasant little airport shone out under the late afternoon sun, its two concrete runways and new-looking buildings neat and trim. There were rows of aircraft at tie-downs, and even a few in the circuit.

After making a low flypast along the runway, the Champ settled in for a smooth and well-behaved three-pointer. Taxying up to the pumps, we stopped and switched off, to be welcomed by Frank Evans' smiling face. But then a second set of problems dropped on us, eclipsing any that we had at Niagara Falls!

I had half expected a Customs Officer to be in attendance with Frank, and was certainly unprepared for the look of blank amazement on the latter's face when we asked where to go for Customs. Amazement was replaced by horror when he realised that we really had come straight into Guelph without landing anywhere else. According to Frank, there never had been any Customs clearance at Guelph, the nearest regular attendance being at Kitchener.

Telling us to stay by the aircraft, Frank went to phone the Customs for us, in order to find out what to do next. The answer was to wait on the tarmac for an Officer to drive over from Kitchener. Meanwhile we asked the Flight Office to close our Flight Plan, to avoid having a search party sent out to look for us. They informed us that they had no knowledge of a Flight Plan being filed for our flight. That explained why there was no Customs man waiting for us: Niagara Falls Air Traffic Control had not after all activated our Flight Plan when we took off, and obviously had not notified Customs either!

That was to cost us dearly, both in time and cash. After an hour and a half the Customs man arrived, and we finally started the formality of having our passports stamped; he was not interested in us or the aircraft, so there really was no reason why we could not have flown over to Kitchener to meet him. Instead we had to pay his expenses in driving to and from Guelph, his time there, plus after-hours excess. He finally presented us with a bill for Can$246 which created another crisis: we had no Canadian money, intending to change some travellers' checks the next day. Customs could not accept travellers' checks: impasse. In the end, he agreed to accept US$, but only after I suggested he would have to put me in jail for the night!

Having tried very hard to play it by the book, and failing miserably to do so, we determined not to get caught out on returning to the US. What made it worse was that we had wasted Frank's time, caused him so much concern and severely curtailed his plans for us. But we all quickly put that behind us!

CHAPTER 23
CANADIAN CAPERS

Whatever Canadian Customs might have lacked in the way of welcoming spirit (at least their representative was most apologetic about the action he had to take, and no doubt we had unwittingly broken enough rules for them to have taken a very much more awkward line), our host and his charming wife more than made up over the next three nights and two days. They invited us both to stay with them at their beautiful home in Kitchener – ah! the luxury of home comforts and home cooking.

During the course of the next two days, Frank and Tom had planned several road tours of local airfields and aircraft museums. One port of call was to Mount Hope airfield at Hamilton, to view the large collection of aircraft forming the Canadian Warplane Heritage, which includes the unique, one-off Fleet 21K biplane and a Fleet Fawn RCAF trainer. Another was to the small private airfield of English expatriate Watt Martin, who built his airstrip, his house and his hangar himself, then filled the latter with DH Moths and Tiger Moths. He found that even in Canada he could not entirely escape bureaucracy, as he was under threat of having his land commandeered for use as a rubbish tip!

Elsewhere were more beautifully maintained old vintage biplanes to see, including a Waco Ten and another Fleet Finch. Back at Guelph, George did some local flying and we carried out a 100-hour check on the Champ. This involved jobs like changing the engine oil, cleaning and gapping the sparking plugs, washing out fuel and oil filters, and lubrication of the airframe components appropriate to our having flown the aircraft one hundred hours since leaving Sky Manor. How time flies!

While at Guelph, we met a young man who was engaged in building new replicas of the prewar German Bücker Jungman and Jungmeister biplanes from scratch, using jigs built around existing airframes. The Guelph Bücker Works! By a remarkable coincidence, he came into contact with a retired Chinese engineer who had been studying in Germany at the outbreak of WW2, was conscripted into the German aircraft industry building Bücker aircraft and, postwar, emigrated to the USA. As he said, a unique example of international co-operation – an American assisted by a Chinaman, building in Canada a German aircraft designed by a Swede fifty years previously!

All too soon it was time to be on our way again. There was one more aircraft collection I was anxious to see whilst in this part of the world, the Canadian National Aeronautical Collection at Rockcliffe, near Ottawa. This would require a 265-mile detour north-east, entailing flying across the fringes of the Canadian 'bush' – those endless stretches of timber-covered, marshy swampland, interspersed with lakes and waterways.

When we left Guelph the weather was still fair, but thin alto-cumulus was spreading across the sky, borne by the north wind still blowing in our face. After a low circle over the airfield and a departing wing-waggle to the little knot of new-found friends who had come to see us off, we headed north-east to skirt Toronto's control zone.

This leg took us across the fertile plain between Lakes Ontario to the south and Huron and the much smaller Simcoe to the north. Here was undulating farm land, green and pleasant, with the sprawling city of Toronto initially forming the skyline to our right. Gradually, the nature of the terrain changed, with more small lakes, rivers and an increasing coverage of trees. Only one refuelling stop was needed, but choice was limited, only Peterborough being anywhere near halfway. We landed there after 1 hour 40 minutes flying.

The airport nestled among the trees in a well-wooded stretch of country, with one long runway almost at right angles to the now quite strong wind. Although there was supposed to be a minor crossing runway, we could not see it whilst circling the field. As we dropped down below the level of the trees for landing, they protected us from the worst effects of the wind, so that what had looked likely to be a problem landing passed off innocuously enough. We had barely stopped at the pumps before a very efficient young lady appeared on the scene to fill us up.

While I was seeing to the fuel, George wandered into the offices of Trentair Aviation, the resident Flight Training School where, several years earlier, one of our Club members had trained for his Commercial Pilot's licence. They remembered him well (who could forget Andy?), and were pleased to have an update on how he had been faring. It made for a small world to be talking here, in the middle of nowhere, to complete strangers about a mutual acquaintance.

But we were anxious to get on, having a long leg ahead of us, and perhaps the worst of any as far as making an emergency landing was concerned. What was more, the residual effects of Hurricane Charlie, which had passed several hundred miles east of here just a week previously, were still being felt, with the forecast of unsettled weather ahead.

It was a long, long taxy to the far end of the runway for take-off, and on the way we encountered training aircraft taking off on the hitherto unseen short runway. No wonder we had not seen it from the air: we had been looking for a tarmac runway, and it turned out to be a grass and dirt strip, barely distinguishable from the rough grass either side of the main runway. Keeping a very wary eye open for any further Training School aircraft using the cross runway, we got off without incident and headed for the nearby town of Peterborough.

Andy had mentioned the unique boat lift on the Trent Canal just outside Peterborough, so we detoured a mile or so to have a look. It proved to be an attractive-looking town, with plenty of trees and open spaces among the houses on the outskirts, and we soon spotted the boat lift. This was an unusual solution to the problem of taking boats from one level to another without the need for a whole succession of locks to deal with the considerable height variation involved. There was a pair of interconnected boxes in line with two waterways at each level. Boats sailed into the boxes, gates closed off the ends of each box and the canal, and one box went down as the other rose, the gates being opened again when the boxes were in line with the canal. An elegant solution.

Heading east from the town, we were almost immediately flying over a stretch of forest, interspersed with multiple small lakes and waterways, which extended as far as the eye could see ahead and to each side. A railway, a main road (the famed Trans-Canada Highway 1) and several power transmission lines pointed the way for the first 22 miles as far as the small town of Havelock. There we saw the road and railway bear away to the right, leaving us just the power lines to follow for the next 20 miles to Bannockburn. For another 38 miles to Fernleigh there was a minor road as well [Fig. 150], and then 40 more miles with only the power lines for company. That took us to the small town of Almonte on the Canadian Mississippi (same spelling but no connection with its US counterpart!).

In all that way, the only significant breaks in the trees, other than over open stretches of water, were where great swathes had been cleared for the power transmission lines, and these could be seen stretching ahead to the horizon. There was little possibility of getting lost, but an emergency landing would be another thing altogether! For much of the way, there were two sets of power lines, each with its own cleared way through the trees, one with a single set of lines, the other, much broader, with five sets of lines and pylons.

George and I conjectured occasionally about the possibility of side-slipping in beneath the cables in the wider of the two, but there was probably little to choose between them, as the pylons of the multiple sets often got out of step. In the event of a loss of power, it is probable that I would have chickened out and gone for a wet but not so shocking dunking if there was water near enough. Where there were roads, sometimes these ran through wide-enough clearings through the trees to think about a landing, but often they were twisting and turning, making a good approach doubtful. Often, the glint of sun reflecting from water under the trees told of swamps or marshes to add to the discomfort of anyone lucky enough to walk away from pancaking among the soft tree tops!

So there were two pairs of ears acutely tuned to the even beat of the motor though, fortunately for our peace of mind, the engine had never given any cause for misgivings. Compared with the somewhat similar but much shorter forays over the unbroken woods of the Allegheny National Forest, or the solidly tree-clad slopes of the Cascades south of Mount Hood, the former probably caused us more concern. Then, we had still to learn of the reliability of the little engine in front. That, coupled with the poor visibility, low cloud base and complete lack of navigation features, gave more food for thought than the Canadian tree-covered wastes!

Even so, there was a noticeable feeling of relief abroad in the cabin when the trees finally gave way to open parkland, then to grass or cropped fields. The power cables would have led us all the way to Ottawa but, to avoid penetrating the Control Zone round the main airport, we gradually diverged as we cut across to the north of the city. Crossing the broad waters of the Ottawa River, where it sweeps round through 90 degrees to the west of the city, we flew along the north bank [Fig. 151] before sighting the single, long, broad runway of Rockcliffe Airport, within the north-eastern bounds of the city.

This was an old ex-RCAF station, with a long and proud Service history. The old hangars now house the National Collection and its workshops, while on the opposite side of the runway are the Clubhouse and hangars of a flying Club, with long lines of tied-down aircraft signifying a high activity level. The windsock showed the wind to be well off the runway and quite strong and gusty, forcing a crabbing arrival from over the river, kicking straight at the last moment. The wind had increased in strength considerably during the day. The further east we went the more threatening the weather in front of us became; the alto-cumulus now formed a top cover to formidable banks of cumulus, in places breaking out into towering cu-nimbus.

At the pumps we got out and attempted to unravel a very complex set of instructions on how to book and pay for the fuel. At least they had 80-octane petrol and it came in good old-fashioned Imperial gallons. The instructions soon resolved themselves into 'help yourself, log how much taken and tell them at the desk when you pay.'

Inside the wooden hut serving as Clubhouse and flight reception etc. was an absolute madhouse of milling people, gesticulating arms and raised voices in both French and English. As in walking from bright sunlight into a darkened cinema which at first resembles a black hole, where vision quickly returns to show aisles and seats and people, so after a few minutes could we identify someone more or less in charge.

This turned out to be a young lady whose Martha Raye-like voice had greater penetrating power than all the others put together. Perhaps because we just stood quietly at the desk, somewhat bemused and amused by it all, and noticeably different in that we were neither shouting nor gesticulating, she eventually recognised that there were strangers in their midst. From that point on, she could not do enough for us: arranging where we should tie-down; enabling us to telephone the US

Customs from the peace and quiet of the CFI's office so that we could make arrangements for clearance the next day; perhaps most important of all at that stage, giving us a lift out to the nearest motel. She waited patiently while we did all that was necessary at the airfield, and then at the motel while we confirmed that the room was acceptable. What would we have done without her?

Any hopes we had of visiting the museum that afternoon were swept away by the rapid passage of time. Landing at 15.40 gave no time to complete the formalities at the Aero Club and still get over to the other side of the airfield, to the museum hangars, sufficiently before their closing time to make it worth while. Besides we would have lost our lift to the motel. So we planned to visit the next morning and try and get down to Old Rhinebeck in the afternoon.

The next morning dawned reasonably clear but with a very strong northerly wind, of almost gale force. The forecast was even worse; if we could finish our visit by 12.00 we might just get away before a nasty looking cold front (a last relic of Hurricane Charlie) moved in, and ride the wind south. If not, we would be stuck until the following day at least. Of course, at 12.00, we were still deep in the most interesting part of the Collection, and soon became aware of the darkening skies and pattering of rain on the roof. We had muffed it!

What had delayed us was a marvellous opportunity offered to see behind the scenes in the Museum workshops. Here we were able to look over, at close quarters, the magnificently rebuilt Curtiss HS-2L twin-engined flying boat used on the Laurentide Air Service. This flying boat made Canada's first commercial flight in June 1919, but crashed into a lake in Ontario in 1922, from where the remains were recovered in the sixties. Though the rebuild was completed when we saw it, it had not then been placed on public display, so we were particularly fortunate.

As for the aircraft in the main display hall, these covered many unique examples that cannot be seen anywhere else in the world. When I was a young lad the discovery that there was a WW1 German twin-engined bomber still in existence in Canada, and on public display, had me yearning to see it one day. Here it was at last, the AEG G.IV, now fully up to display standard, the only obviously non-original items being the wheels and the radiators. There was also a Vickers Vedette single-engined flying boat, a Sopwith Snipe, Junkers, Bellanca, Stinson and Beaver floatplanes, Stearman Mailplane and many more. How could we possibly turn our backs on that lot for the sake of a little rain?

The rain, low cloud and mist were expected to clear through by late afternoon, but had not done so at dusk, visibility then having reduced to about two miles. Meanwhile, we got a lift back to the Clubhouse on the opposite side of the field with an American visitor and his young English grandson, who were most interested in our Oregon Trail trip. Not only that but, in order to take us on to our motel, they waited while we contacted US Customs to cancel the arrangements for that afternoon. I actually managed to contact the Customs Officer who would be on duty at the airfield we were to use as a Port of Entry, and he confirmed that if we met him on the airfield at 9 o'clock the following morning (Sunday) there would be no overtime or special call-out charges. We wanted no repetition of the Guelph fiasco!

Early Sunday morning we took a taxi out to the airfield (and this one charged us only half as much as the one we had used the previous morning for the same trip!), and were ready to go by just after 08.00. There was quite a knot of people in the Flight Office again arguing heatedly. This time it was about the weather, one chap in particular, who wished to travel in the same direction as us, having heard that the wind was gusting 50 knots and that the cloud cover would worsen before it improved! We had the general forecast which inferred that conditions would improve, so went on that. If we wanted to see Cole Palen's Flying Circus in action at Old Rhinebeck, we had to depart immediately. Also, we had arranged to meet the US Customs man at 9.00 at Ogdensburg; any changes would mean a major reshuffle of our plans!

The weather was definitely flyable at that point, but we could see a bank of dark clouds, mist, lightning and rain bearing down on us from the north. If we were going to go, it had to be straight away – even a few minutes delay could see us grounded indefinitely. Now the wind was almost straight across the runway, but I reckoned it was strong enough to get us airborne in the short distance available to us if I angled across the runway at 45 degrees. The worst part was taxying round the perimeter track and wondering whether the wind would blow us over, and it was much too far to expect George to run alongside holding down the wing struts. So, much to the consternation of the '50 knots' man, we went.

As we taxied, George was ready to leap out if disaster should threaten, with belts undone and door open, but surprisingly, we had no real problems. Even in taking off, the wind swung our way so that there was no need to angle off as much as planned. Once off the ground and above the shelter of the trees, I turned into wind and across the top of the Clubhouse. By now, the murk was closing in rapidly, the blanket of rain being no more than five miles to the north, but at least we could run before it. Initially we had to turn east to clear the Ottawa Control Zone, crabbing 30 or 40 degrees off track, and even then were blown south before we were absolutely sure of our position.

Once clear of the Zone, we turned almost due south, straight for Ogdensburg. What with the slight uncertainty about the exact point at which we turned, and a ground speed considerably in excess of anything previously experienced, I gave up trying to check our exact position and concentrated on flying a compass course. This required much concentration, as the heading was roughly midway between the two major deviations, which meant that even the slightest turn would send the rose swinging wildly on a greatly magnified reading. At least we could depend on crossing the St. Lawrence Seaway at some point, and would then only have to recognise where, in order to decide whether to turn left or right!

At first, it seemed as if the rain would overtake us before we progressed very far, but the Champ gradually pulled away from it, as one would expect when flying downwind. Miraculously we were almost exactly on track as we crossed the seaway and found the airfield straight away, to the south of the town. We scudded round to select the most into-wind runway and landed smoothly enough in view of the unpredictable nature of the gusts. As we taxied up to the terminal building and switched off, it was with the greatest satisfaction that I noted the time as being exactly 09.00 – this was the only occasion we ever arrived absolutely on time to our ETA.

As George got out, a gust threatened to turn us over and we manoeuvred the aircraft closer to the building, found some tie-downs and secured it. It was now just beginning to rain hard, and we rushed over to the office door, only to find it locked! There was not a soul in sight, and every other door we tried was also locked. The rain was now sweeping across the airfield, the wind continued to blow and there was nothing for it but to run back to the aircraft and sit and wait, either until the rain blew over or someone turned up. And there we sat, avoiding the occasional drip through the windscreen and canopy, wondering what to do next.

If you have never experienced it, let me tell you dear reader, that there is no more desolate sight than a locked-up and deserted airfield in the rain, no matter what country you are in, especially so on a windy Sunday morning!

CHAPTER 24
A FLYING CIRCUS

We did not have long to sit and listen to the dismal drumming of rain on fabric. A car drew up and a most un-Customs Officer-like figure got out and hurried over to the Flight Office, unlocked the door, paused to wave to us, and went in. Action at last! It was still only ten past nine, but seemed much later. I was feeling a little hurt, not at his being late, but that there had been no one to see us arrive on time – it was such an unusual occurrence that it seemed only right that it should have gone on record somewhere!

He greeted us cordially enough, despite a rather solemn air, but his next words threatened to eclipse the Guelph Customs debacle, particularly as I had spoken to him only the previous afternoon to confirm our arrangements. It seemed that because it was so unusual for anyone from Canada to clear Customs on a Sunday morning, he had not appreciated the full impact of some recently introduced changes. As a result of these changes, Sunday was now treated as overtime working and he should be charging $265 plus the new annual charge of $12.50. He was late because he had been phoning his superior to try and get the excess waived, in view of the assurance he had personally given us that there would be no additional charges, which I thought was very good of him.

The good news was that he had managed to get agreement to a special payment of $25 under some remote loophole. He was obviously very upset about it and even had me feeling sorry for him as I parted with another precious $37.50 which we had not reckoned on! Leaving us to lock the door behind us while we tried to phone the next airfield, he scuttled off into the gloom. It could have been worse!

As we were about to lock up, the first sign of other life materialised as two men drove up. "Going to fly?" we enquired.

"Not b***** likely – we're working on a car in one of the lock-ups," was the reply.

Which did not exactly fill us with good cheer as we contemplated the prospects. The rain had stopped but the wind was still trying to tear the wings off the Champ, while the all-enveloping mist to the north still threatened to engulf us at any moment. However, the cloud base, which had been at about 2,500 feet a.s.l., certainly looked no higher and this was the factor that was our biggest concern.

Our direct route to Rhinebeck, roughly south east of Ogdensburg, would have taken us straight across the Adirondack Mountains. These were not very high at around 4,000 feet where we would have crossed, but that was several thousand feet too high for the cloud conditions. We had no wish to tangle with any clouds having solid centres! The alternative was to go round the mountains, and there were two ways to go.

Rhinebeck is in the Hudson River valley, which could be reached either by flying south down Lake Champlain, or east along the Mohawk River valley, in each case after diverting round the Adirondacks. The best route from the point of view of low ground was over the lake, the highest point crossed being around 500 feet a.s.l., whereas the Mohawk route entailed crossing 700 ft-high ground with a great deal of wiggling about to avoid 1,000 feet and over. But the latter route at about 270 miles was 50 miles shorter, and more importantly, could be made with only one refuelling stop. With time not on our side, it did not take long to decide to try the shorter route.

There were a number of airfields on our route, and we would decide which to use depending on how conditions developed. The halfway mark was at Frankfort, NY, with Kamp some 25 miles nearer to make a good alternate. Our first leg lay south west along the St. Lawrence, roughly at right angles to the wind, then a dog-leg south to Oneida Lake, and another to the south-east along the Mohawk.

It was 10.00 before we got away from Ogdensburg, under conditions no better than when we had arrived – if anything the wind was stronger. Once airborne, the hills to the south of our track could be seen disappearing into the low stratus hanging down over them, and they were little over 1,000 feet high. Ahead, the clouds were still probably 1,500 feet high and there was a clear way through so long as we stayed away from the hills.

A check on our ground speed indicated that the wind was so strong that it looked to be doubtful if we would make it to Frankfort. Although now a crosswind, it was necessary to crab so much (around 30 degrees) to counter the drift that our ground speed fell to less than 50 mph. It was gusting quite strongly, so much so that occasionally we could hear the momentary roar of the wind through the struts and around the gaps in the door. George had stuffed some rags down the rear of the door in attempt to stop the drafts, a trick he had learnt when we were over the Rockies (that had been to keep the cold out!).

Suddenly, in the middle of a particularly vicious gust, there was a deafening report by my right ear, followed by a high-pitched whistle, as the aircraft kicked to the right. We both visualised some sort of drastic structural failure, expecting the wing to fall off. A quick scan of the visible structure revealed nothing amiss, power was still present in the required amount, as was the oil pressure. The Champ was still bucking and crabbing along unconcernedly, though now the door was rattling even more than usual.

"What the hell was that?" we asked each other, and both noticed the reason for it at the same time. The wind had blown in the large and unbraced, slightly convex, perspex door window so that it was now concave, and was threatening to push it out of the door altogether. A smart blow in the middle produced another loud 'crack,' the window popped back to its normal shape and the weird whistling stopped. Another minor crisis over!

We never became entirely used to the disconcerting effects of the window banging in which, now that the wind had learned how to do it, was repeated a number of times. Anyone seeing us from below may have wondered why the aircraft seemed to have occasional bouts of hiccups as my blow on the window produced an equal and opposite reaction on the stick!

In the end I flew with my left hand on the stick and my right arm braced against the centre of the window panel – the last thing we needed was to have the window blown out of its frame! When we turned downwind, the percussion instrument was silenced for good – the wind had done its worst! On the next crosswind leg, the wind would be on the opposite side and the left-hand window was nothing like as large an area as the door window.

Our straight-line track would have taken us two or three miles inland from the St. Lawrence, but it was obviously more interesting to fly along the shore, with hardly any additional mileage. There was very little activity on the water, due largely no doubt to the poor weather conditions, but we had expected to see more large commercial boats, which should have been unaffected by the day of the week or the weather. After all, this was one of the world's major waterways, connecting the cities on Lake Ontario with the North Atlantic.

Our first turning point was the small private airfield of Maxson, near Alexandria Bay, where we turned almost due south, and immediately noticed the difference in the effect of the wind. Now the Champ was flying in the direction it was pointing, and progression over the ground was noticeably faster, even double what it had been before turning, now that the wind was on our tail. There was a good navigation fix after eight miles, as our track brushed Interstate Highway 81 where it curved east in a great loop, and soon we were abreast the large town of Watertown.

It had taken 40 minutes of flying to cover the 34 miles from Ogdensburg to Maxson. On that basis, George was gloomy about our prospects of making it to either of our hoped-for refuelling stops. Rather than risk running out of fuel before reaching them, he suggested that we detour to Watertown New York International Airport, a non-tower controlled airfield, where we would not be shot for landing without radio or prior arrangement. He was not as confident as I was that, in flying downwind, we would more than make up for the time lost on the first leg. But it was obviously the wise thing to do.

The airfield could be seen off to our right, so it was simply a matter of edging into the circuit, noting that there was nothing in sight in the air, and no movement on the ground. In fact I simply let the aircraft drift across to line up with the most into-wind runway, to avoid the possibility of being blown too far downwind on a conventional circuit pattern. At the last moment, just before slipping off the last few hundred feet, a very low-flying helicopter slid into view beneath us, on a convergent course. Although we had been closer to the airfield, he was on finals and already lined up, whereas we were still heading into wind, at 45 degrees to the runway, intending to turn onto the runway heading at the last possible moment.

Cursing my luck, I abandoned the approach, and circled back the way we had come, watching in disgust as he continued on past the airfield, probably blissfully unaware of our presence, thinking that no one else would be idiot enough to be airborne in this weather. After a very tight circuit, well within the airfield perimeter, we slipped in to land, and again were relieved that the Champ now seemed to know how to handle cross-wind landings!

Taxying was another matter, and I had to do a little waltz in front of the main passenger terminal buildings, where a group of people were enjoying the free entertainment. As we reached the intersection of two runways, where we had to turn 60 degrees across the wind to go to the refuelling point, the Champ refused point blank to turn right, even with full right rudder and brake. We had met this stubborn reaction before, and turned left through 300 degrees to get round. The taxyway made a long S-curve into and across the wind, which required two more turns in the wrong direction to get the Champ to turn just a small way across the wind. I felt like going over to the watching group and explaining why we kept going round in circles!

On the way to the pumps we passed a parked Catalina amphibian – a very large flying boat with a retractable wheeled undercarriage that enabled it to land on airfields – which towered over us, the first example that either of us had seen for a very long time. At the pumps, George had to carry out one of his spectacular 'leaping out of a moving Champ' acts in order to hold the aircraft steady into wind before I switched off. The wind was actually blowing us backwards when the throttle was closed, the brakes apparently being effective only when the aircraft was moving forward!

After filling up, we pushed the Champ into the lee of a large hangar, where it settled down out of the wind. When I went into the office to pay the bill, it appeared that our arrival had caused quite a stir in the club house, where the people at the bar very wisely thought it prudent to wait for conditions to improve (which they were now forecast to do) before venturing out for fun flying. In most other circumstances, I would have done exactly the same, but we very badly wanted to get to Old Rhinebeck before they closed the airfield to visiting aircraft.

It was a pity that we were unable to stay and do a spot of hangar-flying with the friendly locals, but it was going to be touch-and-go whether we would make it in time, so we quickly got under way again. This was one of our more rapid turnarounds, ground time being just less than half an hour. At the runway intersection, it was necessary once more to turn through 315 degrees in order to swing just 45 degrees across the wind. Using the short runway straight from the intersection, and facing across the runway straight into the wind, kited us up after a run of only a few yards, positively our shortest ever!

Our route continued south, with the shore of Lake Ontario appearing in and out of the mist to the west. On our left, the fertile green fields were sloping up to the foothills of the Adirondacks, still clear of the patchy cloud base. Beyond, the higher ground was cut off by curtains of rain or the lowering base of the rolling black-grey clouds driven over them. We followed the foothills, over ground rising above 1,000 feet, as they edged round to the east, past Oneida Lake, to fly over the broad, flat, twisting valley of the Mohawk. The river valley was bounded by ranges of hills varying between 2,000 and 3,000 feet high, and our most direct route along the south side of the valley took us over ground up to 1,500 feet high.

Ahead, according to the map, lay Schenectady, a name perhaps more romantic-sounding than the industrial sprawl warranted. I recalled the excitement of listening on a short-wave radio at home to broadcasts from Radio Schenectady, the name barely audible through the bursts of static; that was 45 years earlier but the memory of the wonderment felt then, at picking up recogniseable dance music in war-torn London from an unheard-of town 3,000 miles away, still then at peace with the world, remains vivid to this day. Any suggestion then that one day I would pilot my own aircraft over that city would have been beyond credulity!

To our great relief, the cloud layer was now breaking up, separating into varying-size patches which rushed across the valley to bury themselves in the bank of clouds over the southerly hills. As they scudded overhead, they were leaning forward in their haste, always a sure sign of high wind speeds, but fortunately for us, at our lower level, the wind was channelled along the valley, and we were achieving a groundspeed of 105 mph! This despite a drift angle of 20 degrees to offset the side wind component.

Visibility alternated between clear with sunny patches to dull and misty, improving steadily as we progressed east. By the time we sighted the valley of the Hudson River, passing the industrial plain around Schenectady and Albany, the gap between the cloud base and the hills had increased to several thousand feet, with cloud cover less than 50%.

This enabled us to cut across the last of the hills rather than fly round them in order to reach the Hudson. Now we were faced again with the old bogey of downdraughts, as the rollicking wind raced over and down from the crown of the hills, until we finally shook clear of them as we turned once more due south down the valley *[Fig. 152]*.

Past the smoky town of Catskill, with the 4,000 ft-high Catskill Mountains towering above us to our right, we were soon looking for the mile-long bridge over the Hudson at Kingston. That would pinpoint the forest road leading past Old Rhinebeck airfield. We spotted the airfield only as we flew over it, the narrow gash in the woods being screened by the trees surrounding it. It was now nearly 1.30 pm, and any faint hopes we might have entertained of being able to follow in behind any other latecomers were dashed on seeing tractors moving about on the airstrip, hauling aircraft and equipment into place.

That low cloud which, in forcing us to fly round rather than over the mountains, had added 70 miles to our route, slowed us on the crosswind leg and reduced our range; that, and the time we had spent extra at Ogdensburg, plus the refuelling stop at Watertown, effectively killed any possibility of our getting into Rhinebeck before their twelve o'clock deadline!

The planned alternate was the nearby airfield of Sky Park, just a mile or so away over the trees to the north-west. This also was a single narrow airstrip carved out from among the trees, but its dirt runway was straight and level, and ran along the crest of a shallow ridge so that the surrounding trees seemed lower than at Rhinebeck. The wind was perhaps 30 degrees to the runway, but as we dropped through the buffeting turbulence on the approach, the trees funnelled it into a straight headwind. I refuelled while George made arrangements to get a taxi down to Rhinebeck. The airfield operators sold us a tie-down space, insisting that the Champ be secured while we were away – they need not have bothered to preach to the converted!

The taxi quickly whisked us some four miles over winding roads through verdant woods, and we had time to join the melée at the ticket office (it is true – Americans don't queue!), ogle at and take photos of the display-line aircraft and still find a seat in the stand! There followed a highly amusing and entertaining show of air clowning and skilful flying, despite the severe wind conditions which threatened to severely curtail the display. The evil Black Baron flying his Albatros D.V *[Fig. 154]*, was eventually vanquished by Sir Percy Goodfellow (Sopwith Dolphin) after stealing the latter's girl friend Trudy Truelove, with the help of dashing Dick O'Day in a Tiger Moth! Also flown were a Curtiss Fledgling, New Standard, Fleet Finch, Fokker Triplane and Curtiss Jenny.

Although the wind continued blowing almost unabated across the strip, and swung sufficiently during the afternoon to cause a change in landing direction during the display, the sun shone most of the time, even though the clouds threatened unsuccessfully to deluge us at any moment. We determined that come what may, we would return in the morning before departing south, both to enjoy the satisfaction of having landed at this world-renowned airfield and to view more thoroughly the very rare original and replica aircraft that lived there.

At least we had a worm's eye view of the ground and could appreciate what we would never have realised from the air – just how steeply the ground dropped from the northern threshold before ascending towards the south. By watching the line taken by the display pilots we could see the best approach to take. Perhaps it had not been a bad thing that we were too late to land on the day of the display – I could easily have made a mess of landing from 'cold,' and though the public might have enjoyed my resulting embarrassment I certainly would not have done so!

Our taxi came back to pick us up after the show was over, and on return to Sky Park we decided that, as there were no motels nearby, we would hop across the Hudson River to Kingston Ulster, still within easy reach of Old Rhinebeck. By the time we took off, the wind had dropped considerably, and it was not until we were above the level of the treetops that we caught the turbulence swirling across the trees.

Kingston Ulster was another single-runway airstrip, hiding among the trees on the west bank of the river. We spotted it from low level when crossing the river, and almost turned round and went back to Sky Park! The threshold of the runway was cowering down, perhaps 20 feet below the approach ramp of the big road bridge, with tall concrete lamp standards strung along either side of the road. At least, the asphalt runway was a long one, at 3,270 feet, so there was in fact plenty of room for the Champ. The Airports Directory entry said: "Obstructions: buildings rwy 33, hills rwy 15, trees rwy 33 & 15," and that was if anything an understatement; they failed to mention the bridge running across the end of Runway 33 and the accompanying lamp posts!

After tying down for the night, we were offered a lift to a motel on the outskirts of Kingston, the only snag being that the nearest restaurant was a mile distant. We were again lucky in the morning, as we ran into the airfield operator as we walked out of the restaurant after breakfast, and he drove us back to the airfield via the motel. The weather had changed for the better, the wind having dropped considerably, and the sun shining from a cloudless blue sky. Taxying back to the southern end of the runway, we marvelled again at the approach over the bridge ramp road and the high lamp standards. There were no problems in getting off over the trees, the Champ revelling in the low altitudes and mild temperatures.

Within five minutes we were back over Rhinebeck, and remembering what had been learnt from watching the experts getting in and out the day before. It had not gone unnoticed that while the biplanes generally had no difficulty, a little Funk high wing monoplane looked to have only just cleared the trees across the end of the field, and had veered to the right when airborne. The strip is entirely surrounded by trees, and on the approach looks like a tiny emerald green rectangle amongst the dark green trees. It suddenly struck me that this was why small airstrips are sometimes referred to as 'postage stamps' [Fig. 153] – that was exactly what it looked like as we lined up to land.

The all-grass field, some 300 feet wide and 2,200 feet long, curves west towards the southern end. It runs quite steeply down from the northern threshold to the lowest point some 300 feet in from the end, then slopes gradually up to the far end. It was obviously most desirable to sideslip in over the trees and try to touch down before reaching the bottom of the slope, and that was just what we did, the wheels kissing the grass just before the lowest point so that the transition to uphill was a gentle one! The undercarriage complained loudly as we bounded from one grass tussock to the next, and even taxying slowly was a wildly wing-rocking affair.

We ran the Champ back up the slope as far as the end of the public enclosure fence, having to use bursts of full power to keep it moving on the rough grass. No wonder American biplanes came to be fitted with large fat wheels and softly-sprung, long-travel oleos if they had to cope with fields like this one. The Champ was designed in an era when smooth flat runways were the order of the day and did not take kindly to such rough pastures! Our Tiger Moth and Jackaroo would have loved this field – what a pity they could not have tried it!

We had a long look round the collection of aircraft and engines, cars and motorcycles – there was even an early, vee-twin Morgan 3-wheeler, looking very out of place. We met several of the staff, who were most interested to learn of our connection with the Shuttleworth Collection at Old Warden, and finally with a New Zealander who, like us, could not visit this part of the world without sampling this fabulous field. He was a pilot but regretted that he had no aircraft with which to try his hand at landing here.

Take-off was as interesting as we expected it to be! At just past one o'clock, the sun was quite hot in the full heat of the day. More full throttle work was required to get us moving again up the slope to the threshold, even requiring George to get out and push. Turning at the end of the runway, pulling back to gain every last inch, I ran up to full throttle against the brakes, before letting the aircraft run free. The Champ did not exactly respond with an impulsive leap forward, but I liked to think we had helped it as much as possible. We had almost achieved take-off speed by the time we reached the bottom of the slope, but not quite enough to entirely damp out the thud as the oleos bottomed when the slope reversed direction.

I pulled the Champ off so that the wheels skimmed the surface, so reducing the drag of their running through the grass, flying up the slope and then holding down to build up speed as quickly as possible to give the best chance of clearing the trees at the end of the field. At the last moment we pulled up over the tops, veering to the right as I had watched the others do the previous day. Sure enough, as we skimmed over the treetops, those off to the right seemed a little lower than the ones straight ahead. We had enough in hand not to be too concerned, but I never like being that close to trees on take-off, as there is always a slight down-draught over the cool of a wood.

Our track for the first half dozen miles was down the mighty Hudson, again with barely a boat of any type sailing its broad smooth waters. As we progressed south-west, the river edged away to the left until we lost sight of it altogether, by which time we were flying over quite high hills and steep-sided valleys. Gradually, a haze was forming, tightening the encircling horizon to around ten miles. At the same time, the scene beneath became more rural with fewer trunk roads and railways. The civil engineers were evidently one step ahead of the cartographers in that we came across new roads and even reservoirs that were not on our charts.

Then we saw several small airfields that we could not locate on the maps, and once the pattern is broken, it becomes increasingly difficult to match map and ground until some major feature appears. Ours was an airfield which displayed its name in large white letters on the runway, and immediately knew once more where we were. But what were we doing right over there, nearly ten miles off track in the twenty miles since our last positive check? Despite flying at just under 3,000 feet, which usually aids navigation, we were thrown by changes unmarked on our charts and had not noticed the westward drift, the wind now having dropped and swung easterly while I was still steering against a non-existent west wind!

We were skirting west of Newark and New York City and, what with the drift and the haze, saw nothing of the famous skyline. There were sufficient major recognition features from then on that we had no more difficulties with navigation, though the wind appeared to be swinging about quite a lot. Our aim was to work our way down to the coast in order to fly a short way out over the Atlantic before returning inland. The most convenient field for refuelling and proximity to the coast was Lakewood, just a short distance from the old Navy airship base at Lakehurst.

Still home to balloons and blimps, the base had not seen a rigid airship since the tragic 'Hindenburg' disaster in 1937. It was a sobering moment, looking down on the airship base, with its circle of blimp tethering rings, to reflect that here had been enacted the final chapter in the story of the giant, passenger-carrying, rigid airships. The only other time I had seen pictures of the field was when watching the newsreels of the horror of that conflagration, which had effectively consumed in its flames any hope of keeping alive Count von Zeppelin's dream of commercial operation of airships.

When we reached Lakewood we had the usual problem of finding the windsock; with two runways to choose from and a wind that had been swinging about all day, it was more important than usual. When we spotted it, it showed that the wind was straight down the main runway, but in any case there was someone else for us to follow round the circuit. Unlike most other airfields we had used, there was a quite a stir of activity here, with several active flying schools.

Our route map and flags on the side of the aircraft attracted much inquisitive attention, especially as we were now able to answer questions such as "how many airfields have you visited?", "how many hours flown?", "how much gas used?", etc. etc. As at everywhere else, whenever a knot of people gathered, there was always at least one person who had owned or learnt to fly on a "little old Airknocker." They were as usual a very friendly crowd, and we were soon offered plenty of advice on where was the best place to cross the coast. In the end we settled on our original plan to go straight to Breton Woods and fly north along the coast for 5 or 6 miles before turning back inland to New Garden.

We approached the coast over two lagoons separated by a lifting bridge. As we flew over, the bridge hinged up to allow a medium-sized yacht and two power boats through, by which time there were queues of cars on each approach to the bridge. The latter connected the towns of Manasquan and Point Pleasant, the latter on a straight and narrow south-pointing peninsular *[Fig. 155]*, many miles in length, just wide enough to accommodate a road, an endless line of houses and a fine sandy beach. And then the steely blue-grey waters of the Atlantic!

We kept straight on out over the water, clear of the beach, to complete our full crossing from the Pacific to the Atlantic, the final fulfilment of the great dream. We celebrated by turning north to chase a speedboat which was bouncing off the crests of the waves; I felt like flying alongside and shouting: "We've just flown over from the Pacific" but, even had anyone heard and believed us, the reaction would probably and rightly have been: "So what?"!

There were isolated, Sunday afternoon beach parties, sheltering behind windbreaks, and a few dog-walkers, but virtually no bathers or children playing on the sands as we swept north along the beach. This was a repeat of the scenes on the Pacific coast – beautiful beaches but quite deserted – don't Americans like the seaside? No doubt the chill wind and overcast sky must have sent many scurrying for home before we arrived. We edged towards the beach and waved at a few of the strollers, but were completely ignored. Back home, everyone in sight on a beach would have been waving their arms off in return! Perhaps when the weather is fine, beachgoers on these sands are plagued by "look-at-me" fliers and have now become quite blasé about us all? We persisted and were finally rewarded by an enthusiastic wave from a youngster just before we turned back inland between Manasquan and Asbury Park – he was probably a visitor from England!

Now we were heading west again to proceed round the northern outskirts of Philadelphia. The ground was fairly level, there were sufficient landmarks to save us wandering far off track and we were flying into a lowering watery sun – very soporific. I was jerked out of any ideas of a nap by the sight of a gigantic C-5 Galaxy lumbering up at an impossible angle from a large military airfield complex off to the south. Shortly after that, we saw a Hercules which was much lower, faster and nearer. Of course they were well out of our way, but we had grown accustomed to having all the air to ourselves!

Nearing the north of Philadelphia, we picked out the Howard Johnson motel we had stayed at five weeks earlier (only five weeks? – it seemed more like five months!). There was the driveway between the chalets round which our wives had taken their first cautious driving lessons in the 'tank,' and the sharply-angled ramp into the main road where the suspension bottomed, no matter what line the driver took!

We followed a trunk road to a selected intersection, turned left towards a railroad, and there turned right, expecting to see New Garden airfield a mile or so ahead. But of the airfield there was no sight. We beat up and down the railroad, circled once and then again, and still no airfield. Every feature fitted the maps, and yet . . .! Suddenly, I realised there was another similar set of landmarks four or five miles along, and there sure enough was the airfield. Now the sun had struggled clear of the cloud and was joyfully peering in through the windscreen as I lined up with the runway, just to keep me on my toes to the last. Once again I breathed a silent "thank you" for the long-peaked caps we had been given. There was just enough vision below the peak, when pulled sufficiently low to cut out the sun's golden glare, to view the runway for landing.

After filling up with fuel, we were directed to a sheltered grass patch to tie down for the night. There we met a cheerful bunch who showed us round the hangars (containing many interesting old aircraft, including those of the RFC – the Rural Flying Corps!) and offered to wheel us out to the nearest motel. We had a marvellous evening with them at a local diner, and were then driven to a back-of-beyond motel for the night. Next morning, the sun was shining again out of a hazy blue sky and all was right with the world. After posing for pictures in front of the tallest maize plants we had ever seen, we were soon back at the airfield.

There had been nowhere to get breakfast either at the motel or at the airfield, but we were not unduly concerned. It had been suggested that we should visit an airfield on the other side of the Delaware River, where they did excellent meals right on the airfield. We had not written down the name of the airfield, but it sounded something like Bridgeport. Sure enough, there was an airfield of that name to the south-west of Philadelphia, just over twenty miles distant, so off to breakfast we went.

Our route took us over the outskirts of Wilmington, Delaware, with a good reference point in the sprawling tank farm at Marcus Hook, then south across the river to the airfield. This was easily identified, being alongside a major highway leading from a mile-long bridge spanning the river at Chester. Dropping down over the road, with its built-in approach hazards of tall lamp standards, we noticed a cemetery between the road and the runway – somehow it seemed to fit in with what we found on the airfield. Obviously, this was not the airport our friends had told us about the night before – we must have got the name muddled as no one would play this sort of joke on strangers?

It probably ranked as the most run-down airfield we had visited. The concrete apron and taxyways were badly cracked, sometimes dropping many inches at the breaks, weeds grew freely in the cracks and the buildings were dominated by the twisted, red-rusting skeleton of a blister hangar that had obviously burnt out. Most of the buildings were in a bad state and there was certainly no cafeteria. What we took to be a Club-house turned out to be the flight offices of a small training school. There was an air of total desolation about the whole place, and at first it was completely deserted.

The driver of a passing pick-up truck told us that there was a small truckers' café on the road running past the airfield, but nothing else in the vicinity. There was no fence round the airfield, so at least we didn't have to walk miles to a gate, and we soon found the café. It was run by a woman who turned out to be a real homely character. Tickled pink by having us visit her diner, she could not stop talking long enough to get us a meal until someone else came in and stopped the flow. Fast food it certainly was not, though we enjoyed the experience!

Sky Manor was our next and final destination. No need to refuel as we had only an hour's flying to do at most. Visibility had been a hazy five miles all morning, and now the haze was forming up into thin broken clouds. Retracing our track until clear of the tight Philadelphia Control Zone, our altitude was initially restricted to 1,500 feet in our band of the Zone. Once clear of the Zone, we drifted on up to just to see where the cloud base was. Although there was a thickish ground haze, navigation was no problem with numerous features with which to check position.

Our route entailed crossing the Delaware twice, as it turned through 90 degrees to the north-east of Philadelphia, and when we crossed it for the second time we had climbed to 6,500 feet, with the cloud base looking tantalisingly close. Sky Manor was almost in sight, and would have been were it not for the haze. Knowing it was so close, we circled and climbed until we finally broke through the cloud layer and came out into the clear at about 8,500 feet. Here was a truly beautiful cloudscape, and we played around and above it for ten minutes, always keeping the big river in sight below through the patchy cloud.

Despite the sun, it was getting cold, which surprised us at first, until we remembered that it was now the end of August, and getting close to the Fall. All too soon, we had to give up and drop back below the clouds, finding a convenient cloud canyon to sideslip down. As we emerged below the clouds, well throttled back, we could see Sky Manor ahead. With just an occasional burst of power to prevent the plugs oiling up, we slid gently down into the circuit, noting Bill Smela's Bird Dog just landing, no doubt from an aero-tow, followed shortly after by a sailplane landing on the grass.

The Bird Dog taxied close to the sailplane and switched off. Nothing else was in the circuit, so we made a low pass up the runway just to let everyone see that their Champ had returned safe and sound, then settled in for the last landing. As always hoped for on an occasion such as this, it was a real smoothie, probably the best I ever achieved, the wheels touching so lightly that we hardly knew they were down. It was as if the Champ was pleased to be back and was determined to show it.

We trundled down to the pumps and switched off for the very last time. For a final few reflective moments, we sat listening to the tick, tick of the cooling engine, and the soft creaking as the wind gently rocked the wings, the ailerons nudging the stick in my hand – a sort of farewell handshake. Was it really possible that we would never again take to the air in this little bird, that we would not be out early next morning, stowing our gear, settling in and starting up? We had been through such a great deal together, but sadly it was so. At least, as George and I walked away, we felt we had left our mark on the Champ if only, fortunately, in the form of a few transient words and decals.

It had certainly left a more indelible one on us – flying would never, ever, seem quite the same again!

EPILOGUE

We settled up with Bill Smela the following day, hired a car locally and drove back to Philadelphia to sort out everything there. It proved imposs-ible to return the car from Philadelphia, so we hired another, drove both back to hand in the original, and then returned to the city. If that sounds a complicated way of doing things, it has to be said that there was absolutely no form of public transport which could have got us back! Although Bill Smela had offered to fly us back to Philly, the weather was pretty awful and we were not keen on hauling him out under such conditions (it would have been IFR all the way!). It didn't stop us doing a little more sightseeing along the waterfront, George particularly wanting to see the old clipper ship, the "Moshulu."

We spent a last evening dining out with Gerry and Ronnie Schwam, when we tried to recount some of the highlights, but our stories must have seemed a bit of a jumble to them. Once the flying stopped, we were probably suffering from a form of non-jet lag! We arrived home on the Saturday (to the obvious relief of our wives who, when we left them at Salt Lake City, were convinced that something nasty would happen to us), spent most of Sunday sleeping, and were back at work on the Monday. Within two days, it all seemed to have receded into a fantastic dream!

Our great adventure was kept alive to a degree by the work that had to be done in identifying, sorting and cataloguing the 1,000 ft of films and approximately 2,000 slides and prints which we had taken between us, after these had been processed. All of the ciné film and about 500 of the stills related to the Oregon Trail or associated features. As half expected, a high percentage of the film and the air-to-ground slides was under-exposed to a greater or lesser extent, but there was sufficient that was good to have made the effort worth while.

The under-exposure was due to the automatic exposure controls on the cameras trying to cope either with the glare from the sun reflecting off the bright yellow surfaces of the Champ's wing struts (which managed to sneak into many of the shots from the hand-held cameras), or from the ground. Had we been able to run even one test film on each camera under the conditions encountered, we might have improved significantly on this. This was no reflection on the three cameras which were unfamiliar to us, indeed, the quality of the slides successfully exposed on the Leicas was everything one would expect from such cameras. It was notable that with our own, familiar cameras, we achieved a very high success rate, though the definition was not in the same class as that of the Leicas.

Before leaving the UK, I had marked on my roller map just over 300 places of interest associated with the Trail. These included 189 prime features of which I wanted film or stills. Of these we achieved roughly 75%, including some shot on my earlier visits. In addition, we had many shots of ruts, some clear and unequivocal, others no more than shadows in the vegetation, as well as much other supporting material . As a result, it has been possible to make up a working set of roughly 350 slides from which to select combinations suitable for showing to a variety of audiences. There are enough, in conjunction with some of the film, to one day make up a two- or three-hour video tape showing the Oregon Trail as we saw it in 1986. So, the camera work has to be counted a moderate success.

There are one or two other questions left to be answered. One, perhaps, is whether I would enter another competition such as the Club Challenge, and if so, are there any lessons to be learnt from this exercise. The answer to both parts is "yes." But I would make certain that I obtained a set of the Rules governing the competition, and read the small print very carefully. The main thing I would want to know would be to what extent the organisers had made provision for their effecting drastic last-minute changes to agreed plans.

If fortunate to be chosen as a winner, I would also be inclined to seek professional legal advice as to my standing, at a very early stage. I certainly would not care to suffer again the financial and personal worries that the Club members did on this occasion.

The other lesson learned is to make sure that any estimates given state firmly what tolerance factors are assumed, and to try and live with them. In my hurry to get the entry posted off, it was not possible to update the basic figures to suit the competition. Had there been time to do so *before* instead of *after* being declared a winner, we may well not have had the problems we did.

A further question is one that I have agonised over ever since we made the decision to go ahead with a local aircraft in the States. That is, of course, would we have made it with the Tiger Moth and the Jackaroo? The answer is perhaps "yes," as the three aircraft had roughly the same performance capabilities, but not to the same time scale. There are two reasons for saying this.

The first is that, after our return, in flying circuits and short legs in the UK we suffered plug oiling problems with the Jackaroo engine, which finally forced us to replace it with the spare engine. That would have cost us a couple of days once we had made the decision to change the engine, though it is possible that, over the long stages flown in the States, we would simply have accepted that the plugs on number 1 cylinder had to be removed and cleaned before each flight.

The second reason is that the very strong crosswinds sometimes encountered would have prevented us landing the biplanes on airfields having only hard surface runways. This would have cost us several days on the westbound stages and thus shortened the time available for the return flight. Under those circumstances we could not have stayed the extra days at Blakesburg and Dayton, and would have had to miss flying up into Canada.

One thing is absolutely certain. Had we flown the two biplanes instead of the Champ, the resulting story would have been totally different! Perhaps, one day, I'll yet get the chance to write that one?

I did get an opportunity to make a second flight over the Trail in 1993. It seems that from 1989, a group of pilots in Oregon (the Oregon Flying Farmers) started what became an Annual Flight over the Oregon Trail. First just a trickle, but by 1993 this had grown into almost a flood with participants from all over the States and even Canada. The flight was mentioned in the booklet produced by the State of Oregon listing events and activities being staged for the official Oregon Trail sesquicentennial year (our sesquicentennial celebrations were commemorating the Whitman's journey in 1836). I could not resist writing and offering use of my roller map to anyone interested, and in return Lloyd and Viola Nisly generously offered me a seat in their Mooney as navigator. Over 40 aircraft participated, but with such a large group it was not feasible to fly low and slow as we had done, circling for evidence and following every twist of the Trail exactly. But what an enjoyable experience and what bonhomie amongst the crews. Unforgettable.

One last sad note. Our faithful and hard-working little Champ, to which we had become very attached, is alas no more. Having survived trials and tribulations which most thought it would not, and having returned us safely to Sky Manor, it was totally destroyed in a landing accident there in the snow of the following winter. All that is left of it is a length of fabric from the fuselage carrying George's map and inscriptions, now safely in George's care, thanks to Gerry Schwam.

BIBLIOGRAPHY

OREGON TRAIL
"Maps of the Oregon Trail," Gregory M. Franzwa, Patrice Press.
"The Oregon Trail Revisited," Gregory M. Franzwa, Patrice Press.
"Historic sites on the Oregon Trail," Aubrey L. Haines, Patrice Press.
"The Wake of the Prairie Schooner," Irene D. Paden, Northern Illinois
University Press.
"The Great Platte River Road," Merrill J. Mattes, Nebraska State
Historical Society.
"Marcus and Narcissa Whitman and the Opening of Old Oregon,"
Clifford M. Drury Pacific N'West National Parks & Forest Association.
"The Oregon Trail, Yesterday & Today," William E. Hill, Caxton
Printers Ltd.
"Powerful Rocky," John W. Evans, Eastern Oregon State College.
"The Overland Migrations," National Parks Service, US Government
Printing Office.
"Exploring the American West 1803-79," National Parks Service,
US Government
Printing Office.
"The Overland Journal," Various authors, Oregon-Californian Trails
Association.
The *"National Geographic"* Magazine, August 1986, National Geographic
Society.

OFFA'S DYKE
"Offa's Dyke Path," J.B. Jones, HMSO.

FLYING
"Pilots' Weather Handbook," CAA Tech., FAA, US Government Printing
Office Manual No. 104.
"Song of the Sky," Guy Murchie, Secker & Warbury.
"Fly the Biggest Piece Back," Steve Smith, Montana Press Publishing Co.
"Spirit of St. Louis," Chas. A. Lindbergh, Chas. Scribner & Sons.
"Biplane," Richard Bach, Granada Publishing Co.
"Nothing by Chance," Richard Bach, Granada Publishing Co.

APPENDIX 1

FLIGHT LOG (N.B.Times below exclude all local flights)

Day	Date	Airfield	Near	Hr. min.
Wed	23/7	Sky Manor	Pittstown NJ	
		Schuylkill	Pottsville PA	1.15
		Penn Yan	Penn Yan NY	2.00
		Canandaigua	Canandaigua NY	0.25
Thu	24/7	Olean Municipal	Olean NY	1.25
		West Penn	Tarentum PA	2.15
		Kindelberger	Pittsburgh PA	0.20
		August Acres	Columbus OH	2.00
		Hamilton	Cincinnati OH	1.35
Fri	25/7	Brownsburg	Indianapolis IN	2.05
		Shawnee	Bloomfield IN	1.15
		Highland-Winet	Highland IL	2.10
		BiState Parks	East St.Louis IL	0.35
Sat	26/7	Jefferson City Meml.	Jefferson City MO	1.45
		Independence Meml.	Independence MO	1.35
Sun	27/7	Philip Billard Muni.	Topeka KS	2.00
		Hebron Municipal	Hebron NE	2.30
		Kearney Municipal	Kearney NE	1.30
Mon	28/7	Clinch	North Platte NE	2.25
		Shelburnes	Ogallala NE	1.05
		Scottsbluff County	Scottsbluff NE	2.20
Tue	29/7	Thomas Memorial	Glendo WY	2.30
		Drag Strip	Douglas WY	0.30
		Converse County	Douglas WY	0.10
		Natrona County Intl.	Casper WY	1.25
Wed	30/7	Split Rock Mill	Jeffrey City WY	1.50
		Webster	Farson WY	1.55
		Fort Bridger Municipal	Fort Bridger WY	1.40
Thu	31/7	Tigert Airport	Soda Springs ID	2.05
Fri	1/8	American Falls	American Falls ID	1.30
		Jerome County	Jerome ID	1.45
Sat	2/8	Nampa Municipal	Boise ID	2.25
		Baker Municipal	Baker OR	2.00
Sun	3/8	Walla Walla City Co.	Walla Walla WA	2.05
Mon	4/8	Wasco State	Wasco OR	2.40
		The Dalles Municipal	The Dalles	0.40
		Beaver Oaks	Portland OR	2.35
		Evergreen	Vancouver WA	0.30

Tue	5/8	Pearson	Vancouver WA	0.10
		Newport Municipal	Newport OR	1.35
		Bandon State	Bandon OR	1.35
Thu	7/8	Lebanon State	Eugene OR	2.00
		Albany Municipal	Albany OR	0.15
		Bend Municipal	Bend OR	1.40
Fri	8/8	Burns Municipal	Burns OR	2.00
		Mountain Home Muni.	Mountain Home ID	2.15
		Glenns Ferry Muni.	Glenns Ferry ID	0.35
Sat	9/8	Burley Municipal	Burley ID	1.40
		Salt Lake Skypark	Salt Lake City UT	2.30
Mon	11/8	McCarley	Blackfoot ID	2.10
		Fanning County	Idaho Falls ID	0.25
		St. Anthony Municipal	St. Anthony ID	0.35
Tue	12/8	Gallatin	Bozeman MT	2.10
		Oscars	Billings MT	2.10
		Sheridan County	Sheridan WY	1.50
Wed	13/8	Mondell	Newcastle WY	1.50
		Kadoka	Kadoka SD	2.05
		Gregory	Gregory SD	1.25
Thu	14/8	Martin	Sioux City IA	1.40
		Winterset Madison Co.	Des Moines IA	1.50
		Antique (Blakesburg)	Otumwa IA	1.05
Sat	16/8	Bloomington Normal	Bloomington IL	2.40
		Frankfort	Frankfort IN	1.40
		Sheridan	Frankfort IN	0.15
		Randolph County	Winchester IN	0.55
Mon	18/8	Ashland County	Ashland OH	2.35
		Erie County	Erie PA	2.20
		Dunkirk	Dunkirk NY	0.50
Tue	19/8	Niagara Falls Intnl.	Niagara Falls NY	0.50
		Guelph	Guelph Ontario	1.20
Fri	22/8	Peterborough	Peterborough Ont.	1.40
		Rockcliffe	Ottawa Ontario	2.25
Sun	24/8	Ogdensburg Intnl.	Ogdensburg NY	0.40
		Watertown NY Intnl.	Watertown NY	1.00
		Sky Park	Rhinebeck NY	2.05
		Kingston Ulster	Kingston NY	0.10
Mon	25/8	Old Rhinebeck	Rhinebeck NY	0.10
		Lakewood	Lakewood NJ	2.05
		New Garden Flying	Toughkenamon PA	1.55
Tue	26/8	Bridgeport	Bridgeport NJ	0.30
		Sky Manor	Pittstown NJ	1.25

APPENDIX 2

SECTION: II STAGE: 3 DAY No.: 6 DATE: 29th July DAY: Tuesday

From: Mitchell, Scottsbluff

To: Webster, Farson

Stage Length: 345 miles   Time (assuming 15 mph headwind), Hrs/Min. 5:45
                                         "   20 mph   "   "   6:15
                                         "   30 mph   "   "   7:40

LEG: 1 AIRFIELD: Harford   NEAR: Casper   p522   MST
       Tel: (307)234-6656   Hrs: 24
       LAT: 42.55 LONG: 106.18 ELEV: 5308 FUEL: 80 RWAYS: 07/25* 4000/100 Dirt
       Cct.: 800   Unicom: 122.8 App.: 120.7   /   /
                  Weather (FSS): 235-1555   /   /
       TRACK: 300 VAR: 13E DIST:160m TIME: 2.40   Parachuting

---

ALT: 1A AIRFIELD: Converse County   NEAR: Douglas   p523
                                         Hrs: Daylight
       LAT: 42.44 LONG: 105.21 ELEV: 5220 FUEL: 80 RWAYS: 05/23 3200/100   Turf
       Cct.: –   Unicom 122.8 App. : –   10/28 5066/75
       TRACK: VAR: DIST: 107m TIME:

LEG: 2 AIRFIELD: Split Rock Mill   NEAR: Jeffrey City   p523
       Tel.: (307)544-2291   Hrs: Unattended
       LAT: 42.29 LONG: 107.49 ELEV: 6325 FUEL: Nil RWAYS: 02/20 4850/100 Dirt
       Cct.: –   Unicom 122.8 App.: –   /   /
                 Weather(FSS): 324-3241   /   /
       TRACK: 249 VAR: 14E DIST: 92m TIME: 1.32

ALT: 2A AIRFIELD: Riverton Regional   NEAR: Riverton   p524
                                         Hrs: Daylight
       LAT: 43.04 LONG: 108.27 ELEV: 5509 FUEL: 100 RWAYS: 10/28 8200/150 Asph
       Cct.: 1000   Unicom: 122.8 App.: 122.1   /   /
       Food   /   /
       TRACK: VAR: DIST: 150m TIME: 35m off Trail

LEG: 3 AIRFIELD: Webster   NEAR: Farson   p523
       Tel.: –   Hrs: Unattended
       LAT: 42.05 LONG: 109.26 ELEV: 6594 FUEL: Nil RWAYS: 06/24 2600/60 Turf
       Cct.: –   Unicom: –   App.: –   05/23 4500/60 Dirt
                 Weather: (FSS) 307-362-2121   /   /
       TRACK: 252 VAR: 14E DIST: 93m TIME: 1.33

POINTS OF INTEREST
Leg 1: Robidoux Pass, Gratton Mass. Mon., Fort Laramie, Guernsey Ruts, La Bonte Xing
Leg 2: Fort Caspar, Independence Rock, Devil's Gate, Split Rock
Leg 3: Ice Slough, Willie's H'cart Mem, Burnt Ranch, Sth. Pass, Parting of the Ways

APPENDIX 3

COMPASS DEVIATION CARD

FOR	STEER	DEVN
N	325	-35
030	035	+5
060	098	+38
E	130	+40
120	155	+35
150	174	+24
S	190	+10
210	204	-6
240	225	-15
W	245	-25
300	268	-32
330	293	-37
N	325	-35

LIST OF FIGURES

INDEX

Bold type entries are those associated with the Oregon trail or the flight over it.

S

Sager, Henry, 158
Sager, Naomi, 158
Saint Anthony airfield ID, 206
Salmon Falls ID, 155
Salt Lake City UT, 11, 27, 94, 120, 139, 145, 195, 201, 203, 262
Salt Lake Skypark Airport UT, 203, 267
Sand Hollow OR, 175
Sandy OR, 185
Santa Fe Trail, 73
Sawtooth Mountains ID, 202
Schenectady NY, 253
Schoch, Edwin, McDonnell test pilot, 67
Schuylkill County airport PA, 37, 39, 266
Schwam, Gerry, 3, 10, 24-34, 204, 262, 264
Scott Spring KS, 78
Scotts Bluff NE, 98-101, 106, 114, 203
Scottsbluff City NE, 104
Scottsbluff County Airport NE, 99, 266
SE.5E, 230
Shawnee airfield IN, 58, 226, 266
Sheep Rock ID, 145
Shelburne, Rod, 95, 179
Shelburne's airfield NE, 87, 91, 95, 266
Sheridan airfield IN, 227, 267
Sheridan County Airport WY, 213, 267
Shoshone Falls ID, 154, 155
Shoshone Indians, 104
Shutler Creek Historic Marker OR, 178
Shutler OR, 177
Shuttleworth Collection, Old Warden airfield, England, 256
Silver Creek Reservoir WY, 125
Sioux City IA, 219
Sioux Indians, 80, 104
Sioux Lookout NE, 87, 90, 91
Sky Manor airfield NJ, 12, 28-40, 53-57, 84, 110, 225, 260, 266, 267
Sky Park airfield NY, 254, 255, 267
Smela, Bill, 28-37, 43, 54, 121, 261, 262
Smith's Creek WY, 136
Smith's Ferry KS, 77, 78
Smith's Fork Crossing WY, 140
Smithsonian National Air and Space Museum, 30
Smock Prairie OR, 183
Snake Indians, 151
Soda Point ID, 145
Soda Springs ID, 136, 140-142
Sopwith Dolphin, 254
Sopwith Snipe, 246

South Pass WY, 100, 117, 124-126, 135, 203
Spalding, Mrs Eliza, 100, 115, 126, 148
Spanish Hollow OR, 179
Spearhead Chapter, KPA, 68
Split Rock Mill airstrip, Jeffrey City WY, 115, 121, 128, 266
Split Rock WY, 120
St. Anthony Municipal Airport ID, 267
St. Lawrence Seaway, 248, 250
St. Louis MO, 57-67
St. Mary's Stn. WY, 125
St. Marys KS Catholic Indian Mission, 78, 84
Stanley KS, 74
Star ID, 161
Steamboat Rock NE, 99
Steamboat Rock WY, 119
Steamboat Spring ID, 142, 145
Stearman C-3R, 223
Stevenage Flying Club, 14
Stinking Water Creek OR, 199
Stinson Detroiter, 223
Stinson Reliant, 84
Strawberry Creek WY, 125
Stricker's Store ID, 153, 157
Sublette Cut-Off, 115, 127
Sublette Mountain WY, 140
Sublette, William, 104
Sunflower Ordnance Works KS, 75
Swales, 81, 94, 106, 140, 159, 160, 163, 175
Sweetwater Rocks Hills WY, 120

T

Table Rock NE, 99
The Dalles Municipal Airport OR, 177, 181, 266
The Dalles OR, 10, 179-182
Thief Valley Reservoir OR, 167
Thomas Memorial airfield, Glendo WY, 107, 266
Thomas' Fork Crossing ID, 140
Thousand Springs ID, 157
Three Crossings WY, 120
Three Forks MT, 209
Three Island Crossing ID, 159
Three Island Crossing State Park ID, 200
Three Sisters Mountains OR, 197
Three-Fingered Jack Mtn OR, 198
Thruxton Jackaroo, 14, 15, 19, 21, 22, 29, 172, 256, 263
Tiger Moth, *see* DH.82A Tiger Moth